FLY FISHING GUIDE
to
NEW YORK STATE

FLY FISHING GUIDE
to
NEW YORK STATE

Experts' Guide to Locations, Hatches, and Tactics

MIKE VALLA

STACKPOLE
BOOKS

Essex, Connecticut
Blue Ridge Summit, Pennsylvania

STACKPOLE BOOKS

An imprint of Globe Pequot, the trade division of
The Rowman & Littlefield Publishing Group, Inc.
4501 Forbes Blvd., Ste. 200
Lanham, MD 20706
www.rowman.com

Distributed by NATIONAL BOOK NETWORK

British Library Cataloguing in Publication Information available

Library of Congress Cataloging-in-Publication Data

Names: Valla, Mike, author.
Title: Fly fishing guide to New York state : experts' guide to locations, hatches, and tactics / Mike Valla.
Description: Essex, Connecticut : Stackpole Books, [2023] | Includes index. | Summary: "A complete guide to the best fly-fishing streams and stillwaters in New York including detailed information on where to go, current fly patterns, and advice from local experts"— Provided by publisher.
Identifiers: LCCN 2023003850 (print) | LCCN 2023003851 (ebook) | ISBN 9780811771689 (paperback) | ISBN 9780811771696 (epub)
Subjects: LCSH: Fly fishing—New York (State)
Classification: LCC SH456 .V35 2023 (print) | LCC SH456 (ebook) | DDC 799.12/409747—dc23/eng/20230411
LC record available at https://lccn.loc.gov/2023003850
LC ebook record available at https://lccn.loc.gov/2023003851

♾™ The paper used in this publication meets the minimum requirements of American National Standard for Information Sciences—Permanence of Paper for Printed Library Materials, ANSI/NISO Z39.48-1992.

Contents

NEW YORK STATE FLY HATCHES

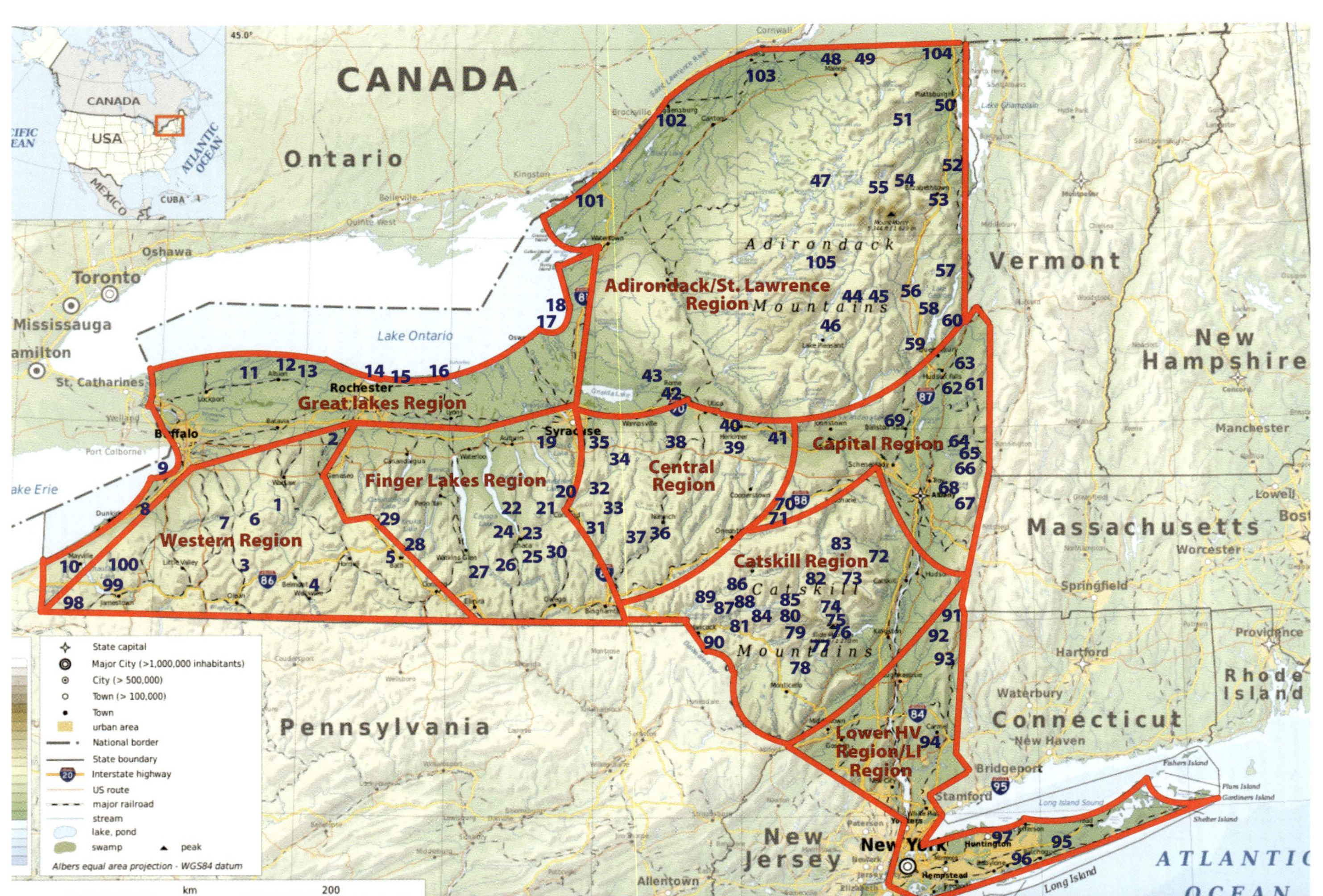

CANADA
CANADA
USA
MEXICO
CUBA
PACIFIC OCEAN
ATLANTIC OCEAN
Ontario
CANADA
Toronto
Mississauga
Hamilton
St. Catharines
Oshawa
Kingston
Belleville
Quinte West
Lake Ontario
Lake Erie
Port Colborne
Welland
Buffalo
Rochester
Syracuse
Vermont
New Hampshire
Massachusetts
Connecticut
Rhode Island
New Jersey
New York
Pennsylvania
Manchester
Lowell
Boston
Worcester
Springfield
Hartford
New Haven
Waterbury
Bridgeport
Stamford
Providence
Albany
Schenectady
Montpelier
Adirondack Mountains
Adirondack/St. Lawrence Region
Great lakes Region
Finger Lakes Region
Western Region
Central Region
Capital Region
Catskill Region
Catskill Mountains
Lower HV Region/LI Region
Long Island
Long Island Sound
Fishers Island
Plum Island
Gardiners Island
Shelter Island
Huntington
Hempstead
Oneida Lake
Mount Marcy
5,344 ft / 1,629 m
ATLANTIC OCEAN
45.0°
State capital
Major City (>1,000,000 inhabitants)
City (> 500,000)
Town (> 100,000)
Town
urban area
National border
State boundary
Interstate highway
US route
major railroad
stream
lake, pond
swamp
peak
Albers equal area projection · WGS84 datum
km   200

Many stream maps showing PFR stretches are available free online at NYSDEC (https://www.dec.ny.gov).

Map Locator

1. Wiscoy Creek/East Koy Creek
2. Spring Creek/Oatka Creek
3. Ischua Creek
4. Genesee River (upper)
5. Cohocton River/Neil Creek
6. Clear Creek/Mansfield Creek/South Cattaraugus Creek
7. Cattaraugus Creek (upper main stem)
8. Cattaraugus Creek (lower—steelhead section)
9. Eighteen Mile Creek
10. Canadaway Creek/Chatauqua Creek
11. Johnson Creek
12. Oak Orchard Creek
13. Sandy Creek (Orleans/Monroe Counties)
14. Genesee River (lower—steelhead/salmon section)
15. Irondequoit Creek
16. Maxwell Creek
17. Salmon River (Pulaski)/Grindstone Creek
18. Little Sandy Creek/South Sandy Creek/North Sandy Creek/Lindsey Creek
19. Nine Mile Creek
20. Grout Brook
21. Factory Brook
22. Salmon Creek
23. Fall Creek
24. Taughannock Creek
25. Cayuga Inlet/Enfield Creek
26. Cayuta Creek
27. Catharine Creek
28. Keuka Lake Inlet
29. Naples Creek
30. Owego Creek
31. Main Stem Tioughnioga River
32. East Branch Tioughnioga River
33. Otselic River
34. Fabious Brook
35. Butternut Creek/Limestone Creek/Chittenango Creek
36. Chenango River (upper)
37. Genegantslet Creek
38. Oriskany Creek/Chenango Canal
39. Steele Creek
40. West Canada Creek
41. Mohawk River (lower)
42. Mohawk River (upper)
43. Fish Creek (East and West Branches)
44. Siamese Ponds Wilderness Area (Thirteenth Lake, Peaked Mountain Pond, Hour Pond, Puffer Pond)
45. Upper Hudson River/Mill Creek
46. West Canada Wilderness Area (Spruce Lake)
47. Saranac Wild Forest Region/Saint Regis Canoe Area
48. Salmon River (Malone)
49. Chateaugay River
50. Saranac River (Landlocked Salmon section)
51. Saranac River (Inland Trout section)
52. Boquet River (Landlocked Salmon section)
53. Boquet River (Inland Trout section)
54. East Branch Ausable River
55. West Branch Ausable River
56. Schroon River
57. Pharaoh Lake Wilderness (Rock Pond, Pharaoh Lake, Grizzle Ocean, Gull Pond)
58. Lake George Wild Forest (Jabe Pond)
59. Lake George (Million Dollar Beach)
60. Mettawee River
61. Batten Kill
62. Lake Lauderdale/Dead Lake
63. Cossayuna Lake
64. Hoosic River/Little Hoosic River
65. Walloomsac River
66. Black River
67. Kinderhook River
68. Poesten Kill/Quacken Kill
69. Kayderosseras Creek
70. Schenevus Creek
71. Charlotte Creek
72. Catskill Creek
73. Schoharie Creek
74. Esopus Creek
75. Woodland Valley Stream
76. Traver Hollow Brook/Kanape Brook/Bushkill Creek
77. Rondout Creek
78. Neversink River
79. Willowemoc Creek
80. Big Pond
81. Beaver Kill
82. West Kill
83. Batavia Kill (Greene County)
84. Barkaboom Stream/Mill Brook
85. East Branch Delaware River (above Pepacton Reservoir)
86. West Branch Delaware River (above Cannonsville Reservoir)
87. Town Brook
88. Little Delaware River
89. East Brook
90. Delaware River (main stem)
91. Roeliff Jansen Kill/Bash Bish Brook
92. Wappinger Creek
93. Wassaic Creek/Ten Mile River/Swamp River
94. Croton River Branches/Amawalk Outlet
95. Carmans River
96. Connetquot River
97. Nissequogue River
98. Findley Lake
99. Chautauqua Lake
100. Bear Lake/Cassadaga Lake
101. Upper Corridor Saint Lawrence River (Thousand Islands)
102. Middle Corridor Saint Lawrence River (Ogdensburg)
103. Lower Corridor Saint Lawrence River (Massena)
104. North Branch Chazy River/Great Chazy River
105. Lake Durant

Acknowledgments

Many friends, old and new, stepped forward to help with fly-tying needs. Flies they tied are effective on New York's waters. Among the tiers are Bob Adams, Andreas Andersson, Dave Agness, Tom Baltz, John Bonasera, Seth Cavarretta, John Checchia, John Collins, Bruce Concors, Chuck Coronato, Pat Crisci, Jeffrey R. Deshefy Jr., Joe Fusco, Ron Frost, Gregg Heffner, Bob Herson, Michael Johnson, John Kavanaugh, Bob Lindquist, Tom Mason, Dave McNeese, Bill Newcomb, Ted Patlen, Frank Payne, Ayumi Ozecki, Dave Rockwell, Steve Silverio, Mike Stewart, Stan Tabaka Jr., Ray Tucker, and Paul Weamer. Special thanks to John Pitarresi and Rob Streeter, talented fly anglers and writers. John and Rob are considered two of the most admired and knowledgeable outdoor newspaper columnists in the Capital and Central New York regions. Rob also tied a couple of flies for this book. Outdoor journalist Don Meissner, a peach of a guy, came to my rescue up in his territory, on the St. Lawrence River Massena area. Others, such as Joe Mecca in the Cattaraugus steelhead area, Dave "Rocky" Rockwell on the Salmon River, Ron Bierstine on Oak Orchard Creek, and Tom and Sue McCoy on Long Island, instantly helped me out with various needs. My good friend and neighbor here in Batten Kill country, sporting artist and fly guy Adriano Manocchia, also threw help my way, as did Stu and Laura LaDue, Ed Ostapczuk, Rich Redmond, and Dan Wanczyk. Thanks also to Alex Krywanczyk and Julie Ferro for introducing me to "muskie hunting." Friends Harry Leichtweis, Tom Burr, and my Cornell University fisheries major classmate Dave Bornholdt helped rekindle college-era outings. New York State Bureau of Fisheries regional staffers and their outstanding information and data sources were of great help. Thanks to the Stackpole team, including editors Jay Nichols and Stephanie Otto, production editor Meredith Dias, copy editor Sean Sabo, proofreader Virginia Bridges, layout artist Wendy Reynolds, and cover designer Amanda Wilson.

I cannot express fully just how helpful my wife, Valerie, was throughout this entire project. There was never an issue during numerous occasions when her husband decided to head out the door, on short notice, for yet another trip to some water around New York State.

Introduction

New York State is fortunate to have an enormous number of waterbodies available to both fly anglers and conventional tackle-fishing enthusiasts. With over 7,600 freshwater lakes, large ponds, small ponds, reservoirs, and some 70,000 miles of rivers and streams, my first thought in undertaking this project was what waters I should include. Plenty of gamefish besides trout, both fresh and saltwater species, also provide anglers with enjoyment all over the state's enormous amount of available water.

You name it—trout, landlocked salmon, bass, northern pike, muskies, tiger muskies, carp, fallfish, even catfish—have been enticed with fly gear. From the big Lake Ontario cohos, chinooks, and steelhead that run the tributaries to colorful little wild brook trout that swim in tiny brooks in New York's inland streams, the state has it all. Saltwater species—false albacore, stripers, bluefish, and others—are also popular fly-angler targets. It's quite a challenge to cover everything New York State has to offer in one book, and no attempt was made to do so. However, there's enough here to keep any fly fisher interested in exploring unfamiliar waters where fish wait to be tempted by their fly patterns.

New York fly angler Lindsay Agness with a Lake Ontario tributary steelhead. A licensed New York State fishing guide, Lindsay has enjoyed sustained success bringing many beautiful Lake Ontario tributary steelhead and brown trout to her net. When she's not enjoying the sport with her husband Dave, she volunteers with groups such as Trout Unlimited, Project Healing Waters, Casting for Recovery, and other nonprofit fly-fishing organizations. (PHOTO DAVE AGNESS)

Wild brook trout that willingly take flies inhabit some of the smallest waters that flow in New York. The majority of fly anglers bypass the numerous woodland trickles throughout New York that inhabit wild brookies, yet good sport can be enjoyed along stream reaches that also provide solitude.

Smallmouth Bass are ubiquitous throughout New York, including this catch taken on the lower Mohawk River. When trout-fishing success begins to fall off during summer, many New York fly anglers cast their favorite bass patterns on many productive warmwater lakes, ponds, and rivers. (PHOTO ROB STREETER)

A few years ago, when the idea of writing this book was discussed, I gulped and stepped away from it after crafting an outline of selected waters, a number far less than what's presented here. Time passed, and I revisited the idea. A refreshed yet expanded outline of waters seemed manageable, so I held my breath and jumped in. Once I got started, it seemed one stream, lake, or pond led to the other. I revisited and fished one stream on the list only to realize that I had forgotten about another one close by I had fished years ago or still fish today. Memories and experiences fishing waters throughout New York kept resurfacing.

The list grew. My fly-fishing memories proved to be both a blessing and a curse. I gulped again many times through the course of tackling this book. It could have been more aptly titled "my favorite fly-fishing waters." There are so many more streams, ponds, and lakes—both coldwater and warmwater fisheries—that could not possibly be covered in one book. I'm sure some will wonder why such and such stream or pond wasn't covered. I'm equally certain some will lament that such and such a stream, pond, or lake *was* mentioned. The truth is hardly any water is truly a "secret." My hope is by discussing my own favorites that others will venture away from the most crowded waters (yes, good fishing does exist beyond the oft-crowded upper Delaware River system).

It occurred to me, as the list grew, there were reasons I had fly-fished so many waters over the past 55 years, in many regions around the state. A combination of childhood fishing experiences with my dad and grandfather and their friends in Central New York, my own solo Catskill region explorations during teenage years, exposure to new waters during college years as a fisheries biology student in the 1970s, career changes and relocations, marriage life, and additional family moves have all helped deliver me to many new places to cast a fly around New York.

I relocated to the Ithaca area in the Finger Lakes region, back and forth, three times alone. There were two years when we lived in the City of Geneva at the north end of Seneca Lake, in range of Lake Ontario and its tributaries. Another move brought us to the City of Saratoga Springs in the Capital District, where we lived for many years raising a family. We built a second home in the Adirondacks only to move back to the Capital District in the Village of Ballston Spa. During that time, we owned a fishing cottage in the Batten Kill area, in the hamlet of Shushan.

A final move (we hope) is now in the Town of Cambridge, still in Batten Kill country, in Washington County, not far from the Vermont border. Whew! That was a lot of moving, which resulted in exposure to many new fly-fishing waters. Much of that story pops up and is sprinkled throughout this book as it relates to fly fishing in New York.

Over all those years, changes took place on some of my favorite waters. Some degraded, while others were improved and enhanced through increased attention and

Author (far right) and Cornell University fisheries major classmates sampling brook trout with Professor Dwight A. Webster (center with white sweater) on an Adirondack region pond, in the fall of 1974. Classmate and friend Dave Bornholdt's role that day was weighing brook trout captured by setting gill nets. Dave (mentioned elsewhere in this book) is pictured here at the weighing scale. Bob Wilberding is at the far left. Graduate fisheries biology student Bob Sopuck is standing to the left of Webster.

managed care from both the New York State Department of Environmental Conservation (NYSDEC) and conservation organizations such as Trout Unlimited. The NYS Bureau of Fisheries and its passionate staff have devoted many years to help ensure anglers are receiving the experiences they desire, yet driven by sound management practices. Some very exciting stream management changes took place during the last few years, including the development of a new state fisheries management plan.

New York State Trout Stream Management Plan Stream Categories

Beginning in May 2018, NYSDEC went to work developing a new management plan for the state's inland trout fisheries. The existing management plan, at 30 years old, was out-of-date and did not reflect changed angler expectations. It was also unnecessarily too complex. A total of 16 public meetings were held to receive angler input on the desires and thoughts. Like any new management plan, lots of discussion and controversy surfaced. Anglers, as expected, often had different opinions on the matter.

The outcome resulted in increased opportunities for fly anglers fishing inland trout streams. Stream regulation changes resulted in year-round fishing on streams that were previously closed to angling between October 16 and March 30. Additional Catch and Release, artificial-lures-only months were added, allowing fly fishers to continue fishing on their favorite streams during those months.

However, the new management plan does not include stream reaches dependent on migratory fish (Finger Lakes, Great Lakes, and Lake Champlain tributaries). In March 2022, ponds and lakes were brought into the year-round, open-season fold. However, some small water bodies, including brook trout ponds and smaller ponds inhabiting lake trout, are still under public input discussion and, at the time of writing, are not open to year-round angling. Check for updates to fisheries regulation changes. Open season date changes were also made to existing warmwater species waters. The bottom line is to make sure you review updated NYSDEC seasonal regulations and other fishery management changes before venturing out on New York's waters.

Lake Ontario coho salmon run tributaries such as the Salmon River during early fall. Typical 3- to 8-pound cohos, along with larger 15- to 30-pound chinooks, start staging in the mouth of Salmon River during late August, although the peak spawning in the river usually occurs in late September into October.

Inland Trout Stream Categories

One of the most useful outcomes Inland Trout Stream Categories of NYSDEC's management plan is the new categorization designations on New York's inland trout streams. You'll encounter new signage along trout stream reaches that alert anglers of the stream categorization they're fishing. Throughout this book, references are made to the categorizations found on inland trout stream reaches.

Highlights of the stream reach categories are as follows. Additional criteria for reach categories, along with information on many inland trout streams, can be found in the *Categorization of New York State Trout Stream Reaches* document available online.

Inland trout stream reaches are now categorized as Wild, Wild-Premier, Wild-Quality, Stocked-Extended, or Stocked. Anglers fishing trout streams throughout New York State will encounter the new signage recently posted along Public Fishing Rights (PFR) stretches.

WILD

Public Access; a large number of unnamed streams flow throughout New York. If a stream reach isn't listed, it's likely categorized as Wild or uncategorized.

WILD-QUALITY

Wild trout biomass >40 lbs/acre or ≥300 yearling or older trout per mile; public access; mean width >10 feet.

WILD-PREMIER

Wild trout biomass >60 lbs/acre or ≥500 yearling or older trout per mile; abundance of wild fish ≥9 inches; potential to catch memorable fish; significant public access; mean width >20 feet.

STOCKED

Survival to the end of May; does not already support adequate fisheries for black bass or walleye, even though technically a trout stream; public access; mean width >10 feet.

STOCKED-EXTENDED

Reach conditions offer potential for spring-stocked trout to survive into summer; temperatures generally suitable for regular stocking through mid-June for two consecutive months. Significant public access of at least 3 miles of cumulative reach length. Mean width >20 feet.

New York State's vast number of public access lands available for not only anglers but also outdoor enthusiasts of all kinds is one of its greatest assets. The Adirondack Park alone has thousands of acres available to hikers, boaters, hunters, and fly-rodders. Of particular importance to inland stream anglers are the state-acquired public-fishing easements acquired since 1935. NYSDEC has worked with private landowners to ensure access to some of the best fishing waters in the country. Some 1,300 miles of

Many public fishing access parking areas are identified by large hanging signs. NYSDEC has recently replaced many of the old, worn signage with new signs along many stream, pond, and lake access sites.

Public Fishing Rights (PFR) easements have been purchased on over 400 streams across the state.

NYSDEC's yellow signs posted along stream reaches, and large hanging signs at official parking lots, serve as welcome mats to fly fishers. Use caution in interpreting the public frontage available as some stream reaches run in and out of public access, interrupted by private property inaccessible to anglers. However, access to private, unposted stretches is often available to anglers who ask for permission to fish.

You'd be surprised how much additional water is available to fish by just politely asking a landowner permission to do so. The best course is always to ask permission when posted signs are encountered. My friend Bill Newcomb often asks permission, informing the landowner he brings

Yellow Public Fishing Rights signs are posted along angling access areas on both streams and stillwaters. Anglers will sometimes encounter these signs posted next to no trespassing signs, causing confusion. Landowners who own public easement fishing waters are still allowed to post their property to prohibit other activities such as hunting.

along a small bag to retrieve any trash he might encounter along the stream. Besides official public easements and permissions often available on private property, New York additional fishing access is available along many of the best waters.

Good trout fishing in wilderness settings is available on State Forest Preserve land. You'll encounter the Forest Preserve signage that is nailed to trees along roads. While sampling waters in the Catskill region, and in the Lower Hudson Valley, plenty of access

New York State holds extensive forest lands, open to public fishing access. Some of the best brook trout waters flow through State Forest Preserve lands in the Adirondack and Catskill Mountains.

Free permits are available online from the New York City Department of Environmental Protection (DEP). Not all waters that flow through DEP lands require a permit. Signage along the various waters that are connected to New York City's water supply reservoirs clearly indicates when a permit is required. Such cooperative access efforts from DEP have opened many miles of productive fishing waters.

is available through the generosity of the New York City Department of Environmental Protection. You'll encounter their white and blue signage. Many trout holding tributaries that flow into their many water system reservoirs are available by obtaining a free permit, easily available online. Also in the mix are the many town and county public parks that abut streams, ponds, and lakes.

I'd be remiss not to mention one additional suggestion before delving into the streams, lakes, and ponds that follow, as it's in my mind equal in importance than merely netting a big trout or bass, or any other fish on a favorite fly pattern. Take time to appreciate the natural environment around you.

Whether it be a snake slithering over a rotten log, or some interesting land feature like old stone walls running along a stream built in a time now long past. Or a Trillium springing up from the earth, encountered while trekking along a woodland path to a creek. Or a field of wildflowers surrounding your waders along the way. Historical signage is everywhere along the waters we fish and enjoy—like naturalist John Burroughs's gravesite and the "thinking boulder" I encountered years ago, with its inset plaque, situated up a lonely Catskill country road. All of these distractions that interrupt your primary mission—to catch fish—will add so much more to your experiences while on New York State fly-fishing waters.

A marker honoring Al Prindle, who once served as postmaster in the Hamlet of Shushan, was placed near the Batten Kill around the corner from the old post office. Batten Kill fly fisher Lew Oatman (1902–1958) created a now-classic-yet-effective streamer fly aptly named "Shushan Postmaster" as a tribute to his friend.

Naturalist John Burroughs (1837–1931) sat on his "Thinking Boulder" during boyhood, contemplating his natural world. It's located at his burial site on a Catskill mountain near Roxbury, near the East Branch of the Delaware River headwaters.

Wild Columbine (*Aquilegia canadensis*), typically found on rocky outcrops or open slopes from April to July, is just one of many flower species fly fishers might encounter while exploring New York's waters.

NEW YORK STATE FLY HATCHES

Anyone interested in determining roughly when a certain aquatic insect emergence will occur, on average, on a particular inland trout stream, in a certain geographic area, should get their hands on Paul Weamer's book *Pocketguide to New York Hatches* (2013). I concur with my good friend Paul and his assessment of hatching charts. It's very difficult to project precisely when you'll encounter a given hatch.

As Paul aptly recognized and described, lots of variables must be considered, even on the same stream. What geographical area is the stream flowing through? Is it a headwater reach, or a lower reach located miles downstream? Is it a cloudy, cool day, or a bright sunshine day? Is there a seasonal temperature, water level, or other factors that are different from an average or typical year? Paul had it right when he wrote that the order of hatch appearances during the season is probably more important to be aware of than projecting exact timing. For certain, you'll encounter *Ephemerella subvaria* (Hendrickson) before you'll encounter *Isonychia bicolor* (Slate Drake) during the calendar year.

Something else I noticed over the years is the tailwaters below the Catskill reservoirs can experience hatch duration and timing differences from freestone trout streams flowing in the same vicinity. My now-faded journal notes from my teenage years on May 20, 1970, on the West Branch of the Delaware River tailwater, indicated Hendricksons were hatching. After all these years, I still remember that hatch downstream from Deposit

General New York State Hatches Emergence Dates

Common Name	Latin Name	General Emergence Ranges Early to Late	Sizes
Little Black Stonefly	*Taeniopteryx nivalis*	Late February to Early April	#18–20
Early Brown Stonefly	*Strophopteryx fasciata*	Early March to Early April	#14–16
Little Blue-Winged Olive	*Baetis*	1st—March to April 2nd—Late September to October	#18–20
Little Black Caddis	*Chimarra* spp.	Mid-April to Early September	#16–18
Quill Gordon	*Epeorus pleuralis*	Mid-April to Mid-May	#12–14
Spring Blue Quill	*Paraleptophlebia adoptiva*	Mid-April to Mid-May	#16–18
Grannom	*Brachycentrus* spp.	Late April to Early May	#12–14
Apple Caddis	*Brachycentrus Appalachia, B. Spinae*	Early May to Late May	#14–16
Hendrickson/Red Quill	*Ephemerella subvaria*	Mid-April to Mid-May	#14–16
Spotted Sedge	*Hydropsyche*	May to September	#14–16
March Brown	*Maccaffertium vicarium*	Mid-May to Mid-June	#10–14
Big Sulphur	*Ephemerella invaria*	Mid-May to Late June	#14–16
Giant Stonefly	*Pteronarcys dorsata*	Late May to Late June	#6–8
Golden Stonefly	*Isoperla* and *Acroneuria* sp. and *Paragnetina immarginata*	Late April to Late July	#6–12
Dark Blue Sedge	*Psilotrata labida* and *P. frontalis*	Mid-May to Late June	#12–14
Little Sulphur	*Ephemerella dorothea dorothea*	Late May to Late June	#18–20
Green Drake	*Ephemera guttulata*	Late May to Early June	#10–12
Brown Drake	*Ephemera simulans*	Late May to Late June	#10–12
Blue-Winged Olive	*Drunella lata*	Early June to Early July	#14–16
Cream Cahill	*Maccaffertium* spp.	Early June to Late June	#14
Dun Variant (Slate Drake)	*Isonychia bicolor*	1st—Late May to Late June 2nd—Mid-September to Early October	#10–14
Pink Cahill	*Epeorus vitreus*	1st—Mid-June to Late June 2nd—Early September to Mid-September	#14–16
Yellow Sallie, Lime Sallie	*Isoperla, Alloperla*	Mid -May to Mid-July	#14–16
Light Cahill	*Stenacron interpunctatum*	Mid-June to Mid-July	#14
Yellow Drake	*Ephemera varia*	Late June to Mid-July	#10–12
Golden Drake	*Anthopotamus distinctus*	Late June to Mid-July	#10–12
Trico	*Tricorythodes* spp.	Mid-July to Mid-September	#22–26
Hebe, Pale Evening Dun	*Leucrocuta hebe*	Early August to Early October	#16–18
White Fly	*Ephoron leucon*	Mid-August to Early September	#12–14
October Caddis	*Pycnopsyche* spp.	Early October to Late October	#12

Little Black Stone Fly
(*Taeniopteryx nivalis*)

Little Brown Stone
(*Strophopteryx fasciata*)

Quill Gordon
(*Epeorus pleuralis*)

Little Blue-Winged Olive
(*Baetis tricaudatus*)

Spring Blue Quill (Mahogany Dun)
(*Paraleptophlebia adoptiva*)

Hendrickson (Female
Ephemerella subvaria)

Red Quill (Male
Ephemerella subvaria)

Grannom (*Brachyentrus numerous*)

Golden Stonefly
(*Acroneuria* sp.)

Yellow Sallie
(*Isoperla* sp.)

Apple Caddis (*Brachyentrus appalachia*)

Big Sulphur
(*Ephemerella invaria*)

Little Black Caddis
(*Chimarra* sp.)

Spotted Sedge
(*Hydropsyche* sp.)

Cream Cahill
(*Maccaffertium* sp.)

Light Cahill (*Stenonema interpunctatum*)

Green Drake
(*Ephemera guttulata*)

Coffin Fly
(*Ephemera guttulata*)

Little Sulphur (*Ephemerella dorothea dorothea*)

Slate Drake
(*Isonychia bicolor*)

White Fly
(*Ephoron leukon*)

Golden Drake (*Anthopotamus distinctus*)

Trico (*Tricorythodes* sp.)

because of the massive number of duns emerging. That date would be considered on the late side for Hendricksons on some streams.

Spin forward to May 25, 2019. I ran into Nick DelleDonne on that very same stretch. We both marveled at the large number of Hendricksons hatching; he took a fine brown trout on a Hendrickson Comparadun because he had the sense to have the fly pattern with him. In 2018, while on the upper Beaver Kill at the covered bridge pool, I encountered a strong emergence of Quill Gordons beyond mid-May—the normal hatch timing for that bug hatch begins in April, usually lasting into the first week of May or mid-May.

Timing can go the other way, too, and show up when least expected. After the unusual, almost winterless winter of 2011–2012, I ran into Batten Kill regular Rich Norman fishing below the Buffam's Bridge in Shushan. It was April 8, the water level was low, and the pool was covered with Hendrickson's—way early for that river. Rich noticed Hendricksons emerging on April 1 during that weird year, so he was prepared with the flies he needed. I watched Rich from my vantage point on the bridge entice a fine brown trout feeding on the duns.

The point of this is to consider emergence tables and the hatch duration bar graphs you'll often see with an understanding of the variabilities that exist. During April, you'll want to carry patterns in your box for emergences that can appear from March into early May. Once mid-May arrives, lots of hatches begin to overlap, so be ready for anything. During the "bug week" that begins in the Catskills in late May into June, you'll encounter all kinds of hatches.

I use a more simplified approach, something Paul Weamer pointed out, by understanding that emergences typically occur later in the Adirondacks than in the Catskills. Western regions can experience hatches that might be considered early when compared to other streams around the state. I've listed here *general* date ranges for some of the more important hatches and *general* emergence times during the day. You'll encounter many others on New York's streams and ponds. Check Paul Weamer's book for a complete list.

Western Region

ounded by Lake Erie and the upper Niagara River to the east, areas of Lake Ontario to its north, the core of the Finger Lakes Region to its east, and the Pennsylvania border on the south, New York's Western Region can satisfy the interest of most any fly rodder. However, defining exact boundaries of the region can be a head-scratcher.

There is considerable disagreement, and confusion, among state agencies about which New York State counties should be included as "Western New York." Some state agencies include only five to eight counties in their Western New York description. Travel guides include as many as 17 counties. It has been written that inhabitants sometimes can't decide if they're from Western New York or the Finger Lakes region that lies to the east since a couple of those outlying lakes extend into their area. This blending of one region into another, of course, occurs statewide. Such agency boundary confusion isn't confined to only "Western New York." I used some degree of liberal license in what waters are included in this section and what waters spill over into the core Finger Lakes Region. (I faced this same challenge with all other New York regions, throughout this book, and took the same liberal approach.)

That said, the certainty is Western New York includes streams and stillwaters that provide a wide variety of fly-fishing opportunities. The western extreme of the region

Productive trout streams scattered throughout Western New York, such as Wiscoy Creek, flow through picturesque rolling hills and farm country valleys. Wiscoy Creek, including its North Branch, along with neighboring Clear Creek, has benefitted from habitat and stream bank projects that include tree sapling plantings like those shown here on Wiscoy's Arbor Road reach. (PHOTO VALERIE VALLA)

is known for its steelhead that run tributary streams that dump into Lake Erie. Muskellunge inhabit both stillwaters and big rivers, rivers such as the Susquehanna and upper Niagara. Anglers of all persuasions, both conventional tackle enthusiasts and fly fishers, know Western New York is "muskie country." Sizeable bass can also be enticed with flies on these same waters.

Big muskies, bass, and steelhead aside, Western New York's rolling inland countryside streams provide excellent brown trout fishing, with good fly hatches, in some of the most productive waters found in New York. Efforts from New York State Department of Environmental Conservation (NYSDEC) have provided sustained attention to its inland waters, as have local Trout Unlimited chapters. For certain, good fly-fishing experiences can be had in Western New York.

Wiscoy Creek

Anglers seeking streams in Western New York that are managed as wild trout fisheries should head to Wiscoy Creek. In the hamlet of Bliss, located in Wyoming County, the North and West branches of the creek merge, sending their combined water on a 20-mile journey to a confluence with the Genesee River. Popular among many fly anglers, Wiscoy Creek is located within an hour's drive of Buffalo and Rochester, two of New York's largest cities. The stream is considered by fisheries biologists as one of the most productive wild trout waters in New York.

Abundant spring seepages keep the water cool all summer, a feature that contributes to Wiscoy Creek's healthy wild trout population. However, water temperatures aside, the stream has enjoyed plenty of attention from conservation organizations that helped contribute to the quality trout stream that it is. NYS Bureau of Fisheries Region 9 staff have also done an outstanding job providing a significant amount of sustained focus on this gem, over many years. The Western New York Chapter of Trout Unlimited has also helped enhance the stream's wild trout potential.

While Wiscoy Creek was historically a brook trout fishery, and although anglers today occasionally report netting a colorful brookie in the stream's upper reaches, it's the wild brown trout that bring fly anglers to the creek. From the 1940s through the late 1960s, Wiscoy Creek received liberal hatchery trout stockings. Over time, annual fish-stocking practices were eliminated as the creek's self-sustaining potential improved.

Stream management changes that helped Wiscoy Creek were made possible through a combination of regulation changes, habitat enhancement, and water-quality improvements. Trout populations in Wiscoy Creek have been intensely studied over the last 70 years.

The major trout sections are located in the creek's upper 17 miles. Anglers will have no problem gaining access to the stream via nearly 13 miles of Public Fishing Rights (PFR) easements. While some water is interrupted by private mileage, much of the stream flows through long, continuous PFR reaches. PFR stretches on the main branch of Wiscoy exist from its headwaters in Bliss some 10 miles downstream to near the intersection of Lapp Road and Pond Road. Many stretches are accessed via designated footpaths that lead from roads to the creek.

The North Branch: Two PFR sections located on the North Branch of Wiscoy Creek can be accessed via footpaths that lead from State Route 362 to the stream. Anglers can access the first path that leads to the PFR water by driving north just south of Gary Road along State Route 362, about 1.2 miles from its intersection with State Route 39 in Bliss. Two additional access footpaths lead from State Route 362 to a PFR stretch upstream

The Camp Road reach has some of the nicest Wiscoy Creek stretches flowing in a woodland setting. Several access points are available along Camp Road via designated footpaths that lead to the stream. (PHOTO VALERIE VALLA)

from Gary Road Drive 0.5 mile north on State Route 362 from the Gary Road intersection and watch for a small New York State Department of Environmental Conservation (NYSDEC) footpath sign on your right. You'll pass a large white and green metal garage on your right just before arriving at the sign along a cornfield and row of evergreen trees. The path will lead to the lowermost extent of the North Branch PFR water.

Drive an additional 0.5 mile north on State Route 362 to reach another NYSDEC footpath sign. You'll pass a large red barn on your left before arriving at the NYSDEC hanging sign on the right side of the road. Even if the fishing is slow, a walk to the creek in this uppermost extent of the PFR water is worth the short trek. You'll admire the stream habitat improvements that have made a difference in the creek's wild trout productivity. Electrofishing data collected in 2019 showed improved adult wild trout numbers.

In 2011, the North Branch PFR reach located upstream from Gary Road was greatly enhanced with significant habitat improvement work, involving over 2,000 feet along the stream. Deep pools were lacking, as well as appropriate overhead shade. A large number of "Lunker" structures (wooden cribs) were placed in the stream to create artificial undercut banks. Over a thousand shade trees saplings were also planted in grow tubes.

The collaborative effort involved the Western New York Chapter of Trout Unlimited, US Fish and Wildlife Service, NYSDEC, Department of Transportation, Wyoming County Soil and Water Conservation District, Wyoming County Highway Department, Wyoming County Fairgrounds Association, the Elm Research Institute, and Finger Lakes–Lake Ontario Water Protection Alliance.

The Main Branch: Leaving the North Branch behind, the uppermost formal NYSDEC angling parking area on the main branch of Wiscoy Creek is located on State Route 39 0.5 mile east of the State Route 362/State Route 39 intersection in Bliss. The lot is at the upper extent of the stream's Catch and Release area that runs a half-mile upstream to a half-mile downstream of East Hillside Road Bridge. A nice little riffle and pool are located directly alongside the parking lot, but the narrow headwaters flow through a stretch confined by bankside alders that's difficult to fully negotiate with a fly rod. However, drifting small wet flies, such as a Partridge and Orange soft-hackle pattern, through the riffles and runs along this stretch can elicit strikes.

Continue driving east on State Route 39 from the first parking area, and in just short of 2 miles, you'll encounter another formal NYSDEC angling parking lot. The small parking area isn't located directly on the stream. Access the creek by walking 150 feet or so along a tree line and farmer's field toward the creek. The stream that flows along this reach is pleasant and a bit easier to fish since it's not quite as narrow and confined as water located upstream.

You'll get into even easier water to fly fish by continuing east on State Route 39, a little over 2 miles to a large angler parking turnout on the right side of the road. An easy entry/departure loop off State Route 39 makes the parking area convenient for delivery vehicles and others seeking a good place to pull off the road. Anglers also find the parking loop convenient since it provides a good location to access both Wiscoy Creek and Trout Brook, a major tributary that also holds wild trout. Trout Brook joins Wiscoy Creek at the State Route 39 bridge crossing, very close to the parking lot.

Uninterrupted, continuous PFR water flows downstream from Wiscoy Creek's junction with Trout Brook, some of which can be accessed at bridge crossings on the way to the hamlet of Pike. Arbor Road, located 0.2 mile east of the State Route 39 Trout Brook bridge crossing (1.5 miles west of the State Route 39/County Road 19 intersection if driving from that direction downstream), is worth throwing a few casts. A small parking area is located next to the bridge. You'll notice a significant number of tree sapling grow tubes along both sides of the stream near the large dairy barn (the grow tubes themselves might be removed by the time you visit the area but the growing saplings should be visible). The 2020 plantings were part of the ongoing area collaborative streamside habitat improvement efforts.

Driving east from Arbor Road and then turning right onto County Road 19 will deliver you to Pike, where you can access the creek. A formal NYSDEC sign is hanging at the bridge crossing a mile from the State Route 39/County Road 19 intersection, just beyond the US Post Office on Main Street. This is not the most pleasant reach to fish, unless you're not bothered by the commotion that exists along a storefront and residential area. Fly anglers are better served by relocating well downstream from the town, along Camp Road, where both formal NYSDEC angling parking lots as well as officially designated footpaths are located.

Drive back in the direction of State Route 39/County Road 19 on Main Street to a right turn on County Road 24 (East Koy Road), then drive 2 miles to a right on Camp Road. The first of two formal NYSDEC parking lots on Camp Road is located 0.2 mile down Camp Road from the previous intersection.

The parking lot is not that far from the stream, much closer than other access points along Camp Road. Your minor challenge will be to get down a long and substantially steep hill to the creek. After parking, stroll through a mature hemlock stand that ends at a steep precipice (your first reaction might be, "Do I really want to fish here?"). There's usually a "community" rope tied to a large hemlock tree that enables anglers to get down the steep hill along a well-worn path that leads to the bottom. My wife Valerie was able to get down without too much trouble holding the rope as she descended, standing upright. I found myself holding the rope but electing to slide down on my rear end.

If it's there, double-check the rope to make sure it's absolutely secure to the tree if you intend to use it. The rope doesn't extend to the extreme bottom of the hill, but it drops down far enough to make your life easier. Once you reach the bottom of the path, and the creek, you'll realize the effort was worth it—it's a beautiful reach, in a secluded woodland setting, with very nice pools, runs, and riffles. Fishing downstream, nymphs and streamers can often entice small wild brown trout. Fish upstream with dry flies.

Of course, there are other ways than descending down a rope to access the creek reach in this general area. Continue driving down Camp Road south of the Babbitt Road intersection and you'll encounter designated official footpaths, some longer than others, to reach the creek, marked by small signage along the road. You'll pass by one before arriving at the second formal NYSDEC parking lot that's located 1 mile from the East Koy Road/Camp Road intersection. Another footpath is located beyond the parking lot as well as a long path past the intersection with Graham Road. The long footpath is located on Armison Road beyond the Wyoming County/Allegany County Line.

Wiscoy Creek has an assortment of common mayfly and caddis emergences commonly found on other fertile New York streams. You'll encounter the usual batch of aquatic

Partridge and Orange (tied by Tom Mason)
An early soft-hackle wet fly pattern, Partridge and Orange originated in England during the 1800s. It's a great pattern to swing through riffles along most any trout stream, including Wiscoy Creek. New York fly tiers such as Tom Mason and John Shaner are passionate followers of old British soft-hackle patterns that work well on New York streams.

Sawyer Pheasant Tail Nymph (tied by Bob Herson)
Sometimes called simply the PT Nymph, this old British nymph pattern is attributed to Frank Sawyer, who developed it on the Hampshire River Avon, in the late 1950s. American fly fishers embrace the fly, and its several variations, coast to coast. Bob ribs his pattern with copper brown UTC Ultra Wire. He likes the wing case tied with dark-shade turkey fibers.

ParaNymph (tied by Tom Baltz)
Tom Baltz's ParaNymph is his signature pattern. Tom is a Pennsylvania fishing guide and commercial fly tier from Boiling Springs, Pennsylvania. The ParaNymph Orange is a general-use dry fly. While Tom ties his ParaNymphs with yellow, pink, or black calf body hair posts, orange is his favorite.

Tricos (tied by Mike Valla)
Wiscoy Creek provides good *Tricorythodes* dry-fly fishing during late season on many of its pools during July and August. Anglers sampling Wiscoy during early morning hours that time of year should carry a supply of Trico dry flies in their boxes.

insects—little black stoneflies in very early spring, followed by Blue Quills, Hendricksons, Caddis, Sulphurs—right down the list. Green Drakes (*Ephemera guttulta*) pop up in late May or early June but not in the numbers you might encounter on other New York streams that are well-known for that mayfly emergence. Area resident and artist Tom Daly, whom I met 11 years ago on Spring Creek in Caledonia, once wrote that the catastrophic 1972 flood (Hurricane Agnes) impacted Green Drake populations and other bugs for some time after, but they slowly returned. Tricos are in abundance from late summer into September.

East Koy Creek

While most consider Wiscoy and its wild trout population and water quality superior to other nearby streams, East Koy Creek provides fly anglers an opportunity to fish for both wild and hatchery-raised brown trout. Unlike Wiscoy Creek, East Koy Creek is heavily stocked with both yearling browns and larger two-year-old, 14-inch fish. Typical plantings total close to 14,000 trout. Access is not an issue along the creek's 13 miles of PFR water. NYSDEC categorized East Koy Creek as Stocked-Extended.

If fishing Wiscoy Creek along the Camp Road, you're very close to East Koy Creek. A short three-minute, 1.2-mile drive from the Camp Road/Babbitt Road intersection along Babbitt Road will get you to a formal NYSDEC angling parking lot and PFR water. It's located next to a bridge crossing on Overholt Road. This reach of East Koy Creek, and the PFR stretch downstream accessed by an official footpath along Clute Road (0.3 mile from the Clute/Overholt intersection), can sometimes warm up significantly. The stream reach is best fished in late April into May or early June.

East Koy Creek at Overhead Road bridge crossing. A sister stream in the neighborhood of Wiscoy Creek, East Koy Creek can provide a different angling experience since its stream reaches receive brown trout stockings. Some 13 miles of public fishing easement stretches are available to anglers. NYSDEC classifies East Koy Creek as Stocked-Extended water from the Wyoming County Line upstream to Green Bay Road. (PHOTO VALERIE VALLA)

Bead Head Hare's Ear (tied by Bob Herson) Bead Head patterns, such as Bead Head Hare's Ear, work well on Easy Koy Creek. This example tied by Bob Herson is scraggly and insect-like in appearance, a sure bet fished along East Koy's riffles and pools, particularly during May.

Other access points upstream can be reached at bridge crossings and along official footpaths along Lamont Road. From the formal NYSDEC parking lot above, drive 0.4 mile east on Overholt (a seasonal dirt road at this point) to Wiscoy Road (County Road 29). Take a left on Wiscoy 0.4 mile, then a left to a bridge crossing on E. Koy Road. Lamont Road is 0.3 mile west of the bridge crossing. You'll notice a large NYSDEC sign hanging next to the bridge. You can't park there (a dwelling owner had problems with anglers blocking his driveway), but the PFR stretch is nice. You can park up the road a distance from the bridge, along the road shoulder.

You'll encounter several official footpath access signs located along the 7.3 miles between East Koy Road and County Road 19 on Lamont Road that will lead to the stream. These are located 0.3, 0.8, 2.3, and 4.4 miles north of the East Koy Road/Lamont Road intersection. The paths are long, running along tree lines or open farm fields. They are not difficult to trek.

You'll see a large NYSDEC sign next to the bridge crossing at the County Road 19/Lamont Road/Shearing Road intersection. The water is nice, but make sure you don't park directly next to the open field area next to the bridge; it's used by the fire department during situations when they need to pump water from the stream.

Other easier areas to park are located upstream along Shearing Road, located 0.2 and 0.5 mile north of the intersection. The first large road shoulder turnout that provides parking right next to the stream undoubtedly gets heavy use early in the season after fish stockings, due to the very easy stream access. Some fly anglers prefer to fish East Koy Creek instead of Wiscoy Creek. Much of the season, East Koy Creek doesn't encounter the same degree of fishing activity once general angling pressure subsides shortly after trout are stocked early in the spring. Many of the same hatches that emerge on Wiscoy Creek can be encounterd on East Koy Creek. Use any fly patterns that you would cast on the Wiscoy Creek or other waters in the general area. Hare's Ear patterns work well.

Spring Creek

Spring Creek in the Village of Caledonia is within range of a large city—Rochester—yet the challenge of catching fish here seems to thin the crowds. A NYSDEC angling parking area is located on State Route 36 (North Street) just beyond the historic Caledonia Fish Hatchery. The Caledonia facility was the first hatchery operated in the Western Hemisphere; it was founded by the "father of fish culture," Seth Green. From the state access parking area, a short trail leads to some 1,000 feet of accessible water, below which the stream flows through private property (club water).

Spring Creek offers fairly easy wide-open casting. The Creek ranges from 50 to 75 feet wide with few casting obstructions. The shoreline is quite mucky, with buried deadfalls just waiting to trip anglers, so wading care is in order. The best way to tackle the creek is to ease into the white-sand channels where wading is easy. A primitive path along the creek's right stream bank offers entryways into the downstream section.

While the fishing reach shares the same massive spring as the hatchery, the quarry is not dumb hatchery trout. Spring Creek trout are very brightly colored and very difficult to entice. One angler remarked, in an 1884 *New Your Times* story, that the fish "can only be taken with a fly, and their taste as to them is exceedingly epicurean."

Fly fishers new to the creek will immediately become frustrated by spotting so many trout, often darting under their legs while they wade, that are disinterested in quickly rising to a fly. This is not a place for a size 12 deer hair ant that produces so well on other New York cold-spring waters, and it's not the place for an impatient angler. Summer fishing involves 12-foot leaders and 8X tippets, along with midge flies as small as size 32.

Thomas Aquinas Daly and Bruce Kurland (1938–2013), two talented artists, two dear fly-fishing friends, who enjoyed decades of experience on Spring Creek, called their

Tom Daly plays a fussy Spring Creek brown trout that took a Kurland Midge. The creek's public fishing stretch inhabits fussy trout. Flowing out of the Caledonia Fish Hatchery, anglers are often surprised when they learn its colorful resident brown trout are not as easy to catch as they might have assumed. Pods of fish will readily show themselves within feet of the stream bank, paying no attention to an angler's fly offering.

Spring Creek offers wide-open casting to hypercritical brown trout. (PHOTO VALERIE VALLA)

favorite slice of water "the laboratory." It's a place to study the dimpling trout and a water to continue their search for optimum summer fly designs. I ran into the two on the creek, over a decade ago. Our pleasant streamside chat was most enjoyable.

"We prefer overcast days," Bruce explained to me on the stream that summer during a 90-degree day (Daly was in the middle of landing a fine 13-inch brown). "The line will not cast a shadow over the fish and lessens (the chance of) spooking them."

Bruce designed a midge pattern that seems to take trout fairly regularly during the heat and midday. Tom, who is well known for his landscape and sporting paintings, explained the development of the fly while we chatted at streamside. "We had been using myriad small flies, including Jassids, to no avail. We found the actual insect [*Diptera*] that Bruce copied with a unique wing design. Any type quill on the body seems to work."

Tom uses a size 28 TMC 518 hook, which has a short shank, straight eye, a 3X fine wire, and a wider gap than other small hooks on the market. The midge fly wing is created by clipping a dun hackle into two very narrow, splayed-out hackle barb wings. The barbs are attached to the quill, on each side, and secured to the hook shank. The brownish hackle is trimmed top and bottom. The two enjoyed fishing the Blue-Winged Olive hatches together on Spring Creek, as well as the Sulphurs, at other times during the season. But they recognized that Spring Creek's fertile, ultra-cold spring water offers good sport during the summer.

There is no doubt one of the most knowledgeable Spring Creek anglers is Bob Herson. Bob, a commercial fly tier, fishing guide, and ardent Spring Creek fly fisher, is known for helping keep fly bins full at the Dette Fly Shop in the Catskills. However, he lives a couple hundred feet from Spring Creek, in Caledonia, and if anyone understands the challenges of netting a trout on that stream, it's Bob. The flies he recommended and tied are awesome. He's also a very knowledgeable Oatka Creek fly fisher. Spring Creek dumps into the Oatka in Caledonia.

Kurland Midge (Tom Daly) Tom Daly, along with his fishing partner Bruce Kurland, developed a midge pattern in 2009 that brought consistent fish-catching results. Small Jassid patterns didn't work well for the two, which led to the development of their very tiny fly that better matched the Diptera trout sipped on their favorite stretch. Tom ties the fly on a size 28 TMC 518 hook.

Burkhart Nymph (tied by Bob Herson)
Bob Herson also embraces a Burkhart Nymph when asked about Spring Creek fly choices. A Daiichi 1120 hook is a good choice when tying the pattern. Bob hangs wood-duck flank fiber tails off a grey goose biot body. In communication, Bob described how he ties the thorax: "The Burkhart's thorax is grey goose that I like to twist while wrapping forward as the fibers seem to stand out better. I then bring the fibers up to the eye of the hook, make a couple wraps, and then draw it back to the start of the thorax, make a few thread wraps, and draw it back to the eye of the hook and tie off. The wing case is situated on the top of the hook as always. Same technique you would use in the Sawyer Pheasant tail. I always add to coats of thin lacquer to the wing case."

Bonbright-Improved (tied by Bob Herson)
Commercial fly tier Bob Herson, who lives on the banks of Spring Creek, is the angler to ask when contemplating an outing on Spring Creek. Patterns such as his Bonbright-improved combine a 6/0 purple Uni-thread body, lacquered twice. He ties the thorax with Ice Dub UV Purple. A bit of pearl flash adds some sparkle. It's tied both with and without a beadhead. If he ties it with a bead, Bob prefers black.

Spring Creek Scud (tied by Bob Herson)
Scud patterns are always popular on spring creeks, including this water. Bob Herson designed this interesting version. Its body combines orange and olive rabbit fur, ribbed with ultra-small gold wire. UV wader repair adhesive is used to form the dorsal part of the fly.

McBride Nymph (tied by Bob Herson) Tied on a Daiichi 1560 hook, using 8/0 olive thread, Bob tails the fly with a few barred wood-duck flank fiber that exit a body created with 2-4 turkey tail fibers. The turkey tail thorax is built up with black wire, with flash pulled over the top, lacquered two to three times. No doubt a good all-purpose nymph.

The Oatka "Trail" section provides easy access to the stream that's popular with both conventional tackle anglers as well as fly fishers during early to mid-spring. Categorized as Stocked by NYSDEC, the "Trail" reach is best fished during spring. (PHOTO VALERIE VALLA)

Oatka Creek

Flowing through four counties—Wyoming, Genesee, Livingston, and Monroe—the 58-mile-long Oatka Creek changes its character by the time it reaches its confluence with the Genesee River near Scottsville, a dozen or so miles south of Rochester. Oatka Creek has sections categorized by NYSDEC as Stocked, Stocked-Extended, and Wild-Quality.

The headwater stretches near Warsaw are not prime fly-fishing waters. Not until the creek makes its turn from flowing north to flowing east near the County Road 19/Oatka Trail intersection near North Le Roy does it transform into better trout water. Cold springs on the Oatka from what is called the "Blue Hole" change the stream enough to attract fly anglers along the Oatka Trail. However, the "Trail" reach is still mainly supported by hatchery trout stockings. A few wild fish are in the mix. Prime wild trout water picks up once the cold waters of Spring Creek join the stream at Mumford a few miles downstream.

Whenever Oatka Creek pops up in a discussion, I immediately think back to an episode on the stream years ago with my friend Harry Leichtweis. I had recently transferred from a research support position on the Cornell University campus in Ithaca to their Experiment Station, 50 miles north at Geneva, New York. That's where I met Harry, in 1980, who was working on a joint collaborative research project. Sometime after, Harry suggested we fish one of his favorite streams. I recently spoke with Harry and asked him if he recalled the Hendrickson hatch fishing outing we enjoyed years ago on Oatka Creek, during a spinner fall. "Oh, yes! It was epic!" Harry replied.

It *was* "epic." The Hendrickson spinner fall was one of the most impressive we had ever experienced. The trout went nuts when the bugs dropped to the water surface, in a

Oatka Creek at the lower Catch and Release section. Oatka Creek, which reaches downstream from Mumford, attracts most fly anglers who visit the stream. Access is plentiful and easy along the creek's 1.7-mile Special Regulations reach that is well cared for by the Seth Green Chapter of Trout Unlimited and other conservation groups.

feeding frenzy. Multiple hook-ups had me going nuts, too. Meanwhile, I was hollering for Harry to join me upstream on my stretch where the action was. Harry was in water a couple hundred feet downstream, still fumbling with leader material. I briefly left my spot and waded down to help him out, still trying to convince him to relocate upstream. Harry stayed put, but I waded back upstream to resume where I left off. However, the 18-inch colorful wild Oatka brown trout I showed him in my net made him think he should have listened to me. It was a gorgeous fish.

Oatka, like many New York trout streams, has experienced its ups and downs over the last decades, but organizations such as Trout Unlimited and others have helped it with habitat improvements. Merganser waterfowl preying on trout, lack of suitable habitat protection, and other factors have impacted the creek since my early days on the Oatka. However, the stream has enjoyed a rebound.

The stream reach where I experienced that initial Oatka Hendrickson action is along Oatka Trail, a popular stretch because it receives ample brown trout hatchery fish stockings. It's also popular because a couple of parking turnouts are located directly next to the stream. A formal NYSDEC angling parking lot marked by a large hanging sign is located on the Oatka Trail stream reach.

If approaching from the Mumford area, near Caledonia, go 0.5 mile west on State Route 36 from the State Route 36/State Route 383 intersection to County Road 245 (Oatka Road). Keep on Oatka Road. It eventually changes to County Road 17 (Oatka Trail). The creek flows next to Oatka Trail about 2.9 miles from Mumford. (Incidentally, I caught that big brown at the creek's bend on that stretch.) A few well-worn short paths lead into the water from the road shoulder where parking is easy. The formal parking lot is located next to a dwelling another 2.5 miles or so up the road on the left. A path leads to the stream. If approaching from the west, the lot is located a half-mile from the Circular Hill Road/Oatka Trail intersection.

You'll want to fish the Oatka Trail stretch primarily in the spring. Hendricksons (*Ephemerella subvaria*) still emerge along that stretch. I've never found the Oatka Trail section particularly productive during the summer months when the water levels drop and the temperatures rise. Oatka Creek's action can pick back up in the fall, especially downstream from the Mumford area where some mighty nice wild browns inhabit the stream. Commercial fly tier Bob Herson, who knows that stream well (because he lives next to Spring Creek), showed me photos of some awesome big lower creek browns. He's one heck of good tier, and like his knowledge of Spring Creek patterns, he knows what flies are effective for the Oatka.

Pheasant Tail Dry (tied by Bob Herson) While Bob Herson lives on the banks of Spring Creek, he's most enthusiastic about fishing Oatka Creek downstream from its confluence with Spring Creek. Bob recommends several patterns, including an easy-to-tie Pheasant Tail Dry. With light dun hackle wings, darker dun hackle tails, darker dun hackle collar, and darker brown pheasant tail body (ribbed with wire), it has the appearance of a Catskill-style dry fly.

Sulphur Parachute (tied by Bob Herson) Sulphur hatch encounters on Oatka Creek require fly anglers to have a supply of their favorite Sulphur patterns on hand. Many effective Sulphur dry fly patterns have been created and every fly angler has a favorite. Bob Herson's parachute version is effective on Oatka Creek. Bob likes to tie his with a white poly post, lightly hackled, and prefers microfibbet tails, two on each side. His body is a beaver fur mix.

Cree Caddis (tied by Bob Herson) Caddisfly patterns, including dry flies, are effective on Oatka Creek, as they are on all New York State trout streams. Bob Herson's Cree Caddis, tied with cree hackle, clipped underneath, floats well. Its wood-duck flank wing also contributes to the mixture of shades that gives the pattern a very insect-like appearance.

Zug Bug (tied by Bob Herson) A few different versions of the famous Zug Bug, including beadhead styles, have kept both anglers and trout happy for many decades. Attributed to Pensylvanian Cliff Zug, going back to 1930, it's still a very popular fly that is easy to tie.

Most of the experienced Oatka fly anglers don't have much interest in the "Trail" section; they cast lines in stretches that hold wild, big browns. The creek downstream from Mumford is enhanced and, in many ways, much different from the Oatka Trail reach. The stream's influx from Spring Creek provides water temperatures conducive to wild trout management. Restrictive harvest as well as Catch and Release regulations are in place, practices that help ensure the Oatka's wild trout sustainability.

Prior to October 1, 2000, a section of the wild reach allowed for high minimum trout size and minimum creel limits. However, the 1.7-mile stretch along Oatka Creek County Park, categorized as Wild-Quality, was changed to complete Catch and Release after that date. The Oatka Creek County Park section is located off Union Street. The reach in the park from Union Street upstream to Wheatland Center Road falls under the Oatka Creek Special Regulations as year-round Catch and Release and artificial lures only.

There are a couple different ways to get into Oatka Creek's Special Regulations section. Unless you're interested in a very long (yet pleasant) walk along a trail through the main section of the park, much easier access is available. Most anglers park at the designated fishing access lot, located on the north side of the Union Street bridge crossing, down the road from the park's main entrance. It's marked by an Oatka Creek Park sign at its entrance. A maintained footpath leads down the hill to the stream. Check out the little "Flybrary" at the parking area kiosk, where anglers can take a fly and leave a fly. It was placed in memory of fly angler Joe Verdone.

A pleasant walk down the wide path will lead to a smaller yet well-used path that directly follows the creek. You'll instantly recognize that the stretch is well cared for. A significant number of bankside tree sapling grow tubes are located along the stream. The Genesee River Trees for Tribs program was initiated to help replace dead or dying ash trees impacted by Emerald Ash Borer insects. The Seth Green Chapter of Trout Unlimited along with the Oatka Creek Watershed workers and other conservation groups did the plantings. You'll also notice other habitat improvements along the stream reach categorized as Wild-Quality. Some nice riffle/pool structure exists upstream toward the railroad bridge crossing, along the rocky bank on the opposite side of the stream. A small streamside bench is located directly downstream from the bridge where anglers can watch for anticipated rises during the hatch.

Special Regulations also apply downstream of Union Street to Bowerman Road. It's Catch and Release between October 16 and March 31, artificial lures only, but a two-fish harvest with 12-inch minimum size is allowed April 1 through October 15. New York State also allowed the same regulation upstream of Wheatland Center Road to the mouth of Spring Creek in Mumford.

During the early season, you'll encounter Little Black Stoneflies (*Taeniopteryx nivalis*), followed by the usual variety of mayflies and caddis flies that inhabit other area streams. Be sure to have Sulphur patterns when that mayfly appears later in the season.

Ischua Creek

I asked my friend, Harry Leichtweis, how to correctly pronounce the local trout stream where he first learned to cast flies. I wrongly pronounced the stream that originates in the Town of Machias, Catteraguas County, "Ish—oo—wah." Harry would know. After the creek flows 20 miles downstream from its source, it eventually dumps into the Allegany River at Olean. Harry grew up in Olean and attended college in the same city located less than 10 miles from the Pennsylvania border. The stream is pronounced "ISH-way."

Ischua Creek, at the Cooney Road NYSDEC angling access area. While some wild trout inhabit its upper reaches, NYSDEC categorizes the Ischua as Stocked.

Access is not a problem on this stream that's inhabited by both hatchery and wild brown trout, although NYSDEC categorized the stream Stocked. Most of the encounters are with stocked fish that anglers net along the 17 miles of PFR water from Machias downstream to Maplehurst, just short of I-86. The PFR reaches are not continuous as the stream traverses through the upstream reaches around the hamlet of Machias and the Village of Franklinville. Ischua continues downstream through the small hamlets of Cadiz, Fitch, and its namesake Ischua. The creek intermittently flows through posted and private sections.

Along its stretches, Ischua Creek receives around 7,500 brown trout between 9 and 15 inches. Anglers might be surprised to latch into large Randolph Fish Hatchery breeder trout and surplus browns that are usually stocked in late September into October in the Ischua and other area waters. NYSDEC reported that the adult wild trout population around Franklinville has varied from around 100 fish per mile to upwards of 500 per mile in some years.

The uppermost PFR reach is located north of Franklinville near Machias. Drive 5 miles north of the intersection of Plymouth Street and North Main Street (State Route 16) to State Route 242. (You'll notice a small, official fishing-access footpath sign directly across from Barbara's Maple Haven Restaurant at this intersection. Bypass it for now.) Take a left on State Route 242 and head west to Maple Avenue Drive a little less than a mile to the bridge crossing.

You can park on the far side of the bridge, on the road shoulder beyond the guardrail, near a NYSDEC large hanging sign. Get into the water by making your way down a short, steep, grassy hill at the bridge crossing. After exiting a small pool directly below the bridge, the stream flows down around a bend behind Gary Herman Memorial Park. If you're after wild fish, there's a chance you'll get one along this reach.

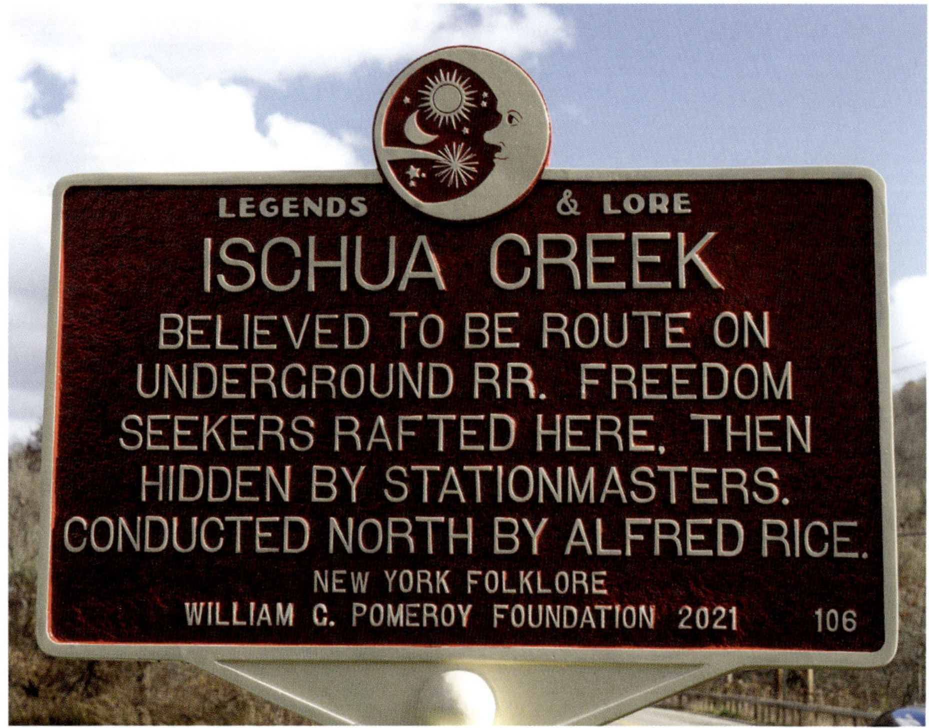

Ischua Creek has greater significance than trout fishing. The creek is thought to be part of a network of clandestine routes established during the nineteenth century that enabled African Americans to seek refuge in free states and Canada.

Working your way downstream, the next PFR reach that's worthy of a couple casts is located back down at the State Route 16/Plymouth Street intersection, across from Barbara's Maple Haven Restaurant. A short official footpath beginning at the small sign will lead to the stream. Long, slow-moving pools that typify Ischua Creek throughout its length flow through this section.

A longer PFR reach with similar slow-moving pools in Franklinville is located a short drive downstream at a formal NYSDEC angling parking area on Factory Street Drive 0.6 mile south on Main Street to Elm Street. Take a right and go a couple hundred feet to Factory Street on the left. You'll encounter a formal NYSDEC angling parking area marked by a hanging sign a couple hundred feet down the road. Walk across the mowed area between the spruce trees to the water. You might see a massive log jam once you arrive at the creek. It'll take one heck of a flood event to move the jumble of broken trees, limbs, and woody debris. If that stretch doesn't elicit fish strikes, head further downstream.

The stream winds and turns as it makes its way south to the State Route 98 bridge crossing. To reach it, drive 1.3 miles south from the Elm Street/State Route 16 intersection to the State Route 16/State Route 98 intersection in Cadiz. You can park at the intersection and walk a couple hundred feet to the stream at the bridge. (There's not a lot of room to park near the large hanging NYSDEC sign at the bridge.) The more interesting feature about this area is a historical sign located near the bridge. Ischua Creek is believed to be a route on the Underground Railroad, where freedom seekers rafted.

Water somewhat more fly-fishing friendly is located a short distance downstream at a second formal NYSDEC angling parking area located on Cooney Road. Drive just short of a mile south on State Route 16 where you'll see a large NYSDEC hanging sign at its intersection with Cooney Road. Drive a short distance down Cooney Road (a short dead-end road) to the large streamside parking lot. The stream enters slower-moving water from a nice yet short upstream run then continues downstream into reaches typically strewn with deadfalls that provide fish habitat cover. The creek here, located directly in front of the parking area, is very popular with early season anglers, largely because it's so accessible. Expect company during April and May.

Ischua Creek's low-gradient nature continues downstream, passing under bridge crossings that generally feature the same flatwater structure, typically with slow water and often deep pools. Some crossings, such as at Coal Chutes Road, have tailouts downstream from the bridge pools that harbor nice fish. Coal Chutes Road is located 1.7 miles south of Cooney Road off State Route 16.

The PFR reach at Coal Chutes Road is upstream from the truss bridge. However, a run a hundred feet or so downstream is apparently not posted, other than "no littering" signs located at the downstream sides of the bridge. Other bridge crossings off State Route 16 at Pierce Hill Road, Five Mile Road, Dutch Hill Road, and others downstream provide access to PFR reaches.

The Pierce Road bridge crossing, located a mile south of Coal Chutes Road, off State Route 16, has the typical, long flatwater above the bridge, but there's a nicer stretch that flows on the downstream side. The reach quickly reverts to the stream's characteristic pool structure, then snakes and winds downstream to the Five Mile Road crossing, located a half-mile south of Pierce Road, off State Route 16. What makes this crossing interesting are the very large parking turnouts that surround both sides of the bridge.

The stream structure isn't very remarkable until it gets down to the Dutch Hill Road crossing located 2.5 miles south of Pierce Road off State Route 16. At the State Route 16 intersection, take a right then in 0.2 mile, cross the bridge. Park on the road shoulder on the far side of the bridge, beyond the guardrail. The PFR water located downstream from the bridge has water worth trying.

Anglers who are willing to trek into reaches well away from roads and bridge crossings can access Ischua Creek via two additional NYSDEC footpaths marked by small signs along State Route 16. They both roughly follow overhead power lines. One is located 0.7 mile south from Cooney Road. The other path is located just short of the State Route 16/Hatch Road intersection approximately 1.7 miles south of Dutch Hill Road. A green Olean Airport sign is located just a few feet from the small official footpath sign, near a utility pole. Ample area for parking is located across State Route 16 on the corner of Hatch Road.

The "footpath" (hang tight to the left of a cultivated cornfield under the power lines) leads to a nice downstream riffle stretch that roughly parallels the railroad tracks along the stream at that point. You'll encounter a freshly posted NYSDEC Stocked section categorization signage along the stream bank. Other nice structures are located upstream. After flowing a short distance, the creek bumps back next to State Route 16, along a rocky embankment, then quickly flows away from the road. Anglers who wish to sample the slow-moving stretch where the stream briefly flows along the embankment, as well as stretches downstream, can do so by parking along the wide road shoulder located directly across State Route 16.

The creek soon vanishes from sight and resumes snaking its way south toward the Farwell Road bridge crossing. Farwell Road is located less than a half-mile from where the stream bumped against State Route 16 along the stone embankment. There's enough

Black Trude (Mike Valla) When fly anglers hear of Trude flies, chances are they would think of dry fly patterns with that name. Original Trude flies, however, were hairwing patterns fished subsurface. Ischua Creek is a long way from where the original Trude fly was first originated in 1901 on the Buffalo River, a tributary of the Snake River in Idaho. Carter H. Harrison tied the first Trude, using red spaniel hair for a wing. Harrison tied variations of his original that included a black pattern, tied with black squirrel tail for a wing. The original black version, or a contemporary version tied with a conehead, is perfect for some of Ischua's deeper pools.

Muddler (Mike Valla) Angler Harry Leichtweis, who grew up in Olean, New York, on the Ischua, recalls fishing the famous Muddler Minnow on the stream as a hopper pattern, dressed with floatant. Muddler Minnows, first tied by Don Gapen (1907–1986) in August 1936 while fishing in Nipigon, Ontario, looked a bit different than modern versions. The heads were loosely spun with deer hair, not well-compacted, and shaped as it is usually tied today.

Kings River Caddis (Mike Valla) Kings River Caddis, a simple turkey wing pattern developed by Wayne "Buz" Buszek (1912–1965) on the Kings River in California, was one of the first dry fly caddis patterns developed many years ago. Originally named Rio de los Santos ("River of the Holy Kings"), Kings River below Pine Flat Dam in the San Joaquin Valley near Piedra, California, looks nothing like the Ischua Creek. However, this old pattern will still entice fish on most any stream.

room to park near the railroad tracks. The creek doesn't look that enticing directly around the Farwell bridge crossing.

Modest structure and riffles are encountered again once the stream reappears and bumps close to State Route 16, about 1.5 miles from the Farwell Road intersection, just upstream before it approaches Kent Road. A challenge is finding a safe place to park along the meager road shoulders. Ischua Creek maintains its monotonous feature, with its long, slow-moving flats flowing along expansive agricultural fields at the Kent Road bridge crossing.

Harry Leichtweis fondly recalls the times when he was a young man fishing the Kent Road reach with salted minnow rigs, enjoying catching rainbow trout that were once stocked in the stream. Harry recalls fishing Muddler Minnows as hoppers with his fly-fishing mentor. They treated the Muddlers with fly floatant. While dry flies, particularly caddis dry fly patterns, undoubtedly can entice the brown trout during modest mayfly and caddis hatches, the Ischua is a nice creek to cast streamers, wet-flies, and nymphs. Black Woolly Buggers or similar patterns and Conehead Muddlers or regular Muddler patterns should be fished through deeper runs and pools.

Genesee River (Upper)

It has been written water from rains that fall on the modest hill in northcentral Pennsylvania, in Ulysses Township, Potter County, might flow in one of three directions. The water might end up in the Allegheny River, then flow west to the Mississippi. Or the droplets might contribute to hydrology that heads southeasterly to Pine Creek then into the Susquehanna River. Or water that the rains provide to the hillside might end up flowing north into the Genesee River, then into New York, ending up in Lake Ontario and the St. Lawrence River. The "triple divide," as such watersheds are called, sets apart the Genesee from other major rivers in New York; it's also a unique and diverse fishery.

The trickle seepage that begins in Gold, Pennsylvania—marked by a simple sign mounted on a metal pipe post—is the birthplace of the mighty and historic Genesee River that flows nearly 160 miles before it dumps into Lake Ontario in Rochester, New York. At the river's mouth and upstream to what is called the "lower falls," anglers cast lines for lake-run chinook salmon, coho salmon, brown trout, and steelhead (see Lower Genesee River segment, page 72).

However, the Genesee River reaches in its headwaters, just across the Pennsylvania border and downstream, is a completely different fishery. Anglers enjoy fly fishing for typical stream brown and rainbow trout using conventional fly-fishing equipment and fly patterns. NYSDEC categorized the stream as Stocked-Extended and annually stocks over 20,000 brown trout and over 16,000 rainbow trout along its 18 miles of PFR water. Both official NYSDEC angling parking areas as well as official footpaths will get you into the stream.

From the New York/Pennsylvania State Line (just south of Shongo, New York), drive 1 mile north along State Route 19 to the first official footpath access. A small sign leading to the path is on the road shoulder. Only an ambitious angler who desires to get off the

Tim Didas, Flymph-pattern aficionado, on the upper Genesee River. Tim and friend Ray Tucker enjoy fishing the upper Genesee together with not only sinking soft-hackle Flymphs but also dry flies. (PHOTO RAY TUCKER)

beaten waters will choose to take the footpath that leads a few hundred feet distance to the stream. At its beginning, the footpath leads down a very steep hill. Be sure to have a wading staff or walking stick ready in-hand to help you down the slope. Some decent riffles and runs flow through that reach.

Anglers who would rather get into the river more quickly can do so by driving north along State Route 19 another mile to a bridge crossing where a formal NYSDEC angling parking lot is located on the right, on the north side of the bridge. You'll see a large NYSDEC hanging sign that alerts anglers that the location is the upstream boundary of the 2.5-mile-long Special Regulation Catch and Release section. A few runs downstream from the bridge can provide decent fly fishing.

Another option for anglers who wish to sample waters well upstream from the bridge is to relocate to nice riffle and run stretches along Hawks Road. Hawks Road runs along the opposite side of the stream from where the long official footpath on State Route 19 (mentioned previously) led to that general stream area. Depart the formal angling parking lot at the bridge then drive a few hundred feet to Hawks Road. Take a right on Hawks Road and drive 1.5 miles to a large parking turnout on the right. The parking area is one of a handful that provides access to the 9-mile Wellsville, Addison and Galeton (WAG) trail that runs along the Genesee River. (You'll also pass an access site shortly after turning onto Hawks Road, but bypass that one to get to better water upstream.) A kiosk is located at the turnout that includes a trail map and other information.

The WAG trail is a multi-use recreational trail that runs between the Village of Wellsville and the Pennsylvania State Line. It follows the direction of the former WAG Railroad along the upper Genesee River, hence its name. Be sure to view a NYSDEC map of the trail, available online.

The stream here, located not far downstream from the Pennsylvania State Line, runs directly in front of the parking area and WAG trail at this location, allowing quick access. Watch for private property posted signs very close to this official WAG access sites. The PFR on that side of the river is short but enough to get you into the stream and very close to the WAG trail where you won't encounter any issues. (The far side of the stream has continuous PFR access.)

Incidentally, the WAG also provides access to other PFR reaches downstream that flow well away from road. The WAG leads very close to the second formal NYSDEC angling parking lot on Graves Road. Drive 0.6 mile north of the last bridge crossing mentioned above on State Route 19 to Graves Road. Take a left, and go 0.3 mile to the angling parking lot at the bridge crossing marked by a large NYSDEC hanging sign.

The popular Graves Road reach is still within the Special Regulation Catch and Release stretch. The water upstream from Graves Road takes a sinuous course through small island-like features before it straightens out and flows in more continuous, slow-moving fashion under the bridge. The river continues below the bridge into a long flat. A nice run exits along the flat a couple hundred feet downstream, still flowing through PFR water as it does above the bridge.

The river then winds and turns north, well away from the WAG trail for about a mile before it rejoins it again a mile or so upstream from the terminus of the Catch and Release stretch at the County Road 29 bridge crossing. Drive north along State Route 19 2.1 miles from its intersection with Graves Road, and then turn left onto County Road 29. You'll encounter NYSDEC parking lot signage that designates the lower boundary of the Special Regulation Catch and Release section. Ample parking room is located on both sides of the bridge.

Lil' Dorothy (tied by Ray Tucker) Created by Mark Libertone, a friend of many, including this author, lived in Wellsville before his untimely passing several years ago. Mark's all-time favorite pattern that he loved to cast on the upper Genesee was his Lil' Dorothy. A fitting tribute to Mark, his good friend and fishing companion Ray Tucker tied this beautiful example of the pattern. Mark used pale orange embroidery thread (#722) for its abdomen, cahill color hare's ear dubbing for the thorax, cream or pale ginger hackle, and Mustad 3906 or 3399A hooks.

Diving Caddis (tied by Ray Tucker) All kinds of Diving Caddis patterns have been created over the years. However, simple Diving Caddis patterns, such as the example Ray Tucker tied here in memory of Mark Liebertone, who created this version, works well on the upper Genesee River. Mark preferred to tie the fly on Mustad 3906 or 3399A in sizes 12 to 16. He used olive floss or embroidery thread as an egg sac tag behind a hare's ear fur body that contained plenty of guard hairs. Fine gold wire served as a rib. Olive thread tied off its brown partridge hackle. Mark created the soft-hackle fly to represent some caddis that dive below the water surface to deposit eggs.

Zebra Midge (tied by Bob Herson) Fly fishers heading for the upper Genesee River should tuck a few Zebra Midge patterns in the fly box. Zebra Midge is said to have been originated in 1996 by Ted Welling along the Colorado River. A great tailwater and stillwater pattern, it's also found to be effective most anywhere trout are feeding on tiny Diptera. It's also effective when fished as a dropper fly along with a dry fly on-point along slow-moving pools.

After departing the Catch and Release stretch, the stream flows out of and then back into PFR water, picking up Ford's brook near the WAG. I've never fished Ford Brook's junction with the Genesee, but a local spin fishing angler told me it has produced nice trout. It flows into the river not far upstream from another formal NYSDEC angling parking lot located at the Jack Bridge Road bridge crossing. A couple of picnic tables are located next to the river at the lot, a nice place to stop for lunch. Swing wet flies and nymphs along the nice run upstream from the bridge. It's also decent dry fly water when the stream isn't running too high.

Try additional locations that provide nice fly-fishing water downstream at the Wiedrick Road and County Road 31A bridge crossings. Wiedrick Road is located off State Route 19 about 1.6 miles north of Jack Bridge Road. Turn onto Wiedrick, and drive just past the Wellsville Rod and Gun Club to the bridge. Fish upstream with dry flies, and swing wet flies through the riffles near the little dam located a few hundred feet upstream. The County Road 31A bridge crossing along Back River Road is located about 10 miles downstream from Weidrick Road in Belmont.

Get into your waders at Genesee River Wilds Amity River access site, located at the bridge just down the road from State Route 19. It's a large recreational area, complete with a pavilion and streamside parking. Anglers are welcome at the nice facility area. A very large roadside sign identifies the access site.

My friend, Mark Libertone, who lived in Wellsville before he passed away a few years ago, enjoyed fishing his soft-hackle Flymphs at the Wiedrick Road and Back River Road reaches with friends, among many other stretches along the Upper Genesee from Belmont upstream to the Pennsylvania State Line. A peach of a guy, and an angling companion to many, Mark was a founding member of the Upper Genesee River TU chapter and the Flymph Forum. His Lil' Dorothy, Diving Caddis, Newton's Flymph, and Black Stonefly Nymph, among many other soft-hackle patterns, were favorites to cast on his beloved Upper Genesee River.

Incidentally, the word "Flymph" was coined by Vernon S. (Pete) Hidy. *In the Art of Tying the Wet Fly and Fishing the Flymph* (1971) by J. E. Leisenring, Hidy described it as "a wingless artificial fly with a soft, translucent body of fur or wool which blends with the undercolor of the tying silk when wet, utilizing soft-hackle fibers easily activated by the currents to give the effect of an insect alive in the water, and strategically cast diagonally upstream or across for the trout to take just below or within a few inches of the surface film."

You'll also want a selection of dry flies in your box if fishing the Upper Genesee when the caddis and mayflies are emerging. A selection of Sulfurs, Hendricksons, Light Cahills, Olives, and general attractor patterns such as White Wulffs should be handy.

Anglers interested in fishing the Genesee River downstream from trout water reaches, along sections that inhabit warmwater species, should carry a selection of bass patterns, too. A very nice section of the river for those anglers looking for both bass and scenery is at Letchworth State Park and the Genesee River Gorge (the "Grand Canyon of the East"), some 30 miles downstream from Belmont near the village of Castile.

Cohocton River

Nearly 60 miles in length, flowing from its headwaters in Livingston County not far from Dansville, the Cohocton is a favorite among many fly anglers. Fly-fishing friends, such as Bath residents Tom and Martha Mason, have enjoyed the stream. Greg Heffner, also a Bath resident, who, like Tom, ties some awesome-looking and effective flies, has guided more than a few fly fishers on its waters. Tim Didas, another friend and Flymph-pattern lover, considers the Cohocton one of his very favorite streams. My fellow Cornell University fisheries classmate and friend Dave Bornholdt, who lives not that far from the river, in the Finger Lakes area, has taken some nice fish out of the river, too.

While the Genesee River takes its course north to Lake Ontario, the Cohocton (aka Conhocton River) flows southeasterly, into New York's southern tier area at the bottom of New York. In its lowermost reach, its waters combine with the Tioga River, creating the Chemung River, a Susquehanna River tributary.

Along its path, the stream flows past the hamlet of Atlanta then through its namesake Village of Cohocton, then down through the villages of Avoca and Bath. It picks up small tributaries, such as Neil Creek, that contribute to its growing width as it meanders through the beautiful countryside, not far from the Finger Lakes that lie to its north.

While the Cohocton inhabits wild brown trout, along with brook trout in its headwater reaches, the river relies on hatchery stockings. NYSDEC typically stocks the river with

The Cohocton River's Special Regulation stretch upstream from Avoca features trout-inhabiting deep pools, runs, and riffles. NYSDEC categorized Cohocton River as both Stocked-Extended and Wild-Quality. (PHOTO VALERIE VALLA)

several thousand brown trout between 9 to 15 inches, along with a few thousand 9-inch to 10-inch rainbows. The Avoca area gets heavily stocked.

The PFR reaches are numerous from its headwaters near Atlanta downstream to Bath. The lowermost NYSDEC angling parking lot along formal public easement water, located within the stream's Special Regulations stretch, is located about a mile northwest of Bath at the Knight Settlement Road (County Road 15)/State Route 415 intersection bridge crossing. The lot is right next to the river, with a stone memorial bench that overlooks the stream. A memorial plaque inset placed by the Cohocton Valley Chapter of Trout Unlimited remembers local angler Milt Nehrke as a "true friend of the Conhocton."

The lowermost extent of a Special Regulation artificial-lures-only section is located just downstream from the Knight Settlement Road bridge crossing at the northern boundary of the US Veterans Facility. It extends upstream to the State Route 415 Bridge in Kanona. A formal NYSDEC angling parking area is located at the uppermost extent of the Special Regulation reach.

Drive 1.2 miles north of the Knight Settlement Road intersection, along State Route 415, to a traffic circle. Exit the traffic circle, cross the bridge, and pull into the large parking lot located on the north side of the bridge. A large NYSDEC hanging sign is located at the parking lot (this formal access lot is relatively new). The river here is typically slow-moving water, with deep pools. The Cohocton along this reach flows through a mixed-use area, with dwellings and small businesses interspersed with agricultural fields.

A very nice stream reach is located a couple of miles north of the previous parking area. Drive 2.5 miles north along State Route 415 to Owens Road. Take a right and follow the short road to a pleasant NYSDEC angling parking area next to the bridge and large hanging sign. Another memorial bench, erected by Cohocton Valley Chapter of Trout Unlimited, Canandaigua Chapter of Trout Unlimited, and Southern Tier Float Stockers, overlooks the stream.

The brass plates honor Don Graham (the co-founder of the float-stocking program) and Bill Lavris, whose many friends also contributed to the nice remembrance. Besides being honored for his conservation-minded efforts, he was recognized by the United States Geological Survey (USGS) by naming an Antarctic peak in his honor. He was a career National Weather Service meteorologist who did weather-related research on that continent. The bench is a fitting tribute for the two.

A nice dry-fly stretch is located just downstream from the memorial bench. Owens Road continues a short distance past the parking area. Walk past the dwelling and badly weathered barn along a rough dirt road (difficult parking) that ends at a railroad bridge (you'll notice sapling grow tubes along the stream).

Neil Creek

Things get more interesting once you continue upstream from the Village of Avoca, where you'll enjoy some very pleasant fishing in a reach where you'll have a good chance of netting wild brown trout. A second Special Regulation stretch exists from the northern boundary of Avoca upstream to the mouth of Neil Creek. This reach isn't stocked and is managed as a wild trout fishery. Two formal NYSDEC angling parking lots will get you into the Special Regulation artificial-lures-only water that allows reduced creel limits and minimum 12-inch trout length size. One is located near Neil Creek, just north of the County Road 15/State Route 415 intersection. The other is downstream on Wallace Avoca Road.

A quick 5-minute, 4.5-mile drive on State Route 415 north of the Owens Road access lot will get you to the upper official parking area. The NYSDEC lot is marked by a large sign located at the bridge (0.3 mile after crossing Neil Creek and just beyond the railroad track road crossing). Long, slow pools flow both upstream and downstream from the bridge crossing.

To reach the Wallace Avoca Road NYSDEC angling parking area, continue north 0.2 mile on State Route 415 to a right on County Road 105 (Henderson Street). Take

Caddis patterns of all types, including Elk Hair flies, will entice brown trout on the Cohocton River. Skittering a good floating Elk Hair pattern across riffles will elicit strikes. Local angler and fly tier Greg Heffner prefers a High Viz Caddis.

Neil Creek, an important Cohocton River tributary, inhabits wild brown trout. When fishing Cohocton River, anglers can be well served by making a trip over to Neil Creek, a much smaller water. (PHOTO VALERIE VALLA)

Henderson Street to Wallace Avoca Road. A large streamside parking lot, marked by a large hanging sign, is about a mile south on Wallace Avoca Road. It's no doubt a popular early season angling destination. A very nice run departs a pool then turns the bend and feeds a riffle into likely trout hold water. It's a very nice location.

In 2019, NYSDEC biologists reported findings of their electrofishing within the Special Regulation reach, at the Wallace Avoca Road site and downstream at Cross Road. As they expected, most of the browns captured were wild fish. They also electrofished upstream from Neil Creek, in stocked sections at the NYSDEC parking area site and further upstream at Wentworth and Jones roads. Wild trout were also captured in those areas, too. The NYSDEC Survey #8190 recommended habitat improvement in the unstocked reach to help elevate the wild trout biomass to 40 pounds/acre. Such habitat improvement could help maintain the entire river stretch that was sampled as a wild trout fishery.

Ample PFR stretches exist upstream from the previous NYSDEC parking lot that's located just north of Neil Creek. A couple are accessed via footpaths. You'll find that some of the footpaths that are indicated on the Cohocton NYSDEC PFR maps are poorly marked or not marked at all. One path follows the railroad tracks from Wentworth Road to a railroad bridge crossing. Wentworth is located about 2 miles north of the Neil Creek area parking lot on State Route 415.

An unofficial parking area is located at the Wentworth Road/State Route 415 intersection at the bridge crossing. PFR water exists downstream from the bridge. A small PFR gap exists upstream from the bridge. The upstream reach can be accessed by driving a short distance down Wentworth Road, to the railroad crossing. NYSDEC maps indicate footpath access along the railroad track leads to the stream.

Anglers wishing to get into upper reach sections a bit easier can access the stream at another formal NYSDEC angling parking lot located upstream above the Village of Cohocton. From the Wentworth Road/State Route 415 intersection, drive north into

Cohocton then keep straight onto State Route 371 at an intersection in the middle of the village. The parking area is at a bridge crossing a little over a mile north on 371, marked by a large hanging sign. PFR water (a long, flat stretch) is available on the left side, upstream from the bridge. It flows along a well-manicured home lawn upstream. PFR is available on both sides of the now small water downstream from the bridge. There's a nice riffle and run downstream from the bridge, along the parking area.

The Cohocton River headwater reaches upstream from the hamlet of Atlanta, which is now classified as Wild-Quality by NYSDEC and will no longer receive hatchery stockings. PFR stretches can be accessed via Beecher Street and Parks Road crossings. If you're after wild brook trout and wild browns, try fishing the small water above Atlanta.

You'll encounter many of the important fly hatches found on other important New York trout streams, everything from Hendricksons during April into May, Sulphurs from May into July, and an extended appearance of Tricos from July into September. Greg

Hi-Viz Caddis (tied by Greg Heffner) Local Cohocton angler and fly tier Greg Heffner was introduced to this pattern by local tier and angler Tom Mason years ago. Greg reports that tied in several sizes and colors High-Viz Caddis will fish all caddis hatches on the river.

Quill Dun (tied by Greg Heffner) Greg Heffner is a big fan of Quill Wing Dun dry flies. Tied in different sizes and colors, Quill Duns are his go-to pattern for most Cohocton hatches.

Sulphur Parachute (tied by Greg Heffner) Greg Heffner also reports his Sulphur Parachute, like his Quill Wing Dun, will fish any hatch by simply changing its color and size. Of course, many other Sulphur patterns have been created to fish that hatch. Anglers should bring along their own favorites when sampling the Cohocton during that mayfly's emergence.

Rusty Spinner (tied by Greg Heffner) Rusty Spinner patterns are highly effective on most any trout stream throughout New York. Very large trout on New York streams have been taken on the simple Rusty Spinner. Another great fly of choice by Greg Heffner should be no surprise to fly anglers.

Partridge and Yellow (tied by Greg Heffner) Like the classic Partridge and Orange classic, Partridge and Yellow soft-hackle "spiders" are from old British descent. Both have been embraced by American fly fishers as a good general purpose wet fly. Often effective when fished on the swing, Greg Heffner's wet fly choice can elicit strikes from Cohocton and Neil Creek brown trout.

Atherton #5 Wet Fly (tied by Mike Valla) Created by illustrator John Atherton (1900–1952) for fishing his home water, Batten Kill in Arlington, Vermont, his #5 wet fly was tied using the same principles of impressionism found in his classic dry fly series described in his book *The Fly and the Fish* (1951). The pattern calls for bronze mallard wings and tails and a reddish-brown muskrat fur mix. It's ribbed with oval gold wire. Swing the pattern through riffles on both Cohocton River and its tributary Neil Creek.

Woodruff (tied by Mike Valla) Woodruff is a classic Catskill pattern that goes back to the 1920s. Chester Mills of the William Mills & Son tackle house in New York City named the fly for Johnny Woodruff. Woodruff did well with it on the upper Beaver Kill, in the Catskills. Tied in small sizes, the dry fly floats well along riffles and runs and is well-suited for streams such as Neil Creek. Tied with spent-wing grizzly hackle wings, a blend of dark olive, olive-brown, and pale yellow rabbit fur for the body and brown hackle collar.

Heffner carries a variety of generic patterns, like Quill Wing Duns, his go-to pattern for most of the hatches, varying the sizes and colors. He likes a Hi-Viz caddis pattern that Bath neighbor Tom Mason showed to him years ago. Greg also varies the fly's dressing, tying it in different shades and sizes. Small soft-hackle wet flies are also effective. It's also a good idea to carry Elk Hair Caddis dry flies, Hare's Ear Nymphs, and Pheasant Tail Nymphs tied in different and sizes.

Neil Creek tributary (aka Neils Creek) deserves added mention because of its importance to the Cohocton River fishery. Mentioned earlier as a boundary for the upper Cohocton River Special Regulation reaches, the quaint Neil Creek tributary is a great place to give your lighter 3-weight to 4-weight rods a workout. NYSDEC categorizes Neil Creek as a Wild-Quality stream. Its waters inhabit a goodly number of wild brown trout. About 9 miles of PFR water, broken into long and short segments, is available from its mouth at the Cohocton to upstream above the small community of Greenville.

One of the nicest stretches is located downstream from the formal NYSDEC angling parking lot located a quick 1.5 miles from the State Route 415/County Road 6 intersection. Take County Road 6 about 0.9 mile to a right turn on Neil Creek Road. The parking lot is marked by a large hanging sign at a bridge crossing 0.6 mile up Neil Creek Road. Fish down the riffles and runs with small nymphs, dark shaded wet-flies, and streamers. Use Elk Hair Caddis or spent-wing patterns that float well if fishing upstream through moderate riffles.

Clear Creek

More than one stream in New York is named "Clear Creek," but the little gem that flows northwesterly through Cattaraugus and Wyoming Counties then weds Cattaraugus Creek in the Village of Arcade stands high among them all. Of course, there's also another nice "Clear Creek" tucked not far away in the extreme southwest corner of New York, near Ellington, that's also a favorite. Both are categorized as Wild-Premier streams by NYSDEC. Neither receive hatchery stocked fish and are managed as wild trout fisheries.

The "Arcade" Clear Creek, a short stream that flows a little over 6 miles, hasn't been stocked for 30 years. Through careful management and excellent attention directed to the small creek, wild rainbows and browns swim in its quaint riffles and pools. Over 5 miles of PFR stretches await fly fishers who desire a wild trout angling experience.

The rainbows that typically average around 7 inches are scrappy and willing to slam small-size bucktails, wet flies, and nymphs. You might be surprised to net larger 'bows, but most likely, the fish you'll encounter are in the smaller size ranges. The brown trout average larger in size, around 9 inches, but a few hefty 12-to-16-inchers inhabit the creek. The Elk Hair Stonefly that my friend Ed Ostapczuk designed for fishing small Catskill region streams will entice the browns.

The PFR mileage closely follows State Route 98 from the hamlet of Freedom area downstream into the Arcade area. The long public easement mileage is essentially continuous, aside from a brief interruption in its headwater reaches upstream from Galen Hill Road. Anglers interested in sampling Clear Creek in its headwaters can park at the NYSDEC angling parking lot located on Galen Hill Road.

Beadhead Prince Nymph (tied by Shorty Bartholomew) Tim "Shorty" Bartholomew, a talented fly tier from Pennsylvania, ties a nice Prince Nymph beadhead variation that is perfect for streams like Clear Creek. The pattern gets down into the water column quickly, and its small bit of flash behind the bead no doubt attracts rainbow trout. Shorty is an amiable tier who ties at many fly-fishing shows.

Elk Hair Stonefly (tied by Mike Valla) A great choice for a floating pattern on Clear Creek is Ed Ostapczuk's Elk Hair Stonefly, aka EHSF, as Ed likes to call it. Usually tied on hook sizes #14 to #16, the pattern's red floss tail, yellow dubbing body along with hot orange thread makes it easy to spot on water. To create the pattern, Ed combined features found in Craig Matthews's X-Caddis, red floss used in an old fly called Mormon Girl wet fly, and hot orange thread Fran Betters used for his Ausable Wulff. Easy to tie, EHSF is a good late-season pattern for small, crystalline streams.

Habitat improvement stretch on upper Clear Creek. A collaborative effort between the Great Lakes Restoration Initiative, US Fish and Wildlife Service, NYSDEC, Western New York Trout Unlimited Chapter, Red House Brook Trout Unlimited Chapter, and Seneca Trail Resource Conservation and Development Council resulted in some very nice stream habitat improvements.

Galen Hill Road is located less than a 10-minute drive south on State Route 98 from the Main Street in the Village of Arcade. Turn onto Galen Road, and drive past the cemetery a short distance. The parking lot, marked by a large hanging sign, is on the right, next to the steel-decked bridge. You'll notice posted signs on the left side of the road as you approach the bridge crossing. Keep in mind the PFR reach at that location is downstream from the bridge. It's small water and sometimes difficult to fly-fish, but using a short rod drift wet flies and nymphs downstream through the riffles can entice small rainbows.

Much better fly-fishing water is available at my favorite reach on the entire stream, at the NYSDEC angling parking lot located across from the expansive Gernatt Asphalt Products gravel plant on State Route 98 (0.4 mile north of Galen Hill Road and about 4.5 miles south of Main Street in Arcade).

A large Great Lakes Restoration Initiative sign at the lot will lead to a short path to the stream. The habitat improvement, with its large rock structures carefully placed into the creek, created a beautiful little pool that the wild trout must love. Fish Prince Nymphs, including beadhead styles for this pattern, are a good choice for this type of water.

Three additional NYSDEC angling parking lots that straddle State Route 98 side road bridge crossings are located downstream north of Sandusky along Jones Road, Sparks Road, and Bray Road. Jones Road is a gravel road that leads to the parking lot just after the bridge on the left. The creek flows a relatively short distance downstream toward the Sparks Road crossing and parking lot. Jones Road and Sparks Road are separated by only 0.1 mile.

The stream length that connects the two bridge crossings is only about a half-mile. If fishing with a companion, a good strategy would be for one angler to begin fishing at Jones Road down through the many gravel bank areas and eventually meet the partner who would fish upstream from Sparks Road.

The PFR water downstream from the Sparks Road crossing briefly flows close behind a State Route 98 dwelling but then quickly winds and turns away into more isolated locations as it makes its way to the Bray Road crossing. Bray Road is located about a mile and a half north of Sparks Road on State Route 98. The NYSDEC angling Bray Road parking lot is on the right side just before the bridge, marked by a large hanging sign. A short path that leads from the lot will get you into water below the bridge.

The run below the bridge flows through likely trout water, along a stone embankment, before it continues along an expansive agricultural field, and down toward Arcade. Cast small streamers through the riffles structure before heading upstream from the bridge. Just upstream from the bridge a couple hundred feet, the creek makes a sharp turn into a nice fish-holding pool. Try casting Prince Nymphs through the run that enters the pool that deserves serious attention.

Once Clear Creek departs Bray Road and the flows beyond the abutting agricultural fields, it enters the more congested Arcade village area, then dumps into the Cattaraugus River. Bray Road is about 1.5 miles south of Main Street in Arcade. Throughout its brief journey to the Cattaraugus, the little creek will provide pleasant fishing, regardless of successful fish-netting.

Mansfield Creek/South Cattaraugus

Mansfield Creek is a little stream that runs through a beautiful farm-country valley on its short journey west to join South Cattaraugus Creek. Two formal NYSDEC angling parking areas are located on the creek, separated by just a couple of miles. The uppermost lot is located at the intersection of Toad Hollow Road and Otto Maples Road. It's located a half-mile north of the Mansfield Town Clerk's Office (located on Toad Hollow Road). The lower formal lot is also located on Otto Maples Road, 1.7 miles west of the upper lot at a bridge crossing. A little over 6 miles of PFR water exists along both sections. NYSDEC categorizes the stream as Stocked and Wild-Quality.

Iron X-Caddis (tied by Tom Baltz) Pennsylvania fly tier and fishing guide Tom Baltz ties an easy-to-spot-on-water caddis pattern. A spin-off of the original X-Caddis created by Craig Matthews, Tom's Iron X-Caddis was designed to help clients he was guiding see the fly while fishing. Tom says the fly collar adds bugginess and helps tame the deer hair flare. Tom had this to add about his pattern: "My guests had a difficult time seeing the X-Caddis, thus the sighter I added. The collar is a blend 50/50 grey squirrel and CDC clippings. Ice dub adds bugginess and helps tame the deer hair flare."

Letort Cricket (tied by Mike Valla) Pennsylvania great Ed Shenk (1927–2020) held both his Letort Hopper and Letort Cricket dear to his heart. Fished on his beloved Letort Spring Run, in Carlisle, Pennsylvania, Ed said he preferred his cricket over all other terrestrials he fished, and it performed well for him East Coast to West Coast. There's no doubt it's a good choice for Mansfield Creek during summer.

Upper Mansfield Creek at the upper formal parking lot intersection of County Road 14 (Toad Hollow Road) and County Road 13 (Otto Maples Road), just downstream from the Town of Maples, in Cattaraugus County.

NYSDEC reported some interesting facts about the stream that inhabits wild brown trout and wild rainbow trout. (The downstream 2.5-mile reach is annually stocked with a few hundred brown trout between 9 to 15 inches.) Recent sampling revealed that the wild brown trout population approached 400 fish per stream mile. The wild adult rainbow population was estimated at a little over 300 fish per mile. "You have to fight the willows on the upper wild trout stretch," Joe Mecca told me. "But it's well worth it." I met Joe while fishing Cattaraugus Creek, a while back.

Local fly angler, and dentist, Joe Mecca, who you're more likely to run into on the Cattaraugus River steelhead stretch or its steelhead holding tributaries, has fond memories of his early years on Mansfield Creek when he fished it in his youth with his dad and uncle. "It was my go-to spot for opening day when I was starting my trout career," Joe said.

Mansfield Creek eventually weds the South Branch of the Cattaraugus Creek a little over 4 miles downstream from the upper formal parking lot in Mansfield. The confluence is at the County Road 12 (East Otto Road) bridge crossing, at Christmiller Road. PFR easements exist on both sides of the stream bank all the way upstream to the lower formal parking area. Plenty of PFR easements along both streambanks provide fishing access downstream from the bridge crossing quite a distance, as well as PFR up into the South Branch of the Cattaraugus upstream from its junction with Mansfield Creek.

The stream continues flowing now as the South Branch of the Cattaraugus River. It continues on as traditional trout water until it arrives at steelhead stretch far downstream.

With the addition of Mansfield Creek, the South Branch of the Cattaraugus River flows wider, with runs that enter slow-moving pools. You'll encounter plenty of gravel at the stream bends, along with plenty of the ubiquitous Japanese Knotweed overtaking the banks. Its pools hold trout that will rise to a variety of dry flies.

When sampling Mansfield Creek and the upper South Branch of the Cattaraugus, bring your usual assortment of spring mayfly and caddis patterns. Try terrestrials along the slow stream pools on Manfield during summer, such as LeTort Crickets, and ant patterns in late summer.

Cattaraugus Creek (Upper Main Stem)

When Cattaraugus Creek pops up in discussions among fly fishers not familiar with trout streams inhabiting Western New York, the chatter is almost always focused entirely around the steelhead section, from the Village of Springville downstream 34 miles to Lake Erie. And justly so—the big lake-run fish attract anglers from near and far. We'll get to that important fishery momentarily (see "Great Lakes Steelhead" section). A now out-of-use, defunct, impassible dam keeps the steelhead from migrating farther upstream from Springville, at least for now. Plans are in place to partially lower and modify the defunct dam to allow additional steelhead upstream while still keeping the lamprey eels out.

However, an important and heavily used trout fishery also exists along the Cattaraugus Creek for miles upstream from Springville. The "Up Catt," as it's sometimes called, provides some really nice fly-fishing experiences for resident trout in the creek itself and also along its tributaries. The creek extends upstream from the Springville Dam another 30 miles or so, to its source at Java Lake. Both stocked hatchery and wild brown trout inhabit the creek, as well as wild rainbow trout. NYSDEC categorizes the stream as Stocked and Stocked-Extended, although Wild-Quality tributaries feed the upper stream reaches.

Studies have shown the first 15 miles or so above Springfield Dam hold stocked and wild trout, but the numbers are limited by thermal warming. Upstream at river mile (RM) 46 at Elton Creek tributary area to RM 58 at East Arcade the Cattaraugus supports wild resident rainbows, wild browns, and stocked browns. Lower densities of browns inhabit the remaining stream miles to Java Lake. A total of 14 mostly all-continuous PFR miles are available on the stream running from the East Arcade area to downstream of Arcade toward Springville. Plenty of PFR water is also available on a couple important tributary streams.

The first formal parking area is located about 1.5 miles upstream from the I-219/State Route 39 intersection in Springville, located at the Hake Road bridge crossing. The lot is very large, large enough to accommodate many vehicles, making this stretch popular with early season bait anglers (you'll likely come across forked sticks along the stream bank gravel bars, used to hold up bait rods). My guess is this area will become important among fly anglers once steelhead are able to migrate upstream through the modified Springfield dam fishway into the upper waters.

Another formal NYSDEC angling parking lot is located just a couple of miles up the road, on State Route 39. A large NYSDEC hanging sign is located at the large parking area. The short PFR stream reach isn't located directly next to the road; a designated footpath leads to the stream located a few hundred feet from the parking area. Depending on the time of year, and water levels, you'll encounter expansive bank gravel bars that typify the stream, along with a couple runs. Many fly anglers bypass this reach also and locate more upstream to the reaches where trout densities are higher.

Access that is more direct to the creek is located a couple of miles upstream at a bridge crossing and parking area off County Road 225 (Savage Road), located just short of a mile south from the State Route 39/Savage Road intersection, at the Cattaraugus County Line. What makes this reach more interesting than areas downstream is the creek's confluence with Hosmer Brook (you'll see the brook entering the creek on your left, as you cross the bridge, assuming you're driving south). Elton Creek tributary is also in the same area. You'll cross it by driving less than a mile past that last bridge.

A little over 1.5 miles of PFR on the 4.5-mile-long Hosmer Brook provides fly fishers with an opportunity to catch wild trout. The stream isn't stocked. NYSDEC biologists

Hurdville Road reach on Upper Cattaraugus Creek. The "Up Catt" and its tributaries provide angling opportunities for stocked brown trout, wild brown trout, and wild rainbow trout.

estimate the productive brook inhabits 700 wild brown trout and rainbow trout per mile. The browns mostly range in size from 6 to 12 inches, although recent surveys have turned up a few fish up to 15 inches. The rainbows are smaller, reaching up to about 9 inches. Unlike Hosmer Brook, the lowermost 6 miles of Elton Creek is stocked with browns. However, the creek inhabits both wild rainbows and brown trout. There is 5.5 miles of PFR water found on Elton Creek. NYSDEC sampled Elton Creek in 2019 and turned up browns from about 5 inches to 22 inches. The rainbows ranged from 5.6 to 13 inches.

Adequate Cattaraugus Creek PFR stretches also exist upstream from the confluence of Hosmer Brook and Elton Creek. Three additional formal NYSDEC angling parking lots are available.

One upstream parking area provides easy access to the creek, at a bridge crossing on State Route 16. Some really nice water flows upstream from the bridge. If approaching from the State Route 39/Savage Road intersection, drive 1.6 miles east on State Route 39 to the Olean Road (State Route 16) intersection. (You'll cross over Hosmer Brook in 0.3 mile on the way, marked by a large hanging sign at the bridge, but parking is difficult on the narrow shoulder.) Take a right on Olean Road and go 0.2 mile to a side road on your left before crossing the bridge (Hutchinson Road) that leads directly into the long parking area marked by a large hanging NYSDEC sign. Try fishing upstream along the nice stream rock structures with dry flies in May.

Another access is located in the Arcade area only a couple of miles away from the previous parking area. The location of the formal parking area shown on the NYSDEC map of the creek is confusing. The map doesn't indicate it's on Hurdville Road. Continue south after crossing Olean Road/State Route 16/State Route 39 until you get to Main Street (State Route 39). Take a left, then drive east on Main Street to Hurdville Road. Take a left on Hurdville. The parking area marked by a large NYSDEC angling sign is located 0.3 mile up the road at a bridge crossing near the Arcade Village Sewage Plant.

Stocked and wild brown trout inhabit the Upper Cattaraugus Creek that originates at Java Lake in Wyoming County. Nearly 14 miles of Public Fishing Rights easement water is available along with 1.6 miles of PFR on Hosmer Brook tributary.

You can get directly into the stream and explore a series of riffles and runs downstream from the bridge.

While in the Arcade area, try fishing Clear Creek, another important tributary featured and discussed previously (see Clear Creek page 32). It joins the Cattaraugus in Arcade and is a great choice to fish if action isn't happening on the Cattaraugus Creek. Stream reaches with easy access near Arcade are also located upstream. You can sample the creek upstream from Arcade at a formal designated footpath access on State Route 98 and at a formal parking turnout upstream from the footpath access point.

If approaching from Arcade, return to Main Street (State Route 39) and drive east 2 miles through the village, then bear left on State Route 98. A small NYSDEC sign is located up State Route 98 along the road shoulder, next to the creek, directly across from the Air Tech company buildings. Fish dry flies upstream through the gentle pools. Nicer water can be found 0.8 mile up State Route 98 from the footpath access. (It's located just past the Arcade Center Farm buildings.) The small parking turnout directly next to the stream is marked by a large NYSDEC hanging sign. The stretch downstream from the parking area has some nice water structure with runs and riffles. Slow-moving water is located upstream from the site. You'll notice a sign that indicates this reach is categorized by NYSDEC as Stocked-Extended.

A couple of additional access options occur upstream, on Cattaraugus Creek itself, also on the PFR stretch that flows along Spring Brook. Continue northeast on State Route 98 past the Arcade Highway Department 1.7 miles to East Arcade Road (County Road 11). The small formal NYSDEC footpath sign is located on East Arcade Road, 0.4 mile from the State Route 98/East Arcade Road intersection. It's just past the commercial gravel pit, on the right. The creek is located a few hundred feet down the footpath from the road shoulder, so it takes a small effort to get into the stream, but the reach gets you off the beaten track.

Spring Brook is just up the road and worth fishing. PFR water is located a short drive from the "gravel pit" access area. Continue on East Arcade Road another 2 miles to Allen

Road, just past a bridge crossing. Drive 0.4 mile to Sullivan Road. (Up Allen Road 0.1 mile you'll notice a formal angling access footpath sign on the right. Bypass it for now; explore it later.) Take a left on Sullivan. A NYSDEC angling access large hanging sign is right next to the small brook 0.1 mile up Sullivan Road. Park on the road shoulder and not the private paved dwelling parking area next to the brook. You'll notice that NYSDEC posted a sign that indicates Spring Brook is categorized as Wild-Quality. You'll have a good chance of netting a wild trout in this stretch. It's small water, difficult in areas to manage with a fly rod, especially in summer.

Yet another designated footpath access to the upper creek's more isolated reaches is located at a formal NYSDEC angling parking area lot at the East Arcade Road/Tyler Road intersection located 1.2 miles from the East Arcade/Allen Road intersection. The nice lot is marked by a large hanging sign. The stream flows well away from the road in this reach.

The trek to the creek via the footpath at the Tyler Road lot is a few hundred feet but can be worth the effort. I've not fished it back in there, but local fly fisher Joe Mecca recently mentioned the mud-bottom stream reach inhabits a few brook trout.

Mixed Baug Dry Fly (tied by Ayumi "Rocky" Ozecki) Ayumi's version of an Elk Hair Caddis, with its interesting name, mixes whitish and brown hair shades. "Mixed Baug" is Rocky's play on words. The name combines "mixed bag" with "mixed bug." Ayumi likes Tiemco 103BL or heavier 113BLH hooks for this pattern. It can be tied with any brown body material, synthetic or natural, along with brown or ginger hackle that's palmered around the body.

JC's Electric Caddis (tied by John Collins) John Collins, a commercial fly tier and talented fly fisher, created this pattern after reading about a technique called the "Internal-ribbed Tubing Body" described in Ted Leeson and Jim Schollmeyer's book *The Fly Tier's Benchside Reference*. John's fly displays translucency and segmentation found in natural caddis larvae. He employed ostrich herl legs to mimic the small legs and thorax on naturals. Tied on Daiichi 1120 hooks, fluorescent green Antron yarn forms the abdominal claw. The abdomen is formed by inserting Chartreuse Ultra Wire into hollow Waspi Stretch Tubing. The pronotum section is formed by burning off the top herl then coating with Solarez UV resin.

Leatherneck Streamer (tied by Mike Valla) Pennsylvania fly tier Chauncy K. Lively (1919–2000) introduced his Leatherneck Streamer in the April 1981 issue of *Pennsylvania Angler* magazine. A simple pattern that sinks well, it's tied with fur strip wings and a copper wire body. Lively believed it to be a good alternative to Marabou. The fly sinks well and its fur strip provides action to the fly that elicits fish strikes.

Your fly box should have a variety of nymphs (beadhead and regular), caddis larvae, pupae and dry fly patterns such as Elk Hair Caddis (and variants), early black stonesflies, Hendricksons, Sulphurs, Tricos, and terrestrial patterns. Small streamers work well fished through the runs and riffles along the upper reaches.

Once you're that far upstream, at the Tyler Road lot area, you might also consider heading east to Bliss and Wiscoy Creek (see Wiscoy Creek section), where we started this Western New York fly-fishing section, coming full circle. It's located less than 10 miles away. However, no doubt the most exiting fishing on the Cattaraugus Creek beginning in late September can be found on the stream's steelhead stretch, downstream from Springville (see Great Lakes Steelhead section).

The Great Lakes Tributaries Region

Modern sport fishing opportunities aside, New York has always benefitted from having two of the five Great Lakes bordering its lands. The retreating ice sheets from the Last Glacial Period, some 14,000 years ago, sculptured basins that filled with icemelt. New York's Lake Erie and Lake Ontario—like Lake Michigan, Lake Huron, and Lake Superior—were of paramount importance for transportation, migration, and commerce. The mid-nineteenth-century "free-for all" commercial fishing industry had a devastating impact on fish populations, including anadromous species. One can only imagine the vast numbers of spawning Atlantic salmon that once ran Lake Ontario tributaries during pre-commercial fishing exploitation years.

Fortunately for many communities along the shorelines that depend on sport fishing for economic well-being, the tributaries that feed both Lake Erie and Lake Ontario harbor annual spawning runs of non-indigenous anadromous fish. Fly anglers eager to latch into big chinooks, Cohoes, and the much-sought-after steelhead can find plenty of action along many miles of public fishing streams, particularly on Lake Ontario tributaries.

Snow squalls and steelhead go hand in hand on New York's Great Lakes Tributaries. "Jersey Jan" Beliveau played this big steelhead during a December outing on the Salmon River. Providing water levels are safe and fishable, anglers who brave winter fishing can find success on several New York State Great Lakes tributaries.

Action begins during September with early chinook and coho runs, followed by steelies and big brown trout later on in the fall. Steelhead fishing continues through winter into spring, enjoyed by many who brave freezing temperatures that ice-up rod guides and snow squalls that can be almost blinding, for the chance of netting a fish in seemingly improbable conditions. The Salmon River that feeds Lake Ontario and the Cattaraugus River that feeds Lake Erie are considered by many the crown jewels of the system.

However, many other smaller, less-publicized tributaries that spill into Lake Erie and Lake Ontario attract lake-run fish and are sometimes free of crowds during times "fish are in." Some tributaries, such as Keg Creek and Black River that feed Lake Ontario, have limited formal public access, although private landowners often allow fishing.

Lake Erie Tributaries

CATTARAUGUS CREEK (LOWER—STEELHEAD SECTION)

While the Upper Cattaraugus Creek, above Springville Dam, is a brown trout and resident rainbow trout stream, the 34 miles below the dam to Lake Erie is a completely different fishery. To many fly anglers, the Lower "Catt" is Lake Erie's crown jewel steelhead tributary. Many fly fishers only know Cattaraugus Creek as a steelhead destination because of the celebrity status it enjoys as one of the best in New York in terms of angler catch rates. The stream receives a significant amount of angling attention when the big steelies begin their annual migration to the creek, starting sometime in late September or early October. The fish depart back downstream to the lake as late as June. Most of the best action occurs during October and November. Unlike some of the Lake Ontario tributaries, the Catt attracts only occasional lake-run brown trout and Pacific salmon.

The creek undoubtedly will receive even more attention from steelheaders once modifications are made to the impassible dam. A fish passageway project long in the planning will bring steelhead into many additional miles of good habitat upstream. An added blessing to extending the steelhead range to over 50 miles of good habitat water is the abundant Public Fishing Rights (PFR) easements that are already in place on the "Up Catt" above Springfield and along its tributaries.

For what seems like eternity, fly fishers have been waiting anxiously for the dam modifications that will include lowering the defunct dam's structure to a minimum level that will still keep lamprey eels migrating from the lake to reaches well upstream from Springville.

A fish passage weir will allow steelhead upstream. NYSDEC also wants to ensure the Upper Cattaraugus Creek will continue to thrive as a quality year-round resident

Cattaraugus Creek from its mouth at Lake Erie upstream to Springfield Dam is best known as an outstanding steelhead fishery, one of the best in New York. (PHOTO JOE MECCA)

Zoar Valley gorge, nested in the Zoar Valley Multiple Use Area and Unique Area, a breathtaking scenic area on Cattaraugus Creek upstream of Gowanda, is accentuated by 500-foot cliffs, soaring bald eagles, and steelhead. (PHOTO VALERIE VALLA)

trout fishery with an enhanced opportunity to experience the thrill of fishing for lake-run steelhead. Biologists close to the project are well aware of the uncertainties and unforeseen consequences that may occur once steelhead are able to migrate upstream into the resident trout communities.

The present steelhead water downstream from the Springville dam provides about 4 miles of PFR stretches and some 8 miles in the beautiful Zoar Valley Multiple Use Area. Some of the best and most popular water flows through the Seneca Nation of Indians (SNI) reservation, but it's entirely open to the public via an easy-to-obtain fishing license. The most convenient place to get a license is at the Seneca One Stop convenience store and gas station in Irving on State Route 5/US-20. You can't miss the big purple-painted facility right near the traffic circle.

When you purchase a license, you'll be handed a map (not the greatest quality) of the reservation that indicates the locations of side roads that will lead anglers to the stream. The reservation reaches flow through mostly all of the 14 miles downstream from the Village of Gowanda almost to Lake Erie.

A couple of the more popular stretches are located just a couple miles from the Seneca One Stop, on State Route 438. Get on State Route 438 at the traffic circle next to the Seneca One Stop, then drive east just over 2 miles to Hawk Meadow Road on the right. The road passes a small neighborhood then enters an expanded, cleared area. You can park within view of the stream just beyond the cleared area. The stream flows downstream through an open area that's a nice fly-swinging run. Anglers will encounter wide-open pools with substantial gravel along the glacial outwash plain—more gravel than you'll ever encounter on other New York steelhead streams.

A second access point is located only a mile up State Route 438. The unnamed dirt road that leads to the stream is on the right, between Woodchuck Road and South Sulphur

Local steelheader Joe Mecca at the Hawk Meadows Road access point on SNI lands. Steelhead can begin entering the stream as early as late September. SNI stream sections can be accessed by obtaining a license at the Seneca One Stop convenience store in Irving on State Route 5/US-20.

Springs Road (about 0.6 mile east of Woodchuck). The dirt road leads to a parking area. If the road isn't too muddy, you can also continue past the parking area to a smaller lot. The stream here appears something like you'd encounter in Montana—wide-open spaces with wide, long, flat pools snaking through the valley accentuated by considerable amounts of gravel along the banks.

The pools downstream, 80 to 100 feet wide, are perfect for swinging flies when the water levels are around 400 to 500 cfs. A good discharge for dead drifting flies is around 300 cfs. When it gets into the 600 cfs range, head to one of the tributaries or the lower South Branch. Another option is to check out Eighteen Mile Creek, another Lake Erie steelhead tributary not far from Irving. Chautauqua Creek also attracts steelhead runs and has PFR water.

Water discharges aside, another major malady of the Cattaraugus is its frequent turbidity experienced after heavy rains. Back in history, the Native Americans named the stream Cattaraugus, the word for "bad smelling banks" caused by natural gas leaking from rock seams. A more appropriate stream name would have been something that means "dirty running water."

While steelheaders fishing Lake Ontario tributaries such as the Salmon River are quick to check USGS water discharge rates, Cattaraugus regulars check both flow conditions as well as turbidity levels. Thankfully, USGS posts both for the Cattaraugus at their online site. Many fly fishers won't touch the stream if turbidity levels are above 20. Some prefer even lower levels, 15 down to 10. The problem with high turbidity levels is the likelihood steelhead will see your fly. Fly shade becomes important; use darker flies in the higher turbidity range and lighter shade patterns once the runs are down to 15 or lower. The stream turbidity level changes from a brownish shade to a murky green and then finally a lighter green appearance once the stained water improves.

Chum Fly (tied by Dave McNeese) Many variations of Chum Flies have been developed over the years. Not only are they effective for catching chum salmon, but because of the pink and purple shades, many Chum Flies also attract steelhead. Creative Oregon fly tier Dave McNeese ties his beautiful version, which combines Chartreuse Angora on the rear with hot pink on the front three-fourths. Hot pink and hot purple fine bucktail forms the wing. Fluorescent orange floss creates the tail that hangs off fine silver flat tinsel tag. The body is ribbed with medium flat silver tinsel. Red 6/0 Danville thread ties off the hot purple hackle.

Chartreuse Beadhead Estaz Egg (Whittaker Fly Shop) Estaz egg patterns are considered almost a staple when heading out to fish Great Lakes tributaries for steelhead, although many other style flies will attract fish. Some Estaz-style flies are tied as beadheads to get the fly down in the water column.

White Bunny Spey—Based on Rick Kustich pattern (tied by Steve Silverio) Steve is a fan of traditional salmon and steelhead patterns that utilize jungle cock eyes. Many effective steelhead patterns utilize purple materials, such as purple crystal chenille found here.

Egg Flies (Pineville Sporting Goods/Whitakers Fly Shop) Egg patterns are available at virtually every fly-fishing shop located near Great Lakes tributary streams that have runs of steelhead or other salmonids.

While the SNI reaches are the most popular, other stretches are accessible outside the reservation lands, upstream of Gowanda. Access areas around Gowanda itself are limited; its best to bypass the couple of bridge crossings where you can cast a line without being thrown off. Instead, head upstream a few miles to the scenic Zoar Valley gorge area.

The Zoar Valley gorge—located in the 3,000-acre Zoar Valley Multiple Use Area maintained by NYSDEC—is located in stretches along both the South and Main branches of Cattaraugus Creek. Bald eagles soar above the breathtaking cliffs reaching up to 500 feet. The stands of old growth timber add to the area's charm, as do waterfalls that spill from the heights into the stream. Access is easy but requires a moderate trek down to the gorge to reach the stream.

Whether approaching from the east, from the Springville area, or from the west down near the SNI lands, head for Gowanda and routes to Point Peter Road. Out of Gowanda, two access points are just a short drive away. The Valentine Flats access parking lot is located on Valentine Flats Road, off Point Peter Road about 3 miles from Gowanda. The Forty Road parking area, that will get you on the South Branch of the Cattaraugus gorge area, is just 1.4 miles down from Point Peter Road/Valentine Flats Road intersection.

The Valentine Flats parking area, located at the end of Valentine Flats Road, has ample room for several vehicles next to an informational kiosk and trailhead to the stream. The trail follows a steep grade downhill to the bottomlands, but it's very manageable. The trail then follows an easy level grade walk a few hundred feet to the stream. (You'll notice the grove of mature walnut trees that will have you wondering if you should have worn a hard hat if visiting the area when the large nuts are falling.)

The gorge streambed has more bare shale bedrock than gravelly areas. Steelhead that move into the area seek the areas that have decent gravel substrate. Fish the runs that occupy obvious holding areas. The gorge reach is best fished from October into November or at least before the harshness of winter with its ice and snow sets in.

A couple of other access points upstream from Zoar Valley gorge are at the formal NYDEC Cattaraugus Creek Water Way access lot on North Otto Road bridge crossing and the Hammond Hill Road bridge crossing. If approaching from Gowanda, drive 6.5 miles up Zoar Valley Road to reach the Waterway access lot and another 4 miles or so upstream to the Hammond Hill Road crossing. If approaching from Springville, get on Zoar Valley Road at the State Route 39/US-219 intersection. Hammond Hill Road is about a 6-mile drive. PFR frontage at Hammond Hill Road is on the right side of the stream only (looking upstream), except directly under the bridge area.

OTHER LAKE ERIE STEELHEAD TRIBUTARIES

While Cattaraugus Creek receives most of the attention as the primary destination for Lake Erie tributary steelhead fishing, for good reasons, a few other tributaries in that region also receive steelhead runs. Eighteen Mile Creek, Canadaway Creek, and Chautauqua Creek are also worth sampling if activity is slow on the "Catt."

Eighteen Mile Creek: One of the better Lake Erie steelhead tributaries is located a short distance from Irving, near the Town of Hamburg. The creek traverses a spectacular gorge along much of its length. Access is provided by a combination of 1.4 miles of PFR water and over 2.5 miles of stretches along Eighteen Mile Creek County Park. The park area is managed as Catch and Release, artificial-lures-only fishing. Other stretches along the creek also provide angling access.

The County Park, located off South Creek Road, attracts both hikers and anglers. A trailhead begins at the large parking lot. Follow the blue reflective trail markers for a distance until the trail splits. Take the trail to the right, now marked by green reflective markers, that leads down the hill into the gorge and stream. Swing flies through the runs and glides. Like all the Lake Erie tributaries, the fish at the County Park attract many anglers, both fly fishers and others. A couple other formal PFR areas are located downstream.

Hobuck Flats stream reach, popular because of its easy and quick stream access, is located downstream in the North Evans area, off Versailles Road. Directly across from the North Evans Fire Department, take Versailles Road down a steep curved hill to a

Chris Vesperman on the Hobuck Flats reach, in North Evans area off Veresailles Road.

small parking area. Parking can be difficult, because of the small lot. You'll see the large hanging NYSDEC Hobuck Flats sign at an old iron bridge. Long pools and pleasant glides are nice stretches to drift or swing flies. Plenty of stream access is available along footpaths, but respect the posted private frontage upstream from the iron bridge, on the right side.

After exiting the iron bridge at Hobuck Flats, the creek flows downstream short of a mile to a somewhat isolated railroad overpass. The stream reach can be sampled by driving 0.6 mile west of the North Evans Fire Department, on South Creek Road. Park on the left, next to the railroad tracks. A footpath on the opposite side of South Creek Road leads to the creek, but you'll have a 1,000-foot trek to reach the railroad overpass and the nice gorge area.

If you're not up to the walk, and getting down into the creek gorge at the railroad overpass, continue driving west on South Creek Road another 1.2 miles to Lakeshore Road, crossing State Route 5 on the way. Take a right on Lakeshore Road to reach a large formal angling parking area directly next to the creek. Steelhead often hold under the Route 5 overpass at the lot. Expect crowds at this stream reach, since creek access is direct and easy.

One final stream reach to explore, but again if you're up to a trek to reach the creek, is located off Basswood Road at a formal NYSDEC angling parking lot. From the State Route 5/South Creek Road intersection, drive 0.5 mile (crossing the bridge on the way) to North Creek Road. Take a right turn, and take your first right onto Basswood Road. The parking lot marked by a large NYSDEC hanging sign, is at the road's dead end. After peering over the precipice at the lot, and viewing the stream flowing through the gorge far below, you'll wonder how on earth you'll be able to get down to the creek. A footpath that leads from the parking area a little less than 900 feet or so leads down to the stream and its nice water.

This fresh-run steelhead was netted along 18 Mile Creek in the North Evans area, during an unusually warm mid-February day.

Canadaway Creek: This one is located in Chautauqua County near the City of Dunkirk. Steelhead run from the mouth of Lake Erie to Laona Falls. Steelhead PFR stretches are limited, but anglers can easily access the stream off State Route 5 south of Dunkirk. Take a left just before the bridge crossing at Temple Road. A pull-off area is next to the stream. Only 0.6 mile of public water access is available via the State Route 5 pull-off area at the bridge crossing. (The upstream inland fishery section has 1.6 miles of PFR water near the hamlet of Griswold. It's stocked with brook trout and brown trout.)

Chautauqua Creek: Located near the Village of Westfield, this has 8.5 miles of PFR water, including a 1.3-mile Catch and Release stretch. The Westfield Water Works Dam fish passageway completed in 2012 provided 10 additional miles of steelhead water. A large formal NYSDEC parking area marked by a hanging sign on County Touring Route 21 (County Road 74) is located 1 mile south of the US-20/County Touring Route 21 intersection, a couple of miles south of Westfield. The creek also attracts brown trout during fall runs.

Lake Ontario Tributaries

SALMON RIVER (PULASKI)

While New York's Salmon River experiences brief early fall runs of coho and chinook salmon, fly anglers anxiously await the arrival of steelhead that soon follow into the river from Lake Ontario at Pulaski, New York. Steelhead provide sport through late fall into winter and into spring. Winter steelheaders are among the most enthusiastic, eager to latch into the fish, despite sometimes frigid conditions.

I landed my first steelhead on New York's Salmon River more than 40 years ago. The beautiful 9-pound, chrome-bright fish that came to the net that cold, snowy day in January 1980, fresh out of Lake Ontario, took a size 12 Abbey, a classic wet fly. The

Salmon River upper fly-fishing-only stretch often receives snow by the time that reach closes on November 30. Paradise Pool is a steelhead favorite on the stretch. A lower fly-fishing-only reach is located a few miles downstream at Altmar.

fish slammed the red-bodied, tinsel-ribbed fly that I fished deep on the swing through Sportsman Pool, one of the most popular pools on the river in those years. (Sportsman's Pool formal NYSDEC angling parking area is located 3 miles southeast on State Route 13 from the State Route 13/I-81 intersection in Pulaski.)

Dozens of other anglers, fishing everything but fly tackle—often with snagging ("snatching") rigs—watched in disbelief as I pumped long casts off my 10-foot Powell rod rigged with a crudely crafted, homemade, slow-sinking shooting-head line. I should have been wearing a hard hat while dodging bank anglers casting lead-weighted treble hooks into the pool. Some shook their heads after I landed the fish. I'm sure they thought I was some kind of crazy person, wading chest deep through the pool with a fly rod in hand. But it didn't take long for the sentiment to change.

Fly fishing for steelhead and Pacific salmon was next to nonexistent on the Salmon River back then, yet today, the fishery is one of the most popular fly-angling destinations in the East. I was a skeptic myself back then, until my fishing partner, Ed Schmidtmann, convinced me that Lake Ontario–run salmonids could be taken on fly tackle. Even though New York had first stocked Pacific salmon and steelhead in the Salmon and other rivers in the 1960s, fly fishing for these fish was considered a West Coast pursuit.

Schmidtmann had been a California steelheader until he ended up in New York as an assistant professor of entomology at Cornell University. "I can't get excited about the East Coast pound-size browns," he said the first time I met him, when he interviewed me for a research support specialist position under his supervision (that's no doubt how I landed the job with him—fly-fishing bonding works). However, he was quite excited about fly-fishing possibilities on the Salmon River. He convinced me to give Lake Ontario tributary steelhead fishing a try. We did.

Steelhead are the crown jewels of New York's Salmon River. Mike Lazzaro netted this one on November 30 at Paradise Pool on the Upper Fly Section, the final day of the open season on that reach. The Lower Fly Section is open September 15 through May 15; it extends from Beaverdam Brook 0.25 mile down to the Oswego County Road 52 bridge.

Other East Coast anglers soon rushed to the Salmon River with their fly rods and experienced the thrill of catching multiple-pound fish on flies. Even more arrived on the river after the State of New York blew the whistle on legal snagging on the Salmon and other Lake Ontario tributaries, a decision that led to lawsuits. In 1992, the state attempted to shorten the legal snagging season, but area businesses, fearing loss of revenues from a perceived disappearance of visiting anglers who came to the river in large numbers, took the decision to court. They won that small battle, but their elation was brief as snagging was banned for good in 1995 by the governor-appointed state Conservation Fund Advisory Board.

Snagging was initially allowed on the Salmon River because it was believed Pacific salmon entering the stream couldn't be taken on lures, and certainly not on flies, because they stop feeding during spawning activity. It was the inadvertent impact of snagging on nontarget species, such as steelhead, that helped change the law, not the weight of fishing ethics or snagging in and of itself. It didn't take long for fly anglers to disprove or even laugh at the notion that Pacific salmon can't be taken on flies.

The elimination of snagging wasn't the only positive change that encouraged additional fly anglers to visit the river. The same year that I caught my first steelhead, 1980, saw the opening of the enormous state-of-the-art Salmon River Fish Hatchery in Altmar. Designed to raise Pacific salmon and steelhead, the facility greatly enhanced the Lake Ontario fishery and its tributaries. Today the facility also serves as an educational destination for anglers and nonanglers alike.

The positive impact of the new hatchery aside, Salmon River anglers benefitted from other changes that enhanced the fishery, especially changes in river flow releases from the three upstream dams. Minimal flow regulations went into effect in 1997 as a result of the 1995 Federal Energy Regulatory Commission relicensing. The river was routinely reduced to a trickle as a result of power-generation fluctuations, impeding natural reproduction of salmonids and retarding the proliferation of macroinvertebrate populations to sustain fish.

One of the fishery's most passionate anglers, Dave "Rocky" Rockwell is a no-nonsense, fine-cigar-smoking retired lieutenant colonel and veteran of two tours in Iraq. His infectious good humor, sprinkled with occasional blasts of ribald wit, is both entertaining and welcome when you're wading next to him in the river at first light. He loves the fishing, enjoys guiding clients on the river, and likes studying the Salmon River's rich history.

"The minimal flows turned the fishery around completely," Rocky told me during an enjoyable midwinter chat when I should have been fishing and not gabbing. "There was inconsistency. The erratic releases out of all three of the dams affected the system. The fishery before the minimal-release regulations was sometimes good and sometimes not so good. Before those changes, the river was totally dependent upon the hatchery for fish. There was virtually no natural reproduction at that time. The changes have been good for everyone, especially for the region's economy."

Over the past few decades, the Salmon River fishery has seen many positive changes, which have contributed to its growing popularity among fly fishers who come to the river in hopes of landing a trophy-size chinook or coho salmon, steelhead, Atlantic salmon, brown trout, or even bass. What has not changed over the years are the great numbers of anglers who converge on the 13-odd fishable miles between Lighthouse Hill Reservoir and Port Ontario when word is out that fish are running the river.

Pulaski, headquarters during salmon and steelhead season, comes alive beginning in mid-September, when chinook and coho runs are generally expected in the Salmon River, swimming through the Port Ontario estuary and on upriver. Outside the many lodges, motels, and eateries, roadside signs prominently welcome anglers. Well before daybreak, anglers in waders and headlamps line up for coffee at a local convenience store, their objective to be first on some of the best runs and pools in the river.

Coho salmon are among the first salmonids that run the Salmon River in September. While not as large as the big chinook salmon that are in the river at the same time, cohos are beautiful fish that also strike colorful egg flies.

Encountering large numbers of anglers is inescapable on the river that offers such a high probability of landing such large fish. As one angler said to me while he was gearing up next to his vehicle, "You have to recalibrate your fly-fishing experience expectations. Sure, there are crowds, but where else can you hook into a 10-pound steelie or 25-pound chinook on fly tackle? And often get into multiple hookups?"

Some have called the Salmon River a world-class fishery. Others say that while that may be true, for them, it's not a world-class fly-fishing experience, particularly if you prefer solitude on the water. The Salmon seems to appeal to many fly anglers who are not bothered by so many people fishing in such close proximity. It's rare to encounter a fly angler on the river who complains about all the company, even those fishing almost shoulder to shoulder.

Salmon River first-timers either love the river or loathe it. The anglers who enjoyed their first experience on the Salmon River almost always return. Many, if not most, revisit annually. Some avoid the heavy weekend crowds by fishing only on weekdays. The largest numbers of visitors, especially conventional tackle anglers, are on the river for the Pacific salmon runs. For one thing, the weather is nicer in September and early October. And the chinook run large, some approaching 30 pounds.

I tagged along with Rockwell and Mike De Rosa in late September and again in early October a few years ago during what was expected to be the height of the chinook and coho runs. We were on the Douglaston Salmon Run (DSR), 2.5 miles of the lower river a couple of miles downstream from Pulaski on County Road 5. The DSR is a pay-to-fish stretch just upstream from the estuary in Port Ontario. The fish that enter the run are fresh and lively. It's common to witness pods of chinook rooster-tailing up through the shallows, announcing their presence.

Some may frown at the pay-to-fish concept, but there's some worth in the clean, civil, and friendly environment that a controlled system can offer. You're likely to encounter River Walkers on the Run, staff members who patrol the DSR mileage. They're unobtrusive and courteous, and beyond a quick hello, and sometimes a brief chat about the fishing, they move on. The DSR limits the number of anglers who can purchase a pass, and the number varies depending on the season.

A half dozen of us, wearing headlamps and gripping wading staffs, thrashed across a DSR stretch well before daylight one day. It's best to be on the water as early as possible. Multiple hookups didn't happen, and the group called the fishing slow. It's common to call fishing slow when only a few anglers in a group get into a fish. A couple of anglers in the group that day landed large, bright salmon on chartreuse Estaz egg patterns, popular flies on the river. Hardly slow fishing by my definition.

Spey fishing has grown in popularity over the last decade, and it's common to see more anglers swinging flies using traditional steelhead-fishing technique. On the Salmon, it can be difficult to squeeze your way into the crowds to swing flies. Some steelhead Spey casters seek out the less popular river stretches to perfect their casting and fishing techniques, avoiding the normally crowded fly-fishing-only designated area.

Most steelhead fly casters who are not fishing the DSR frequent the two designated fly-fishing-only zones in Altmar. Altmar is located about 6.5 miles east from the I-81/State Route 13 intersection in Pulaski. The Lower Fly Zone is open September 15 through May 15; it extends from Beaverdam Brook 0.25 mile down to the Oswego County Road 52 bridge—not a lot of water to accommodate the number of fly casters who like to fish this reach.

If approaching from Pulaski, drive 6 miles east on County Road 13 to Pulaski Street on the left. Take Pulaski Street less than 1 mile to its end at Bridge Street (County Road 52).

You'll find two large parking areas at the bridge, one on each side. If the fish are in the river, the lots will be packed with vehicles. One of the best runs to fish is about 50 to 100 feet directly upstream from the County Road 52 bridge. I've consistently witnessed, over a couple decades, many steelhead brought to net on that run and many hook-ups where the steelhead won the battle. The downside is many anglers know that to be the case; expect competition for that slot. Make a point to stop in at Melinda's Fly, Spey and Tackle Shop located within sight of the bridge, at 3 Pulaski Street, in Altmar. Owner Melinda Barna briefly considered closing her shop but all is well and she's decided, thank goodness, to remain in business. I stopped by the shop in February 2023, and spoke to her about the rumors. Access the river downstream from the bridge via a footpath next to the lower parking lot. During periods of higher-water flows the stream reach in that section can be productive. Swing flies through the run. The footpath along the stream bank can get you into water for quite a distance. Tailwater Lodge, a high-end accommodation that welcomes anglers, owns frontage on the opposite bank. Guests have free access to that side of the river. Complete with an indoor wader washing area, the rooms and dining area are tastefully decorated in fly-fishing themes.

The Upper Fly Zone, located along County Road 22 and open from April 1 through November 30, extends from the Lighthouse Hill Reservoir tailrace down to a marked boundary upstream of the fish hatchery. If approaching from the County Road 52/Pulaski Street intersection at the Lower Fly Zone area, drive 0.2 mile south on County Road 52 to a left on County Road 22. Follow County Road 22 1.3 miles or so to the large formal NYSDEC angling parking area on the left. (You'll pass by the Salmon River Fish Hatchery on your way.) A well-used path will take you to both upstream and downstream areas along the stream bank.

The popular Paradise Pool is one of the favorites among Upper Fly Zone regulars. Once you arrive at the river bank from the path that leads from the parking area, walk along the path a short distance downstream. The path eventually goes down a slight slope next to the river and the run that enters the pool. You're more likely to encounter fewer anglers enjoying the section during the last few days of November when the reach is open to fishing before it closes at the end of the month. Other good stretches to try are downstream from Paradise Pool several hundred feet to another good run that produces nice steelhead every year.

The Upper Fly Zone is also considered by some prime Atlantic salmon water—indeed, steelhead, big browns, and bass are not the only fish that anglers might hook into on the Salmon River. If I had one wish while fishing the stream, it would be to land a hard-fighting, 16-pound Atlantic salmon like the fish my friend Rocky Rockwell took in June 2011 on a Hornberg streamer. That dream hasn't come true yet. Incidentally, the Salmon River got its name not from chinook and coho, but instead from the Atlantic salmon, a species indigenous to the river but long ago extirpated here.

Atlantic salmon in the Lake Ontario watershed were able to run to the Atlantic Ocean before geologic changes landlocked the species. They were once present in all 25 Lake Ontario tributaries except the Niagara River, but wild runs were extirpated in the late 1800s. Since 1995, hatchery-raised Atlantic salmon have been part of the usual stocking regimen for the Salmon River, but adults have seldom returned in numbers anglers would love to see. Still, there's always a chance you might hook one. They start entering the Salmon River in May and stick around the upper river all summer.

No matter what fish you target on the Salmon River—Pacific salmon to Atlantic salmon—make sure you check out the NYSDEC official Salmon River regulations. While the stream is open to fishing all year, the fishery is regulated by a variety of rules, including tackle restrictions; some regulations vary by season.

Tackle Selection

Speaking of tackle, first-time fly fishers often ask what type of rods, reels, lines, and terminal tackle to use and flies to carry. Steelhead fishing results can be enhanced by using effective setups that are different from regular fly-fishing tackle. Lots of changes in rods, reels, terminal tackle, and even fly patterns have developed over the last 22 years since I first took that big steelie in Sportsman Pool.

Switch rods that vary in length from 10 feet 6 inches to 11 feet 6 inches with 7-weight to 8-weight lines make you a better fly fisher immediately, something I learned from Rocky a while back. I've netted plenty of Salmon River fish on my 9.5-foot, 7-weight rods. However, the upgrade is well worth the expense. As Rocky insists, such rods will enable easier roll casts, easier mending, longer presentations, and an advantage on hook setting.

Fly Selection

Egg patterns are popular but by no means the end-all when it comes to fly-pattern selection. The sheer number of patterns in the fly bins at major fly shops in the Pulaski area—such as Whittaker's Sport Store on State Route 13, Malinda's Fly & Tackle on Pulaski Street, and Pineville Sporting Supply also located on State Route 13—is rather overwhelming. Chinooks will strike most any fly colors at one time or another, from hot colors to drab shades, including streamers (believe it or not) and even the smallest of flies. I prefer to swing traditional steelhead hair-wing patterns, such as a Brad's Brat, modified with a hot-orange head. Other anglers have experimented with nontraditional patterns and had good results. You'll also need to carry a variety of nymph patterns, from small sizes to larger sizes. Jeffrey Deshefy Jr., a Salmon River regular and guide, created an interesting and effective Double Ribbed Golden Stonefly that proved its worth on the river.

Angler Dave "Rocky" Rockwell on the lower Salmon River DSR stretch during the coho and chinook run. A passionate Salmon River angler, Dave is a retired military man who now limits his guiding to assist and instruct active-duty military, veterans, wounded warriors, and Healing Waters veterans.

Dave "Rocky" Rockwell's fly box is fully stocked with a variety of bright patterns, Estaz eggs, and other attractors, perfect for both Pacific salmon and steelhead.

One talented angler I met several years ago on the river, who goes by the name "Jersey Jan" Beliveau, consistently takes chinook and steelhead on simple, slender, flashing-bodied size 14 and 16 patterns that resemble caddisfly larvae. I ran into Beliveau on one of his favorite stretches, and despite the fact I witnessed him take what was no doubt a 25-pound chinook on his tiny fly, he, too, called the fishing slow by Salmon River standards. And that wasn't the only fish he landed that day.

Whether you are making your inaugural visit to the Salmon River or you're an old hand on these waters, make time to enjoy the area; visit attractions and check out all the local businesses that cater to anglers. Stop by the Salmon River Fish Hatchery, the Salmon River Falls Unique Area (located a few miles from the hatchery off Falls Road), and the Salmon River International Sport Fishing Museum (located on State Route 13 between Altmar and Pulaski).

The Salmon River Hatchery is a great place for the whole family during the spawning runs in October. The viewing deck at the entrance to the fishway allows visitors to watch fish swim out of Beaverdam Brook and up the hatchery fish ladder. For anglers and nonanglers alike, it's a view to a revitalized river; where landlocked Atlantic salmon once flourished, their anadromous brethren from the Pacific Coast now offer both the prolific fisher a premier fly-fishing experience.

Dave Rockwell's Typical Steelhead and Salmon Setups: The leader length should be approximately the length of the rod or up to a foot longer. Tippet length is a maximum of 4 feet on Salmon River, and if you are checked by a NYSDEC Conservation Officer, he will probably measure it! I use a 4-foot tippet for dead-drifting nymphs and egg patterns. For indicator fishing where I want to ensure the fly is on the bottom, I cut the tippet in half and tie both pieces together with a blood knot and place a very small split short above the knot. This assists in the fly staying down and leading the presentation.

Double Ribbed Golden Stonefly (tied by Jeffrey R. Deshefy Jr.) This interesting pattern was handed to me at one of the fly-fishing shows where Jeffrey was busy at his tying table displaying his steelhead creations. Beautifully tied, it's a very effective steelhead catcher. Jeffrey, a registered NYS Fishing Guide, designed his stonefly to fish under high Salmon River conditions, something that could quickly reach the bottom. He was unable to locate a fly in any of the shops that could fill that need. Jeffrey likes tying the pattern with a 5/32-inch gold bead and 15 wraps of 0.020 lead wire to get the fly down to the fish. He favors a Mustad S82-3906B hook in sizes #6 to 8.

Brad's Brat (tied by Dave McNeese) Oregon fly tier Dave McNeese is a big fan of this classic steelhead pattern. In this authors book *Tying and Fishing Bucktails and other Hair Wings*, McNeeses's full step-by-step tying sequence is shown for this pattern. Like any fly that's been around since the 1930s, there are several versions of Brad's Brat, first tied by Enos Bradner in Washington State. In his book Classic Steelhead Flies (2015), John Shewey provided interesting history behind the fly and Bradner himself. John, like Dave McNeese, also retooled the fly a tad. Shewey's version appears in his book.

Al's Special (tied by Dave McNeese) Al Knudson's steelhead pattern that goes back to the 1930s was tied much differently than Dave McNeese's version shown here. Early versions, as shown by John Shewey in his book, were tied with yellow chenille bodies. McNeese's style uses yellow angora or wool, among other material differences. Either way, it's still a good pattern to try on the Salmon River when in the mood to try classic patterns on the swing.

Flesh Fly (tied by Dave Rockwell) Flesh Flies, popular on the Salmon River, are tied to suggest hunks of flesh that break down from decaying Pacific salmon that entered the river and eventually died. Many types and versions of Flesh Flies exist, some with bead heads.

Comet Fly-orange (tied by Dave Rockwell) Comet-style steelhead patterns, with their characteristic bead-chain heads, have been around since the 1940s. In his beautiful book *Classic Steelhead Flies* (2015), John Shewey writes that its "genesis is murky." Evidence seems to point in the direction of Eureka, California, and its surrounding steelhead rivers. They were once called "popeye flies." Comet-style steelhead flies are popular swing flies on the Salmon River.

Dave "Rocky" Rockwell's Suggested Salmon River Leader:

SIGHTER: 12 to 18 inches, 15- or 20-pound test Amnesia Mono (red)—Attach to fly line with a "Perfection Loop."

LEADER: 6 to 7 feet, 12-pound Mono—Attach to Sighter with a "Blood Knot."

MINI-SWIVEL: Attach to leader with an "Improved Clinch" or similar. Leave a very short tag end with an "Over Hand Knot" for split shot, if needed.

TIPPET: 3 to 4 feet Fluorocarbon (line test based on conditions).

THE SANDYS: SOUTH, NORTH, LITTLE

Fly anglers who prefer to stay clear of sometimes heavy crowds on the Salmon River often relocate to one of "The Sandys"—a short drive from Pulaski. South Sandy, North Sandy, and the Little Sandy Creeks still attract lots of both conventional tackle anglers and fly fishers. However, there are times the anglers are spread out. Or, if you're lucky enough, you'll even have a stream stretch to yourself.

South Sandy Creek

South Sandy is most crowded during the chinook salmon runs in September into early October. You'll know if fish are in the river when you pull into one of the parking areas near the stream. I've been on South Sandy after the height of the chinook run, and during times the first steelhead are in the stream, and see few vehicles at angling access parking areas.

If you're after steelies, late October into November is a better time to begin fishing the stream for that species, preferably before the water temperatures dip below 40 degrees. However, steelhead can be enticed all winter; they're just not as interested in feeding or moving. A fly is more effective if it passes by their nose. After they're done spawning during March and April, the fish are again on the hunt for food. More than a few anglers look forward more to fishing for the "drop backs"—steelhead on their way back down to Lake Ontario in spring. Brown trout are sometimes caught along the banks in late

Chinook salmon run the South Sandy in September into October. They can weigh up to 30 pounds. A variety of fly patterns are effective for chinooks on the Sandys. Estaz egg flies are among the most popular.

South Sandy Creek at State Route 289 bridge crossing in Ellisburg. Chinooks were being caught in the creek when this photo was taken in late September. Once the chinook run dwindles down to nothing, the stream can be almost devoid of anglers until steelhead show up later in October.

November into the winter months, too, but anglers have better luck fishing for browns over on Little Sandy Creek.

The reason for angler presence fluctuations on all the Sandys has to do with the requirement of sufficient water flows that will bring fish into the stream from Lake Ontario, a much different situation from Salmon River where the upstream reservoir provides water storage and sufficient, if not constant or even too much, release. Steelhead on the Sandys will arrive in pulses and even drop back to the lake when water levels decrease and fish sense they need to move downstream. It can be a "back and forth" fish migration situation, of sorts.

Plenty of public access via formal NYSDEC angling parking areas can be found that will get you into water. Some access points are directly on the stream, and some require a short to moderately long trek along designated footpaths. The uppermost parking area on South Sandy is located at a bridge crossing off Monitor Mill Road about a mile upstream from the Village of Ellisburg. Monitor Falls, located upstream from the bridge, is impassible to migrating fish. Ellisburg is about 13 to 15 miles north of Pulaski, depending what route you take (US-11 or I-81).

All of your South Sandy angling will take place from the Monitor Falls area downstream to the lowermost parking lot located 4 miles, give or take, downstream at South Landing, not far from the stream mouth at Lake Ontario on State Route 3. But there's plenty of formal parking access areas along the way to South Landing.

One popular parking area and access point is located in Ellisburg, a mile or so downstream from the Monitor Falls lot next to the State Route 289/State Route 193 intersection near the bridge crossing. You can park at the streamside lot graciously allowed by the Ellisburg Fire Department. There's an honor system request for a $5.00 donation at the lot. Some nice chinooks are caught downstream from the bridge along the runs, but upstream can be good, too. An unofficial path located across the road from the parking lot leads to the reaches downstream from the bridge.

Other formal NYSDEC parking areas are located just a couple of miles downstream on South Landing Road. Get on the South Main Street corner located at the State Route 289/State Route 193 intersection near the Fire Department building. South Main Street continues as South Landing Road as it follows the creek downstream toward the lake.

The first formal NYSDEC angling parking lot is less than 1 mile down South Landing Road, on your left. The large lot will accommodate plenty of vehicles. A pleasant yet long walk across a large open field from the NYSDEC parking leads to the stream. Very nice runs and pools account for good numbers of chinooks and steelhead every year along this reach. You'll have lots of angling company along this stretch when the chinooks are in. The stretch is frequently blessed with logjams that help provide stream structure.

Another smaller official NYSDEC parking lot is located 2 miles down South Lansing Road from the last parking area. It's directly across the road from a long dairy barn with green gable ends. This reach produces fish, but it isn't as nice as the upstream stretch. A designated footpath leads from the parking area down a very rocky moderate slope to the creek.

Back on South Lansing Road, drive another 2.4 miles to State Route 3 and take a left to the lowermost formal NYSDEC angling parking area, marked by a large hanging sign. It's also the parking area for the Lakeview Wildlife Management Area. A boat launch is located at the bridge crossing. Long, slow-moving pools are located both upstream and downstream.

One other formal NYSDEC parking area is located on Nash Road. This parking lot provides access to the opposite side (southside) of the creek via a designated footpath. From the State Route 3 Lakeview Wildlife Management Area bridge crossing, drive less than a half-mile south on State Route 3 to a left on Nash Road. The parking lot is marked by a NYSDEC hanging sign on the left. The river is located a few hundred feet from the parking lot.

South Sandy Creek at the access point less than 1 mile down South Lansing Road from Ellisburg. This photo was taken during the chinook run in late September. Most of the anglers were positioned out of site both upstream and downstream from this location.

If targeting chinooks, many fly anglers stick with garish Estaz egg patterns that have sustained effectiveness for enticing Pacific salmon in this creek and other Great Lakes tributaries. Steelheaders drift egg patterns with an appropriate amount of small split shot to get the fly down to the fish. Nymphs work well for both steelhead and the occasional brown trout that wander into the system, especially during the spring months. Small, bright pink or purple Matuka patterns will bring fish to the net on pools appropriate for swinging flies.

Estaz Egg (Whittaker's Sport Shop) A variety of egg patterns fill the bins of Salmon River area fly shops. Some of the beadhead versions are very colorful, and they are no doubt enticing to steelhead and Pacific salmon that enter the area tributaries.

Golden Stonefly (tied by Dave Rockwell) This Golden Stonefly is particularly interesting given its rubber legs. It's tied with amber dubbing and turkey quill section wing cases. Anglers fishing the Salmon River and its nearby tributaries should carry a supply of various stonefly patterns.

Swing Fly-Yellow (tied by Dave Rockwell) This beadchain head swing fly, with its yellow strip wing, is yet another interesting pattern fished on the Salmon River.

Pink Matuka (tied by Dave McNeese) Dave McNeese's Pink Matuka provides good feather action while swinging the pattern through steelhead water. Its creamy pink fur ribbed with silver tinsel along with its long purple hackle and pink bucktail wings and tail is an interesting pattern to fish on the swing. Dave ties off the head with 6/0 red Danville thread.

Estaz Egg-Chartreuse (Whittaker's Sport Shop) Yet another Estaz egg pattern, tied with an orange body and sparkling chartreuse Estaz Chenille. Estaz egg patterns are easy to tie, and the materials are readily available for tiers who prefer to fish with self-tied flies.

North Sandy Creek, at the Woodville bridge crossing looking downstream. The creek flows over a significant amount of bedrock along this reach. Chinooks often hold under bedrock ledges and show themselves by rooster tailing.

North Sandy Creek

Most fly fishers that head for one of the three Sandys that flow north of Pulaski prefer South Sandy, largely because of the number of easy access points available via formal NYSDEC angling parking lots. North Sandy has only a couple formal access points: one just downstream of Woodville, and the other at the North Landing bridge crossing parking area located on State Route 3. (Incidentally, the North Landing parking lot is located only 1.5 miles north of the South Landing parking area that serves South Sandy Creek. If you're fishing South Sandy in the lower reach, you can easily and quickly get on North Sandy Creek stretches.)

If approaching from Pulaski and you wish to start fishing North Sandy Creek along its upper reach first, head for the hamlet of Woodville. It's located about 15 to 20 miles north of Pulaski, depending on the route. Woodville is only 2.5 miles north from the State Route 193/State Route 289 intersection in Ellisburg, on State Route 193 (see South Sandy Creek section). If driving north from Pulaski on I-81, take Exit 39 to County Road 90 to County Road 87 to Ellisburg. You'll pass over South Sandy Creek in Ellisburg on your way to Woodville.

If gazing both upstream and downstream from the Woodville bridge, you'll notice the creek flows over an expansive amount of shale bedrock. It's not the best fish holding water, especially directly upstream from the bridge. However, on one occasion, I saw big chinooks rooster tailing a couple hundred feet downstream from the bridge along an undercut midstream ledge. It's better to go downstream a short distance.

Once you arrive in Woodville, drive south 1.2 miles on County Road 120 from the County Road 120/State Route 193 intersection (it's near the south side of the bridge). A formal NYSDEC angling parking area is on the right and will provide better access to the south side of the creek reach downstream from the Woodville bridge crossing.

North Sandy Creek, upstream from the State Route 3 North Landing bridge crossing NYSDEC angling parking area on the creek's lower reach. The run upstream from the bridge provides excellent steelhead fishing when fish are in the stream. Early run chinooks also hold in the stretch under the bridge.

The creek structure and holding water is improved down that way. However, you'll be trekking a designated footpath several hundred feet across an expansive field to reach the steep bank along the stream. Here you'll find better runs and pools that exist directly upstream and downstream from the Woodville crossing, but it will take some effort to sample that reach.

Steelhead begin making their presence known by late October or early November, depending on seasonal conditions and water flow levels. Water flows out into the lake mouth are largely dependent on rainfall amounts that bring fresh fish into the stream.

Little Sandy Creek at the Norton Road bridge crossing. Fly anglers desiring smaller Lake Ontario tributary water should make a few casts on Little Sandy Creek. Chinooks, brown trout, and steelhead are caught in the stream. (PHOTO VALERIE VALLA)

If you're not inclined to walk and fish a distance to get on the water, especially if the winter weather conditions are brutal, another creek access option is located downstream at a formal NYSDEC parking lot directly on the streambank. Continue driving 0.7 mile down County Road 120 to the State Route 3 intersection. Take a right, then drive less than a half-mile to the parking area at North Landing bridge crossing. It's a very long parking lot on the downstream side of the bridge. You'll want to position yourself at the nice run located a couple hundred feet upstream from the bridge, on the right side of the creek looking upstream. Steelhead hold best at the head of the pool run and at the tailout.

Little Sandy Creek

A favorite among both conventional tackle anglers and fly fishers, Little Sandy Creek is just that: "little." However, its size belies its potential to attract both big chinooks and big steelhead, with a few brown trout joining the migration from Lake Ontario. Of the three Sandy Creeks in the area, Little Sandy is the closest distance to Pulaski. Drive to the Village of Sandy Creek via US-11, County Road 15, or I-81 out of Pulaski. The village is only 7 to 9 miles from Pulaski, depending on the route. In addition to chinooks and steelhead, brown trout also run the stream.

Little Sandy Creek provides 3.6 miles of PFR water in addition to a couple of unofficial stretches at side road bridge crossings. Make sure you're not fishing posted property. A couple of formal NYSDEC angling parking areas are on (or off of) County Road 15 east of the village. If you're taking US-11, drive north to the US-11/County Road 15 intersection in the village. Take a left, and drive about 1.5 miles to a NYSDEC angling access parking area on the right side of the road, just before a utility building and large red barn. The designated footpath leads a few hundred feet to the stream.

If you're not into trekking a long path to reach the creek, try fishing the reach down at the Norton Road formal NYSDEC angling parking lot. It's right next to the creek. Drive 0.7 mile down County Road 15 from the previous access lot (2.2 miles down County Road 15 from the Village of Sandy Creek) to Norton Road on the right. The bridge crossing and parking lot is located a couple hundred feet down the road. The large hanging sign simply says "Sandy Creek," but it's actually Little Sandy Creek.

PFR stretches are available both upstream and downstream from the small bridge. Fish along the runs and pools. Some mighty big browns have been caught downstream at the State Route 3 bridge crossing. The brown trout you might encounter during late fall into winter often hang out under deadfalls, woody overhangs, or undercut bank areas. Browns can be enticed by small Woolly Bugger-style patterns. The creek is posted upstream from the bridge but is open to public access downstream. NYSDEC signage states it's closed to fishing between March 16 and the first Saturday in May.

LINDSEY CREEK/SKINNER CREEK

Lindsey Creek, along with Skinner Creek, are what I call "blown out" Lake Ontario salmonid tributaries. The smaller Pulaski area tributaries are where you want to locate during times the larger streams, such as the Salmon River, are blown out with unfishable high and stained water conditions. Chinooks enter the stream in September. Steelhead follow later on in November and stick around into spring. Like the Sandy creeks, water flow levels are an important factor in drawing the fish into the stream from Lake Ontario.

Lindsey Creek is located about 10 miles north of Pulaski. Drive to the Village of Sandy Creek via US-11 or I-81. A good place to begin fishing Lindsey is at a formal NYSDEC angling parking lot about 3 miles from the village on County Road 87. In the village, take a left on Ellisburg Road (County Road 22A). You'll be driving past the Oswego County Fairgrounds. County Road 22A eventually becomes County Road 87 just past Scott Road. The angling parking lot is located about 0.8 mile from the County Road 87/Scott Road intersection. Parking is directly next to the stream at a bridge crossing. Lindsey Creek picks up additional water from Jacobs Brook just downstream from the bridge. PFR water is available on both streams.

Lindsey Creek and its extensive PFR water can also be accessed downstream at the McDonald Hill Road bridge crossing 2 miles from the above formal parking lot. Drive back on County Road 87 to Scott Road. Take a right on Scott, and drive less than a mile to a right turn on McDonald Road. The bridge crossing and PFR water is 0.4 mile up McDonald. I can't say I favor that reach, and I am more inclined to bypass it in favor of sampling Skinner Creek.

Skinner Creek can run very clear when other streams in the area are blown out. Skinner Creek is a quick 1-mile drive north from the formal NYSDEC parking lot described earlier. Drive north 1-mile on County Road 87 to a bridge crossing. You'll notice a small NYSDEC "anglers park here" sign on the road shoulder, with an arrow directing visitors to the stream. It's small water here, for sure.

More interesting PFR stretches are located upstream that can be accessed from another formal NYSDEC angling parking lot on County Road 89. Drive another 1.1 miles up County Road 87 to Ellis Road then take a quick right on County Road 89. The parking area is 0.8 mile up County Road 89, on the right side of the road marked by a hanging sign. You'll have an interesting trek down a designated footpath to get to this stream reach that flows a few hundred feet away from the parking lot.

Lindsey Creek during a day that the Salmon River was largely unfishable due to high water levels. When the larger area Lake Ontario tributaries are blown out—running high or stained—head to the smaller streams. (PHOTO VALERIE VALLA)

The footpath heads down a very steep hill, at first well identified by trail markers, to the woodland floor below. The challenge is locating the formal NYSDEC small square trail markers that vanish once you're down below the hill, on flat ground. You won't have any trouble locating the stream by continuing your walk a couple hundred feet in the same direction.

However, when you reach the bottom of the steep hill, I recommend that you glance back up the hill at the parking area so you can make a mental note of landmarks of where the steep hill path is located. Logging activity in recent times has created some slash from the cuttings; perhaps the designated trail markers have vanished for that reason. The stream back in there is very nice, with runs and pools, perfect for drifting egg patterns, and even swinging flies through some of the longer runs. Fish the tailouts and heads of pools.

Another reach worth sampling is located at a formal parking area upstream, a short drive away. From the last NYSDEC parking area, drive 0.8 mile to a right on County Road 90 then continue 0.3 mile to Brown Road (you'll cross over I-81 on your way to Brown). You'll arrive at a parking area 0.4 mile down Brown Road with a cell tower in sight. The stream is located a few hundred feet from the parking lot. Once again, a footpath leads down a very steep hill to the area below and the creek.

GRINDSTONE CREEK

Brushy Grindstone Creek, located only a couple miles south of Pulaski, is a small stream that spills into Lake Ontario at Selkirk Shores State Park. Selkirk Shores State Park is just around the corner from Pulaski, a couple of miles south of Port Ontario on State Route 3. Most of the stream, with its 5.4 PFR miles, is along County Road 28 and County Road 41A. The brushy, smallish creek receives runs of chinooks, steelhead, and browns out of Lake Ontario. NYSDEC annually stocks the creek with some 5,000 steelhead fingerlings. Access is via four formal NYSDEC angling parking lots along the creek, as well as downstream at Selkirk Shores State Park.

The lowermost parking area is located on County Road 28 1.2 miles south from the County Road 28/State Route 3 intersection, marked by a large hanging sign. A footpath from the parking area leads to the stream located a couple hundred feet from the road.

Another formal lot is located about a half-mile upstream on County Road 28. From the previous parking area, drive 0.2 mile to a left turn on Salisbury Road. Cross the bridge and continue with a quick right on County Road 28. The lot is less than a half-mile up the road. Again, the creek requires a short walk along a designated path that leads through an open area before the creek comes into sight. It's not a very appealing stretch for fly fishing. Like most of the creek, it's popular with conventional tackle anglers. Two additional parking areas are located upstream, one on Krebs Road and another smaller parking spot farther upstream on County Road 41A next to a private residence. Both are marked by large hanging signs. If you're not interested in taking a long trek to the stream, try the downstream access points.

What I find more appealing about Grindstone isn't the stream itself; it's the mouth of the creek where it dumps into Lake Ontario at the Selkirk Shores State Park. My fishing partner Ed Schmidtmann and I explored the mouth area and its potential many years ago, during the spring of 1979. Ed, a West Coast steelheader who moved to New York when he accepted an assistant professor position at Cornell University, enjoyed casting with shooting tapers on big water. He was probably one of the first fly anglers I knew who discussed using a stepladder, planted firmly a distance from shore, to help him deliver long casts out into the expanse of the big water.

One thing that will quickly become apparent is the amount of angling activity at Grindstone's mouth, especially during September. A large parking lot along the lake shore where Grindstone's tongue flows out into the lake attracts many confident anglers hoping to latch into a big chinook or other salmonid. Spring also brings anglers back.

Grindstone Creek on the left, flowing out into Lake Ontario at Selkirk Shores State Park. Grindstone Creek receives steelhead and some brown trout runs. It's a small, brushy creek in some sections and often difficult to fly fish. However, PFR access exists along the creek. (PHOTO VALERIE VALLA)

Frequent head winds at Selkirk Shore at the mouth of Grindstone Creek can be brutal. Fly fishing is best done on the inland tributaries during such unfishable conditions.

When the lake water begins to warm around Selkirk Shores State Park, baitfish are attracted to the favorable water temperatures near shore. Big brown trout follow, for an annual feast. Anglers visiting Lake Ontario in spring will notice fishing boats trolling lures relatively close to shoreline, particularly around Selkirk Shores and a few miles south at Mexico Bay. The browns wander in close enough at times that fly anglers can reach them casting from shore. The fishing seemed to be better years ago, before zebra mussels appeared, but that's an uncertainty as a reason and just conjecture.

Bringing fish to the net doesn't always happen and, in recent years, somewhat episodic, but it's worth fishing Grindstone's outflow into the lake during early spring. You'll need plenty of punch with a shooting taper, specialty line, or faster action rod to reach the browns when they're cruising the shoreline, especially if its moderately windy. There are some days in early spring when the winds are coming in directly so strong that it's not worth the effort and outright impossible to cast flies. A slight chop on the water is manageable; when you see whitecaps, it's time to head to a bar or diner.

Wind plays a big part in determining success. A slight wind isn't a problem; use slender baitfish patterns and not the big meaty flies, wind-resistant patterns if you're having trouble getting the distance you'd like. The browns aren't too particular concerning what fly pattern to cast; anything with a bit of flash, sparkle, or something that suggests a baitfish will work.

If you're crowded out by conventional tackle anglers who gather directly where Grindstone enters the lake, cast with a shooting taper to the tail of the outflowing water, from the long concrete pier. It's sometimes not possible, unless you want to risk slapping one of several conventional fishing anglers occupying the pier with your fly on a backcast.

You can also fish from shore at Mexico Point State Boat Launch, a couple of miles down State Route 3 from Selkirk Shores, where browns also congregate in early spring, looking to feed on baitfish that congregate in the warming waters. Drive south from the entrance to Selkirk Shores State Park on State Route 3 to State Route 104B. Take a right on County Road 40 to the boat launch area.

Brown trout can be caught close to the shore of Lake Ontario at Selkirk Shores State Park during early spring, when baitfish are frequenting the warming waters. Mexico Point State Boat Launch nearby also has shore fishing access.

CF Baitfish White (tied by Andreas Andersson) Swedish fly tier Andreas Andersson created an interesting series of baitfish patterns he calls CF Baitfish. "CF" stands for craft fur, a material he often combines with natural bucktail. Andreas ties the general design in many ways—hook size and colors can be varied, as are materials. His CF patterns provide good movement in water and are relatively easy to cast.

Fathead Minnow (tied by Keith Fulsher) In its normally smaller hook sizes, Fulsher's Thunder Creek baitfish patterns are no doubt a little small to entice big salmonids that hang off the mouth of Grindstone Creek. However, they are very easy to cast into a mild wind coming off the lake, a big advantage. Keith Fulsher (1922–2017) developed his now-classic baitfish series in 1962. A complete chapter on Fulsher, along with examples of Thunder Creek patterns, is included in the author's book *Tying the Founding Flies* (2015).

Black Blonde (tied by Ralph Graves) In the December 1963 issue of *Outdoor Life* magazine, Joe Brooks (1901–1972) wrote, "If I had only one pattern for all big fish in both fresh and salt water, I'd choose the Blonde." In his story, titled "Those Deadly Blondes," Brooks wrote how he landed every conceivable gamefish on his Blonde flies. Big Atlantic salmon on the Aurland River in Norway "busted their spots going for Blondes." Included in the series is a Black Blonde, a fly that's actually relatively easy to cast out quite far into large water bodies.

MAXWELL CREEK

Maxwell Creek brings back lots of memories of the first years I fished it in 1981 with friend Tom Burr, a plant pathologist (now retired) from Cornell University's experiment station in Geneva, New York. I don't think I would have ever fished that stream had I not transferred to "The Station," as it was formally called, from a laboratory at the campus. Maxwell Creek/Maywell Bay is located 1.8 miles east of the State Route 14/County Road 101 intersection in Sodus Point, on Lake Ontario.

When I left my Research Support Specialist position at Cornell's campus, 50 miles south, for a joint appointment with both the entomology and plant pathology departments, I didn't have an inkling what new fly-fishing experiences would be at hand. My supervisor and fishing partner professor Ed Schmidtmann sent me off to my new job with sound advice: "Look up Chuck Eckenrode; he's an entomology professor up there in Geneva and an enthusiastic Seneca Lake and Lake Ontario angler." So I did.

Geneva, located at the north end of Seneca Lake, is a 40-mile drive north up State Route 14 to Lake Ontario. I started working at the Geneva experiment station in March 1980, before I changed professions a couple years later. Perfect timing, fishing wise, to get to know Eckenrode. Chuck was a conventional tackle angler who trolled Rapalas off the lake shore near Sodus Point. In short time, I was in Chuck's boat by April, with my fly rod, trolling large streamers close to the shoreline not far from Maxwell. We both got into multiple steelhead hook-ups.

It wasn't long after that I asked about the tributaries along the lake in that general area. More than one angler in the coffee room at the experiment station mentioned Maxwell Creek and its mouth. Harry Leichtweis (who is mentioned elsewhere in this book) fished it. So did other Geneva anglers. About that time, I became friends with Tom Burr, who was also interested in the stream. Tom Bonetti, an accomplished Geneva angler who I met soon after, also knew the stream well.

While Maxwell Creek near its mouth during summer months appears like algae-filled dead water, changes occur once the weather cools. The stream rids its summer condition, and by October, brown trout migrate into the lower creek area in both fall and spring.

Maxwell Creek flows through trout-holding slow water a few hundred feet upstream from its mouth on Lake Ontario. The lake is located just over the tree line in the background. (PHOTO VALERIE VALLA)

There was the time in mid-December 1981 Burr and I wandered down to the stream's mouth and spotted two steelhead, in water about 3 feet deep and 6 feet wide. We both landed one. The steelhead stage at the mouth before they move up into the slow-moving estuary water, as do brown trout. Tom Burr recently pulled out the photos of those fish. Together, we both shared a nice remembrance of that outing.

I was more interested in the estuary's potential than the lake itself at that time. That's when I decided to fish it during the spring, with Tom Bonetti. A handsome 4-pound brown trout came to my net one sunny day in March, while swinging small nymphs through the long, seemingly lifeless pool just downstream from the small County Road 101 bridge crossing.

The estuary is difficult to fish with flies because of the deep muck that makes wading a challenge. Burr recalled the time I sunk in so deep he had to pull me out with a tree branch. It will swallow up an angler in no time. Years ago, you could access the estuary from both the west and east sides of the creek, immediately downstream from the bridge. The east side along a dwelling is now posted, directly below the bridge, but only for a short distance. Today, you can access the estuary via a very long formal NYSDEC Maxwell Bay parking lot on the east side of the stream off County Road 101, something that didn't exist during the years I first fished Maxwell. A maintained and operational apple orchard was once located in what is now the large parking area next to the estuary. The dwelling at the bridge didn't exist either.

Most of the activity, by conventional tackle anglers, occurs along a footpath that leads from the lot to the estuary and along the water. It's possible to wade out a few feet in the mucky bottom, and cast far enough to drift or swing flies. Use fairly small size nymphs, rusty or black. An AP Black Beaver Nymph, created by Andre Puyans, in size 12 is good, drifted off a weight-forward line. In years past, I always swung flies through the water from the west side of the creek, but the east side is manageable, too.

Lake Ontario shoreline, a short distance west of Maxwell Creek's mouth, near Pultneyville. Browns come in relatively close to shore in late fall and can be enticed with flies. (PHOTO VALERIE VALLA)

If wading out into muck doesn't appeal to you, fish upstream from the County Road 101 bridge crossing. A small parking area is located right next to the south side of the creek, the only parking lot that existed years ago. The little 8-to-10-foot-wide creek here is completely different, with its small riffles and run reach where egg patterns can be drifted through the holding water. The stretch has never been good to me, but many anglers prefer it to fishing the estuary or the lake shore. During times I didn't fish the estuary, I fished out into Lake Ontario itself.

What was once an easy stroll down to the lakeshore itself through the orchard is now a battle with overgrown honeysuckle, abandoned apple trees, and growth. The footpaths seem to vanish once you're back in there, but anglers still manage to get to the lakeshore and the creek's mouth. Gone are the days I carried a stepladder down to the lake, pumping out shooting-head lines during early April when both steelhead and brown trout were near shore.

There was an occasion many years ago when I took a walk down to the lakeshore near Maxwell's mouth, at dark with a flashlight. I wasn't fishing—just observing what I suspected. I could not believe the number of browns splashing within a couple feet of the shore, dorsal fins exposed. It was a sight I'll never forget.

Another way we once accessed the lakeshore at Maxwell was through the Girl

Sparkling Dark Nymph (tied by Mike Valla) Dark Nymphs, with a touch of sparkle, work well on Maxwell Creek. Sparkling Dark Nymph is a general pattern that can be tied with any rusty-brown dubbing mixed with materials such as Waspi Prism Dubbing. The fly tail is tied with guinea hen feather fibers. The front collar is tied with a couple sparse wraps of partridge feather.

Scout Camp lands on the west side of the estuary. It was private but shut down by late fall. Today, it's completely abandoned and called "Beachwood State Park," an undeveloped New York State Park. I'm not sure what possibilities lie ahead once that area is operational, but it will be something positive for anglers.

GENESEE RIVER—(LOWER—STEELHEAD/SALMON SECTION)

The lower Genesee River just upstream from its mouth at Lake Ontario is a much different fishery than the upper headwater inland trout reaches that flow downstream from Pennsylvania (see page 23). Lake Ontario sends big cohos, chinooks, brown trout, and steelhead into its reach downstream from what is called the Lower Falls, in the City of Rochester. Lower Falls is 6 miles, give or take, upstream from Lake Ontario.

NYSDEC ensures a healthy run of the fish into the river through abundant stockings near the stream mouth. Typical annual stockings include 155,000 chinooks, 22,100 steelhead, and 22,000 coho salmon. The fish are big and feisty, something not uncommon on Lake Ontario tributaries. What makes the lower Genesee interesting is not the size of the fish; instead, it's the location right smack in the middle of Rochester, one of New York's largest cities.

When you're down in the Lower Falls gorge reach, suddenly all the noises and commotion up above on the streets of Rochester vanish; it gives you the feeling you're casting somewhere in a more remote area. If it were not for the fact the 717-foot spandrel braced Driving Park Avenue Bridge is in view (that spans the 200-foot-deep gorge), you'd think you're fishing in British Columbia.

Of course, during the early chinook runs in September there's plenty of activity and commotion from conventional tackle anglers on the reach. But as is true on other popular Lake Ontario salmonid tributaries, once the chinook and coho runs subside by sometime in October, the crowds thin.

Purple Spey Bugger (tied by Dave Agness) For some reason, steelhead and other salmonids are attracted to the color purple. With its striking purple marabou hanging off the hook bend, Dave's purple version of his Spey Bugger also provides good action in water, something that no doubt interests steelhead.

Black Spey Bugger (tied by Dave Agness) Beside his Purple Spey Bugger, Dave ties other color versions of his highly effective pattern. Dave's fly box includes olive, brown, and green versions as well as black. Black performed particularly well for Dave during the fall 2022 season on Lake Ontario tributaries. Tied with copper chenille, and ribbed with copper wire, Dave ties his Spey Buggers on heavy wire, long shank hooks in sizes #2–4, such as his preferred Mustad R749672 4XL model. Black schlappen in front of a conehead provides additional action while swung through the water column.

Lower Genesee enthusiast Dave Agness latches into a steelhead below the Lower Falls reach, in Rochester. Dave and his wife, Lindsay, consistently land big steelhead and brown trout on Lake Ontario tributaries.

The access to the Lower Falls reach is via a small parking lot on Seth Green Drive in Rochester. The only formal access is on the east side of the river, although you'll often spot anglers who traverse down to the west bank via a steep path, from the west side of the bridge. NYSDEC's Lower Genesee River PFR maps online give detailed directions to Seth Green Drive. A macadam road leads from the parking area down a moderate slope to a Rochester Gas and Electric Corporation Hydroelectric Station Building and the river.

Dave Agness with a fine steelhead that slammed his Purple Spey Bugger. Something I noticed about Dave while anxiously waiting for him to latch into the steelie was his obvious confidence in his pattern. Cast after cast, drift after drift went on for some time. His Purple Spey Bugger made me a believer, for sure.

Anglers and hikers are allowed access via walking only. A designated angling walkway leads to a fishing platform directly next to the Station 5 Powerhouse that's popular with conventional tackle anglers during the chinook runs. Better fly-fishing stretches are located downstream a few hundred feet.

A bankside footpath follows the stream down to the slower-moving pools and runs. When water levels allow, you can wade out to the middle of the stream and swing flies. Two of the most accomplished fly anglers on the lower Genesee are Dave Agness and his wife Lindsay.

Dave's persistent yet graceful fly-swinging choreography on the lower Genesee River results in many fine fish that come to his net. Casting technique and stream knowledge aside, "Spey Bugger" flies that he designed and ties also play a large part in his consistent fish-catching success. Dave fishes both purple and black versions that provide confidence. If the fish are in the river, his patterns will elicit strikes from steelhead.

There is one thing you want to be cautious about while parking at the Seth Green parking area. As is true in any major city, make sure you don't leave valuables exposed in your vehicle while you're fishing out of sight for an extended time. The same holds true while fishing nearby Irondequoit Creek (see the following section) at one of the public park areas. Our daughter found this out the hard way during a time years ago when she and her family were living in the Rochester area, in Penfield.

IRONDEQUOIT CREEK

Anglers fishing the Lower Genesee River in Rochester are within quick range of sampling nearby Irondequoit Creek that flows into Lake Ontario only a few miles east of the lower Genesee River. Irondequoit is best known as a steelhead fishery, although NYSDEC stocks 9- to 15-inch brown trout in its Penfield and Pittsford reaches. PFR water is minimal; most access is provided via public parks: https://www.dec.ny.gov/docs/fish_marine_pdf/pfrirondiqck.pdf.

A good steelhead reach is in Penfield (a suburb of Rochester) at the Channing H. Philbrick Park, a public park located at 1 Linear Park Drive off State Route 441. Two walking trails, Honey Creek Trail and Philbrick Park Trail, are located at the 19-acre park. The scenic Philbrick Park Trail follows Irondequoit Creek.

SANDY CREEK (ORLEANS/MONROE COUNTIES)

Fly fishers interested in targeting big fall-run Lake Ontario brown trout have a couple of streams to choose from west of Rochester. One is "the other Sandy," not to be confused with the three Sandy Creeks (Little, South, and North) in the Pulaski area. This Sandy is located near the Town of Hamlin (about 30 miles west of Rochester).

The popular formal NYSDEC angling parking lot access is located about 2.5 miles north of the County Road 234 (Lake Road West Fork)/State Route 19 (Lake Road East Fork) intersection in Hamlin. The parking area is at a bridge crossing, directly next to the creek. You'll know when the big browns are in Sandy, just by the number of vehicles in the lot, and the numbers of anglers spread out upstream from the Lake Road East Fork bridge crossing. PFR water is located from the bridge upstream a good distance.

Anglers can also seek out other reaches on Sandy Creek located upstream from the Lake Road East Fork bridge that are not official public easement water but are not posted. As I've mentioned throughout this book, it's always best to ask landowners if they allow fishing on their stream frontage. Asking permission goes a long way. On your way back

Sandy Creek, north of Hamlin, at the NYSDEC parking area reach off Lake Road East Fork (State Route 19). You'll have plenty of company when the big browns head into the stream from Lake Ontario in October.

out from fishing, pick up any stray trash left along the stream bank by less-considerate anglers. Mention to the landowner your intention of doing so.

One popular, unofficial reach that anglers frequently fish is located upstream from the NYSDEC angling parking lot, downstream from a bridge crossing just around the corner from the Lake Road East Fork access lot, upstream on North Hamlin Road.

Successful anglers use a variety of patterns, many the same that are effective on other Lake Ontario brown trout and steelhead tributaries. Two of the most talented big brown

Tom Novak caught this nice Sandy Creek brown on a Black Stonefly Nymph at the NYSDEC angler parking lot reach in Hamlin, upstream from the State Route 19 bridge crossing.

Otter's Soft Milking Egg-Buff (tied by Stan Tabaka Jr.) The Tabakas also carry a supply of Buff-colored versions of Otter's Milking Egg.

Black Stonefly (Whittaker's Sport Shop) Besides various Estaz egg patterns and other flies such as Otter's Soft Milking Egg patterns, Black Stonefly Nymphs also attract lake-run brown trout during October into November.

Otter's Soft Milking Egg-Flamingo (tied by Stan Tabaka Jr.) Stan Tabaka Jr. and his son, Stan Tabaka III, carry a variety of flies when fishing Sandy Creek. Their boxes are loaded with all styles and types of patterns. However, the Otter's Soft Milking Egg flies are particularly effective. Flamingo color is a good brown trout-getter.

anglers I crossed paths with on Sandy are Stan Tabaka Jr. and his son, Stan Tabaka III. They fish Otter's Soft Milking Eggs, veiled with chartreuse or white yarn. Estaz egg patterns, of course, are also in their fly boxes.

The Tabakas like fishing floating lines with 6- to 8-pound fluorocarbon leaders off 4- to 7-weight Orvis Helios rods. I fish a 9.5-foot Catskill Research rod loaded a bit heavy with 6-weight, WF floating line with nymphs on the delivery end. Split shot is added to keep the fly gently bouncing along the stream bottom, adjusted by size and number according to water conditions.

Stan and his son know enough to realize if one stream in the area isn't fishing, well its best to relocate to another nearby tributary. One year nearby Oak Orchard or Johnson Creek might be fishing well, and the next year, they're not. The Tabaka pair will relocate somewhere else, such as Sandy Creek. Water conditions during the annual October brown trout runs on the tributaries can change from week to week and from year to year. Good brown trout and steelhead action can occur during mid-November, depending on conditions and water levels.

A good place to contact to get an accurate report of what's happening on Sandy, Oak Orchard, or Johnson Creek is Oak Orchard Tackle and Lodge in nearby Albion.

OAK ORCHARD CREEK (AKA OAK ORCHARD RIVER)

Oak Orchard Creek's 6 miles of water from Waterport Reservoir Dam to Lake Ontario at Point Breeze has the reputation as being New York's premier lake-run big brown trout destination. However, as true as that may be, "the Oak" also attracts chinooks, cohos steelhead, and a few Atlantic salmon. It also attracts plenty of anglers who descend on the stream when the fish are in. As is true on other Lake Ontario tributaries, the chinooks arrive first (sometime in September), followed by the browns and then the steelhead.

Fly fishers interested in sampling Oak Orchard Creek, and its small tributary Marsh Creek, should head to Albion, a village located in Orleans County about 30 miles or so west of Rochester and about 15 miles north of I-90 at Batavia. If your fly box is low on effective patterns typically fished on Lake Ontario tributaries, your first stop should be at Oak Orchard Tackle and Lodge located 6 miles north of the State Route 31/State Route 98 (Oak Orchard Road) intersection in Albion. Check in with Ron Bierstine, the owner, who can help select flies that work well on Oak Orchard and other nearby tributary streams. Ample fly-tying materials, leaders, lines, and other equipment is available.

Only the first couple of miles downstream from the hydroelectric dam at Lake Alice is conducive to wade angling and swinging flies. Access to upper reach is at two points separated by less than a half-mile. The uppermost access is at a large formal NYSDEC parking lot on Park Avenue at the dam. The other is located a short distance downstream along Park Avenue Extension along the side of the road. Both access points are just a couple of minutes away from Oak Orchard Tackle and Lodge.

You'll know if the chinooks have arrived when the expansive upper parking lot is loaded with vehicles and conventional tackle anglers are lined up at the dam's chain-link fence along the spillway, casting into the turbine channel spillway currents.

A formal angling parking lot is located at Waterport Reservoir Dam. A NYSDEC large hanging sign is positioned at the entrance to the lot.

Waterport Reservoir Dam and its turbine channel tailrace is the upstream extent for fall-migrating salmon, steelhead, and brown trout. Most of the conventional fishing tackle anglers line up along the fence at the dam spillway area.

Oak Orchard Creek is just downstream from the Archery reach below Waterport Reservoir Dam, along Park Avenue Extension. When the fish are in, anglers park along Park Avenue Extension. A wide footpath leads from the road down to the stream.

Extensive signage warns anglers of dangers inherent with sudden water releases from the dam and risks of drowning. The rules that govern angling access, for safety purposes, are well spelled out on the multiple signs. Warning lights and sirens alert anglers of rising water.

A crushed stone footpath at the parking lot leads down the slope to the turbine channel, the main stream channel that parallels an overflow channel from Lake Alice for several hundred feet before the two combine and widen the flow. There are times the overflow channel is raging and impacting the system with highwater and excessive staining and other periods of time when the overflow contribution is negligible, if anything at all. The annual water level lowering of the Erie Canal in late fall, sending water into the Oak, can impact the system, too.

The Park Avenue Extension access point is popular among fly fishers. Park your vehicle on the side of the road. You'll notice a wide crushed stone pathway, at the green metal gate entrance, that can be accessed by walking only. The easy trek down to the stream will get you on the Archery Pool stretch that flows along the St. Mary's Archery Clubs, property. The Sycamore Hole, another popular spot, is located upstream from the Archery reach, just downstream from the junction of the turbine channel and the overflow channel.

By early October into November, the Archery water becomes increasingly crowded with anglers anxious to latch into big fish. Anglers line up in an almost festive atmosphere. It's difficult to plan for exact dates when the fish are in, but typically late October into early November is a good time to target the browns. Once they complete their own spawning tasks, the browns become aggressive feeders.

Winter holdover fish can provide continued action. Fly-fishing success is often episodic, based on varying winter conditions, but the fish are there without the major crowds

Oak Orchard upstream from the mouth at Point Breeze on Lake Ontario. Fly fishing is done from watercraft in the lower creek reaches.

of anglers after them. Once the first few hints of spring arrive, in March, the fresh steelies arrive out of the lake, along with those that overwintered. While it's true the stream's water level is higher during March, and more stained, the fishing potential can be great. Browns also wander in, on the prowl for food.

As long as the stream isn't completely blown out and beyond just mild to even moderate staining, you can still get into fish. As is true for any major Ontario tributaries, check with local reports. Ron Bierstine at the Oak Orchard Tackle and Lodge provides accurate updates on conditions and exactly what's happening or not happening on the Oak. Check his website for the reports.

Water flow is everything in bringing fish up from Lake Ontario. The colorful chinook-egg-gobbling browns are eager to eat egg patterns or nymphs ticked along the stream bottom with the aid of a couple small split shot. It's not uncommon to hook

Tim Didas with an Oak Orchard steelhead.
While many fly fishers target big brown trout on Oak Orchard, steelhead also keep anglers busy. It's best to check current fishing conditions by checking reports from Oak Orchard Tackle and Lodge.

Carpet Fly (Oak Orchard Tackle and Lodge) Mark Stothard's Carpet Fly is almost synonymous with Oak Orchard Creek. Mark, who passed in 2004, was a local fly tier, angler, and artist. Oak Orchard Tackle and Lodge carries the pattern in their fly bins.

Glo-Bug Sucker Spawn (Oak Orchard Tackle and Lodge) Also popular on other Lake Ontario tributaries, Glo-Bug Sucker Spawn is another pattern to consider fishing on Oak Orchard Creek.

Purple Crystal Woolly Bugger (Oak Orchard Tackle and Lodge) For some reason, lake-run salmonids are attracted to flies tied with purple materials. Purple marabou exiting the rear of the hook provides action that attracts steelhead. Fly fishers heading to "The Oak" should have a few in their fly box.

Egg Sucking Leech (Oak Orchard Tackle and Lodge) Tied with brown marabou projecting from the rear of the hook, along with brown chenille palmered with brown hackle and a yellow chenille head, Egg Sucking Leech is also popular with Oak Orchard fly anglers.

into an early steelhead when targeting browns, or even a chinook living its final moments in the stream during late October.

Most any egg pattern is attractive to the fish; the angler's experience and knowledge has much more impact on success. A homegrown pattern called a Carpet Fly, designed by fly tier and local resident Mark Stothard, has become a part of the Oak's folklore. Mark passed in 2004, but his talents as an angler, fly tier, and artist is still brought up in discussions. You'll find the fly in the Oak Orchard Tackle and Lodge fly bin.

Fly fishers interested in swinging patterns can get into the action at the lower Archery area. Swing your purple and other color marabou-tailed patterns, woolly buggers, muddlers, and the same stuff you'd use on other tributary streams. Spey bunnies can bring fish to the net, and even sculpin patterns will work. The water downstream from the swing stretch becomes too deep to wade fish.

While the 2 miles below the dam are by far the most popular fly-fishing locations, anglers can sample other areas of the stream and the nearby Marsh Creek tributary. Boat floaters fly-fish the big wide Oak at the lowermost extent of the stream near its mouth, upstream from the State Route 18 bridge.

JOHNSON CREEK

Johnson Creek is a small tributary that flows through Niagara and Orleans Counties. Anglers who are in the area fishing Oak Orchard Creek and Sandy Creeks often zip over to Johnson Creek. Chinook salmon, coho salmon, brown trout, and steelhead migrate from Lake Ontario upstream to the impassible 11-foot-high Lyndonville Dam, located at the Village of Lyndonville. Lyndonville is located about 9 miles or so due west of the Oak and about 50 miles west of Rochester.

Impassible Lyndonville Dam is the upstream extent for Johnson Creek salmonids migrating from Lake Ontario. Better sections are found downstream from the Lyndonville Dam.

The Blood Road PFR reach downstream from Lyndonville. A short stretch of PFR water is located upstream from the bridge crossing.

Fishing is allowed at the Lyndonville Town Park, upstream of the South Main Street (State Route 63) bridge crossing next to the Yates Community Library at the dam. However, the reach from the bridge to the dam provides only a couple hundred feet of stream frontage. You'll most likely encounter more conventional tackle anglers casting into the small dam's spillway than fly casters working the water. Big chinooks are dragged out of the spillway every fall. Anglers wishing to cast a fly at that short reach can park on the street in front of the library (across the street from a Dollar General store).

Another popular access point is along Railroad Avenue in Lyndonville. Drive north on Main Street 0.2 mile from the bridge crossing then turn right onto Railroad Avenue (next to the fire department). The access area is located just down the road next to the stream.

Better reaches than the dam area in Lyndonville, for fly fishing, are available downstream. A short reach of PFR water is located upstream from the Blood Road bridge, 2 miles from the town park. Near the town park, take Maple Avenue to Platten Road, then a left on Alps Road to a left on Blood Road. The bridge crossing and PFR water is 0.2 mile from the Alps Road/Blood Road intersection. Parking is a challenge, limited to the road shoulder. Other unofficial access points are available downstream, along State Route 18.

If approaching from Lyndonville Town Park, drive 1.8 miles north on State Route 18 to a right turn on State Route 18 (Roosevelt Highway). In about 6 miles or so down State Route 18, the road begins to more consistently follow the creek. During the fish runs, anglers commonly access the stream near the State Route 18/County Road 62 (Lakeside Road) intersection. Park at the turnout next to the bridge on Lakeside Road. If approaching from near the Waterport Reservoir dam (on Oak Creek), zip up State Route 279 north 3 miles to State Route 18. Take a left and go a half-mile to the bridge crossing at Lakeside Road.

Finger Lakes Region

The Finger Lakes Region in west-central New York is comprised of 11 roughly parallel "fingerlike" waterbodies situated west of north-south running I-81 that cuts the state in half. A couple of outlying lakes, such as Coneseus (a warmwater fishery), blend into the Western Region. It's an area known for spectacular gorges with waterfalls, world-class wineries, and rolling farmland and racecar events. It's also considered an angler's paradise.

Life's journey led me to locate and settle in the region three different times, largely because of its breathtaking beauty. It's that kind of place. University years spent on a hillside "far above Cayuga's Waters," one of my first jobs at the top of Senaca, at Geneva, and an early professional career back on Cayuga, in Ithaca, all provided great memories, including times on waters with a fly rod. Fishing opportunities in the area, of course, had something to do with it, experiences first enjoyed as a young boy.

Canadice, Canandaigua, Cayuga, Conesus, Hemlock, Honeoye, Keuka, Otisco, Owasco, Seneca, and Skaneateles were formed more than 2 million years ago during the Pleistocene Ice Age when glaciers carved out troughs that filled with icemelt. The lakes all vary in length and depth, with Seneca being the deepest at over 600 feet and Honeoye a mere 30 feet deep.

Mouth of Salmon Creek at Myers Point Park on Cayuga Lake. Cayuga Lake is the longest of the region's Finger Lakes. A deep lake that harbors both cold- and warmwater fish species, Cayuga Lake receives water inflow from Fall Creek, Cayuga Inlet, Salmon Creek, Taughannock Creek, and Six Mile. (PHOTO VALERIE VALLA)

Both warmwater and coldwater species inhabit the lakes and the various tributaries that spill into their waters. Stillwater anglers enjoy casting for everything from bass to pike to lake trout to brown and rainbow trout to landlocked salmon.

Well before the Great Lakes salmonid fishery exploded with big fish opportunities, the Finger Lakes were a primary destination for anglers targeting big lake-run rainbow trout during spring spawning migrations. Aside from the lake waters and their tributaries, a number of inland streams can provide fly-fishing experiences for brown trout, brook trout, and juvenile rainbow trout.

Fall Creek

Fall Creek flows some 30 miles from its source near Lake Como in Cayuga County before it dumps into Cayuga Lake, the longest of New York's Finger Lakes. Public fishing access is available along nearly a third of its mileage.

The topography along its route gradually changes. After wandering through the upstream farm country, traversing westerly through Tompkins County, the creek eventually flows through Cornell University located over 20 miles downstream from its source. The stream then tumbles through an impressive 200-foot-deep gorge before creating Ithaca Falls in the City of Ithaca, a destination for both naturalists and anglers. The creek then makes a final quiet run and empties into the Cayuga Lake at Stewart Park.

I have nice memories of first observing the falls and gorge area that go back to the early 1970s when my faculty advisor at Cornell, fisheries biologist Dwight A. Webster, led his "rat pack" of a half-dozen fisheries students to an overlook near the campus. He commented that Fall Creek is a stream composed of two different fisheries: the brief mileage below Ithaca Falls and the mileage upstream from the gorge to its source.

With topography maps in hand, we charted how the gradient and creek's structure changed as we stopped along the stream at several locations before reaching our final stop

Fall Creek at Ithaca Falls, in the City of Ithaca. Fall Creek downstream from Fall Creek Falls attracts a small run of landlocked salmon from Cayuga Lake during the fall. (PHOTO VALERIE VALLA)

Upper Fall Creek, at the State Route 90 bridge crossing. Upper Fall Creek is inhabited by brook trout.

at a tavern, upstream near the source at Lake Como. Webster led his rat pack into the bar and bought a round of beers for the group (that was during the time the legal limit was 18).

We soon learned why we ended up at the tavern. Webster explained it was common practice to arrange fish jaw tag drop-off stations with local taverns. The practice must have justified the final stop at the bar during the outing. Area anglers were instructed to take trout jaw tags to such establishments where proprietors collected them for later pickup. The tags were used in Fall Creek trout population dynamics studies.

The survey along the stream that September day was interesting. However, I've always considered the stream as three separate and uniquely different fisheries, not just two: the headwaters near Lake Como and Groton City; the middle reaches between Mclean and Freeville; and the final stretches below Fall Creek Falls to the lake.

Just below Lake Como, along Lake Como Road, a formal NYSDEC parking turnout exists next to the first signs of the stream. It's a very marshy area not conducive to fly fishing. Beavers have been at work here, damming the small flow, creating great habitat for wood ducks. The stretches below the marsh are very brushy, weedy, and difficult to navigate. Fly rodders are better off sampling the stream a bit more downstream.

A very short drive down Lake Como Road will take you to Peth Road. Here the stream at a small bridge crossing is more fishable. Because of the high streamside weeds and brush, a better time to sample it would be either early or late in the season. It's still small and narrow water, slow and meandering, yet a nightmare for fly fishers. The water at another bridge crossing downstream a short distance at Creech Road is much the same.

Brief stream riffle structure, and relatively easier fly fishing, depending on the time of year, can be found downstream at a very large formal NYSDEC angling parking lot located on State Route 90 at a bridge crossing. The water upstream from the bridge maintains its slow, meandering nature, rife with streamside brush making for difficult trekking during summer months. Intermittent riffles are located downstream from the bridge.

The State Route 90 crossing is popular with early season bait anglers because the access to the stream directly below the bridge is effortless. A short set of timber stairs assists getting anglers down the short slope right next to the stream. The same can't be said of the public fishing reach located a few minutes' drive downstream. Take Hinman Road off State Route 90 to the next formal NYSDEC angling access parking area located next to a farm. It's a small parking lot clearly marked by a large sign.

The isolated stream reach is not located directly next to the parking area. An official NYSDEC footpath leads to the water that flows several hundred feet away from the lot. The path is marked by small yellow circular signage nailed to trees along the way. At first the trail is shrouded with brush and difficult to follow next to an unnamed tiny brook. After a short distance, however, the footpath breaks into an open area along a farm fence.

The yellow path signage becomes more frequent and visible as it leads to the stream. You'll likely have more of a chance being greeted by black angus beef cattle grazing along the adjoining pasture than another angler. At the point the footpath finally joins the stream, you'll encounter larger rectangular yellow PFR signage nailed to trees. The stream is wider in this area but still protected and shaded by saplings and small brush. This is brook trout water, for sure.

While the upstream reaches of Fall Creek below Lake Como area are very brushy and difficult to fly fish, NYSDEC reports it stocks a little over a thousand 9- to 10-inch brook trout in that area. Stockings occur near the intersection of Hinman Road and Hatfield Road upstream to the Peth Road bridge.

Another NYSDEC parking area is located a few miles down County Road 103B to the intersection of Groton City Road and Old Stage Road. Anglers will encounter more bankside brush along the PFR access allowed upstream from the bridge crossing. The stream reach is more open here yet still relatively tiny water. It's an area easier to navigate and fish during early or late season when the brushy weeds die back.

Head downstream to the intersection of County Road 222 and Lafayette Road and further downstream into McLean for enhanced riffle-/pool-structured water that's much easier to wade and fish. Park along the shoulder next to the County Road 222 bridge at a NYSDEC hanging sign. The stream is in open meadow along a farm here and harbors brown trout. It fished better years ago, but it's still worthy of a cast now. Public Fishing Rights exist both up- and downstream from the bridge. A nice stretch can be found a short distance downstream in the hamlet of Mclean, along Champlin Road and Cemetery Lane at the bridge crossings, located a short distance from School Street.

Annually, NYSDEC typically stocks nearly a couple thousand one-year-old 9-inch brown trout and a couple hundred 2-year-old 13- to 15-inch brown trout from School Street (County Road 105) in McLean upstream to Groton City Road (County Road 103) in Groton City.

Once the stream departs the upstream reaches, plenty of PFR water exists downstream from Mclean (look for the yellow NYSDEC Public Fishing signs along those reaches). Additional informal access can be located clear down to Freeville and Etna. It has been quite a while since I've fished those lowermost reaches. While I've netted brown trout along the stream near Freeville, including sizeable brown trout enticed from deep pools, those reaches have not been particularly good to me, on a consistent basis, and not part of my Fall Creek fishing focus.

The big Fall Creek enchilada is the reach below Fall Creek Falls, in Ithaca. Finger Lakes angling Special Regulations that apply to other Cayuga Lake tributaries don't apply to Fall Creek. Tributaries such as Salmon Creek and Cayuga Creek are closed to

Purple Matuka (tied by Dave McNeese) Purple fly patterns, including Matukas, when targeting landlocked salmon that run up from Cayuga Lake during fall. Dave McNeese's version is tied with purple dubbing ribbed with flat silver tinsel. Tail and wings are tied with purple bucktail. For wings, three or four separated increments are tied in along the body, angled to the rear. Purple guinea feather forms the throat.

Green Highlander (tied by Steve Silverio) Classic salmon flies, like Green Highlanders, also attract attention from landlocked salmon. While the old classics have fallen out of favor, they accounted for many landlocked salmon catches on Fall Creek during the 1970s and 1980s.

angling January 1 to March 31. The stream reach in Fall Creek from the downstream edge of the railroad bridge below County Road 13 up to the falls is open to all legal angling methods from April 1 to December 31. Catch and Release, artificial-lures-only angling is still permitted from January 1 to April 1.

During the mid-1970s, during my Cornell University fisheries student years, fly anglers in Fernow Hall (home of the Natural Resources department and fisheries biology programs) openly discussed and shared information surrounding landlocked salmon that ran up from the lake into Fall Creek, primarily during the fall and to some extent in the spring. Landlocks that enter the stream from the lake weren't a secret then, and they are not a secret now. My dormitory was located a short 20-minute walk down the road to Ithaca Falls, so naturally, I was quick to get on that stream reach when word was out that landlocked salmon or rainbows were in.

In *Tying the Founding Flies* (2015), I shared the story of running into Jeff Kurt sometime around 2010 at a regional fly-fishing show. Jeff was a Cornell engineering student who I often ran into while cutting classes to fish for the landlocks. We both fished what we called "the Slot," a holding lie for big landlocked salmon within view of the falls. The best way to reach the Slot was to carefully trek along a foot-wide rocky ledge above the rushing water. It was a balancing act we both now chuckle about when we run across each other at fly-fishing shows. I wouldn't recommend to anyone trying such a dangerous feat—don't even attempt it!

Jeff recalled I fished big Hare's Ear Nymphs along the Slot during those brief years. I fished other patterns on other runs though the pocketwater that flowed downstream from Lake Street bridge. The only thing I managed to catch was my thumb while yanking on my fly line after my fly got caught in an overhanging branch. The line and fly snapped back toward my hand. The staff at the University clinic were a bit puzzled when I walked in still wearing waders, seeking treatment to remove the hook. By the late 1970s, when I was working as a research specialist at Cornell, and again in the late 1980s, when I was once again living and working in Ithaca, I switched tactics and fly patterns.

A couple of Fall Creek salmon enthusiasts, such as the late Ithaca resident Eric Seidler (who passed in 1990), were big fans of classic Atlantic salmon patterns such as the Green Highlander. I watched Eric, a fellow member of Cornell Fly Tiers, swing a Highlander over and over again along the rocky ledge just downstream from the falls. His confidence paid off. He netted a multi-pound landlocked salmon while other anglers went fishless. We also fished those oldies but goodies directly below the falls, where the falls spray coated our jackets and often turned to ice on the colder days.

Matuka patterns, both contemporary and even classic tied with crystal flash and purple-dyed hair or marabou, are effective salmon enticers. I like to fish a drab fly called Orphan or a Hare's Ear Nymph through the area along the rocky ledge below the falls. A flashy claret body Purple Matuka is effective when fished through the slower-moving pool. A good place to try is downstream from Lake Street bridge, near the railroad bridge crossing pool where salmon sometimes hang out.

Of course, landlocked salmon are not the only fish that can be taken on the reach below Ithaca Falls to its mouth at Cayuga Lake. Back in my student years, I recall a typical early spring day when winter returned. It was cold, and the snow squalls were almost blinding as I drifted a Yellow Stonefly Nymph through the water. I hooked into a memorable big lake-run rainbow trout that can also be caught in the stream during that time of year. I've also taken my fair share of suckers, drifting Yellow Nymphs deep in the water columns during April.

It's not unheard of to land big lake-run browns during the spring and also during the fall up into November. During summer months, the late Todd Swainbank, who owned a fly shop in Ithaca, and I caught smallmouth bass directly below the falls, especially after a drenching summer rain. You'll sometimes encounter trout rising to various aquatic insect emergences along the plunge pool where dry flies can bring savage strikes.

Cayuga Inlet/Enfield Creek

Cayuga Inlet, and its major tributary, Enfield Creek, brings fishing memories reaching back to the late 1960s. During those years, the now-vast Lake Ontario steelhead fishing didn't exist; anglers desiring to net large lake-run rainbows turned to Finger Lakes spawning streams such as Cayuga Inlet and Salmon Creek on Cayuga Lake, or Catharine Creek on nearby Senaca Lake. Or other smaller Finger Lakes tributaries. My dad and grandfather's favorite years ago was Cayuga Inlet, since it was not that far of a driving distance from our homes in Binghamton. Naturally, I was dragged along with them.

Around 1970, we were fishing Enfield Creek during the April spawning run. Enfield is not a large creek and was perfect for a youngster to fish the smaller pools, wearing hip boots. Dad and my grandfather had a luckless morning, but downstream, just above the junction with the Inlet, I spotted a rainbow next to the bank. Drifting a Yellow Nymph, soaked in cod liver oil (a common practice back then), the fish smacked it hard. When I landed the fish that was all of about 14 inches, I noticed a shiny jaw tag dangling from its mouth. In very small lettering, the tag instructed that it be sent to Cornell University.

Cornell University coldwater fisheries biologist professor Dwight A. Webster was conducting population dynamics studies on the rainbow trout populations. I was elated when I received in my home mail a packet from Webster that stated the length and weight of the fish when it was tagged at the Cayuga Inlet Fishway, a fish ladder structure Webster helped design with New York State Conservation Department (as it was called back then) as an egg collection facility. It also helped keep lamprey eels from migrating

Cayuga Inlet, at the mouth of Van Buskirk Creek tributary Cayuga Inlet is one of several streams that attract rainbow trout during their spawning season in the spring. The stream dumps its flow into the south end of Cayuga Lake, not far from Cornell University. (PHOTO VALERIE VALLA)

upstream. Webster also included a reprint from a publication he authored that told the story of Cayuga Lake rainbow trout and their spawning runs.

I continued to fish Enfield and the Inlet well after graduating from college. My fishing tactics today, of course, have changed. Enfield Creek flows through spectacular Enfield Gorge at Robert H. Treeman State Park, located 13.5 miles south of Ithaca on County Road 327. A rugged yet scenic stone-staired and often slippery trail through Enfield Glen provides breathtaking views of 12 waterfalls, including the 115-foot Lucifer Falls, along the stream's path before it finally reaches Cayuga Inlet.

There was a time I crawled down into the remote upstream gorge pools to fish for small brown trout that rise to the early morning diminutive *Tricorythodes* mayflies. In recent years, however, I've sampled Enfield in the lower reaches both up- and downstream from the County Road 96 bridge crossing at the intersection with County Road 13 just south of the entrance to Treman Park. A parking area is located on the downstream side of the bridge.

Author at the Cayuga Inlet Fishway, as a Cornell fisheries major, in the fall of 1974. The fishway was originally constructed as a flood control weir and had nothing to do with a fisheries function. Dwight A. Webster, a fisheries biology professor at Cornell, designed a denil fishway constructed of baffles that traps rainbow trout during spawning runs. The fishway, opened in 1969, served as a fish-tagging and egg-extraction facility.

Juvenile rainbows can be caught along Cayuga Inlet. Small juvenile rainbows offer sport in Cayuga Inlet's upper sections long after the spring spawning season. The juveniles eventually migrate down to Cayuga Lake. While many of the small rainbows are from natural spawn, NYSDEC stocks thousands of 8-inch rainbows in Cayuga Inlet during the spring.

Trekking upstream from the bridge will eventually take you to a swimming area below a large waterfall that's been called one of the best swimming holes in New York. During the summer months, the stream is dammed a short distance downstream from the falls to create a larger and deeper swimming area. This reach is best left for late-season fishing.

During the spring, you'll typically encounter many anglers fishing with conventional tackle upstream from the bridge, during the spring rainbow trout spawning runs in April. Most will be drifting egg sacs, using either spinning rods or fly rods with fly reels spooled entirely with monofilament, through likely holding water. The same holds true that time of year downstream a short distance to its junction with Cayuga Inlet. The commotion usually subsides by mid- to late May, my favorite early season time to sample both Enfield Creek and Cayuga Inlet. You'll sometimes encounter large rainbows hanging out under deadfalls or half-submerged logs during clear water conditions. Mid-September is a good time to resume fishing those streams.

Ample PFR water, 8 miles of frontage that runs in and out of private water, is present on Cayuga Inlet. My favorite reaches are upstream, well above the Enfield Creek junction. A formal NYSDEC angling parking is located at State Route 34/96 near Brown Road. A large hanging sign identifies the area, next to a large parking area next to the railroad tracks. PFR stretches occur both upstream and downstream of the Brown Road bridge crossing.

Directly below the bridge, Van Buskirk Creek, a small tributary, enters the stream. Decades ago, when I fished this area with my dad, Van Buskirk Creek was open to fishing but is now entirely posted private

Trude (tied by Mike Valla) In 1901, Carter H. Harrison tied the first A. S. Trude fly with a red body. Trudes were originally tied as sinking flies. Today, modern sinking Trude flies are tied with squirrel tail wings, not spaniel hair as in the original. Trude flies are effective for attracting Cayuga Inlet juvenile rainbow trout.

property. I can recall an April day in my teenage years when I wandered up the tributary quite a distance to a beautiful waterfall in the little gorge and fished it almost until dark. It's a shame the little stream is posted. However, you can still fish Van Buskirk Creek where it joins Cayuga Inlet and fish the Inlet itself downstream from its junction. Fall is a better time to sample the stream since heavy angling crowds fill the stream during the spring up until about May.

Another formal NYSDEC parking area, marked clearly by large hanging signage, is found upstream on Brown Road. PFR frontage exists both upstream and downstream of a bridge crossing next to the parking area. By mid-September, the water here is clear and small, maybe 8-foot wide, and rushes downstream adjacent to the railroad tracks. Deadfalls and other cover provide habitat and cover for developing juvenile rainbows, many of which will eventually migrate by their third year downstream to Cayuga Lake. Short-length rods and small wet flies fished through the riffles and cover can elicit strikes from juvenile rainbows. A variety of fly patterns work well along this reach, mostly wet flies, including my favorite, a Trude wet fly, tied down to size 14. The stretches directly upstream from the bridge flow along a land trust called the Gilman Wildlife Sanctuary, marked by a roadside sign near the bridge.

Other smaller PFR water exists well upstream from the Brown Road crossing at Station Road, much of it challenging to fish with flies.

Cayuta Creek

Located southwest of Cayuga Lake, Cayuta Creek flows a little over 35 miles south from its origins at tiny Cayuta Lake, in Schuyler County. Cayuta Lake, a warmwater fishery, is located a short distance west of Montour Falls and about 20 miles southwesterly of Ithaca.

Cayuta Creek at the State Route 224 bridge crossing, about 1.2 miles south of the hamlet of Cayuta. Cayuta Creek is best fished during the early season. NYSDEC categorizes the stream as Stocked.

While anglers target big 5-pound largemouth bass in the little lake, fly anglers after brown trout head well downstream from the lake's outlet, on stretches between the hamlet of Cayuta and the hamlet of Van Etten. Cayuta Creek relies on a few thousand stocked brown trout between 9 to 15 inches planted during three intervals—late March, the middle of April, and the middle of May and sometimes in late fall. A Special Regulations artificial-lures-only stretch is located upstream from Van Etten. Two formal NYSDEC angling parking lots are located between Cayuta and Van Etten. There are also numerous unofficial areas to park along road shoulders.

The uppermost parking lot is located on State Route 224 about 1.2 miles south of Cayuta just after the bridge crossing. It's marked by a large hanging sign. The creek here flows through a pleasant valley surrounded by rolling hills. The stream reach is best fished during late April and May when the water levels and temperatures are optimal and the trout are eager to strike caddis patterns.

The lowermost NYSDEC angling parking lot is located not far from the State Route 224/State Route 223 (Swartwood Hill Road) intersection, off Swartwood Road. If approaching from the north, drive 6 miles south of the Cayuta parking area on State Route 224, turn right on to State Route 223 (Swartwood Hill Road). If approaching from the south in Van Etten, drive 2.7 miles north on State Route 224 to State Route 223. Swartwood Road is located 0.8 mile from the intersection. (Just after the intersection, you cross the State Route 223 bridge and upper boundary of the Special Regulations artificial-lures-only stretch.)

The large official angling parking area is at an old bridge crossing at the end of Swartwood Road. All that remains of the bridge that's been demolished are the concrete abutments. The slow-moving, large pool is popular with spin anglers. Fish downstream from the lot.

Besides the Swartwood formal access point, several pull-off areas next to the stream are located on Decker Road. Decker Road is on the left, just beyond the State Route 223 bridge crossing. Some nice fly-fishing runs exist along Decker Road. Decker Road eventually joins Wyncoop Road. The lower boundary of the Special Regulation stretch ends at the Wyncoop Road bridge crossing.

By the time the moderate-size creek flows past Van Etten, in Chemung County, it's well on its way to the Village of Waverly in Tioga County. From there, the stream passes under I-86 in New York's southern tier, then enters Pennsylvania, where it finally empties into the Susquehanna River.

An 8-foot, 4-weight rod will take care of most of the casting tasks on Cayuta Creek. During May, fish caddis pupae nymphs through the small runs, especially along Decker Road.

Salmon Creek

During my early teenage years, my grandfather, dad, and my dad's uncle looked forward to the April 1 opening day of trout season in New York. Their opening day destination choice was always Salmon Creek, located only an hour's drive from home in Binghamton. Salmon Creek, a major Cayuga Lake tributary located about 12 miles north of Ithaca, provides both conventional tackle anglers as well as fly fishers an opportunity to latch into one of the big rainbows that head up the stream to spawn during the early spring. However, the crowds of conventional tackle anglers do much better than fly fishers in the very early season.

Upper Salmon Creek at Ludlowville Falls at Ludlowville Park. The 1.1 miles of stream that flows to Cayuga Lake from the falls provides the only formal PFR water. (PHOTO VALERIE VALLA)

My grandfather fished the stream using fly rods mounted with automatic Martin fly reels, spooled with floating lines. My dad enjoyed fishing bucktail streamers, lures, and worms during most of the trout season. However, during the April Finger Lakes rainbow trout spawning run along Salmon Creek, they fished with small round pieces of yellow sponge soaked in cod liver oil and coated with petroleum jelly. It was such a smelly mess when they confiscated our kitchen table while the both of them snipped out the little round sponge baits.

After the rainbow trout runs, by late April or early May, the crowds significantly subside along the stream stretch flowing from lovely 40-foot-high Ludlowville Falls downstream to the lake mouth. The roughly 1.1-mile lower stream stretch provides the only significant formal Salmon Creek public stream access.

Anglers generally access the stream at Ludlowville Park, a little recreation and relaxation area that overlooks the impassable falls. The stream and the falls can be reached via a steep, and often slippery, muddy trail located near the park pavilion. The boulder-strewn stream tail-out below the falls and the plunge pool area harbors rainbows, when they're frequenting the stream. Gazing upstream at the falls, anglers frequently admire the cave-like area tucked underneath the falls.

A second parking area is useful for accessing the middle and lower stream reaches all the way downstream to the mouth at the lake. The lot is located a very short distance downstream from the falls. The formal NYSDEC formal anglers parking area is clearly marked by a large hanging sign next to the bridge crossing along Ludlowville Road. Anglers who visit the stream in April during the rainbow run will have plenty of company at the lot, an access point for fishing PFR water both upstream and downstream from the bridge.

More rainbows are always caught upstream from the bridge than directly below the bridge because the rocky substrate is more attractive to the fish. In years past, newspaper reporters would gather on the upstream side of the bridge where they would photograph anglers who proudly displayed their rainbow trout catches. The water directly below the bridge flows over a bedrock slab, something the stream runs in and out of on its journey down to the mouth at Meyers Point Park.

There was a time I carried a stream sketch I scribbled during the very low water levels in late summer. I shared it openly with others, to help remind them where the stream flowed over bedrock slabs during the higher water levels in spring and where it flowed over favorable cobble and small stones that the trout favored. During the spring, during high water conditions or stained water conditions, it's difficult to make that determination. During low water summer conditions, the entire streambed is within view and allows better understanding of the stream's features. My sketch came in handy during the rainbow run.

Rainbow trout aren't the only fish species that ascend the stream up to the impassable falls. While not in great numbers, brown trout, landlocked salmon, and even smallmouth bass run up and down the stream. On one occasion, I unexpectedly hooked into a lake trout below the Ludlowville Falls during a cold, early November morning years ago.

Depending on the time of year, and the water conditions, anglers can experience such surprises. Rains that raise the stream level, and create a tongue of water flowing out into the mouth at the lake, often rattle the curiosity of lake-dwelling fish. The current flow out into the lake at the stream's mouth brings them upstream.

During the early 1970s, with the support of a federal grant and in conjunction with Cornell fisheries biologists, an artificial anadromous spawning facility was constructed across the stream from Myers Point Park, the first on the East Coast, within view of the stream mouth.

During my fisheries student years in 1974, we performed stream velocity calculations along the concrete, cobble-filled raceways that have now long been demolished and removed from the site. The facility that was intended to support applied fisheries research never became functional as envisioned. However, to supplement natural spawning, NYS-DEC typically stocks some 30,000 3-inch to 6-inch rainbows in the stream, where they'll migrate to the lake and hopefully reward anglers when they return on spawning runs.

Three years later, in 1977, I was introduced to something a lot more interesting from a fly-fishing perspective, at the mouth of Salmon Creek. After a stint in graduate school, out of state, I returned to Ithaca and landed a research position in Cornell's entomology department. The competitive interview went well, especially after I learned during our chat the professor was an experienced West Coast steelhead fly angler. Dr. Ed Schmidtmann was a California Humbolt College graduate who fished steelhead rivers in the area and recently joined the entomology department in Ithaca.

Ed was all about big water, big fish, and shooting taper fly lines. The mouth at Cayuga Lake was good to him on his arrival to the area, where he landed a 4-pound rainbow on a Muddler Minnow pattern. After joining Ed's program, where we researched *Culicoides* midges (no-see-ums), we spent numerous evenings and early mornings wading out into the stream mouth, carefully negotiating the ever-shifting and changing gravel bar.

We usually accessed the stream mouth lake fishing from the right side because it was easier wading in relation to the gravel bar's position. But there are times the mouth can be fished from the Meyers Point Park side of the mouth. The park typically charges a small fee to access that area.

To reach the right side of the lake, drive along a small road on the right directly after the stream bridge crossing along Meyers Road just past the park entrance. Today, the

Schmidtmann-Valla Smelt (tied by Mike Valla)
Smelt populations on Cayuga Lake and other Finger Lakes tanked once zebra mussels became established in the waters. However, during the mid-late 1970s, thousands of smelt ran Cayuga Lake tributaries during spring spawning runs. However, the smelt pattern Ed Schmidtmann first conceived still works well on Cayuga's waters.

Missoulian Spook Muddler (tied by Mike Valla)
Muddler Patterns, such as this white muddler (first called Missoulian Spook), are a good choice for attracting rainbow trout that frequent the mouth of Salmon Creek during fall. Created by Dan Bailey, in Livingston, Montana, it was made famous by cartoonist and fly fisher Vincent Hamlin who illustrated the pattern in one of his *Alley Oop* comic strips.

drive back to the lake on that side has changed over the years and is hardly recognizable. It used to be pretty untidy years ago, with a simple bumpy potholed dirt road that led directly to the lake.

In more recent years, the Town of Lansing developed the site owned by NYSDEC into the Salt Point Natural Area. Crushed gravel paths that wind and turn through the property created easy access to the lake for naturalists, recreationists, and anglers. None of that was in existence when Ed and I fished the water years ago.

If wading out into the lake, casting large streamers and white muddlers with 6-weight and 7-weight rods, and shooting headlines, use extreme caution. The gravel bar formed by Salmon Creek outflow can drop off abruptly and the location where it drops off can change. Its better fished in the fall season than spring when the last thing you'd want to happen is having water go over your waders.

When the lake water is calm and mirror-like, you'll sometimes encounter salmonids surfacing. Most of the fish I latched into were silvery rainbows, some sizeable and very feisty. While angling success is very episodic at the mouth, there are times on an early late September morning that more than make up for blank days. It's for sure hit or miss.

Today, as in past years, almost all of my Salmon Creek angling is at the mouth, or up at the falls, during the early to late fall season. The issue with fishing above Ludlowville Falls, along Salmon Creek Road, has more to do with available public access than trout fishing potential. The reaches have also experienced severe erosion problems that have recently been addressed with stream-channel reconfiguration and stream-bank protection.

During my youngster years in the 1960s, my dad and I sampled those reaches, but I have no recollection exactly where we fished. While NYSDEC typically stocks a number of brown trout at reaches above the falls, the stream flows along private and posted lands that are farmlands. Brief stream fishing access is limited at a few bridge crossings, or along areas where polite anglers approach landowners, seeking permission to fish their frontage. In its headwaters, Salmon Creek is joined by Locke Creek, a small brook that inhabits trout. Upstream from its junction with Locke Creek, and about 3.5 miles above Ludlowville along Salmon Creek Road, visitors to the area will encounter Salmon Creek Nature Preserve signage, a nationally recognized bird-watching area.

Anglers departing that area who are more interested in catching trout than a view of cerulean warblers should consider driving a short distance easterly to the Town of Locke where they'll encounter one of my favorite streams, Owasco Inlet.

Cayuga Lake doesn't stand alone as a member of New York's Finger Lakes that sends egg-laying rainbow trout into its tributaries during early spring. Owasco Lake, Keuka Lake, Skaneateles Lake, and the big sister of them all, Seneca Lake, also grow rainbows that head into their tributaries during annual spawning runs.

Taughannock Creek

Two things I most remember about Taughannock Creek and its confluence with Cayuga Lake. The most memorable is the time during the fall of 1974, as a junior year fisheries student at Cornell, when I was out in a boat with NYSDEC staff setting out gill nets for lake trout. The lakers always congregate during the late fall, off the creek's mouth; it's pretty deep water in that area.

The positive memory is the goodly number of fish we pulled in and the number of eggs we stripped out of the females. Milt from the males was mixed in containers. But, oh boy! The negative memory is the very worst case of boat motion sickness that even today I've never again experienced. I recall wandering back up to my dorm room, so sick I cut afternoon classes.

However, that experience did pique my interest in the creek's fishing potential, just upstream from the streams mouth at the "lower falls." It wasn't until years later that I netted my first lake-run brown at the falls. It's called the lower falls, because the main falls is located a 1-mile trek upstream along the heavily visited gorge trail. Surrounded by spectacular 400-foot-high cliffs, the single drop waterfall is the tallest east of the Rocky Mountains.

The "lower falls" at Taughannock Creek, just upstream from Cayuga Lake. During fall and again in spring, both conventional tackle anglers and fly fishers fish the lower falls.

Rainbow trout, brown trout, and sometimes landlocked salmon venture up to the lower falls during spring and again during the fall. Trout can be taken way upstream at the "big" falls, something that's always surprised me since the lower waterfall appears impassable. The runs are not substantial, and fishing success for me in modern times has been episodic. You'll know when the "fish are in" based on the number of anglers, both conventional lure throwers and fly fishers that compete for a place at the falls. My singular advice is to get in there as early as possible during the morning. I've always preferred fishing it from the right side, looking upstream, casting Matuka patterns. Drifting large nymphs is also effective if the browns are in the mood.

The 215-foot Taughannock Falls is taller than Niagara Falls.

Owasco Inlet

Owasco Lake is one of the smallest of the long and narrow Finger Lakes that are clustered in the west-central region of New York State. Owasco Inlet, a major tributary that pours into the south end of the 11-mile-long lake, provides excellent trout fishing throughout its 25-mile length.

The little farm-country stream runs south to north, flowing through the villages of Groton, Locke, and, finally, Moravia, where it dumps into the south end of the lake. Scattered along its entire length, over 13 miles of PFR water provide anglers with plenty of easy access to its trout-filled waters. Public fishing reaches are also available on its lower reach tributaries, Hemlock Creek located along Route 90, and Dresserville Creek located along Dresserville Road.

Rainbows actively spawn in Owasco Inlet and provide sport for both conventional fishing anglers as well as fly fishers. However, the spawning runs don't match those that occur in neighboring Finger Lakes inlet streams. Owasco is a smaller lake, and its rainbow population is minor by comparison. Moreover, predator fish such as walleyes have impacted Owasco Lake and tributary stream salmonid potential. The situation may improve, since the state decided to cease stocking the lake with walleyes.

During my early Owasco Inlet years, I occasionally netted a few hang-around, spawning-run rainbows. I remember a beautifully colored, wild 14-inch rainbow I took during a Sulphur hatch one May evening in 1978. The fish surprised me since the section I was fishing normally produced only brown trout. A couple of years ago, I returned to that same stretch and was surprised to encounter large numbers of juvenile 3-inch to 7-inch rainbows. Some of these were no doubt a product of the fingerling rainbows stocked by the State, some 20,000. But the smallest fish were probably wild from natural spawn.

Rainbows aside, Owasco Inlet is presently stocked with brown trout from 8 to 15 inches, but it's not uncommon to encounter browns much larger in size. They can be taken on dry flies during early season hatches. Back in the mid-1970s, my friend, Dr. Ron

Marinaro Thorax Dun (tied by Tom Baltz) Sulphur hatches occur on Owasco Inlet, bringing both rainbows and brown trout to the surface. Most any sulphur dry fly can be effective, including Tom Baltz's cut-wing version inspired by Pennsylvania's spring creek titan Vincent C. Marinaro (1911–1986). Spade hackle fibers or CDL fibers are used, tied at right angles to hook shank to act as "outriggers." Tom, a well-known Pennsylvania fishing guide, ties the fly commercially.

Casual Dress (tied by Mike Valla) Brown trout on Owasco Inlet strike fuzzy nymphs such as the Casual Dress. Oregon fly tier Polly Rosborough (1902–1997) created this buggy pattern, tied with muskrat fur for a body and ostrich herl for the head. Polly favored #4-10 Mustad 38941 hooks, but any heavy nymph hook will suffice. (Complete step-by-step tying instructions are found in the author's book *Tying the Founding Flies* [2015].)

Llama (tied by Mike Valla) Llama hairwing fly, popularized by fly-tying author Eric Leiser (1929–2004), is attributed to Miles Tourellot, a Wisconsin Native American. Llamas are tied with woodchuck hair wings. Hen grizzly hackle is used for the throat.

Howard Jr., formally a Natural Resources staffer at near-by Cornell University, made a believer out of me. I often popped into Ron's office on my way to class for his fishing reports. On one occasion, Ron sent me scrambling to Owasco Inlet when I learned of his 18-inch brown he took on a Quill Gordon dry fly on a final cast in the last-light. From that point forward, Owasco Inlet became a favorite.

During my early Owasco Inlet years, I used to favor stretches located a few miles downstream from Groton along State Route 38. Today, there's a formal NYSDEC parking area next to the bridge at that location (something that didn't exist in the 1970s). There's a NYSDEC sign on the road next to the parking area and bridge. Many of the old log and stone stream bank stabilization structures that I remembered are now obliterated, buried in sediment, or washed away, but local Trout Unlimited members have completed some great fish habitat improvement work along the stream in that area.

Another nice area can be reached driving a few miles north along State Route 38 to Locke. Deep pools located both upstream and downstream from the bridge next to the State Route 38 fairgrounds in Locke (located less than a mile north from the intersection with State Route 90) have always harbored nice brown trout. During a recent sampling of

Owasco Inlet downstream from the village of Groton. Owasco Inlet is inhabited by both rainbow and brown trout. The inlet is a major tributary to Owasco Lake. The farm country stream has plenty of public fishing access water.

this section, I hooked (but did not land) a beauty that I had spotted from a vantage point on the stream bank. The big brown sucked in a deer hair ant pattern plopped over its nose.

You'll encounter other good stretches along Owasco Inlet as you work your way downstream from Locke toward Moravia. You can fish most of the stream with a 7-foot to 7½-foot, 4-weight rods. Bring your standard mayfly patterns along with caddisflies and an assortment of nymphs. A weighted Casual Dress Nymph works well, as does Llama streamers, during early season. During May, make sure you have a supply of Sulfur dry fly patterns.

Catharine Creek

The village of Watkins Glen, located at the south end of Seneca Lake (the largest of the Finger Lakes) has been called the spiritual home of road racing. Tucked in the heart of wine grape vineyard country, the village and the area draw tourists seeking wine-tasting experiences. Auto-racing fans look forward to the annual NASCAR Cup Series event that takes place during August. Trout anglers know Watkins Glen for a different reason: Catharine Creek.

A few decades ago, well before Lake Ontario's tributaries became the focus for those seeking large steelhead trout and Pacific salmon catches, Catharine Creek received national attention for its annual spring rainbow trout spawning runs. Hundreds of anglers descended along its 15-mile length that mostly follows State Route 14 north though the hamlet of Pine Valley, the Villages of Millport and Montour Falls, and, finally, into Seneca Lake at Watkins Glen.

As far back as I can recall, going back to the 1960s, my dad and grandfather commented that they avoided Catharine Creek the first few days in April because of the

Catharine Creek is one of the most famous rainbow trout run tributaries in New York. Several digger dam structures are located along the creek. (PHOTO VALERIE VALLA)

extreme crowds. Our local newspapers in the Binghamton area reported 500 to 600 anglers per mile along the creek! Postcards were printed that showed hopeful anglers standing at the stream shoulder-to-shoulder casting into the same fish-holding pools.

Those numbers of spring rainbow trout anglers strung along Catharine are a thing of the past. While early April crowding still exists, it's nothing like it used to be. While it's true some fly anglers jump in with the commotion on April 1—doing well drifting egg flies—I prefer bypassing Catharine until the fall months if I happen to be traveling through the area. During late October lake-run brown trout and landlocked salmon begin sniffing around the mouth of Catharine Creek.

Fall rains that increase water flows out into Seneca trigger fish to run the creek. Some rainbows will do the same, usually in late November. Most of the angling activity for the big browns and landlocked salmon will occur along downstream reaches around Montour Falls. While chances to latch into fish are no doubt better in the lower creek reaches during the fall, I prefer the Millport area because it can be almost devoid of anglers in late November into late December. I've enjoyed drifting flies along an entire mile of stream without sighting another angler. I'll take the solitude anytime over better fish-catching chances.

Plenty of PFR water awaits fly anglers venturing to Catharine Creek, spring or fall. The uppermost headwaters PFR reach can be accessed by parking at the NYSDEC angling lot on Smith Road in Pine Valley. The lot is located 0.1 mile from Smith Road's intersection with State Route 14. You'll see the large hanging sign at the lot that's located directly next to the Catharine Valley Trail, a multiuse trail that follows the old railroad bed down to Montour Falls. A short walk north along the trail will lead to a railed bridge and the creek. A nice pool is located below the trial bridge. The trail eventually parallels the creek.

Driving north along State Route 14 a couple of miles from the Smith Road intersection will lead to Millport. In Millport, turn on Crescent Street off State Route 14, drive across the bridge, and continue to Maple Street, where you'll see a pavilion at the small park-like area next the creek. A digger dam and attached platform provides easy fishing. The deep holding water below the little falls created by the habitat structure is a popular fishing location. A touching memorial monument honoring Andy Walker, placed by the Catharine Creek Chapter of Trout Unlimited, is located at the stream, along with a stone bench. An auctioneer, Andy, donated time raising thousands of dollars for conservation organizations. This location was his favorite fishing location on Catharine Creek.

Just north of the Crescent Road on State Route 14 you'll encounter a second formal NYSDEC angling parking lot. An easy quick walk will get you into the water and at a planked digger dam. During highwater, the platform connected to the small "falls" can be completely flooded. The deep-water habitat created by the small falls holds fish during the spawning runs. As a consequence, you can expect crowds around the structure during early April.

Just 0.5 mile down the road from the last lot, you'll see a large formal NYSDEC parking area that was recently constructed and great stream-access improvement. During previous years, parking was haphazard in muddy areas. Today, a pleasant crushed stone path easily leads anglers to the creek and yet another digger dam, with a platform and small falls. This location is one of my favorites. PFR water exists both upstream and downstream from the bridge. Formal PFR water is short downstream. On a recent trip I didn't review the maps and continued fishing a distance downstream all the way to the junction with Sleeper Creek, a small brook-like tributary. Beautiful fish-holding water is located along that reach. While I didn't encounter any posted signs along the length, it might be best to check with the landowner to determine if fishing is allowed.

PFR water resumes downstream from the mouth of Sleeper Creek, at the junction with Catharine. Just upstream from the junction, one of the most massive logjams I've ever encountered virtually dams the creek. My guess is it will take a series of large water events, perhaps over years, to clear the area. I had a tough time getting around the mess, while fishing downstream toward Sleeper Creek but managed to do so by crawling over the large trees and woody debris that washed into the obstruction.

Located at a State Route 14 bridge crossing 0.4 mile north of the last parking area (just past Seafuse Road), Sleeper Creek produces catches of large rainbows every year. PFR water is located both upstream and downstream of the bridge. Park along the road

Big steelies that run Catharine Creek attract fly anglers to its many public access runs and pools.

shoulder on the south side of the bridge. A well-worn path leads from the road shoulder to the stream and down along its length. The stream runs only a very short distance downstream from the bridge before it dumps into Catharine. Two digger dams constructed a short distance apart provide remarkably deep plunge pools that hold fish. A few other formal NYSDEC angling parking areas are located north along or near State Route 14.

One is located 0.6 mile north of the Sleeper Creek crossing along State Route 14. An informational kiosk is located at the lot. Most of the PFR water is located upstream from the parking lot although a short section is available downstream. A

Chartreuse Egg (Pineville Sporting Supply)
Egg fly patterns fish well on Catharine Creek during rainbow trout spawning runs. Chartreuse is popular, but other colors will interest the rainbows. Materials for tying egg patterns are available from many fly-tying material supply houses. They are also readily available at many fly shops.

beautiful stream reach, with some very nice large-boulder stream habitat improvement, is located 2 miles up the road at another NYSDEC angling parking lot marked by a large hanging sign. A planked platform juts out into the creek from the bank that creates a deep fish-holding pool. Plenty of continuous PFR water exists both upstream and downstream. Very nice runs are located downstream from the planked platform.

A nice creek stretch is located at a Catharine Valley Trail parking area located just off State Route 14 in Montour Falls, on South Genesee Street (look for the high-voltage electrical facility). Turn on to South Genesee. You'll cross Catharine Creek in 0.2 mile. The parking lot is located on the right, just after you cross the bridge. Plank platforms on the downstream sides of the bridge jut out into creek. A second platform pool is located a few hundred feet downstream from the bridge. Below the lower pool, a run attracts both fish and anglers. The now-lower-gradient stream is conducive to drifting egg-flies and Matuka-style patterns during the spring and again in the fall.

During late October into early November many of the brown trout and landlocked salmon caught are primarily from this reach and downstream toward the Catharine Creek Marsh Area. When word gets around that the landlocks are in, expect other anglers who are also after the sizeable fish.

Anglers wishing to sample some of the lowermost reaches can park at the NYSDEC angling access lot located 0.4 mile along State Route 14 from the South Genesee intersection. It's directly across from the Loyal Order of Moose facility. The expansive parking area, complete with a couple of picnic tables, provides very easy access to the stream. A black metal statue of Big Foot will greet you as you make the short walk down crushed stone paths to the stream.

Naples Creek

Naples Creek that enters the south end of Canandaigua Lake, Keuka Lake Inlet (Cold Brook) that enters the south end of Keuka Lake, and Grout Brook that enters the south end of Skaneateles Lake are not considered major fly-fishing destinations. But like Owasco Inlet that enters Owasco Lake, Naples Creek and the others are worthy of a few words since spectacularly large trout are caught on flies every year in those smaller streams, too.

Naples Creek at the State Route 245 bridge crossing. The Village of Naples comes alive every spring when rainbow trout spawning runs attract anglers hoping to latch into a fish. A small stream, Naples Creek attracts sizeable rainbows running upstream from Canandaigua Lake.

It's not impossible to entice the big spawners and their lovesick mates into striking flies, but such action can be difficult yet rewarding. Of course, most of the lake-run beauties are taken by egg-sac drifting anglers who crowd along both streams, almost smothering each other at popular pools and runs. But as is also true on Salmon Creek, Cayuga Inlet, and Owasco Inlet Finger Lakes spawning tributaries mentioned previously, fly anglers can enjoy their sport, too.

Naples Creek, a stream that flows through the picturesque Naples Valley, is a remarkable little creek that comes alive during April. The quaint Village of Naples, located a couple of miles from the south end of Canandaigua Lake, hosts the annual Naples Creek Rainbow Trout Derby, an event sponsored by the local Rotary Club for over 60 years.

The derby draws not only anglers but onlookers and tourists who get glimpses of some of the beautiful lake-run rainbows that are entered in the contest that takes place the first couple of days after April 1. Fly anglers who prefer not to get tangled in with the throngs of anglers who are busily drifting egg sacs should either stay away from the stream in very early April or seek out less popular trout-holding runs. Ample PFR water easily accessed exists along the creek's entire 11.5-mile length along with a very short public water reach on Grimes Creek, a small tributary.

One of the most popular formal NYSDEC angling parking lots, one of six scattered along the creek's length, is located 0.2 mile from the South Main Street/Mark Circle intersection in the village, near the Five Star Bank. A couple hundred feet away from the lot, anglers can also park at the large parking area at the High Tor State Wildlife Management area.

A wide gravel path, handicap accessible, leads from the parking area directly to the creek and a "digger dam" habitat improvement structure. Such structures create remarkably deep pools created by water spilling over the wood planks. Spring lake-run rainbows, and even fall-run browns, hold up in the deep pools. A consequence of the nice habitat are the crowds of anglers who circle the plunge pool on opening day. Fly anglers should relocate elsewhere should they be fishing the creek in early April. However, it's an interesting place to visit and observe the action if not to fish. During late fall, and up until the end of December depending on the weather and seasonal condition changes, there's a chance to net a brown trout around that location, free of crowds.

Another nice reach is located on State Route 245 0.2 mile from its intersection with North Main Street in the village. A large hanging NYSDEC sign is located at the bridge crossing, next to a NYSDEC maintenance facility and informational kiosk. Ample PFR is available both upstream and downstream from the bridge. During the spring, drift egg-flies weighted with a couple small split-shot. During the fall, cast small bucktails and streamers through the runs and pools.

During the late fall, weather and seasonal conditions dependent, lake-run browns can be caught on the lower reaches of Naples Creek. An official NYSDEC angling parking lot, large enough to accommodate 50 vehicles, that's located 0.3 mile south of Parish Road on State Route 21, is a good place to start.

NYSDEC biologists periodically sample Naples Creek during March as a continued effort to monitor the stream's trout population density. The electrofishing activity has been ongoing since 1962. Onlookers frequently gather along the stream sampling sites to observe the action. Recent samplings estimated 14,100 age 1 and older rainbows along with 45,900 young-of-year fish.

Keuka Lake Inlet (Cold Brook)

Keuka Lake Inlet (more often called Cold Brook along its entire length) is a minor Finger Lakes tributary that receives small spawning runs of rainbow trout in the spring and brown trout in the fall. Anglers also catch stream-bred colorful trout throughout the season. But it's the big spawners that attract most of the attention. Ample PFR water exists downstream from the Bath Fish Hatchery all the way down to Hammondsport, where it enters Keuka Lake. Two good access points are located in its headwaters at Cold Spring Road and downstream along Pleasant Valley Road.

Head for the Village of Bath, and take State Route 54 to Hatchery Road that's located about 2 miles from the Village. If you're driving north along State Route 54, you'll see a green NYS Fish Hatchery sign just past the Ford car dealership. Hatchery Road is on the left across from the Pinnacle Rental Center. A short 1.5-mile drive will lead to Cold Spring Road, just past the fish hatchery facility. The NYSDEC angling parking lot marked by a large hanging sign is next to the bridge crossing.

The headwater reach is usually small water, conducive to fishing flies downstream through the riffles and small pools. You'll want to use a 7.5-foot rod in this stretch. As is true with all Finger Lakes tributaries during the spring rainbow trout spawning runs, you'll be competing for the best water by other anglers who are just as eager to net one of the big fish. Fly anglers interested in spring fishing are better off waiting a week or so after April 1 before attempting to drift flies in this reach.

Get into the water at the bridge and fish small flies downstream through the nice riffles that flow along the old, dilapidated habitat improvement structure along the right bank. And watch out for the rusted nails and rebar sticking up from the old wood. The PFR easement (on both sides of the stream) flows about a half-mile downstream to the Taggart bridge crossing. Be aware of the posted signs at the bridge area, next to the dwelling. The PFR easement continues only on the right side (looking downstream) from the bridge, for a short distance.

Upper Keuka Lake Inlet Keuka Lake Inlet, at Cold Spring Road reach just downstream from the fish hatchery. Also called Cold Brook, Keuka Lake Inlet receives a small rainbow trout spawning run during spring. Twenty-mile-long Keuka Lake, a Y-shaped Finger Lake, is better known for its lake trout and smallmouth bass (the dominate species), although other fish species, including rainbows, inhabit its waters.

Plenty of continuous PFR reaches can be accessed at the Pleasant Valley Road bridge crossing. The NYSDEC angling parking lot is located next to the bridge, just past the Pleasant Valley Grange building, marked by a large hanging sign. Pleasant Valley Road (County Road 88) is located at the end of Fish Hatchery Road, about 1.2 miles north of Cold Spring Road. There's ample water to fish both upstream and downstream from the bridge. A plunge pool directly below the bridge provides holding water for rainbows running the brook in April. The runs downstream from the bridge are also nice.

Additional PFR stretches can be accessed in Hammondsport, at the State Route 54A bridge crossing, not far from its terminus at Keuka Lake. The slow-moving, low-gradient stretches in this area are best left alone until fall when there's a chance of getting into one of the lake-run brown trout that start running the stream from the lake.

Grout Brook

One other minor Finger Lakes rainbow trout spawning stream is the small Grout Brook, an inlet to Skaneateles Lake. Yet surprisingly, large fish are caught every spring along its meager 1.9 miles of PFR water broken up into four separate locations. The longest continuous reach is located at a bridge crossing on Glen Haven Road. It's best reached by heading up State Route 41 out of Homer (just off I-81). It's about an 8-mile drive. On the way, you'll pass over Factory Brook (see page 110).

The first thing you'll scratch your head about when you reach the Glen Haven Road bridge crossing, and formal NYSDEC angling parking lot that parallels the stream, is it seems to be flowing the wrong direction, directly south. The lake is located a few miles north. The stream flows south, but it eventually makes a U-turn, and heads toward its mouth at Skaneateles Lake. At the bridge, you'll notice a large sign informing anglers and others that the stream reach benefitted from the Great Lakes Coastal Restoration Program.

Grout Brook at the Glen Haven Road reach. Grout Brook is a small stream that feeds Skaneateles Lake at its south end. A 16-mile-long Finger Lake known for its ultra clean water. Grout Brook attracts rainbow trout from the lake during spring spawning season.

Stream bank erosion structures were installed some time ago a few hundred feet downstream from the bridge. Unless you're not bothered by the dwellings on both sides of the bridge, you're better off heading downstream where you can get away from the neighborhood feeling. Expect crowds here on April 1, since the access is so easy even for kids. The stream is not very wide, maybe 7 to 9 feet and difficult to effectively drift egg-flies. You won't be casting, per se, in this stretch or really any reach along the entire stream, aside from the short stretch directly upstream from the lake.

Departing this uppermost PFR area, pick up the stream again at NYSDEC angling parking area on West Scott Road. It's a quick 0.9-mile drive. Cross the Glen Haven Road bridge then bear left onto Grinnell Road. A parking area is located after the sharp right turn onto West Scott. This reach is pretty short but worthy of trying.

The next NYSDEC angling parking area is located on just a short blip of PFR water, at a bridge crossing located at the corner of Sweeney Hill Road and Glen Haven Road. From the previous angling parking lot, continue on West Scott, then quickly veer right onto Grout Brook Road, then veer onto Glen Haven Road. You'll see the large hanging sign at the formal parking lot that's right next to the small brook a couple hundred feet down Glen Haven Road. Very limited PFR frontage exists both upstream and downstream from the bridge. Plenty of posted signs will let you know when you are approaching private frontage. Nice fish-harboring plunge pools, little waterfalls, exist downstream from the bridge along the very short easement water—just a couple hundred feet, at most. A short area of PFR water also exists upstream from the bridge.

However, as is true on virtually the brook's entire length you'll have other anglers competing for the best water during very early April. It will be nearly impossible to drift a fly through this reach on opening day of trout season. However, once the crowds subside by mid-April there's a chance to work the pools, casting upstream with egg-patterns or nymphs, weighted with a couple of small split shot.

A final PFR reach is located down near Skaneateles Lake. Drive about 1 mile down Glen Haven Road. Stay on Glen Haven where it continues after a sharp turn, passing the Andrew R. Fuller Park. The NYSDEC angling parking lot is just down the road at the bridge crossing. A well-worn footpath leading from the parking area follows the right side of the stream.

The lower gradient stream enters a nice run, a few hundred feet downstream from the bridge, before it continues a short distance to its mouth at the lake. It's a bushy stretch, still not very wide, with plenty of Japanese knotweed crowding the stream banks. Fly fishing is still not easy. It involves swinging your line out a short distance, rather than casting, making short fly drifts just off the stream bottom.

Of course, the hoopla surrounding Grout Brook has always centered on the big spawning run rainbows. However, brown trout inhabit the little stream, as do colorful juvenile rainbows that can provide sport during the more lightly fished fall months. I've fished the stream in November and never ran across another angler the whole time.

Nine Mile Creek

Nine Mile Creek stirs fond memories; my earliest recollections of sportfishing involve my grandfather and father in about 1960, well before I ever wetted a fishing line. A now-defunct paper mill on the creek was operational during that time (and continued to be so for a number of years). Water flowed over a dam at the mill full force, creating a frothing plunge pool.

From my vantage point above the dam, I watched as my grandfather crawled down to the base of the falls, through its cold mist, netting a large trout for my father. The sight of that trout thrashing in the net is something I'll never forget. Over time, from past to present, my own fly-fishing experiences on Nine Mile Creek added to the stream's charm.

Nine Mile Creek begins its journey as an outlet of Otisco Lake, one of the smallest of the Finger Lakes. While most trout streams hold their coldest waters in upstream sections, the opposite is true of Nine Mile Creek. At that location, the stream departs Otisco Lake as an unremarkable warmwater fishery. Not until the stream gathers the cooling waters of springs downstream, near Marcellus Falls, does it transform into nice trout waters. Tumbling off the Appalachian plateau fall line, toward the Lake Ontario lowlands, the creek courses through limestone bedrock and makes its transformation.

NYSDEC categorizes Nine Mile Creek as Stocked and Stocked-Extended. A year-round Catch and Release, artificial-lures-only section is located from Onondaga Lake upstream to Amboy Dam. Although it is stocked, wild brown trout inhabit the fishery. NYSDEC studies have estimated that the stream reach from below Marcellus Falls down to Amboy holds more than 200 yearling brown trout per acre. I've always considered the stream prime trout water once it flows past the old and now-defunct former Marcellus Paper Company paper mill, last operated as the Martisco mill.

Very cold (49-degree) springs feed Nine Mile Creek just upstream from the now breached mill dam. During the time the paper mill was operational, the water flowed over the dam full-force. The plunge pool provided habitat for very large brown trout. Today, the reach both above and below the dam area has changed dramatically.

During the mid-1960s, we fished directly downstream from the dam, tolerating the stench from the mill. Mill workers typically watched from above, admiring my catches. Brook trout that inhabited the mill reach back then came to my net while I fished along the pocketwater that flowed a short distance downstream from the dam. Anglers are not likely to catch brook trout along that same area today.

Nine Mile Creek, at "the cave." Nine Mile Creek receives lots of attention from both conventional tackle anglers and fly fishers because of its relative proximity to the City of Syracuse. Cold springs keep trout happy during summer months. (PHOTO VALERIE VALLA)

The creek downstream from that area has also changed over the years. Easy access is available about a half-mile downstream from the mill site. The first parking area provides access to a particularly nice section of the creek that flows through a shaded cave-like overhanging outcrop—called "the cave" by my father. Other parking areas are downstream, again well-marked with NYSDEC public access signs.

Driving 0.4 mile, farther downstream (north) delivers you to another nice parking area (just after the short tunnel beneath the railroad bed), marked with a Central New York Land Trust sign. A short 100-yard walk down the adjacent path gets you to the stream and some excellent fishing and trout habitat. The stream eventually flows away from the road and through some isolated swampy areas, losing its gradient. Although there are additional public access areas downstream to Camillus, I've always fished primarily the upstream sections in summer months.

Nine Mile Creek fly fishers have used a variety of fly patterns with success. Some like small beadhead flies, scuds, and wet fly patterns. Today, Nine Mile Creek remains one of my favorite summer fishing destinations because it's spring fed and cold. I've always had success with deer hair ant and beetle patterns, popping the morsels along the small pools, tail-outs, and even riffles.

Nine Mile Creek has always produced some extremely large trout during the height of the fly-fishing season, during the time when it's more crowded with anglers. But good fishing can also be had in summer. An ineluctable fact about the stream is its prime-season fishing pressure, but when the early summer begins melding into (and, at times, melting into) late summer, you can find relative solitude on Nine Mile Creek.

Owego Creek

Owego Creek is a small trout stream, born of two branches, that flows southerly through farm country in Central New York State. The East and West Branches eventually join just north of the Village of Owego, where the creek weds the mighty Susquehanna River along the southern tier of the state.

As is true with most small trout streams in that area of New York, the upper reaches hold the best trout water. Both branches flow through similar valleys that are separated by long ridges, yet they are much different in character and the opportunity they offer fly anglers. The drainages feature stocked brown trout ranging in size from 9 to 15 inches. While not present in high numbers along the entire system, wild brook trout also inhabit Owego Creek.

The West Branch, arising in the Hammond Hill State Forest in southeastern Tompkins County, is small, brushy, and often difficult to fish with the fly rod because of dense riparian vegetation. The 1.6 miles of PFR access can be reached from three formal NYSDEC parking areas just south of Route 79, not far from Richford on West Creek Road.

Access the small stream 0.35 mile south on West Creek Road. There's an interesting plunge-pool structure in that area: Youth Conservation Corps volunteers, along with the Tompkins County Soil and Water Conservation District, have improved stream habitat over the years. However, the West Branch offers limited fly-fishing potential so most fly anglers focus attention to the East Branch, just north of Richford, while others prefer the main stem's stocked waters.

More than 60 years have passed since my grandfather dragged his eager grandson along the Owego but never along the West Branch or main stem. It was the East Branch above Richford, along NYS Route 38, that attracted his attention. During my years at nearby Cornell University, in the mid-1970s, I routinely biked to the East Branch with fly rod stretched over handlebars, especially in May and during the summer. Even in recent years, my visits to the little creek have focused on those same stretches.

There are 5.3 miles of public fishing access along the creek. A formal NYSDEC parking area sits just off Route 38, a mile or so north of Richford. Watch for the quaint brook trout sign along the highway, and then turn down a short dirt road to the bankside parking lot. Anglers can explore both up- and downstream along public access stretches.

East Branch of Owego Creek reach at the Town of Richford bridge crossing. Both the East and West Branches are categorized as Stocked.

Red Fox Squirrel-Hair Nymph (tied by Dave Whitlock) Scraggly nymphs, such as Dave Whitlock's Red Fox Squirrel-Hair Nymph, work well on Owego Creek. A general impressionistic fly, Dave tied it in many variations, including as a beadhead caddis pupa, although the Standard pattern is the best for brown trout on streams like Owego Creek. Dave, who passed away in November 2022, sold squirrel hair blends through Waspi. The abdomen uses red fox squirrel belly fur mixed 50-50 with sienna or fox tan Antron dubbing. Thorax is tied with Red Squirrel skin back fur mixed 50-50 with charcoal Antron dubbing. It's ribbed with oval gold tinsel. Dave preferred the Tiemco 5262 hook for the Standard pattern.

Owego Bucktail (tied by Mike Valla) A simple streamer, Owego Bucktail is tied with an Amherst pheasant tippet tail, flat silver tinsel body, orange hackle throat, and wing created by tying olive bucktail over black bucktail. Streamer hook of choice. The pattern worked well for brook trout on the upper West Branch of Owego Creek.

To avoid tripping over each other while fishing with a companion (the creek is relatively small), one angler can fish sinking flies along the bank structures while working downstream. Then they can fish back upstream to the parking area with floaters. The companion can work upstream from the parking area, casting dry flies along the structure riffles, then work back downstream with sinking flies. In the early season, an Elk Hair Caddis is an excellent choice for surface fishing. In summer months, beetles and ants work well, plopped along the bank structures. Sinking flies such as very small streamers and nymphs work well while fishing downstream.

After exploring those stretches, drive again north along Route 38 to an obvious turnout. A trek through an old spruce tree plantation will eventually return the angler to the creek. I discovered this reach while duck hunting at a nearby beaver pond one fall in the late 1970s.

Whether you fish along the more secluded sections of the East and West Branches, or around the more open main-stem stretches, the creek offers a variety of insect activity—from mayflies to terrestrials. Hatches include the Sulphurs, *Isonychias*, March Browns, Hendricksons, and Tricos. Dave Whitlock's highly effective Red Fox-Squirrel Nymph, tied in sizes 12 to 16, will catch fish throughout the year. In its uppermost reaches, deer hair ants are effective during late-season Owego Creek angling.

Anglers will notice large numbers of small baitfish darting around in the creek's shallows, especially in late summer. Some years ago, after noticing so many baitfish, I decided to design and tie to different versions of a streamer, simply called Owego. One is a featherwing version, and the other is a bucktail that's completely different in appearance. I prefer the bucktail.

Factory Brook

Factory Brook is a deceptively productive brown trout stream near Homer. It was one of Leon Chandler's favorite trout streams. Chandler (1922–2004), a fly-fishing icon beloved by the industry, is best known through his 50-year association with Cortland

Line Company, where he rose to the rank of an Executive Vice President. While 2.3 miles of PFR stretches provide access to the stream, only one formal NYSDEC parking area exists, found at the Creal Road bridge crossing near State Route 41.

The stream is reasonably easy to fish along a very short stretch directly upstream from the bridge. However, venturing further upstream can be a fly fishers nightmare, given the overhanging branches and other vegetative obstructions. The stream harbors some very large wild brown trout that probably grew to that size given the protection afforded by sections difficult to fish. Early season fishing is a good time to sample the water, particularly during mid-May.

My favorite memory of Factory Brook goes back to May 1978, when Cornell University Natural Resources Department staffers Ron Howard Jr., Dan Decker, R. J. "Rocky" Gutiérrez, and I enjoyed a spectacular *Ephemerella subvaria* (Hendricksons) spinner fall. The stream boiled with rising brown trout. Ron netted an 18-inch wild fish while Dan and I latched into sizeable yet smaller browns. Sulphur mayfly hatches also bring fish to the surface.

Access can be difficult along other PFR reaches, and much of the brook flows through private lands. Politely asking permission to fish private reaches can often result in a positive response. Back in the late 1970s, we enjoyed access to one of the best stream sections, on private land, off Spencer Road. Cortland Fly-Fishing Club did habitat-improvement work during the early 1970s on both the Spencer and Creal properties, which benefitted both the fish and anglers.

The Spencers, poultry farmers, erected a large sign at a fence-stile crossing directly next to their home. So long as anglers respected their property, and were quiet if arriving at early hours, both Mr. and Mrs. Spencer were happy to allow access and often greeted anglers while they sat on porch chairs. The property has since changed hands, and the formal access courtesy is no longer available along that reach, as I now understand it.

Factory Brook, at Creal Road bridge crossing. Factory brook is a productive yet brushy stream in areas. Access can be difficult. (PHOTO VALERIE VALLA)

Central Region

lso called the Leatherstocking Region of New York, its name derived from leather leggings worn by frontiersmen. Author James Fenimore Cooper brought attention to the term. The area roughly follows or is confined by the Mohawk River, Chenango River and the upper Susquehanna River drainages but extends north along the Mohawk, overlapping into the foothills of the Adirondack Region. Cooperstown, "the Village of Museums," is located in the heart of Central New York. The little village is home to the Baseball Hall of Fame. For the most part, the Central Region is dairy farm country, with its rolling hay meadow hillsides and extensive cornfield acreage. Streams flow through the farmland backdrops that provide a pleasant fishing environment.

Anglers who reside in the region's former industrial-based cities, such as Rome, Utica, and Binghamton, head to many well-known inland streams each spring in hopes of netting a fine trout. My own heritage is centered in Binghamton, a former factory-based city along the Chenango and Susquehanna Rivers. Shoe factory workers and tailors, such as my grandfathers and other relatives, looked forward to weekend trout fishing forays to little streams such as Butternut Creek, Oriskany Creek, and Limestone Creek. My dad's favorite was Oriskany Creek. These are a few of my heirloom waters that still provide good fishing.

Some of the nicest trout streams in Central New York, like Genegantslet Creek, flow along hay meadows and dairy farms. (PHOTO VALERIE VALLA)

Otselic River

Beginning as a trickle out of Torpy Pond, the Otselic River (sometimes called Otselic Creek) meanders 55 miles southwest through the rolling hills of idyllic Central New York farm country. Flowing through the small hamlets of Georgetown, Otselic Center, South Otselic, Pitcher, Cincinnatus, and Willet, the little stream eventually dumps into Whitney Point Reservoir, a warmwater fishery. Below the reservoir, the Otselic meets the Tioughnioga River at Whitney Point.

The Otselic offers various angling opportunities along its 23 miles of public fishing stretches. Smallmouth bass populate the lower section of the stream, just above Whitney Point Lake, while stocked brown trout, wild brown trout, and a few wild brook trout inhabit the upper reaches. The Otselic is stocked annually with 14,000 1-year-old browns (8 to 9 inches) and 2,000 2-year-old brown trout (12 to 15 inches). NYSDEC categorizes the Otselic River as Stocked and Stocked-Extended. My grandfather once told me that, back in the 1950s, the river held rainbows, but those days are gone.

Several public fishing parking lots sit along the creek. Along State Route 26, the first parking area is 3 miles north of the intersection with Telephone Road in Cincinnatus. The lot is next to a bridge at the Cortland County/Chenango County line. Public fishing extends for several miles in both directions from the bridge.

Another formal parking area, serving one of my favorite stretches of the Otselic, is another 4.7 miles north on State Route 26 at North Pitcher. Turn right onto Mill Road, and drive a short distance to the state parking area at a small plank bridge spanning the stream. The Otselic is somewhat isolated in this area, both upstream and downstream. The relative seclusion, as well as the prime trout water, makes for an enjoyable fishing experience. I like to fish this stretch with a 7-foot, 4-weight rod, and I often skitter a small Elk Hair Caddis on the riffles at the pool heads.

Back on State Route 26 north of the Mill Road Turnoff, you'll find additional state-owned formal parking turnouts. A signed parking area 2 miles north of Mill Road is set back from the highway via a short dirt driveway. The stream at that point, located in South Otselic, is interesting for not only its trout potential but also the rich fishing heritage that surrounds the small rural hamlet.

South Otselic was once home to the B. F. Gladding Company, a onetime fishing line manufacturer. During the late 1960s and early 1970s, I fished with Gladding lines, which were known for their quality. The line company, established in 1816, eventually became the oldest in the world; South Otselic, in due time, earned the moniker "Fishing Line Capital of the World." The South Otselic Fish Hatchery, located on State Route 26, is also part of the local heritage.

The hatchery, which rears the entire statewide supply of tiger muskellunge and produces walleye fingerlings, serves as one of the locations for the popular annual Fishing Heritage Day sponsored by the Otselic Valley Fishing & Heritage Association, in partnership with NYSDEC. Anglers sampling the stream in mid-May might want to consider bringing family along for the event, which offers myriad activities and tours for all ages, including fly-fishing demonstration. You can enjoy the event and then explore the stream around the hamlet.

Three miles north of South Otselic on State Route 26 is another NYSDEC parking area at the highway bridge that crosses the now narrowing stream. I've never fished that section, but it looks interesting. Another 2.5 miles up the highway is yet another NYSDEC parking area, the uppermost along the stream, near the intersection of State Route 26

Otselic River at a State Route 26 bridge crossing at the Cortland County/Chenango County line. A major tributary of Tioughnioga River, the Otselic provides fishing for mostly stocked brown trout. The farm country stream has plenty of public fishing access along its mileage. (PHOTO VALERIE VALLA)

and County Road 16 (turn south on County Road 16, cross the river, and park at the lot on your right). Here the stream is very narrow and brushy, meandering through pastoral farmlands. It's quintessential Central New York farm country. The stretch, both upstream and downstream from the bridge, is PFR water. The upstream reach departs from roads and offers secluded though difficult fly-fishing water. I've always been tempted to thrash through the brush in this section of the stream and try plopping an ant pattern along the overhanging vegetation.

Tioughnioga River

Composed of two branches—the shorter 15.6-mile west branch and the longer 34.2-mile east branch—the river with a strange name joins in the City of Cortland to form the larger main stem. Derived from a native word meaning "forks of the river," the Tioughnioga River then continues flowing southeast toward the City of Binghamton. It picks up water from Factory Brook along its west branch and Fabious Brook along its east branch. By the time it reaches Whitney Point, it broadens after receiving the Otselic River. The river finally dumps into Chenango River at Chenango Forks, 10 miles upstream from Binghamton. NYSDEC categorizes both branches as Stocked.

WEST BRANCH TIOUGHNIOGA RIVER

The river's west branch has 0.9 mile of PFR water, although there are no formal NYSDEC parking areas along its stocked reach from the State Route 13 bridge in Cortland upstream to the State Route 11 bridge at Durkee Memorial Park located a half-mile upstream from the center of the Village of Homer. Locating the PFR reaches can sometimes be confusing since the stream hugs I-81 in areas and flows through other congested areas. Once I-81 was constructed many years ago, it made accessing public easement rights confusing

East Branch of Tioughnioga near the hamlet of Cuyler

West Branch of Tioughnioga River, a short distance upstream from its junction with the East Branch, in Cortland

if not difficult in some sections. Anglers are best advised to use NYSDEC's interactive stream locator map accessed at the following link: https://gisservices.dec.ny.gov/gis/dil/index.html?cat=WRL.

Access the stream at unofficial pull-offs at a few of the side roads off South Main Street in Homer between Water Street and Albany Street. Some of the side roads end at small truss bridges that are no longer in service. The stream can also be accessed behind the Homer Recreation Department behind the tennis courts and Homer American Legion located at the intersection of State Route 90 and County Road 11 (between Albany Street and Pine Street).

Nearly 3,000 9-inch to 10-inch brown trout and a few hundred larger 12-inch to 15-inch browns are stocked in the Town of Homer. The pond at Durkee Memorial Park also gets annual trout stockings, as does Casterline Pond, another nice place to introduce kids to angling. Fly anglers encounter a few wild brown trout and rarely a wild brook trout in its upper reaches.

If you don't mind fishing in an urban-congested setting in view of motels, fast food restaurants, fitness centers, and the incessant vehicle noise (not my cup of tea at all) both stocked and wild trout are routinely caught during the May Hendrickson hatches where the stream passes Riverside Plaza Shopping Center, near Clinton Avenue off I-81 in Cortland. It's unfortunate that the stream can be so trashed up along the parking lot but it's for sure easy stream access in that area.

There's not much stream structure in that reach along the shopping center when the water is running high. The stream moves swiftly as one continuous, uniform water column and doesn't provide what I'd call pleasant fishing conditions.

The junction pool, where the East Branch joins the West Branch of the Tioughnioga, is not far downstream from the shopping center. A small road that leads from behind the Wendy's Restaurant can get you close to the junction pool. The unnamed access road parallels I-81 for a short distance and ends at an underpass that leads into Yaman Park. Drive into the park and go right. The road will lead to a boat launch along the East Branch of the Tioughnioga at the south end of Yaman Park, just upstream from the junction of both river branches.

EAST BRANCH TIOUGHNIOGA RIVER

Wandering through agricultural lands in Madison and Cortland Counties, the East Branch flows southeasterly from near the hamlet of Sheds nearly 40 miles before it joins the West Branch in Cortland just downstream from Yaman Park. Yaman Park, located next to I-81 Exit 11, is a public facility open year-round. You can reach it by driving up State Route 13 from I-81 to Kennedy Parkway.

Along its path through dairy country, the East Branch flows downstream past the hamlet of Cuyler before reaching Truxton located a dozen miles downstream from its source. The hamlet is named for Commodore Thomas Truxton, one of the US Navy's early commanding officers. Most angling activity on the upper reaches occurs along the stream's modest formal PFR access points downstream between Cuyler and Truxton along State Route 13. Anglers also fish along unofficial parking areas, such as the reach near the Cuyler highway department garage on Tripoli Road. However, a formal NYS-DEC parking area, marked by a large hanging sign, exists at a bridge crossing a short distance downstream from Cuyler.

Most of the trout angling activity downstream from the bridge crossing at the DEC parking area happens early in the season, by bait anglers, soon after fish stockings occur between Bell's Mill Road in Truxton and Cuyler. Close to 1,500 brown trout are stocked annually in late April. The stream in this area, like most of it, isn't very appealing to the eye, with its slow-moving deep pools. But there is a nice run that enters deeper water downstream from the bridge. You won't encounter many fly anglers around that reach later in the season after the initial stockings take place.

The stream reach in its lowermost area, down near Cortland, receives stockings of approximately 3,500 9-inch to 15-inch brown trout in the area between the lower end of Yaman Park upstream to Youngs Crossing. Youngs Crossing is located about 7 miles upstream off County Road 144.

Like the upper reaches, the East Branch from Young's Crossing downstream to Yaman Park appears unremarkable, with little stream structure attached to its long, low-gradient flatwater pools. It's not pretty water, but as hard as it might be to believe, big brown trout that lurk in some of the deep pools sometimes surprise anglers who fish for bass.

TIOUGHNIOGA RIVER—MAIN STEM

After the East Branch and West Branch meet in Cortland, the river maintains its low gradient, deep-pooled character downstream from Cortland, all the way to the Chenango River. Back in late 1950s up until the early 1970s, the reach downstream from State Route 392 crossing in Messengerville was my dad's go-to trout fishing area on the river. (Incidentally, a formal NYSDEC PFR parking lot, marked by a large hanging sign, is located at the State Route 392 bridge.) The stream in that section was a relatively short distance from our home in the Binghamton area, and he often fished it after work with my uncle and his fishing buddy, George Kurbaba.

There's a very steep hill along a pullover area about a half-mile south of State Route 392 on Route 11. They fished along the river after trekking down the hill to the water. My most memorable moment of tagging along with them while they fished that section, sometime around 1960, was being dropped in the water by my dad after I fell off his back! My uncle George came to the rescue. Dad often carried me on his back up that hill. I also fondly remember the times, when I was 5 years old, that he left me in the car at that pullover area while he fished at daybreak in that stretch. I have a vivid memory of him returning to retrieve me, showing off a creel full of trout.

Main stem of Tioughnioga at Blodgett Mill Road bridge crossing. The main stem is almost entirely a warmwater fishery that was once heavily stocked with both brown trout and rainbow trout. However, trout still inhabit the big water, including some very large brown trout, but not in the numbers when stocking occurred. The stream reach at the Village of Marathon was once a popular section for fly fishing when the hatches were on.

Matuka Sculpin (tied by Dave Whitlock) Dave Whitlock decided to improve his original sculpin by borrowing features found in popular Matuka patterns. Dave's July 1994 *Fly Fisherman* magazine feature article, titled "Fishing Sculpins," provided a review of the many sculpin patterns available at that time.

NearNuff Sculpin (tied by Dave Whitlock) Big sculpin patterns are flies of choice when sampling the main stem pools for large brown trout that inhabit the water, but there they are now few and far between. Warmwater species can still keep fly fishers busy. Dave's NearNuff is a suggestive imitation that is a bit easier to tie than his Matuka Sculpin.

By 1968 or so, I fished that same stretch and recall catching a rainbow trout; dad always caught browns. I often wondered why the area was so productive for him and his fishing partners and theorized perhaps there was some sort of thermal refuge from inflow of Gridley Creek that joins the water from the opposite side of the river. I know that my dad was constantly pouring over topo maps throughout his angling life, seeking out tributary inflows. However, the stream was heavily stocked in those years, and that might have had something to do with it, too.

The main stem of the Tioughnioga has not been stocked since 2000, but large trout are still netted in the lower river. The main stem river is better described as a warmwater bass fishery despite the occasional trout that anglers catch. It's a tough river to wade fish, but there are areas that can be fished in that manner.

Some prefer to float the river, a task made easy via the Town of Cortlandville Public Boat launch at the Blodgett Mill Road bridge crossing. It's also called Hiawatha Landing. A large wooden statue of an Indian greets visitors at the entrance to the large parking area. When the water is low enough, wade fishing is possible in a nice river stretch upstream from the bridge. Most anglers target bass in that section, but trout are sometimes encountered along the deep run. Fish sculpin patterns, such as a Whitlock NearNuff Sculpin or his Matuka Sculpin.

Chenango River

It's not surprising that the 90-mile-long Chenango River progresses from inhabiting trout in its uppermost reaches near the Village of Morrisville to a warmwater bass fishery in its middle to lowermost sections down to the City of Binghamton. For me, during my teenage years when I lived in Binghamton a block from the river, it provided good sport when I couldn't get onto trout water in the Catskills during late summer. The smallmouth fishing near my home on the Chenango River was, and still is, fabulous (see Warmwater Fly Fishing section).

While the lower stretches of the Chenango River hold a special place in my heart, there's much more good fly-fishing water along its 90 miles, as it flows south through Central New York to its confluence with the Susquehanna River in Binghamton. The

Upper Chenango River at the Carey Road bridge crossing. While the lower Chenango River near Binghamton provides good smallmouth bass fishing, its uppermost reaches inhabit brown trout. (PHOTO VALERIE VALLA)

Chenango begins briefly as trout water in Madison County at Morrisville but quickly develops into a warmwater fishery once it flows past Sherburne. In addition to smallmouth, the river holds northern pike, walleyes, muskellunge, and carp.

There's plenty of public access along the entire course of its flow, although years ago, there was much more access upstream in its trout-inhabited reaches near Randallsville. However, three formal NYSDEC PFR sections exist a short distance downstream from Morrisville. Drive down South Street from Morrisville to Hart Road. Take a left on Hart Road, then a right on English Avenue. The uppermost PFR access is marked by a large hanging NYSDEC sign on the right side of the road a couple of miles down English Avenue.

The uppermost PFR parking area isn't directly on the stream. A path that's not all that apparent in sections leads down to the stream a good distance from the parking area. It starts out along a cornfield, heads down a slope through a grove of crab apple trees, and then reaches additional cornfield areas. You'll probably lose sight of the path, but it's not that difficult to sense the position of the stream location. The 10-foot-wide stream is in a very secluded location, full of deadfalls and likely holding pools. It's not easy fishing, but the seclusion is a draw for sure.

After crawling out of the uppermost PFR, try a second formal access point that is located down English Avenue past the intersection with Brown Road. Again, the parking area is marked by a large hanging NYSDEC sign that isn't directly on the stream. An even longer distance must be traversed through fields to reach the stream. The access path is even more poorly marked and hardly apparent; a bit of bushwhacking through high goldenrod and other vegetation is needed to reach the stream that flows off in the distance.

The less ambitious angler will head for the third and lowermost PFR parking area downstream on Carey Road. The most direct way to Carey Road is via its intersection with County Road 73 south of Eaton. Follow Carey Road a short distance to the stream and parking area marked by NYSDEC hanging signage. Hendricksons hatch in that section, along with several caddis species. The best time to fish that reach is in mid-late May and again in the early fall months. NYSDEC stocks nearly 3,000 brown trout in the Eaton area that range from 9 to 15 inches. NYSDEC categorizes the stream as Stocked.

Limestone Creek

Along with two other streams relatively close to Syracuse—Chittenango Creek and Butternut Creek—Limestone Creek is also a favorite fly-fishing destination that is convenient to anglers who reside near the populous city. The stream also attracts conventional bait-and-lure anglers throughout its length that originates south of the hamlet of Delphi Falls. Limestone Creek is primarily categorized by NYSDEC as Stock-Extended.

After leaving the area near DeRuyter Reservoir, a warmwater fishery, the creek traverses northerly 25 miles through farm country before eventually flowing through Manlius and Fayetteville, suburbs of Syracuse. After departing the Fayettville area, Limestone Creek leaves behind optimum trout habitat then picks up water from Butternut Creek. The merged waters join Chittenango Creek upstream from Oneida Lake, the terminus of the collective waters.

While no formal NYSDEC parking areas exist along the stream's meager 1.6 miles of PFR water, anglers find plenty of access at informal parking areas, along the length of the stream, including water that flows through the "suburbs" stretch between Manlius and Fayettville.

Before sampling the lowermost Limestone trout-inhabited reaches located around those two suburb towns, it's worth exploring PFR water near the headwaters. A short PFR reach is located on Limestone's headwaters, on Cardner Road, just north of State Route 80.

The Mill Run Park reach, in Manlius. The stream flows along walking trails at the park that's open for free to the public. Historic remnants of an old stone grain-mill dam built in the 1800s is located near the stream.

East Branch of Limestone Creek, at Delphi Falls. The short stream stretch downstream from the falls isn't prime trout habitat, given its shallow water that flows over bedrock and typically warms significantly in summer. (PHOTO VALERIE VALLA)

(You'll notice orange posted signs tracked on the same trees that also display the yellow NYSDEC public fishing stream signs. I checked with NYSDEC concerning the dual signage on this stretch. I was told landowners can still post their lands against other activities besides fishing. It's common for landowners to not indicate fishing is allowed.) Another PFR section on the main stem is located downstream from a bridge crossing along Tracy Road, located a few miles downstream, north of Delphi off Oran-Delphi Road.

While in the headwaters area, stop by the spectacular Delphi Falls waterfall located at Delphi Falls County Park in its namesake hamlet. The falls were off-limits to the public for many years before Madison County purchased the lands in 2018. The falls plunge water from Limestone Creek's East Branch. The stream that departs from the falls plunge pool flows largely over bedrock and shale. The water is typically shallow, has little fish-holding water in the park, and warms significantly during the summer.

I have yet to net a trout in the plunge pool below at the falls. However, the pool provides potential during early season and again in late season on higher water conditions after rains. Fish might migrate up from Limestone Creek's main stem located a short distance downstream at its confluence with the West Branch. The free park is a great place to stop and eat your lunch and enjoy the scenery.

Suburban sprawl that progressively occurred over the years between Manlius and Fayetteville downstream has changed the character of Limestone Creek. However, many Limestone regulars aren't concerned with fishing in a congested area because the fish are present and willing to take flies in that section. Some of the extreme small head-water areas south of State Route 20 are better suited to bait fishing. Split between two counties—Madison and Onondaga—Limestone Creek receives more than ample stocking of brown trout along with brook trout. Over 10,000 trout are stocked annually between State Route 80 and the Limestone Creek terminus.

Baltz's Deep Emerger (tied by Tom Baltz) Tom created his pattern weighted to get down deep in the water column. "Some mayflies emerge closer to the stream bottom than at the water surface," Tom said.

Soft-Hackle Hare's Ear (tied by Bob Herson) Bob Herson's dandy little Soft-Hackle Hare's Ear is perfect for swinging through Limestone Creek's runs and riffles. Bob's hare's ear body material is loop-spun, then picked out after spinning to provide bugginess. He favors Diiachi 1530 hooks for the pattern.

A very nice Limestone Creek reach flows in Manlius at Mill Run Park, a popular angling access point located at 125 Mill Street in the village. A trail next to the stream leads from a pavilion area. While walking up the streamside path in the park, you'll notice historic remnants of an old stone grain-mill dam built in the 1800s. The free park is open from dawn until dusk. Nymphs, emerger patterns, and small streamers are productive along the riffles and pocketwater runs.

Chittenango Creek

Of the three sister trout streams located near the City of Syracuse, Chittenango Creek is perhaps the most picturesque of the clan. When compared with its siblings—Butternut Creek and Limestone Creek—it holds other advantages besides beauty. Mostly along State Route 13, 4.8 miles of intermittently spaced, easy-to-access PFR water exists along the stream from its headwaters at Nelson Swamp Natural Area downstream to the Village of Chittenango. Included in the PFR mileage is a special regulations Catch and Release area. Beauty is there, too, with its 167-foot Chittenango Creek Falls located roughly 5 miles upstream from Chittenango. NYSDEC categorizes the stream as Stocked and Stocked-Extended.

Besides numerous informal roadside pull-off areas located along the stream, anglers can park at several official NYSDEC angler parking lots. Three official NYSDEC angler parking areas, marked by large hanging signs, are located above the Chittenango Creek Falls. The lowermost formal NYSDEC parking lot is located at the popular Catch and Release section nearly 3 miles downstream from the falls off Olmstead Road. An additional parking area where uppermost PFR water can be easily accessed exists at the Nelson Swamp Unique Area (NSUA) parking lot located some 8 miles upstream from the Village of Cazenovia.

The NSUA parking area, marked by a large hanging sign, is located on Constine Bridge Road directly across from the Town of Cazenovia Highway Department and Transfer Station located at 3425 Constine Bridge Road in Cazenovia. Anglers can park at the lot and access the PFR water in two ways.

A 0.2-mile walk down the road will get you into the stream at a bridge crossing. The better alternative is to walk down the stone dust trail that leads into the NSUA from the

Chittenango Creek, at the Olmstead Road Catch and Release reach. Kudos to NYSDEC and the Madison County Chapter of Trout Unlimited for their involvement in trout population dynamic assessments along Chittenango Creek, particularly in the C&R reach. (PHOTO VALERIE VALLA)

parking lot. Walk past the yellow vehicle barrier gate and go to the right where the trail splits. An 8-minute walk down the trail bordered by horsetails passing through cedar trees will lead to an awesome mature hemlock grove at the stream. You can either fish upstream or fish downstream back down to the bridge crossing, then walk back to the lot. The stream is about 12 to 15 feet wide in the area and well-shaded.

The creek opens up a bit as it approaches the Constine Bridge Road crossing downstream. By the time the upper creek reaches State Route 13, it takes on the characteristic of a meandering stream, passing through open areas. To reach the first official PFR angling parking area, depart the NSUA lot and drive north a half-mile to Ballina Road. Take a left on Ballina (County Road 50), and drive 2.7 miles to State Route 13. Turn right on State Route 13, going north, and you'll arrive at the NYSDEC lot marked by a large hanging sign. A 100-foot path leads from the lot to the stream. PFR water exists along the upstream stretch.

Driving an additional 2 miles north on State Route 13 will take you into Cazenovia, where Chittenango Creek picks up additional water from Cazenovia Lake. State Route 13 weaves through the village, eventually refollowing the stream. Driving approximately 3.8 miles north of the State Route 13/State Route 20 intersection in Cazenovia will bring you to one of the most popular official NYSDEC angling parking lots along PFR water on State Route 13. The large lot is located about 0.7 mile upstream from the entrance to Chittenango Falls State Park.

Fishing is allowed on the stream along the park grounds but not directly below or directly above the waterfall; it's blocked off for habitat protection of the Chittenango Ovate Amber Snail, an endangered species, and for safety reasons. You can reach the creek at the park by trekking down the steep rock and gravel stairs and trail to near the base of the waterfall. The creek downstream from the waterfall in a gorge-like setting

Rusty Llama (tied by Mike Valla) The author's own creation, Rusty Llama borrowed features from Llama hairwing and a Rusty Rat Salmonfly. It's an easy fly to tie (complete step-by-step tying instructions are found in the author's book *Tying and Fishing Bucktails and other Hair Wings* [2016]). It fishes well through Chittenango Creek's swifter runs. Gray Fox Guard Hair and underfur wings provide motion to the fly.

can be a torrent or modest flow or even a relative trickle, depending on seasonal conditions. Chittenango Falls State Park is very nice and a great place to have a lunch break.

To sample additional creek stretches, depart the park and continue driving north on State Route 13. You might want to make a quick stop at another official NYSDEC angling parking lot located off Emnoff Road before continuing down State Route 13. Exit the park entrance, take a left, and drive 0.1 mile to Emnoff, then another 0.3 mile to a very small parking lot marked by a NYSDEC hanging sign. It's not the most popular access point, but it is worth a cast or two, and the fish are there.

Additional access points that are much more popular with fly anglers exist along State Route 13 from the park entrance down to Chittenango. You'll encounter five unofficial large parking turnout areas along State Route 13 in the 4 miles after departing the park entrance. These are in addition to a couple NYSDEC areas marked by hanging signs. You'll want to fish the Catch and Release stream reach on Olmstead Road located just a few hundred feet from its intersection with State Route 13 at the bridge crossing. The NYSDEC parking lot access point is marked by a large hanging sign. The Madison County Chapter of Trout Unlimited maintains a small box at the parking area with printed information. The reach is very popular with Chittenango Creek regulars.

NYSDEC biologists have done an excellent job categorizing the varied stream reaches from its origins located 7 miles or so miles upstream from Cazenovia at Nelson Swamp Natural Area downstream 13 miles to Chittenango. Kudos also to NYSDEC for their painstaking interest and thorough involvement assessing trout population dynamics on Chittenango Creek, particularly on the Catch and Release section.

The 2.2-mile-long Catch and Release section, located from the Town of Sullivan/Town of Fenner line at mile marker 1219 on State Route 13 to mile marker 1237 south of the Village of Chittenango line, was created in October 2010. During August of 2010, biologists performed electrofishing studies to create baseline data for annual trout population assessments in the newly created Special Regulation zone.

The reason for the study was to determine what initial and long-term impact the newly created Catch and Release reach would have on trout density and structure. Surprisingly, or maybe not surprisingly, after studying annual electrofishing results for a decade was the lack of changes in overall trout density or class structure. In their report, NYSDEC concluded, "Currently, it does not appear that the Catch and Release regulation has had any impact on the trout population within the two standard sample sites. Though the regulation doesn't seem to be benefitting the trout population, it does provide a unique and popular angling opportunity and should be continued." However, in 2020, a third electrofishing site was added, a site where some habitat improvement work was completed in 2010, interesting data showed a different trout range.

The creek and its fishing opportunities are sometimes affected by low water conditions. There are years when the stream water levels are more than adequate throughout the summer, but sometimes during periods of regional drought or less-than-adequate rainfall, the stream can drop to very low levels. My cousin Donna has lived on the banks of the creek downstream from the Catch and Release stretch for many years and has witnessed both times of highwater flooding at her home and times when the stream all but dried up. There was an extended period of drought in the 1990s when the stream was so low you could walk across it by stepping on exposed stones, hardly getting your ankles wet.

NYSDEC typically stocks some 13,000 brown trout ranging in size from 9 to 15 inches along the stream. Anglers occasionally net brook trout in Chittenango Creek.

Butternut Creek

Butternut Creek has always been my least favorite stream of the "three sisters clan" that includes Chittenango Creek and Limestone Creek, but I still enjoy fishing a few of the reaches. The creek is not a classic-appearing trout stream, aside from a couple sections in the headwaters and some areas downstream from the Jamesville Reservoir. After flowing north from its origins at a marshy swamp near Apulia Station on State Route 80, it flows 10 miles or so north, mostly along Apulia Road, past State Route 20, and then to Jamesville Reservoir. After existing the reservoir, the creek flows another 10 miles north where it receives Limestone Creek at North Manlius area. NYSDEC categorizes the stream as Stocked-Extended.

Butternut Creek at Fiddler's Green Park, in Jamesville. Fiddler's Green is an 11-acre green space donated to the town in 2007 by Hanson Aggregates. NYSDEC categorized the stream as Stocked-Extended.
(PHOTO VALERIE VALLA)

Upper Butternut Creek at Weller Road (PHOTO VALERIE VALLA)

Some anglers routinely fish the lower reach downstream from the reservoir to just north of Jamesville. If fishing in a suburban area with sounds of moving vehicles doesn't bother you, there's a riffle-filled reach at the intersection of I-481 and Jamesville Road off Exit 2.

A small parking area, marked by a NYSDEC large hanging sign, is located right smack next to the exit ramp at the intersection. PFR signage exists at a well-worn path that leads to the stream. The section is much different in stream structure than some of the slow-moving, low-gradient, meadow-like reaches upstream above Jamesville Reservoir. Trout also inhabit Butternut Creek downstream almost to its mouth down near Kinne Road. Onondaga County's Carpenter Brook Fish Hatchery annually stocks the reach from Kinne Road upstream to the reservoir with 2,160 brown trout (9 to 14 inches) and 500 brook trout (9 inches). Other nicer stretches exist less than a mile upstream, still below Jamesville Reservoir.

From the I-481/Jamesville Road intersection, drive south along Jamesville Road for 0.8 mile to Solray Road. Take a left on Solray, cross the bridge, and take an immediate right into Fiddler's Green Park (4691 Solvay Road, Jamesville). The park was donated to the Town of Dewitt in 2007 by Hanson Aggregate quarry. The 11-acre natural area park, enjoyed by both anglers and trail hikers, is a natural area.

The parking lot directly next to the tumbling stream is very small but adequate for a few vehicles. The streamside picnic table is a nice place to have lunch. While munching on your sandwich, you'll hear water tumbling over a waterfall on the south side of the bridge.

I rarely sample the lowermost reaches downstream from the reservoir but instead have focused on the stream reach between State Route 20 downstream to the Colton Road sections and occasionally two brook-like PFR reaches upstream from State Route 20 along Clark Hollow Road located above from Jamesville Reservoir. The reach from Jamesville Reservoir upstream to Route 80 is typically stocked with nearly 6,000 brown trout and 1,000 brook trout. Those were the stretches that my dad and grandfather preferred from the 1950s into the early 1970s, probably even during the 1940s. Butternut Creek, the eastern-most stream of the three sisters, was convenient to Binghamton, where we lived.

The PFR water on Weller Road located less than a mile north of Dodge Road in Onativia (6 miles north of Apulia Station) is a good place to start. A formal NYSDEC parking lot is next to the stream bridge crossing. During the early spring, you'll be in the company of bait anglers and others using conventional fishing techniques. But there's plenty of water for all to explore and cast a line, including fly anglers. Cast small streamers and nymphs into the water that has structure and deadfalls.

To reach the Clark Hollow Road headwater brook-like stretches, take Exit 15 off I-81 at Lafayette to State Route 20 then drive less than 2 miles to Apulia Road. At the Apulia Road/State Route 20 intersection, drive south 0.8 mile and take a left on Cascade Road. You'll pass a formal NYSDEC angler parking area that's worth fishing. In a half-mile, turn right on Clark Hollow Road, and drive 1.2 miles to the formal NYSDEC angling parking lot located on the left, marked by a large hanging sign. It's located next to a private home. A second formal parking area on Clark Hollow Road is located less than a mile south of the previous lot. Fish the riffles and small pools with nymphs.

Additional PFR stretches next to official NYSDEC parking lots are located both upstream and downstream from the Weller Road parking area. A formal NYSDEC angling parking lot is located at a bridge crossing a half-mile east of the State Route 20/Apulia Road intersection on State Route 20. It's popular with bait anglers early in the spring.

Drive another 0.3 mile along State Route 20 then left on Clark Hollow Road to Dodge Road. A formal NYSDEC angling lot is located a half-mile down the road at a bridge crossing. You'll see major power lines overhead. It's not a particularly good reach for fly angling. The creek upstream from the bridge slowly flows through marshy wetlands filled with cattails.

Fabious Brook

Two certainties come to mind when fishing Fabious Brook, a 6-mile tributary of the East Branch of the Tioughnioga River. The first certainty is some very big brown trout—over 20 inches—inhabit its deep pools that provide great habitat among large tree deadfalls and cover. The second fact is spin-and-bait anglers do a much better job of teasing the big brutes out from water that's more difficult for fly anglers to fish from its banks. However, enjoyable fly-fishing success for both brown trout and brook trout can be achieved along its length if runs and pools are selected that are reasonably fly-fishing friendly. NYSDEC categorizes the stream as Stocked, although some wild trout inhabit the brook.

Many years ago, Fabious Brook was always a favorite of my grandfather and father, who enjoyed fishing it with bait, for brook trout. They used fly rods mounted with automatic Martin fly reels, level fly lines, and twist-on leader sinkers that enabled them to dangle small garden worms over the banks down to the fish. As I recall, they always got fish. I don't recall if they ever netted brown trout—it was a brookie destination.

Some 1.4 miles of PFR water can be reached along several separated stretches, beginning upstream at the Village of Fabious, just a few miles away from the headwaters of Butternut Creek. If you're fishing Butternut's headwaters, it makes sense to also try Fabious Brook, although that little stream isn't as conducive to fly fishing.

A formal NYSDEC angling parking lot is located on State Route 80 about 7.5 miles from I-81 Exit 14 driving east toward the Village of Fabious at a bridge crossing. It's on the right side of State Route 80 0.1 mile before arriving in Fabious. A very short PFR stretch is located on the right side of the stream, looking upstream, across the road from the parking lot. A grassy area that's typically mowed allows anglers to get close enough to the

Fabious Brook at Bardeen Road bridge crossing. Fabious Brook grows some very nice, large brown trout in its lower reaches. Bait-and-lure anglers seem to bring in better catches, but fly fishers can often latch into good fish, too.

water to cast flies from the bank for trout, typically brook trout. Fishing upstream is next to impossible. Beavers have worked hard to dam the creek along the brushy headwaters.

The tiny creek that flows directly downstream from the parking area is also very brushy and not very conducive to fly fishing. Fly anglers are better trying other locations a few miles downstream. Try the PFR stretches by driving west 0.6 mile to Shackham Road. Turn left and drive 0.4 mile to Bailey Road. Take another left, and drive another 0.6 mile to Parker Road. A PFR reach marked by a yellow NYSDEC sign exists at the bridge crossing looking downstream, on the left side of the stream. Parking is difficult along the road.

A couple other PFR reaches are located downstream. Continue on Parker Road to Keeney Road, and go right for another mile to a bridge crossing. You can fish downstream from the bridge on the left side of the stream's PFR water. Another PFR stretch is located downstream at Bardeen Road Drive down Keeney Road a half-mile to Bardeen Road, then take a right, and you'll see a large hanging NYSDEC sign at a parking area at the bridge crossing.

A very large, deep pool exists upstream from the bridge but not conducive to wade fishing. Slow, deep water easier to spin fish also exists along the short PFR reach along the leftside upstream from the bridge. Longer PFR frontage exists upstream from the bridge on the right side, but when the water is high, it's difficult to access.

The stream section that flows downstream from the bridge is much more fly-fishing friendly. While not formal PFR water, it's not posted. It's always best to obtain permission when fishing along private stretches. A modest path that leads from the bridge downstream was obviously created by anglers walking along the stream. A nice run and riffle flows through that section.

Oriskany Creek/Chenango Canal

Oriskany Creek is best explored by arriving in Oriskany Falls, a town situated just a few miles just north of the intersection of State Route 12B-26 and US-20 east of Madison. From the vantage point of the village, fly fishers can sample the creek upstream through its headwaters and its important tributary, the Chenango Canal. The lower reaches of the creek can be fished by heading downstream from the village, in a northerly direction, eventually reaching public access areas in the Town of Kirkland. I've always called the two streams "heirloom" creeks; knowledge of their cold and productive waters was handed down from my grandfather and my father, who fished those waters extensively as far back as the 1940s and 1950s.

A photograph of my father taken in the summer of 1959, smiling in front of his wicker creel and spread of Oriskany brown trout across a newspaper—with one spanning its width (taken in an era when such unfortunate practices were fashionable and accepted)—remains a reminder of the stream's sustained productivity. I'm certain that my grandfather, and father, had no inkling how those two streams were so productive in summer months; to them, they were, in isolation, simply good late-season destinations because of their cool waters.

Although the lower creek is also productive in summer months, the upstream headwater reach, since teenage years, has always been my favorite during warm weather. During summer days when Catskill region waters became too warm to seriously fish, a recess excursion to the Oriskany was always a welcome relief. There was always someone, typically a friend's father or an older fly fisher, who was willing to trade a ride to the stream for knowledge of its good fishing.

The headwaters are easily accessed in just a couple of miles south of Oriskany Falls, driving southerly via State Route 26-S to Valley Road. There are several pull-over areas

Upper Oriskany Creek is known for its population of wild brown trout. One of the author's favorite streams in his teenage years, Oriskany was introduced to him by his father and grandfather many years ago. It's fed by Chenango Canal, a spring creek-like flow that grows colorful brown trout.

along the road, which runs along the creek, as well as a formal NYSDEC fishing access parking lot. The area is well-marked as having public access. Fishing upstream from the parking area, the fly fisher will encounter some stream improvement structures such as deflectors and plunge pools. Valley Road eventually reaches Solsville, where there is additional parking and access by crossing the bridge that leads to a parking area. The headwater areas are not stocked by the state but are still very productive.

Chenango Canal—Tributary of Oriskany Creek

Continuing just a very short drive southerly out of Solsville, now along the Canal Road, the uppermost extent of the Oriskany is encountered at a pull-over area where the Chenango Canal spills its waters over a small waterfall, at the old Lock 76, into the creek. There's a sign near the parking area that alerts anglers of the Special Regulation Chenango Canal waters.

The 97-mile-long canal, constructed by Scottish immigrants, was operational from 1837–1878, linking transportation waters with the Erie Canal. The canal today, in this region, provides several miles of Special Regulation trout fishing along the Canal Road to the Bouckville area on State Route 20. There are easy pull-off areas along the Canal Road and the adjacent towpath trail affords a variety of access points into the water.

At its terminal junction with the Oriskany, the Canal can be accessed by parking at the pull over along Canal Road, walking downstream below its outlet falls, and fording the creek. A short walk through the deadfalls will get the fly fisher up along a maintained canal towpath trail and into the Canal waters. An easier strategy instead of fording the Oriskany, and one I usually use, is to park along the road shoulder 0.2 mile upstream from Lock 76. Walk upstream from the road shoulder a couple hundred feet, then wade across the Canal to the tow path. Trek down the towpath several hundred feet along the towpath to Lock 76. Then get into the water after cussing at the brambles you'll fight getting into the water. Your efforts will be worth it. Slowly make your way upstream, watching for dimple rises. Stop and watch is the tactic. Don't rush along.

The Canal is a deceptive flow of water, not even crotch deep in summer and not very wide. Unlike the Oriskany, with its rubble, stone, and rock substrate flowing through riffles and pools, the Canal is a very clear, smooth, seemingly motionless flow, bordered by brush and filled with water vegetation. It's the kind of water that most might drive by and not realize it is trout water. It's easy to wade, and as long as you're watching your backcast, casting can be long and precise to the dimple rises that can be created by a very large trout. Fishing tactics on the Oriskany is routine, but stealth is the word on the Canal, along with careful and quiet wading.

Chauncy K. Lively's Carpenter Ant (tied by Mike Valla) The author's all-time favorite Oriskany Creek and Chenango Canal pattern during summer is a simple folded deer hair ant. During teenage years, the author carried a sizeable box of Carpenter Ants tucked in the back pouch of his fishing vest. Any fly fisher he might have encountered would receive a few.

Although the Oriskany Creek and its Chenango Canal tributary are vastly different types of water, I've always used the exact same fly pattern for both waters—Chauncey Lively's folded deer hair Carpenter Ant. It's the sole summer fly that I've used on the Oriskany since my teenage years.

The Chenango Canal, a short distance upstream from its terminus at Oriskany Creek, is an interesting slice of water. It's spring creek-like appearance grows beautifully colored wild brown trout. The canal used to produce much larger trout in years past, but the smaller browns typically netted today are just as gorgeous. The stream provides *Tricorythodes* fishing in late summer, along with good terrestrial fly fishing.

I can still recall having a very large plastic bin box; it was so large it occupied the entire back pouch of my vest, with every compartment chock-full of the pattern. If I came upon another Oriskany fly fisher, the box came out, and a few were dropped into waiting hands. Wandering around used book stores in the late 1960s, hunting down fishing books, I came across the *1964 Fisherman's Digest*. An article by Lively described that he originally created the fly for bass fishing but found late-season success with it on the Letort and Young Woman's Creeks in Pennsylvania.

It's a simple 2-minute fly to tie and easy to fish. The only drawback is its lack of sustained durability. The tactic I use is to fish it, in sizes 12 and 14, is to cast upstream along deadfalls and even pocketwater, deliberately creating a wake as it drops to the water. What you don't want to do is crash the entire line tip into the water in an attempt to create the wake from the fly. It takes some practice.

Fishing it on the Canal involves standing patiently along the edge of the water, watching upstream for a dimple rise, marking the spot, then slowly wading forward within casting range. Using 7X on a 12-foot leader, the ant is plopped above the marked area. You can, of course, blind fish the ant—upstream—to obvious trout-holding areas (such as along log jams), the tactic I use on the Oriskany creek itself, including the lower creek areas.

The exception to fishing the Carpenter Ant on the Canal is during last August into September when I visit Chenango canal in anticipation of the Trico hatch. Water that seemed lifeless suddenly comes alive with the dimpling wild browns during the morning, up until about 10:00. It's a good time to spot where the fish are holding. Tricos also emerge downstream on the Oriskany.

The lower Oriskany Creek reaches, below Oriskany Falls, also remain cool during summer months. Driving northerly along State Route 12B will bring you to public fishing access parking areas in the Deansboro/Kirkland area with a formal NYSDEC angling

This wild, beautifully colored Chenango Canal brown trout fell to a Trico pattern. *Tricorythodes* start emerging on the canal during late July into September.

access lot area along Dugway Road. (Dugway Road is located at a right turn where it intersects State Route 12B about 12 miles north of Oriskany Falls.) There's also another NYS parking area where Dugway loops and reconnects with State Route 12B (just a few hundred feet up the road). The area offers some solitude and wide-open casting. The lower sections of the creek are state-stocked waters.

Genegantslet Creek

Genegantslet Creek flows through picturesque, rolling countryside characteristic of many other areas in Central New York. The "Genny," as it is affectionately called, is part of a dendritic complex of small streams that flow south, eventually feeding the Chenango River, a warmwater fishery that weds the upper reaches of the Susquehanna River. Brooks that originate in post-agricultural, large-acreage conifer plantations, created by Depression-era Civilian Conservation Corps activity, contribute water to Genegantslet Creek, transforming it into a splendid fly-fishing destination. NYSDEC categorizes the creek as Stocked, although some wild brown trout and brook trout inhabit the waters.

Wild brown and brook trout inhabit the stream, but it is also stocked annually with around 3,000 to 4,000 browns. The Genny's upper, middle, and lower sections vary in both trout productivity and fly-fishing attractiveness. Three formal public fishing access parking areas are situated along the prime upper and middle sections from McDonough to Smithville Flats.

In its McDonough Township headwaters, the stream eventually widens to a fishable size as it traverses surprisingly secluded areas. Just south of McDonough, along Creek Road, a footpath at the first parking area leads through a verdant stand of mature pine and hemlock to the creek and nice, trouty, bankside glides. There is pleasant fishing along nearly a mile of productive water in this area; other sections, accessible about 2 miles downstream, offer equally good water.

Continuing on Creek Road to State Route 220, then south some 2 miles, delivers you to the Art Lake Road access area. Fishing upstream from the parking area, look for the numerous stream-improvement structures installed decades ago (many are in need of repair, and Trout Unlimited and collaborative groups are addressing these needs).

Genegantslet Creek, a splendid Central New York Region trout stream. A favorite of many Binghamton anglers, the "Genny" has ample fly hatches and willing trout. However, the stream has experienced its ups and downs through the decades and can't match what the author experienced decades ago in his teenage years.

A few miles south on State Route 220, at the second creek bridge crossing, another New York State fishing parking area allows access to the middle sections of the Genny, among the best areas on the creek. Upstream from the State Route 220 bridge is nearly a mile of intriguing Catch and Release water; downstream from the bridge flows another mile of productive and interesting "regular-regulations" water. A view of the creek from the bridge, both upstream and downstream, is deceptive. Trek beyond sight of the road and bridge, into secluded areas, and you will find interesting stream-improvement structures, hemlock-shaded runs, and deep pools.

The lower section of the creek, below Smithville Flats, is not nearly as productive as the upper reaches, where typical peak-season hatches of Blue Quills, Sulphurs, and even larger burrowing mayflies, and caddisflies, entice trout and provide good fishing.

The Genny (tied by Mike Valla)
Tied in the Catskill-style, the Genny dry fly still entices brown trout along the creek's riffles and runs. In *American Trout Stream Insects* (1916), a Catskill region angler wrote, "To name flies after rivers, places or people is provincial, commonplace, and utterly in bad taste." Whether in bad taste or not, this Genny pattern was modeled after an older gentleman's dry fly that was handed to the author and was a similar dry fly on Genegantslet Creek in the early 1970s.

One local dry fly, which I dubbed the Genny, always seems to do well in peak season: the first time I saw this pattern was in the early 1970s, when a kind fly angler, much older than I, came up from the stream to where I had been watching him and handed a couple of the flies to me, saying, "Try these." Remembering his kind gesture, I, too, made a habit of giving away a few flies to fellow anglers. The Genny sports a tail of dark ginger hackle barbs, canted upward; a dubbed body, dark, muddy, yellowish-olive in color, ribbed with small gold oval tinsel; wings of lemon wood duck; and light ginger hackle. Of course, these days, fly anglers use beadhead nymphs, a variety of parachute-style dries, and, in late season, terrestrial patterns worked along the stream-improvement structures.

The little stream has changed greatly since my first encounter with it in my teenage years; I can remember a 20-plus-fish day in 1971. Changed stocking policies, recent extensive and damaging flooding, and other factors have no doubt made such episodes unlikely today. But it is still a nice little creek that will not disappoint anglers, tight line or not.

Steele Creek

The Village of Ilion, located off the Mohawk River, about 3 miles or so from the Village of Herkimer across the river, is no doubt better known for the historic and now-defunct Remington Arms Company than for Steele Creek. The old Remington factory buildings in the town still stand, a reminder of an industry that shaped the village. Steele Creek flows through the village, not far from those remarkable old buildings.

From its headwaters in an unnamed swamp 10 miles south near the hamlet of Cedarville, it drops down through Ilion Gorge, finally flowing through the village flats before its dumps into the Mohawk River. Its elevation changes from around 1,200 feet at the Cedarville area to about 400 feet at its mouth. NYSDEC categorized the stream as Stocked. The tiny stream usually receives a handful of small rainbow trout.

The precipitous drop creates a charming little stream with riffles and runs that follow State Route 51 almost its entire distance. The tumbling stream is perfect for little rainbow trout. Steele Creek isn't a major fly-fishing destination, but it's worthy of fishing if passing near the area on the way to other trout streams. Oriskany Creek or nearby West Canada Creek across the Mohawk are not far away.

Plenty of informal road turnoffs along the shoulders next to the little stream will get anglers on water. In fact, the access is so easy along its flow, aside from a few posted and private areas in its upstream reaches, plenty of anglers enjoy the creek, mostly during spring.

The formal NYSDEC angling parking lot along the stream, upstream from Ilion, is located 2.8 miles south on State Route 51 from the State Route 5S/State Route 51 intersection at the Mohawk River. On the way up State Route 51 to the formal lot marked by a large hanging sign, you'll pass three other informal road shoulder parking areas at 2.1, 2.3, and 2.5 miles. Additional parking areas are located upstream from the NYSDEC lot, at 2.9 miles and 3.0 miles.

Upstream from those easy access road shoulder areas, the stream flows through intermittent posted areas but there are long stretches of unposted stretches. Just be on the lookout for obvious posted water near dwellings. Asking permission to fish is always the best approach when desiring to access private yet unposted waters.

As you continue to drive upstream along State Route 51, you'll pass County Road 16 (Jerusalem Road) on the right side of the road, blocked off with barriers. Herkimer County decided the constant road repairs due to annual flooding of a small brook along

Steele Creek flows some 10 miles north from a swamp near the hamlet of Cedarville, dropping precipitously to the Mohawk River flats, at the Village of Ilion in Herkimer County. (PHOTO VALERIE VALLA)

the road wasn't worth the effort. The road was closed 40 years ago. Any vehicles parked at the blocked off entrance are probably rock and mineral enthusiasts after travertine rocks. The old macadam road is all but washed away. The important thing about the area besides the interesting calcite rocks are the series of springs that exit the shale along the little flow that help cool Steele Creek.

NYSDEC routinely stocks the creek with a few hundred rainbows annually in April. It's presently classified as a stocked inland water. In the past, it was described as a wild trout stream. The creek was recently given "high priority" for fish population sampling by NYSDEC. Steele Creek is a nice place to shed waders and wear hip boots while casting your 3-weight rods.

West Canada Creek

A transitional stream connecting two of New York's regions, West Canada Creek is considered one of New York's best trout streams. Before dumping into the Mohawk River and Erie Canal at Herkimer in Central New York, West Canada traverses nearly 80 miles through three counties from its headwaters in the southern Adirondack Mountain region. After its brief life in the fringes of the Adirondacks, it meanders through downstream farm country where most of its important fly fishing happens. The stream is most noted for its annual *Ephoron* White Fly hatch.

Several decades ago, during my teenage years, my dad and I annually fished the river during very late September, closing out the final days of the formal New York trout fishing season. I had no idea what hatches might have emerged earlier in the season; the stream seemed devoid of emergences when we fished it. It wasn't until years later that I heard of its annual *Ephoron* White Fly hatches that come off the "creek" during August into early September. While a variety of caddis and mayfly hatches add to the stream's charm, its signature blizzard-like White Fly hatch is what it is most known for. However,

Trenton Falls marks the upstream boundary of the Special Regulation Catch and Release section. The Special Regs reach is the most popular stretch on the river, although some mighty big brown trout are landed farther downstream, in the deep pools. West Canada Creek is known for its annual White Fly hatch.

plenty of action can take subsurface along its deep and expansive pools while fishing big muddlers and similar flies.

Other factors besides an impressive fly hatch define and affect West Canada Creek's potential as a great trout stream. Fly anglers and recreational floaters are both at the mercy of Niagara Mohawk Power Corporation. Dramatic water fluctuations caused by dam releases at Trenton Falls and Hinckley dams send anglers to the stream banks. Even the White Fly hatch is impacted.

Danger from rising water signage is posted along the stream. Sirens blast when the water releases are imminent but the safe thing to do is be mindful of rising waters while fishing. The *"Waterline"* online site will provide useful flow rate information. It's very difficult if not impossible to wade the stream when the levels are up, even around 1500-CFS. If I had my choice, the river would be at about 600-800 CFS levels.

More aptly called a big river than a creek, this stream is considered one of New York's premier trout waters. It's stocked annually with several thousand brown trout in the mid and lower reaches along with ample brook trout stockings in its headwaters. With nearly a dozen parking areas along the stream, and several miles of accessible water that includes a 4-mile Special Regulation Catch and Release trophy stretch, there's plenty for fly fishers to explore.

The Special Regulation Catch and Release, artificial-lures-only section—popular among fly fishers, stretches from Trenton Falls downstream 4 miles or so to the first bridge crossing below the mouth of Cincinnati Creek. The lower boundary of the section is about 4.5 miles north from the center of the Village of Poland, on State Route 28. Poland is located about a half-hour drive north on State Route 28 from I-90 (the NYS Thruway) in Herkimer.

Good fishing is located both in the Catch and Release stretch itself as well as along stream reaches downstream, north of Poland. At the State Route 8/State Route 28 intersection in Poland (at the Stewart's convenience store on the corner), drive north on State

West Canada Creek downstream from the Village of Newport. Water levels can rise and fall throughout a 24-hour period, due to Niagara Mohawk Power Corporation releases. It's good practice to check water release schedules before venturing out on the big water. Always carry a wading staff. (PHOTO VALERIE VALLA)

Route 28/State Route 8 about 1.5 miles to a sharp right at a bridge crossing where the road continues at just State Route 28.

Just after crossing the bridge crossing, try the stretch along the large parking area that parallels the stream. It's a good area for fishing the White Fly hatch. Depart the parking area and drive just over 2.5 miles to Gravesville Road/Partridge Hill Road and a bridge crossing at the formal NYSDEC angling parking lot. When the White Fly hatch is on, the lot will be full of enthusiastic fly anglers (we'll get to more on that hatch momentarily).

The stream reach at the NYSDEC parking lot is located about a mile downstream from the Cincinnati Creek mouth and lower Catch and Release boundary. You can reach the upper boundary of the Catch and Release stretch at Trenton Falls by driving another 3.5 miles north on Partridge Hill Road to Dover Road. The dam bridge crossing is on the left.

A footpath at the bridge crossing leads down to a nice riffle and run. Take notice of the sudden water release warning sign as you walk down the short path to the stream. On low water levels, the stony bank makes for pleasant casting and wading. The small parking lot is located on Trenton Falls Road, on the west side of the bridge. Instead of returning downstream via Partridge Hill Road, you can get back to State Route 28 by driving 1 mile down Trenton Falls Road. A short drive south on State Route 28 will get you back to the NYSDEC parking lot and a favorite White Fly hatch location both upstream and downstream from the bridge.

Getting back to the White Fly hatch, I don't know how many times during "White Fly season" I checked the flow level projections at *Waterline*, waiting for the stream to drop below 1000 CFS. White Flies can begin emerging anywhere from early to mid-August into early September at around 7:00 p.m., but high water can delay the action, making wading impossible. The bugs probably wait for lower levels, too.

Something else I experienced about White Flies: they could be emerging in small numbers on a more shaded stream reach and at the same time a white blizzard could be

Large brown trout inhabit West Canada Creek. Some of the largest brown trout are caught out of the deep pools during night fishing. But again, check water release schedules before venturing out on the river in darkness.

starting on another pool more exposed to sunlight. I was on the pool at the long parking area at the State Route 8/State Route 28 bridge crossing area when nothing was happening.

The water levels were not perfect but definitely wadable, and it was late August and about 7:30 p.m.—"White Fly zone" for sure. I stumbled back up to my vehicle mumbling to myself, ready to call it quits. Valerie suggested, as usual, to not reel in but instead have a quick look up at the NYSDEC angling parking lot, just up the road.

The blizzard was just getting started up there. I geared up and threw out a small, short shank Silver Opossum streamer. A big brown grabbed it on the first cast. Other anglers were casting below the bridge, smashing into their faces. It all gave more meaning to the words "ears, nose, and throat." Subsurface flies, such as the Silver Opossum and Tom Baltz's White Fly Emerger, work during White Fly hatches. A White Wulff and a pattern I created years ago called Moose Tail White Fly work well on top.

Of course, West Canada has much more to offer than the White Fly hatch on its upper reaches. Plenty of action is available downstream from Poland as well. My dad preferred the Poland area and downstream below the Village of Newport. I recall one day many years ago during a hard rain my dad insisted on fishing the Poland reach. The water was high, but he waded out anyway and caught a brown before he thought it wise to depart the water.

Driving south from Poland about a mile on State Route 28 you'll pass a large formal NYSDEC angling parking turnout next to a very wide and deep pool. Some huge browns have been yanked out of West Canada's big pools, on the lower stream reaches. John Pitarresi, who devoted more than 40 years to Utica area newspapers as a sports writer, shared a photo with me of a 25-inch, 6-pounder a local friend of his caught on a tadpole fly. The photo of the angler wearing a headlamp, walking out of the deep pool with the fish, is an eye opener. I'm not sure where he caught it, and I didn't ask.

Further downstream, about 1.4 miles south on State Route 28 from Bridge Street in the Village of Newport, a parking turnout next to the stream will get you quickly into

Silver Opossum (tied by Mike Valla) The author's Silver Opossum is fished an hour or so before White Flies begin to emerge on West Canada Creek. The opossum hair behaves well in water, its motion eliciting attention from browns in wait for the emergence. A simple tie, oval silver tinsel forms the body. Red hen or saddle hackle creates the throat. A wad of opossum guard hair and underfur forms the wing. Any streamer hook of choice will work fine.

White Fly Emerger (tied by Tom Baltz) During mid-August into September, fly fishers heading to West Canada Creek should have an ample supply of White Fly patterns, a headlamp, and bug repellant. It's no wonder commercial tier and fishing guide Tom Baltz developed his White Fly Emerger. Tom lives in Boiling Springs, Pennsylvania—limestone stream country. The annual White Fly hatch on his home Yellow Breeches draws many fly fishers to the stream. His interesting emerger is both unique and effective. The abdomen is crafted from Austrailian opossum, ribbed with copper wire. Tom mixes a 50-50 blend of gray squirrel and CDC fibers, with some ice dub flash to form the thorax. Its deer hair head positions the fly exactly where it should ride in the water column.

Moose Tail White Fly (tied by Mike Valla) The author's own creation, the dry fly is tied with white hen hackle tip wings, moose body hair tails, and badger hackle. Wings can also be tied in spent position, for better floating.

water on a nice riffle and run that can be productive. A streamside picnic table is a good place to have lunch or arrange your fishing gear. But again, fishing this reach depends on water levels. This is the stretch you'll want to fish streamers.

About 3 miles downstream from the parking turnout on State Route 28, you'll enter the Village of Middleville. It's a good place to gas-up and grab a sandwich at the corner Stewart's convenience store at the State Route 29 intersection. Once you get downstream of Middleville, you might be more interested in what all the hoopla is about the famous "Herkimer Diamonds." Signs along the road will lead you to the Herkimer Diamond Mine, a resort-type area good for kids and families to "mine" for the big quartz crystals. How I wish my dad would have allowed me to put my rod aside back in those years and let me dig "diamonds" while he fished those very low stream reaches in the area.

Besides White Flies and "diamonds," West Canada Creek offers a few other hatches. A caddis emergence that comes off in July attracts fly fishers to the stream. I've never encountered Green Drakes, but I'm told they also sometimes make an appearance during early June.

My rod of choice is a 9-foot, 5-weight. The West Canada is big water; 6-weight rods are also useful when punching out big streamers into the deep pools. You'll want flies that get down deep during higher water flows, and weighted Matukas are good.

Mohawk River (Upper Trout Section)

Drums along the Mohawk was one of my favorite high school reading selections. The interesting tale surrounding its characters during the American Revolution, centered in the Mohawk River valley, was one of the few book assignments back then that grabbed my attention. Like Walter D. Edmonds's 1936 classic, the river that bears the same name also has interesting history, of a different kind.

In *Tying and Fishing Bucktails and Other Hair Wings* (2016), I described in detail early fly fishers who cast their flies on the river. William E. Scripture Jr., who was, for decades, thought to be the "father" of bucktail flies (an incorrect notion, in his own words), wrote in his unpublished 1954 memoir his experiences fishing "Scripture" bucktails on the upper Mohawk. The river at the hamlet of North Western was a favorite.

Reading about Scripture's forays on the river with Catskill luminary George Parker Holden (1869–1935) and Princeton theologian Henry Van Dyke (1852–1933) was nothing less than captivating. Netting 7-pound brown trout seems also an unlikely notion, but his words were as exciting as Edmonds's, in a fly-fishing context. Scripture, from Rome, New York—a city located in the Mohawk valley where the mighty river contributes water to the New York State Barge Canal (aka Erie Canal)—deserves his place in Mohawk River fly-fishing history.

It's unlikely (but possible) that modern fly fishers will routinely net the multiple-pound brown trout that Scripture described (including brown trout like the 7-pounder netted at North Western), but the Mohawk can still provide a variety of fly-fishing experiences. From trout on the upper to mid-reaches to warmwater species on the lower river, particularly on the canal, there's something for everyone. NYSDEC categorizes the upper Mohawk as Stocked and Stocked-Extended.

Upper Mohawk River at North Western, several miles upstream from the City of Rome. While the lower Mohawk River many miles downstream along the Barge Canal is known as a great smallmouth fishery, trout inhabit its reaches upstream from Rome.

Pixley Falls on Lansing Kill at the Pixley Falls State Park, a 375-acre natural area with hiking trails that follow the stream. (PHOTO VALERIE VALLA)

The upper headwaters in the Adirondack foothills near the Town of Ava where the East and West Branches of the Mohawk receives water from small flowages, including the Lansing Kill. You'll encounter both brown trout and a few brook trout along those reaches and brook trout in Lansing Kill. The river widens after it receives the Lansing Kill along Hillside Road, located 13 miles or so upstream from Rome on State Route 46, the main route that roughly follows the Mohawk all the way downstream to the barge canal.

The midsection that flows from the river's junction with Lansing Kill, downstream past North Western into and out of Delta Reservoir, then through the City of Rome, finally joining the barge canal. The reach downstream from the reservoir is among the most popular brown trout destinations among fly rodders.

Finally, the longest section that includes the barge canal at Rome that carries the Mohawk's waters over 100 miles east through upper Central Region to its terminus at the Hudson River at Cohoes in the Capital Region. This section is prime water for those targeting smallmouth bass, tiger muskies, carp, and northern pike (see Warmwater Fly-fishing section).

The upper Mohawk, along its East Branch in the Town of Ava, receives a small number of brown trout stockings. However, the Rome Fish Hatchery is located about 4 miles north of Rome, ensuring heavier stockings downstream along public easement stretches and ample stockings of brown trout along public access reaches along the river. PFR access is available directly across from the hatchery, on State Route 46, marked by a large NYSDEC hanging sign.

Caddis hatches emerge along most of the mid-upper-river reaches, along with a few Hendricksons and Sulphurs and other mayflies, including *Ephoron* White Flies. If you're looking for substantial blizzard White Fly hatches, head over to West Canada Creek located not all that far from the Mohawk. Streamers and bucktails are favorites on the lower tailrace river below the reservoir. I use a 9-foot, 5-weight rods on the Mohawk below the reservoir and 8-foot, 4-weight rods on the upper reaches. My 7-foot, 4-weight Becker cane rod comes in handy on the Lansing Kill area.

The best way to locate PFR and fishing stocking stretches not only on the upper Mohawk but along the entire river is to use the NYSDEC trout stream tool site, and click on "outdoor" and "inland trout streams." The stream PFR reaches and stocked sections are color coded and highlighted. The site is located at https://gisservices.dec.ny .gov/gis/dil/index.html?cat=WRL.

However, a couple of access points easily found are located at river crossings. You'll want to try the section downstream from Delta Dam located off Golf Course

Scripture Bucktail-C (tied by Mike Valla) One of William H. Scripture Jr.'s bucktail patterns he developed during the early 1900s for fishing the upper Mohawk River, this classic pattern is still effective on the stream's trout reaches. Scripture tied his bucktails on short shank hooks. Red yarn tail tags typify Scriptures bucktails.

Road and located a little over a half-mile north on State Route 46 from the fish hatchery. There's a nice run downstream from the bridge. River Road crossing in North Western, located about 7 miles north of the Golf Road/State Route 46 intersection, is worth a couple casts before heading back on State Route 46 north just over a half-mile to nicer water at the Hillside Road crossing.

On your way to Hillside Road, you'll pass over a small tributary, Stringer Brook, that has PFR. It's a nice little brook to give your 7-foot rod exercise in September. The nice thing about the Hillside Road bridge crossing is the formal NYSDEC angling parking lot located on State Route 46 directly next to the bridge.

Another formal NYSDEC parking lot is on Lansing Kill, a pleasant little tributary stream. From the State Route 46/Hillside Road intersection, a 3.1-mile drive up State Route 46 will deliver you to the nice little parking area. A short footpath leads to an area flooded by beaver activity. Relocate to other stretches upstream at Pixley Falls State Park located another 2.8 miles north of the parking area on State Route 46. A looped hiking trail leads to the falls and stretches downstream.

Adirondack/ Saint Lawrence Region

The Adirondack Mountain region is home to more than 1,500 miles of rivers and an estimated 30,000 miles of brooks and creeks that flow within the Adirondack Park, an area that roughly corresponds to its boundaries. Angling opportunities are limitless, especially when its 2,800 lakes and ponds are added to those numbers.

Many of the lakes, ponds, and streams have been well known to fly anglers for many years. Other waters are lesser known, or possibly unknown to the majority of fly anglers. It's a daunting task—actually, an impossible task—to adequately describe all of my favorites. Some of the tiniest trickles I've wandered along and fished, waters that inhabit wild brook trout, don't even have names.

While there are plenty of stillwater lakes and ponds that inhabit warmwater species (I'll mention a few), it's the remote brook trout ponds that seem to generate the most interest when I bring up the subject of my favorite fly-fishing destinations in the Adirondack region. Of course, not all of my Adirondack fly fishing has been limited to ponds and lakes over the years. Many favorite major rivers have provided equal joy, too.

Thirteenth Lake, gateway to the Siamese Ponds Wilderness Area remote brook trout ponds, is located near North River in Warren County. Because of its easy and direct access by vehicles, it's popular with campers, canoers, hikers, and anglers launching into the remote wilderness waters on extended backpack outings.
(PHOTO VALERIE VALLA)

East Branch of Fish Creek at County Road 46 (Osceola Road) bridge crossing near Swancott Mills. A formal NYSDEC parking area is located at the stream reach. (PHOTO VALERIE VALLA)

East Branch Fish Creek

Like the nearby upper Mohawk River, the East Branch of Fish Creek is also surrounded in fly-fishing history. Bucktail fly guru William E. Scripture Jr. invited fishing guests not only to the Mohawk, but also Fish Creek near Swancott Mills was another favorite stream. George Parker Holden (1869–1935), a significant figure in Catskill region fly-fishing history, described, in his now-classic book *Streamcraft* (1919), Scripture's invitation to fish the East Branch of Fish Creek.

The Swancott Mill stream reach is located upstream from a bridge crossing on County Road 46 (Osceola Road). Just east of the bridge, you'll see a NYSDEC angling access sign on County Road 46. A side road leads off the main road past a dwelling, eventually ending at a parking area just off the stream. You can fish downstream to the bridge through a few runs and riffles with small streamers and bucktails. Incidentally, the relatively newly acquired and managed 14,110-acre East Branch of Fish Creek Conservation Easement Tract is in the area. A large NYSDEC hanging sign that directs visitors to the easement access is located less than a half-mile west of the bridge crossing, at the corner of Gallo Road and Osceola Road. The easement includes the headwaters of the East Branch of Fish Creek and other trout streams.

While exploring the East Branch of Fish Creek in the Swancott area, and also downstream several miles at PFR water located a bridge crossing at the hamlet of Point Rock, you might come across white paper signage posted by Fish Creek Atlantic Salmon Club alerting anglers to the presence of Atlantic salmon in Fish Creek.

The club was started in 1997 with the mission to re-establish Atlantic salmon's historical presence in Fish Creek. Fish Creek originates in the Tug Hill Plateau area, then flows south to Taberg before it redirects itself west, eventually flowing into Oneida Lake. Oneida Lake's waters eventually end up in Lake Ontario. An ambitious group, the club constructed fish hatcheries, raising the Atlantic salmon from eggs. A couple of years ago, because of water flow issues at their hatchery (that ended up being demolished), the club decided to obtain Atlantic salmon fry from the Ed Weed Fish Culture Station in Vermont. Volunteers typically gather in Taberg during late April to coordinate distributing the fry.

The East Branch of Fish Creek, West Branch of Fish Creek, Mad River, and Furnace Creek are stocked. As interesting as the prospect of landing an Atlantic salmon somewhere along the stream and connecting tributaries, anglers target brown trout in the East Branch of Fish Creek downstream in the Annsville and the West Branch at the Village of Camden areas.

West Branch Fish Creek

Nearly 13,000 brown trout are also stocked in the nearby West Branch of Fish Creek along nearly 30 miles of PFR reaches. The bulk of the West Branch stockings occur in the reach between Mill Pond Way in McConnellsville (south of Camden) upstream to the confluence with Thompsons Branch (north of Camden).

NYSDEC lists four formal parking areas in the Oneida County section. No official parking areas exist along the Oswego County stretches (anglers use unofficial parking along roads). The official West Branch PFR section upstream from the Village of Camden at the hamlet of Westvale, categorized as Stocked by NYSDEC, is more of a boat access point into a small impoundment at an impassable dam. Bait and conventional tackle anglers often fish from shore directly above the dam. The stretch downstream from the dam enters a wide, slow-water pool difficult to fly fish during high-water conditions. I prefer two stretches: one unofficial section where fishing is permitted, located in the Village of Camden; and the other located a short distance downstream at the Brewer Road steel-decked bridge crossing located off State Route 69 a couple miles south of Camden.

Alexzander Freywald on the West Branch of Fish Creek, in Camden along the Mechanic Street reach. Mechanic Street stretch is one of the easiest stretches to access water since the stream flows directly next to the road, and parking is easy.

The nice unofficial stretch of riffles that lead to a nice pool is located off Mechanic Street. The reach is also categorized as Stocked. Mechanic Street is located directly across from the large Byrne Dairy convenience store and gas station on Main Street in the village. Parking is available directly at streamside. You'll encounter a quaint little covered bridge over a walkway that leads to Forest Park at the pool that's annually stocked with brown trout. Forest Park is a lovely public town park known for its walking paths and pavilions.

The Brewer Road bridge crossing reach, accessed from either State Route 13 or State Route 69, is located a couple of miles downstream from the village. Fish the run downstream from the bridge with streamers. (No official parking lot exists at this location—park safely on the road shoulder.) An official NYSDEC parking area is located further downstream off Trestle Road at a bridge crossing, about 3 miles south of Camden. Very wide, deep, and often difficult to wade pools are located both downstream and upstream from the bridge. Bait casters fish the big pool below the bridge after trout stockings in spring. The reach is categorized as Stocked.

Siamese Ponds Wilderness Area

The Siamese Ponds Wilderness provides angling experiences for both those seeking single-day outings and those more intrigued with the idea of serious extended-stay backpacking trips to the more remote ponds. In either case, preparation is of paramount importance, especially so for those with meager experience trekking into the backcountry. There are a number of well-marked trails that interconnect all the ponds, some better suited than others depending on individual or group angler plans.

I highly recommend that anglers interested in experiencing fishing the marvelous brook trout ponds to first read *Adirondack Trails: Central Region* (4th Edition of the Forest Preserve series published by the Adirondack Mountain Club). The little book explains all the trails and lean-to shelter locations in the Siamese Ponds Wilderness Area. You'll also want to study the *National Geographic/Adirondack Mountain Club Illustrated Trails Map #736*. Both are indispensable for not only safety reasons but also practical tips concerning access. Day trips are great. But if you're planning an extended fishing jaunt into the Siamese Ponds Wilderness, preparation and safety are primary concerns over what flies to pack and what length rods are best. Many of the trailheads that lead to the most remote ponds have a sign-in kiosk. Make sure you sign in on your intended length of stay, for safety purposes. Rangers often review the log books. It's also important to stay on the marked trails and observe signage and foot trail markers.

Standard backpacking practices are in order, but if you're not an experienced packer or hiker, bone up by consulting experienced wilderness travelers. Weight is everything; pack for the elements and take enough food, but pack as light as possible. As crystalline as the myriad Adirondack brooks and ponds appear, forget drinking directly from them. Girardia and *cryptosporidium* protozoan parasites will give you the worst case of gastrointestinal illness you've ever had. But there's an easy and fast solution. Pick up a Katadyn water filter; they're small, light, easy-to-use, and very effective.

An extended-stay trout expedition to an Adirondack wilderness pond, sleeping if not shivering in a lean-to shelter, is an experience you'll never forget. Fly fishing doesn't get any better than spending a couple of days in the backcountry with good friends, sitting in front of a roaring campfire, and sharing tales and hopes of catching those big, colorful brook trout waiting at our doorstep.

Be sure to sign the log-in book at the kiosk located at trailheads that lead to remote Adirondack waters. Safety is everything when planning a backcountry trip. It's also a good idea to inform others of your destination intention and planned time of return.

Distance signage and trail markers are often encountered along trails into many of the remote ponds and streams. It's best to preplan an outing, and bring a trail map when trekking into wilderness areas. Follow trail markers, and refrain from drifting off said trails.

Trekking into remote ponds for an extended backpacking trip often happens at daybreak. The word is "preplan" and understand exactly where you're heading and the nature of the environment you're heading into. During the particular trip shown in the photo, my fishing partner and I took a wrong turn down in the woods and ended up heading the wrong direction. We had to reverse course to our point of beginning—a half-hour trek back uphill!

The rule most of us follow is to plan the trip around the weakest member of the party (sometimes that happens to be this author). If you're backpacking for a few days to chase those big brook trout with a long rod, you'll need to pay attention. Bears are common, and so are biting insects, such as the dreaded blackflies, which buzz around your face and cause quite an annoyance while you're throwing loops in springtime. Their bites are nasty. You'll run into plenty of mosquitos and deer flies in summer months.

The most effective craft for fishing remote ponds is the lightweight Hornbeck. Backpacks can be bolted to the craft, for trekking long trails into remote ponds.

Hornbeck Boats are Adirondack-crafted Kevlar Craft. They're light and easy to carry, but because of their construction, personal weight limitations can exclude some anglers.

You'll also have to decide what type of floating craft is practical to haul in for ponds not well suited to wade or for bank fishing. Everything from float tubes to small boats to canoes have been hauled in to the ponds. I've fished out of most every floating craft available, but Pete Hornbeck's Adirondack-built lightweight Kevlar "boats" (they look like canoes) are in my opinion indispensable if trekking into the most remote ponds. Hornbecks are so light you can carry one on your shoulder. I mount mine to a metal-frame backpack, which allows me to hike without even putting my hands overhead on the craft itself. My Hornbeck is custom-fitted with oar-locks, ideal for slow-rowing streamers and bucktails.

Various waters in the Siamese Ponds Wilderness Area harbor brown trout, rainbow trout, landlocked salmon, and lake trout as well as a variety of warmwater species. But it's the regions big brook trout that provide the biggest excitement for adventurous anglers. Some ponds and small lakes in the Siamese Ponds Wilderness are remote and difficult to reach, while others, such as those nearby popular Thirteenth Lake, are relatively easy via hiking trails that crisscross the mountains.

A few of the more interesting trout-filled ponds—ponds that require 3- to 6-mile hikes—are reclaimed ponds that were treated with rotenone to eliminate undesirable fish. Waters such as Hour Pond and Peaked Mountain Pond were reclaimed years ago in an effort to improve the fishery on Thirteenth Lake, which is connected to them by tributary streams. The reclaimed ponds were planted with "heritage strain" brook trout that once populated many of the Adirondack ponds.

THIRTEENTH LAKE

Unlike the remote ponds, Thirteenth Lake has drive-in access. It is a gateway location, a jumping-off point for hiking to remote waters such as the aforementioned Peaked Mountain Pond and Hour Pond, as well as Puffer Pond and the very remote Upper and Lower Siamese Ponds. Ready access to Thirteenth Lake assures its popularity; it draws lots of anglers, campers, hikers, picnickers, and day-trippers. A number of campsites are situated along the lake, none of which can be reserved, and a small boat-launch area sits at the head of the lake.

To reach Thirteenth Lake, follow New York State Route 28 to the little hamlet of North River and then go south 3 miles on Thirteenth Lake Road. (At the junction of State Route 28 and Thirteenth Lake Road, watch for the NYSDEC sign directing visitors to the Siamese Ponds Wilderness.) The road begins on the banks of the upper Hudson River, a half-hour drive from Warrensburg, New York.

While Thirteenth Lake's coldwater fishery was reclaimed in the early 1970s with rotenone—ridding the lake of perch, suckers, and baitfish populations—it's not strictly a brook trout fishery. Landlocked salmon, rainbow trout, and brown trout also inhabit the lake. Prior to reclamation, lake trout were also present, but that species no longer lurks in the lake's depths. (Lakers are still found in Lower and Upper Siamese Ponds.)

To rid Thirteenth Lake of undesirable fish species, biologists realized connected waters would also need to be treated with rotenone; it was a substantial undertaking. Vic Sasse, who served as the area's forest ranger prior to his retirement in 1991, recalled the rotenone treatments and what happened in the fishery at that time. I enjoyed a nice chat with him, at his home on Thirteenth Lake Road.

"They tried to kill all the minnows in the adjacent marshlands and brooks. State workers went in with backpacks and applied rotenone to all standing water they could find. But it

Thirteenth Lake near the access entrance. Fly fishing can be enjoyed on Thirteenth Lake itself. Hexagenia mayfly hatches begin mid-late June. Trout can also be taken by slow rowing a canoe, trolling streamers.

wasn't entirely effective to do so anyway. I went in there after the applications and observed baitfish were still present. They made a good effort but it wasn't 100 percent effective."

After Thirteenth Lake was reclaimed, it was stocked with landlocked salmon along with a genetically unique Little Tupper brook trout. The heritage strain brook trout acquired from Little Tupper Lake (another Adirondack water) are direct descendants of the first trout to have reached Little Tupper after glaciers receded about 12,000 years ago. Brown trout and rainbows were stocked in Thirteenth Lake a few years after the brook trout were introduced.

"The fishery blossomed after the lake was reclaimed," Sasse explained. "Brook trout shaped like footballs were routinely caught. One angler took a 26-inch landlocked salmon one week and shortly after took another of similar size. Smelt were also introduced as a food source."

But shortly after this peak, anglers began reporting that the salmon were shaped almost like snakes—big heads and skinny bodies—and the trout exhibited the same nutritional deficiencies. State officials set nets and discovered that suckers had repopulated the lake, affecting the post-rotenone fishery. "By 1979 and 1980, the Thirteenth Lake fishery was done for," Sasse told me.

"The original project to reclaim the lake by removing suckers and perch was supposed to include construction of a fish-barrier dam on Thirteenth Lake Brook, an outflow of the lake that empties into the Hudson River, to keep rough fish out of Thirteenth Lake. But the dam was never constructed because of a last-minute change required by a private landowner who initially approved the barrier on his property. Consequently, suckers simply swam upstream from the Hudson River and repopulated the lake."

Vic is the type of fellow you could sit and talk to all day. His passion for conservation is captivating, and his recollections of his years protecting the matchless natural resource in the Siamese Ponds Wilderness Area made for a most enjoyable visit. His tenure as a ranger, which began in the 1960s, provided him with a perspective that few have; his Siamese Ponds Wilderness Area stories are fascinating tales.

I moved to the edge of my chair when Vic continued his Thirteenth Lake story. In reaction to the health decline in the trout and landlocked salmon population, state biologists introduced seeforellen strain brown trout to help knock down the sucker population. The seeforellen browns, a deep-water lake strain originating in Western Europe, feed heavily on forage fish and grow to monster sizes. "Evidently the plan worked because the fishery recovered," Vic said. But today, the Thirteenth Lake receives annual stockings of regular hatchery-strain browns and landlocked salmon, not the voracious seeforellens.

Brown trout are great surface feeders on Thirteenth Lake, especially during a two-week period at the end of June when the annual *Hexagenia* hatch begins. It's the one hatch that Thirteenth Lake regulars look forward to every year. These large mayflies primarily begin hatching in late evening or even after dark, but I've seen a few of them fluttering off the water in the late afternoon. Some anglers don't fish the water during an emergence until after 10:00 p.m., when, on a calm night, you can hear fish slapping the water while feeding on the inch-and-a-half-long insects.

To effectively fish the June *Hexagenia* hatch, it's best to cast from a canoe and use big dry flies, such as Wulff patterns. If fishing near dark, I like to cast what fly tier Ralph Graves called a Big Fish Fly, mainly because I can spot the yellow hair wings in last-light (the yellow color doesn't seem to deter strikes).

However, in the spring, just after ice-out, trolling streamers and other large sinking patterns out of a canoe is perhaps the deadliest tactic. Row slowly along the shoreline

Black Leech (tied by Ed Ostapczuk) One of Ed Ostapczuk's favorite patterns he now fishes extensively on his home Catskill streams was first created for Adirondack waters like Thirteenth Lake. Ed once owned a camp on neighboring Indian Lake at the time he first tied his leech.

Nine-Three Streamer (tied by Mike Valla) The classic Nine-Three is a good trolling streamer on Thirteenth Lake. Dr. Herbert, of Waterville, Maine, created the fly to imitate smelt. He landed a 9-pound, 3-ounce salmon on the fly, hence its name.

Big Fish Fly (tied by Ralph Graves) Ralph Graves, a noted Catskill fly tier, created this pattern for late-evening fishing at times he was targeting big fish on rivers like the Beaver Kill. It's a good choice while fishing *Hexagenia* hatches on Thirteenth Lake. Tie the fly on most any long shank hook. The wings and tail are dyed yellow calf tail or goat hair. Orange fur or synthetic yarn dubbing body is palmered with dyed yellow grizzly.

using a sinking-tip line. Classic patterns, such as the Green Ghost, Gray Ghost, and Nine-Three, work well, along with the iconic Muddler Minnow. My friend Ed Ostapczuk developed his highly effective Black Leech pattern for fishing Thirteenth Lake during the mid-1980s, during the time he owned an Adirondack camp on nearby Indian Lake.

PEAKED MOUNTAIN POND

A reclaimed water, Peaked Mountain Pond is a favorite and holds some handsome brook trout. A well-marked trail, beginning at Thirteenth Lake, takes you there. You can fish Thirteenth Lake as a day trip, but it's also a beautiful place to camp on an extended visit—worthy of photographers and painters, as well as fly anglers. Primitive Adirondack lean-to shelters are found on some ponds in the Siamese Ponds Wilderness Area, but unfortunately not at Peaked Mountain Pond. However, there's a nice camping spot in the corner of a little bay, an idyllic place to pitch your tent.

Peaked Mountain Pond is not kind to wading anglers; the only effective way to fish the pond is with a floating vessel. A friend of mine, and Adirondack native and probably one of the most accomplished local brook trout anglers, who frequently fishes the region's ponds, was crazy enough to carry in a small boat years ago, all the way up a steep mountain to the pond. But that's a tough task.

If you carry in a canoe (make sure it's a lightweight model), nearly a mile of hiking along a rocky section of the trail that hugs the western shore of Thirteenth Lake can be eliminated. You can row or paddle your craft down the shoreline to the mouth

Peaked Mountain Pond, with its namesake mountain. A long trek uphill from Thirteenth Lake will deliver you to one of the most beautiful of Siamese Ponds Wilderness Area brook trout ponds. You're likely to encounter more hikers than anglers at the pond. (PHOTO VALERIE VALLA)

of Peaked Mountain Brook, where you can pick up the trail to the pond as it turns west from the lake.

One of several designated campsites along Thirteenth Lake, campsite number 9, is near the mouth of Peaked Mountain Brook and the trail that heads up the mountain to the pond. It's a gorgeous location—it overlooks Thirteenth Lake—and makes a good base camp for an overnight stay before resuming your trek up the mountain, early the next morning. The trail rises a few hundred feet in elevation along the 2.8 additional miles to the pond. When you arrive at the pond, after skirting a couple of vleis and admiring beaver activity, you'll thank yourself for making the trip.

Peaked Mountain Pond, overlooked by 2,919-foot Peaked Mountain, is a Special Regulations fishery. Only artificial lures are allowed. I've seen more hikers up there than anglers because of the no-bait rule. Sometimes the pond swarms with bugs and not a single fish rises. But there are other times the water boils with feeding brookies. Sasse once encountered such a feeding frenzy years ago. "I took a young fellow up to Peaked once

Little Brook Trout (tied by Mike Valla) Peaked Mountain Pond brook trout are not particularly fussy when it comes to fly patterns cast or trolled. The colorful Little Brook Trout, part of his "Little Trout" series, was created years ago by Sam Slaymaker II, of Lancaster, Pennsylvania (1923–1989). It's a good trolling choice.

whose grandfather I played golf with. I never saw surface action like he had that spring day," he recalled. "Some 30 trout were caught and released, all taken with surface flies."

Sasse knows he lucked into an unusual experience; more often, trolling subsurface patterns such as classic Little Brook Trout bucktail or a Mickey Finn brings brookies to the net. But it's hard to beat the thrill of catching one of the pond's 2-pound brook trout on a dry fly—if you hit it right. The same situation holds for the other ponds in the Siamese Ponds Wilderness Area—Hour Pond, Puffer Pond, and the Siamese Ponds.

A canoe is the best craft to use on Peaked Mountain Pond to adequately fish the entire extent of the pond shoreline. I've used float tubes, too. The problem with float tubes is you'll get blown around the water, and it's sometimes difficult to stay in a place where fish might be feeding.

HOUR POND

The best way to reach Hour Pond is to drive south on Old Farm Road along the east side of Thirteenth Lake to the signed trailhead at Old Farm Clearing. The trail registry, with

The lean-to shelter at Hour Pond. Unlike Peaked Mountain Pond, an Adirondack lean-to shelter is situated near its shore. The shelter makes extended fishing trips into Hour Pond more enjoyable.

Colorful brook trout inhabit Hour Pond.

Hour Pond, deep in the Siamese Ponds Wilderness Area. The 4-mile trek into Hour Pond is long yet pleasant. Hour Pond offers limited wade-fishing. To thoroughly fish the pond, take in a canoe or float tube, but it's a long trek to get to that water. Use the same fishing technique that is effective on Peaked Mountain Pond, but if you're planning on wade-fishing, it's best to sample the water during early spring and early fall when the fish are closer to shore. Use a shooting taper line and patterns such as Little Brook Trout bucktails or Muddler Minnows. (PHOTO VALERIE VALLA)

additional information concerning hiking distances to the pond, is found just beyond the stone barrier. The 4.3-mile trek passes through a magnificent spruce tree plantation before eventually following a tumbling brook that will capture your imagination. You'll notice old stone foundations half-hidden among the trees, evidence that the area was once farmed (in the 1800s). And during the spring, you'll be greeted by trout lilies, red trilliums, and painted trilliums that grow along the trail.

Hour Pond offers something that's missing at Peaked Mountain Pond: a lean-to shelter. An Adirondack lean-to shelter has always been a welcome sight for weary hikers and backwoods anglers. You can't reserve a lean-to, and you can't claim exclusive rights to one, even if it's unoccupied upon your arrival. Sometimes it's fun to join others who are using the shelter and already have a nice campfire burning, ready to welcome new arrivals. But most of the time, you'll have it to yourself.

PUFFER POND

Adventurist fly fishers can access Puffer Pond via a few different trails. While trekking to Peaked Mountain Pond, you'll come across a branch trail that leads to Puffer Pond, but that route requires over 4 more miles of additional hiking, more appropriate for an extended backpacking trip into the wilderness area. A much closer 2.4-mile trek to Puffer Pond exists via the King's Flow trailhead located at Chimney Bluffs.

I've used the King's Flow trailhead at different times of the year—early spring, summer, and fall. I most remember fighting an icy trail in April and swatting annoying deer flies buzzing around my head during July. Late September provides a most satisfying angling experience, when the trout begin to swim closer to the shoreline. The brook trout go deep during the summer and are more difficult to entice.

To reach the trailhead, drive west along State Route 28 past the Thirteenth Lake Road intersection another 9 miles to County Road 18 then to Big Brook Road. You'll eventually reach a private for-rent Cabins at Chimney Mountain area. A small entrance fee ($5) allows hikers to park at the trailhead area. There's a simple payment box at the grass lot where visitors can slip in a $5 bill, and then continue on the trek. You'll often see more vehicles parked there by visitors who intend to hike Chimney Bluffs and not Puffer Pond. Directional signage exists near the privies located at the trailhead.

The beginning section of the trail to Puffer runs through private yet accessible lands. After a short, pleasant trek, you'll encounter NYS Forest Lands Wilderness signage along the trail that marks the entrance into public lands. The trail is well-marked with small, circular yellow markers that keep hikers and anglers heading in the right direction to the pond.

The first half-mile or so of the trail provides an easy hike past a beaver flow. The trail soon starts an ascent up the mountain, and there's where the pain begins for out-of-shape anglers. The trail, often muddy, rises through washed-out grapefruit- and larger size rocks—ankle-sprain territory for sure, so be careful. You'll need a walking stick or use a wading staff. There will be plenty of huffing and puffing on your way up the mountain to Puffer Pond, for quite a distance. During rainy periods, you'll hike across small brooks and water runoff that cross the trail.

Eventually, you'll reach a good place to rest your weary legs by sitting on a large, 30-inch-diameter fallen sugar maple at a trail intersection marked by encouraging signage nailed to a tree that informs hikers they have 0.8 mile remaining to reach the pond. Stay on the trail clearly marked by the circular red trail markers. (Another trail that leads 3.2

Puffer Pond during early fall is a good time to net brook trout. Brook trout are active close to the shoreline during spring, but fall outings are much more enjoyable, given the fall foliage scenery.

Yellow-Spotted Salamander (tied by Mike Valla) Yellow-Spotted Salamanders frequent vernal ponds during spring breeding season. Vernal ponds are considered wet lands that mostly dry up during summer. However, for whatever reason, Yellow-Spotted Salamanders sometimes wander into connected larger ponds. Some Adirondack fly anglers consider the spotted creatures the first hatch.

Brook trout smack Yellow-Spotted Salamander flies in early spring. Whether Yellow-Spotted Salamanders reach a trout pond or not, wandering from vernal pond habitat during breeding, the fly that the author created to suggest that animal still elicits strikes during spring brook trout pond fishing.

Yellow-Spotted Salamander (*Ambystoma maculatum*) is considered a mole salamander; they spend most of their time underground but wander out to their vernal pond breeding areas.

miles to Johns Pond, marked with blue trail markers, leads to the left at the intersection.) The trail again resumes another fairly steep ascent (your puffing isn't over yet) along more washed-out rocks.

Just about the time you're wondering if you'll ever get to the pond, more sunlight begins to show through the tree line, and you've arrived at Puffer Pond. An Adirondack lean-to shelter, one of two on the pond, is situated where the trail meets the pond. The trail continues to the left and to the right along the pond. Another lean-to shelter, my favorite, can be reached by taking the trail to the left, located several hundred feet up the shoreline (it's in need of repair but still very useable and functional).

I've attempted to fish the pond without a watercraft, but it's next to impossible to sample the water that way. Again, a floating craft is required. The last time I visited the pond, I admired an angler rowing a metal canoe along the shoreline. It's a tough trek in with a watercraft other than a light Hornbeck boat, but it can be done. As is true with other area brook trout ponds, Puffer is best fished by slow trolling bucktails and streamers along the shoreline just after ice-out and again in the early fall. Yellow-Spotted Salamander flies are a good choice in early spring, when the creatures sometimes wander in from vernal ponds.

SIAMESE PONDS

Upper and Lower Siamese Ponds are more known for their rainbow trout than brook trout. While Thirteenth Lake trails eventually connect with the upper and lower ponds, these two waters are better accessed from the trailhead along State Route 8 at the tiny hamlet of Bakers Mills (5 miles south of the intersection of State Route 28 and State Route 8 at Weavertown; a large trailhead sign labeled "ELEVENTH MOUNTAIN/SIAMESE PONDS" is easy to locate at a parking turnout on State Route 8. You'll find a lean-to shelter along the East Branch of the Sacandaga River 4 miles up the trail from the State Route 8 turnout. It's another 2 miles to the ponds; the long trek is suited for an extended backpack trip and not a day hike for sure.

OTHER BROOK TROUT PONDS AND LAKES IN SIAMESE PONDS WILDERNESS AREA (SOURCE: NYSDEC)

- John Pond
- Clear Pond
- Indian Lake
- John Mack Pond
- Long Pond
- Mud Pond
- Second Pond

Mill Creek

More than one "Mill Creek" flows in New York; this one is a small, brook-like tributary of the upper Hudson River, located in the Wevertown/Johnsburg area about 15 miles or so northeast of Warrensburg. It's not a major fly-fishing destination but worth a quick look on the way to the Thirteenth Lake/Siamese Ponds Wilderness area, on State Route 28. You'll pass over Mill Creek at a State Route 28 bridge crossing in Wevertown, located about 10 miles south of the State Route 28/Thirteenth Lake Road intersection.

The best fly fishing is upstream from the intersection, although PFR water also exists downstream from the intersection along Heath Road. While a few wild brook trout inhabit

Mill Creek along the Millwood Road section. Mill Creek receives brook trout stockings from the Warren County Fish Hatchery. Stocked brown trout also inhabit the stream. (PHOTO VALERIE VALLA)

the difficult-to-fly-fish upper reaches of the stream, south of Johnsburg, Mill Creek is dependent on hatchery trout stockings. NYSDEC takes care of stocking less than a thousand brown trout in the lower sections. The Warren County Fish Hatchery stocks over a thousand brook trout up in the headwaters at the Hudson Street/Cleveland Road sections, at formal NYSDEC parking areas. NYSDEC categorizes the stream as Stocked.

My job first brought me to the little Adirondack creek. Over many years, I provided exams annually, for kids at Head Start, at the program's facility in the little town of Johnsburg, located on Johnsburg Road. It's located walking distance to a Mill Creek bridge crossing. Naturally, I always throw a few casts before heading back to Glens Falls Hospital, after a day's work. The section I always fished and still sample today are the PFR reaches, along Millwood Road, and upstream a couple of miles along Hudson Street.

From the State Route 28/State Route 8 intersection in Wevertown, drive south on State Route 8. In 0.8 mile, take a left on Washer Hill Road, a dirt road to Millwood Road. Cross the one-lane bridge that spans Mill Creek. In about a half-mile up the Millwood Road (a bumpy gravel road), you'll run into NYSDEC public fishing signage and a nice PFR section. Continue up the road another tenth of a mile to a section along the road shoulder where you can park. A short path leads directly to the stream that tumbles through interesting pocketwater. Pocketwater along that reach is best fished with small nymphs. The stretch isn't loaded with fish, but it provides a nice, off-the-road location to sample the stream. Millwood Road continues along the stream a short distance until in intersects South Johnsburg Road next to a bridge crossing.

The Hudson Street access site, stocked with brook trout by the Warren County Fish hatchery, can be accessed by relocating to a formal NYSDEC parking lot 3 miles or so from the Millwood Road/South Johnsburg Road intersection. From the intersection, turn left and drive 0.7 mile to a right on Hudson Street. The parking lot is on the left 2.3 miles from the intersection. A small brook that flows under a small bridge next to the parking lot flows a short distance to its confluence with Mill Creek. You won't see the creek from the parking lot. Access the creek via a wide path located just east of the parking area that leads to an old dilapidated structure. The creek comes into view there. Small nymphs and Elk Hair dry flies fished through the runs are effective.

The uppermost PFR stretches located upstream are not particularly conducive to fly fishing. The sections are heavily shrouded with alders and brush. The first formal NYS-DEC parking lot along the headwater reach is easily accessed by driving 0.7 mile from the previous parking lot on Hudson Street to a left on Garnet Lake Road at the cemetery. The formal NYSDEC stream access lot, marked by a large hanging sign, is located 1.7 miles up Garnet Lake Road. A footpath along a page-wire fence leads to the creek and a very large, slow-moving, usually impossible to wade pool created by beaver activity. It's best to bypass this stretch to another formal parking lot access point and stocked section upstream 0.6 mile farther up the road. Wading and fly casting are also difficult on this reach, but it's an improvement over the one downstream.

Upper Hudson River

NYSDEC and the Warren County Fish Hatchery stocks brown trout and rainbow trout in the Upper Hudson River downstream from the Thirteenth Lake Brook outlet, along State Route 28, at the North River area. The Warren County Hatchery also stocks brook trout in the reach a mile downstream from the outlet, in early fall. Providing water levels are conducive to fly fishing, May and again in the fall are the best times to fly fish the scenic upper Hudson River.

I've netted browns upstream from the outlet and rainbows in the riffles and runs downstream. Parking is available directly next to the river at road shoulder turnouts along State Route 28 and at the Thirteenth Lake Brook bridge crossing. Access is very easy. You're more likely to run into recreational river raft and canoe folks than fly anglers during June through summer.

Upper Hudson River stretch, just downstream from Thirteenth Lake Brook outlet.

The river can warm a bit during summer and tends not to be as productive. I've experienced more than a few blank days once July rolls around. Fish Elk Hair Caddis dry flies along the stretch upstream from the brook outlet and streamers through the runs downstream.

West Canada Wilderness Area

Other wilderness areas are located in the area, such as the West Canada Wilderness area. Separated from the Siamese Ponds Wilderness Area by 12-mile-long Indian Lake in its northern aspect, the West Canada Lake Wilderness Area provides some of the most remote outdoor activity in New York's Adirondack Mountains. Experienced wilderness hikers backpack the Northville-Placid trail (NPT) that runs from the south at the Village of Northville some 139 miles north through the heart of the Adirondacks to the Village of Lake Placid.

The sometimes-grueling-yet-inspiring trail passes by beaver swales and through timberlands. Everything from larger streams to small brooks are encountered along the route. In some sections, the trail often dips into mucky, rocky messes before it climbs up hills and mountains that rise above the lowlands. It's truly an area in New York where a visitor can feel one with nature.

Wilderness brook trout ponds can be accessed along the NPT, as it's usually called. These include ponds such as Cat Lake, Cedar Lakes, Kings Pond, and West Lake. Side trails such as the French Louie Trail can get hikers and anglers into Pillsbury Lake and Sampson Lake. And if that's not enough, dozens of brook trout ponds are scattered throughout the wilderness area that can only be accessed by bushwhacking off trails—not something for an inexperienced fly angler to attempt.

SPRUCE LAKE

One of the ponds that I've come to love is Spruce Lake (more of a large pond). Besides the brook trout that can run several pounds in size, there are the loon calls at night that

Sharing a lean-to with my buddies Terry "Tuck" Tucker and Bill Altman at the north end of Spruce Lake. An extended Adirondack wilderness ponds outing is greatly enhanced with fishing companions. There's nothing better than sitting next to a campfire at a lean-to with fishing buddies, solving the days angling challenges or reveling in the days brook trout netting success.

Spruce Lake is a great remote, brook trout pond destination. A watercraft is a must to effectively cover water.

help calm the mind from life's stresses that exist back in the real world. I've been back there during spring, just after ice-out, and again in early fall, when spectacular fall foliage provides the backdrop as I paddle or row my Hornbeck through the waters.

Early spring and mid-late September are the most important periods to have the best chance of netting a brook trout. During summer, the fish hang deep. And you're more likely to have NPT hikers desiring a lean-to stayover. As mentioned, no one has exclusive use of the shelters, and any tired NPT backpacker who wanders through has the same right to use the same lean-to (not that it's a bad thing).

For some, the trouble getting back in there isn't worth the effort. For me, it's never been just about the fish. Some of the happiest times I've had fishing were the times I shared a lean-to shelter at Spruce with by buddies Terry Tucker and Bill Altman, two born-and-raised Adirondack brook trout anglers. However, anglers interested in fishing Spruce Lake need not hike the strenuous 9 miles up the NPT from a trailhead access point located at the north end of Piseco Lake.

A better route that cuts off a lot of trekking is via the Jessup River Road, a rocky, gravel, sometimes muddy, rut-filled, and often not-well-maintained road that runs through the Perkins Clearing Easement, a private timber logging tract. Expect to encounter logging skidders or trucks. Jessup Road and Perkins Clearing is located just short of 3 miles north on State Route 30 from the State Route 30/State Route 8 intersection in Speculator. You'll encounter signage that indicates the 7.3 miles of driving on Jessup Road that will deliver you to a NYSDEC trailhead parking area. A four-wheel drive vehicle is almost always required, but there are times a regular vehicle can get you back into the area.

As I do while getting into other remote ponds, my metal-frame backpack is bolted to the Hornbeck canoe, and off I go with the craft riding over my head, leaving my hands free to negotiate the trails with my wading staff. You can, of course, carry in a light canoe. You'll want to wear a good pair of waterproof backpacking boots, as the trails are usually muddy. (Follow all the safety precautions previously discussed.)

A trail will lead from the parking area. Make sure you stay on the first part of the trail. On one occasion, we made the mistake, in darkness with headlamps on, of veering off in the wrong direction. Not a pleasant discovery having to reverse course uphill, to get back on the trail after a half-hour into what would be a long trek to begin with.

After about 1 mile, the trail finally meets the NPT that heads south to Piseco or north to Spruce Lake. The trail is often very muddy; I wear a good pair of waterproof backpacking boots. Make sure you head *right* on the trail to Spruce Lake, not the left at the junction. An experienced Adirondack buddy of ours who was scheduled to meet up with us the next day never showed up. He had made previous trips into Spruce Lake but didn't pay attention—he went to the left at the NPT junction and ended up at Piseco Lake! Once you hit the NPT, you'll arrive at Spruce Lake at lean-to #1 at the south end, one of three lean-to shelters well-separated along the east shoreline.

The best lean-to is #3, at the north end of the lake, but #2 in the middle is okay. Get into the lake, and row or paddle your craft up the shoreline. Troll streamers using S-curves

This Spruce Lake brook trout was netted just after ice-out, trolling a Shushan Postmaster bucktail along the shoreline. Brook trout cruise close to shore during spring.

Southern Redbelly Dace (tied by Mike Valla) Southern Redbelly Dace bucktails are also effective trolling flies on Spruce Lake.

along the way, up to the north end. On one trip, I barely got my streamer into the water while on my way to lean-to #3 when nice brookie slammed it. Great way to begin an extended stay into Spruce Lake.

The streamer patterns that work well are the Shushan Postmaster and Southern Red-belly Dace. Yellow-Spotted Salamander patterns are also effective during early spring (see Puffer Pond section). A 9-foot, 6-weight fly rod on Spruce Lake, fitted with a sinking-tip line and 3X tippet is a good gear choice.

The *National Geographic/Adirondack Mountain Club Illustrated Trails Map #736* (Northville-Placid Trail) and its companion, Adirondack Mountain Club's *Northville-Placid* book (5th Edition), are very useful.

Saranac Lake Wild Forest Region/Saint Regis Canoe Area

Saranac Lakes Wild Forest, part of New York's extensive Adirondack Forest Preserve lands, is chock full of some 144 small ponds to larger lakes in its 75,000 acres. Both cold-water species and warmwater species provide fly anglers a variety of experiences. Some ponds, such as Lake Colby, are located right smack next to a major village. Anglers can be on water within minutes of launching a floating craft. Other water bodies are remote and require more time and effort to access.

The same can be said of the Saint Regis Canoe Area. However, many fly anglers fish the expansive 18,400-acre regulated pond and lake-filled area. Anglers visit the region largely for one target: brook trout in a wilderness setting accessed by paddling or rowing canoes moderately long distances across various remote ponds that are interconnected with portaging trails.

The 1,800-acre Saint Regis Canoe Area is the only designated canoe area in New York State. Unconfined paddling opportunities, along with its many remote ponds, attracts both adventurists seeking wilderness camping experiences and anglers who target brook trout fishing.

LAKE COLBY

In *Tying and Fishing Bucktails and Other Hair Wings* (2016), I told the story how our small groups of Cornell University fisheries students were en route to sample brook trout populations and water chemistry on several ponds in the Adirondacks. My faculty advisor, Professor Dwight A. Webster, was heavily involved since the 1950s studying brook trout strains and hybrids that might better withstand the acidic conditions on many Adirondack ponds. (Webster's research formed the core of what would eventually become the Adirondack Fisheries Program, which is headquartered at the Little Moose Field Station near Old Forge in the southwestern Adirondacks.)

We arrived at Lake Colby in the afternoon during late September in 1974, escorted by Cornell staffer Dr. Carl Scofield, as a stay-over location. We were not sampling that particular pond but merely needed a place to bunk down for the evening before we continued on our way the following morning to meet up with Webster at another lake.

The ramshackle shed at a NYS environmental camp closed for the season was the perfect place for us to roll out our sleeping bags for the night. Dr. Scofield, a principal investigator in 1972, discovered it was acid rain that was making many Adirondack waters uninhabitable for brook trout. Before we all found a rustic yet cozy corner to sleep in the rustic accommodation (including Dr. Scofield), someone came up with an idea to catch trout for dinner. We were all anglers, not just students, and had brought along our gear.

Classmate Bob Wilberding and others were busy on shore catching brook trout under a dock. Dave Bornholdt found an unsecured canoe, and we both paddled across the pond to the far shore. It wasn't long before I caught a large brown trout that smacked a bucktail streamer, a fly I named, years later, Bornholdt Golden Squirrel. We all convened around a campfire, dining on fresh trout. Someone must have located a frying pan. I don't recall bringing along or finding any dinnerware, yet we managed.

Almost to the day, in late September 2021, I revisited Lake Colby in hopes of repeating the success I experienced that was approaching 50 years ago. I didn't find an unsecured

Lake Colby, located just north of the village of Saranac Lake. Its 286 acres provides fly fishing for a variety of species. Brown trout, rainbow trout, landlocked salmon, smallmouth bass, and largemouth bass swim in its waters. Boats are allowed, but a 10-hp motor limit is strictly enforced.

A Lake Colby landlocked salmon taken hammered this Honey Blonde bucktail during late fall.

Honey Blonde (tied by Ralph Graves) A pattern from the Blonde series created by Joe Brooks (1901–1972), Honey Blondes interest many fish, including landlocked salmon.

Bornholdt Golden Squirrel (tied by Mike Valla) Named for the author's Cornell University fisheries major classmate Dave Bornholdt, the pattern was originally tied on the Mustad 79666 keel model hook. It's tied with the hook bend pointed up. Mustad's keel hook is now unavailable. Aside from bending a Mustad 79580 streamer hook into a keel shape, try the Varivus 2510WB keel streamer hook.

canoe and didn't bring along a watercraft so the only alternative was to wade fish. It was a pretty windy day, and I wouldn't have launched a canoe, anyway.

The DEC Education Camp area isn't open to the public. However, a DEC boat launch area and large parking lot is located off State Route 86, identified by large hanging signage along the road. It's easy to wade out from shore along the sandy bottom. Within a few minutes of casting, a nice landlocked salmon slammed a Honey Blonde bucktail streamer no more than 30 feet from shore. Brown trout and rainbow trout also inhabit the lake.

MOUNTAIN POND

Fly anglers visiting the Saranac Lake region, or other popular fishing ponds at the Saint Regis Canoe Area, should consider fly fishing Mountain Pond if they have a canoe or floating craft with them. It's tough to wade fish, given the pond's mucky bottom, but there are times and places when the trout are close to shore where it can be done. However, a floating craft is almost a necessity. Mountain Pond is a reclaimed pond, under special fishing regulations. It's managed as Catch and Release, artificial lures only.

Mountain Pond is a reclaimed pond off State Route 30, a couple miles north the State Route 30/State Route 86 intersection in Paul Smiths. A unique water, the pond inhabits heritage Windfall Strain brook trout. (PHOTO VALERIE VALLA)

Mountain Pond is located about 2.5 miles north on State Route 30 from the State Route 30/State Route 86 intersection in the hamlet of Paul Smiths. A NYSDEC hanging sign is at the pot-holed dirt road entrance into the pond area. It's possible to get to the pond with a regular car, but four-wheel drive vehicles will serve you better to get to one of several primitive campsites along the pond. A regular sedan will get to the first campsite, right on the pond, without too much problem.

If you hook into a brook trout, it will be a heritage Windfall strain, one of several heritage strains that inhabit Adirondack waters. Only a small percentage will be wild fish; almost all are stocked and fin clipped for identification purposes. The deeper water is at the north end; the south end is shallower. You'll want to fish the deeper end right after ice-out, trolling or casting small streamers. During the fall, the brookies that can approach 20 inches are likely to be more distributed along the shoreline, into the south end.

BLACK POND

Black Pond, located on the northeast border of the Saint Regis Canoe Area, is a brook trout destination easily accessed. Reach the small pond by driving down Keese Mills Road in Paul Smiths, off State Route 30. A small parking area is located right next to the pond at the Paul Smith's College Day Use Recreation Area, identified by a large hanging sign. A canoe can be quickly launched into the pond. Brown trout also inhabit the pond. Signage asks that anglers considering removing them if caught, to inhibit competition with established brook trout populations.

Within sight of Black Pond on Keese Mills Road, NYSDEC signage identifies the trailhead to Saint Regis Mountain, a popular hiking destination. A great view of much of the Saint Regis Canoe Area can be viewed from the summit. Canoes can be launched from a pull-off across the outlet brook from the large parking area trailhead, but much better launching areas exist to get anglers into the heart of the Saint Regis Canoe Area and into brook trout fishing.

Black Pond, at Paul Smiths, is a very easy pond to launch a canoe. Parking is available on-site.

LITTLE CLEAR POND/LITTLE GREEN POND

These two gems, located near the NYS Adirondack Fish Hatchery off State Route 30, are totally off-limits to fishing. Both serve as salmonid brood stock waters for the hatchery, including landlocked salmon. Don't be tempted to cast a line; the ponds are routinely patrolled. They're located about 10 miles south of Paul Smiths and about the same distance north of the State Route 30/County Road 45 intersection. The two ponds sit side by side in a very picturesque setting. However, they are worth mentioning for two reasons.

Little Clear Pond, like Little Green Pond, are off-limits to fishing, but they are mentioned here because they can serve as canoe launch sites that will deliver anglers to other fishable ponds.

Twelve camping sites are available on Little Green Pond (campsite #6 is very nice). Paddling your craft across Little Clear Pond will lead into the formal Saint Regis Canoe Area, and portages between numerous ponds provide brook trout fishing opportunities. Paddle your craft from the launch parking area on Little Clear Pond to its far end. Portages will provide access into Saint Regis Pond and Green Pond.

From Green Pond, portages will get you into Little Long Pond and Bear Pond—the ponds located along the eastern aspect of the Saint Regis Canoe Area. Numbered campsites exist around those ponds. Numbered campsites also exist around Saint Regis Pond, a good launching base to fish ponds, such as Orche Pond, Mud Pond, Fish Pond, Little Long Pond, Lydia Pond, and others located in the remote northwesterly aspect of the Saint Regis Canoe Area.

SAINT REGIS CANOE AREA PONDS: OTHER ACCESS POINTS

However, other canoe launch sites that can provide access to the northwesterly part of the Saint Regis Canoe Area and its remote ponds exist along Floodwood Road, located about 7 miles south down State Route 30 from the County Road 18/Fish Hatchery Road intersection. Floodwood Road can be accessed at its intersection with County Road 46/State Route 30. (It's located about 0.6 mile south from the Santa Clara Town Office Building that's located on State Route 30 and 0.3 mile south of the Saranac Golf Club sign.) You'll see a golf course very near Floodwood Road.

Drive down Floodwood Road 4.2 miles to the end, at a parking lot and Long Pond canoe launch site. The road is paved for its first mile but then continues as a well-maintained gravel road. A hundred feet or so after the road turns to gravel, you'll encounter a canoe-carry sign posted on a tree on the right side of the road. The portage will lead to Hoell Pond. Hoell Pond (part of the Saranac Wild Forest) borders the Saint Regis Canoe Area; it's another gateway water that leads into the Canoe Area and its ponds.

Many of the remote ponds can be accessed by paddling up Long Pond, then portaging. Numerous camping sites are located around Long Pond, providing good base camps for outings to the most remote trout ponds that lie to the north. I highly recommend anglers stop in at Saint Regis Outfitters, located next to the parking area that serves the Long Pond launch.

Maps, advice, and other necessities commonly used by anglers seeking an extended outing into the backcountry ponds can be obtained at the facility. They also rent canoes and have transport services. They no doubt will mention safety issues, especially to anglers unfamiliar with this type of experience. It's important to prepare and also check weather forecasts if planning to stay back in the Canoe Area for an extended period of time. Preparation is even more important if planning to get back into the most remote ponds in the Fish Pond area.

Fish Pond, located at the most northern part of the Saint Regis Canoe Area, can serve as a base camp for fishing trout ponds, such as Kit Fox Pond and Little Long Pond, via portages to them. Two lean-to shelters exist at Fish Pond (one on the north side, and one on the south side). Primitive camping sites are also scattered throughout the region's ponds.

Whether planning a short canoe fishing day trip or a longer outing, you can also use base campsites that you'll encounter on your way into the Long Pond launch site. Numerous campsites, all numbered, exist along the entire length of the road. Site #8 is particularly nice; it's located on the shore of Polliwog Pond. Deciding which base campsite to utilize depends largely on which ponds inside the Saranac Saint Regis Canoe Area or Saranac Lake Wilderness you plan to fish, their locations, and the length of your stay—a day trip or an extended trip.

Anglers not particularly concerned with just catching brook trout found on Saint Regis Canoe Area ponds can paddle a popular loop through warmwater fisheries that begins at Floodwood Pond launch site near the parking area. The Floodwood Pond Loop takes anglers through ponds located in the Saranac Lake Wild Forest, not the Saint Regis Canoe Area.

The loop leads into Fish Creek Pond Camping area, then continues through other waters, eventually leading back to the point of beginning. It involves five portages, taking paddlers through Floodwood Pond, Fish Creek, Little Square Pond, Fish Creek Ponds, Follensby Clear Pond, Polliwog Pond, Hoel Pond, Slang Pond, and Long Pond. Camping sites, available on a first-come basis, are scattered along the route. Polliwog Pond is listed as inhabiting brown trout; Little Polliwog Pond is listed as having brook trout.

FISH CREEK POND STATE CAMPGROUND

Another good base camp for anglers planning to sample the Saint Regis Canoe Area is located at the Fish Creek Pond Campground along with its adjoining Rollins Pond State Campground. Fish Creek Pond is a warmwater fishery. They both share the same entrance located a few miles north of the State Route 30/County Road 45 intersection. Reservations can be made online for one of the numerous camping sites.

In theory, a carefully planned multiday paddle and portage outing from the campground can get anglers into the Saint Regis Canoe Area that lies north of Fish Creek Pond (which lies in the Saranac Lake Wild Forest Region), but that would be an ambitious undertaking. The better alternative would be to access the Saint Regis Canoe Area via Floodwood Pond Road.

FOLLENSBY CLEAR POND

Two Follensby Clear Pond canoe-launching site parking areas, separated by a couple of miles, exist on State Route 30. Both are marked by large NYSDEC hanging signage approximately 5 miles south of the Little Clear Pond/Little Green Pond access and

Follensby Clear Pond is a good canoe-launching site to access other Saint Regis ponds.

approximately 5 miles north of the State Route 30/Route 45 intersection. Follensby Clear Pond is a warmwater fishery located just south of the Saint Regis Canoe Area in the Saranac Lake Wilderness.

BROOK TROUT PONDS IN THE SAINT REGIS CANOE AREA

- Bessie Pond
- Bickford Pond
- Bone Pond
- Clamshell Pond
- Conley Line Pond
- Dry Lake
- Grass Pond
- Green Pond
  (plus splake)
- Kitfox Pond
- Little Long Pond
  (plus splake)
- Lindsey Pond
- Lydia Pond
- Nellie Pond
- Ochre Pond
- Sky Pond

BROOK TROUT PONDS IN THE SARANAC LAKE WILD FOREST

Echo Pond, Federation Pond, Little Polliwog Pond, Meadow Pond, Panther Pond, Saint Germain Pond, Sunday Pond, Sunrise Pond, Track Pond, and Twelfth Tee Pond.

Exploring the myriad ponds and lakes in the Saint Regis Canoe Area are not the only fly-fishing waters worth fishing that far north in New York State. Several streams are located in the St. Lawrence River area, near the Canadian border. There are plenty of streams and rivers 30 miles north of the Saint Regis Area/Paul Smiths, in Franklin County. A half-hour drive on State Route 30 will deliver you to a couple of good streams; Salmon River and Chateaugay River are two streams that flow north into the St. Lawrence River.

The St. Lawrence River itself, a warmwater fishery, is covered in the Warmwater section.

North Country Rivers

Streams that flow through the extreme northern areas of New York, some as far north as the Canadian border, are filled with trout and other fish species that provide fine sport for anglers willing to make long drives to reach them. Two of the most popular are Salmon River near Malone and the nearby Chateaugay River, both heavily stocked trout streams. Other rivers and smaller streams that inhabit both trout and warmwater species flow nearby or within a relatively short driving distance.

SALMON RIVER (FRANKLIN COUNTY)

The "other" Salmon River (not to be confused with the Salmon River in Pulaski) is tucked away in the extreme northern part of New York, in Franklin County. A sister river of the nearby Chateaugay River that flows only a dozen miles to its east, fly anglers traveling to the area often fish both. The Salmon River provides lots of PFR stretches that inhabit some very nice-size brown trout, rainbow trout, and even brook trout that swim in its headwaters. While natural reproduction takes place in the stream, it is dependent on hatchery plantings. NYSDEC typically stocks 13,000 brown trout and 9,000 rainbows annually. The river has both Stocked and Stocked-Extended reaches, marked by signage.

For most New York fly anglers, it's a long drive to reach its waters, some 46 miles of river that begin in the Adirondack Mountains in the Town of Franklin and end at the United States/Canada border at Fort Covington. Once the river reaches Canada, it continues through lowlands until it joins the St. Lawrence River.

The historic runs of large Atlantic salmon that once migrated into the river from the St. Lawrence is a phenomenon of the past. The runs are so large and fish so big they clogged up the mill's waterwheel at Fort Covington. Called "Negentsiagoa" by the

Valerie Valla on the upper Salmon River, at the King Memorial Park reach near Whippleville. Salmon River near Malone, New York, is heavily stocked with both brown trout and rainbow trout. NYSDEC categorizes the stream as Stocked and Stocked-Extended, depending on the stream reach location.

original Mohawk Indian people, which translates to "the place where we catch large fish," the Salmon River, in a modern context, can still surrender large brown trout to fly anglers along many of the river's reaches. However, the river often falls under the radar, perhaps because of its relatively remote location.

The Village of Malone, considered the central location for the river (and very close to the Chateaugay), is a half-hour drive or so north of Paul Smiths and the Saint Regis Canoe Area, on State Route 30. For a better perspective, Malone is over 200 miles from the City of Albany, nearly 200 miles from the City of Syracuse, and about 50 miles east of the City of Plattsburgh. It's about dead center along the top of New York.

NYSDEC breaks up the Salmon River into six general reaches, from the headwaters located south at Mountain View to the northern reach at Westville Center. Westville Center is about 7 miles south of the United States/Canada border. Each of the six sections has its own river characteristics that vary from boulder-strewn rapids to more gentle gradients through farmlands. Generally, brown trout are scattered throughout the reaches, both above and downstream from Malone. But trout populations drop off, and warmwater species—bass, northern pike, and pickerel—make an appearance along the lowermost few miles below the State Route 37/County Road 4 intersection in Westville Center.

Sandbars and lack of good substrate and riffle/run water structure dominate the lower river upstream from Fort Covington until the Westville Center area. More gravel and cobble and better stream structure provides trout habitat although thermal warming can be an issue that far downstream.

Anglers can access PFR water upstream from Westville Center at Fireman's Memorial Drive and downstream at Cushman's Road bridge crossing, both are off State Route 37. Nice riffles exist at the Cushman's Road crossing, but both those stretches are located a little too far downstream for my liking. Unless you're targeting warmwater species, bypass the previous access areas and locate more upstream at Cargin Road and Flat Rock

James Nichols casting flies for rainbow and brown trout at the Flat Rock Road bridge crossing, on the lower river downstream from Malone. James netted numerous rainbow trout and a few brown trout during the May outing.

Road crossings where the stream gradient, forest shading, and stream narrowing creates much better trout habitat.

If approaching from downstream at Westville, drive south on State Route 37 a short distance to Lower Flat Rock Road, then 1 mile to the bridge crossing and intersection with Upper Flat Rock Road. If approaching from Malone, drive 5.5 miles north on State Route 37 to Lower Flat Rock Road, from the State Route 37/US-11 intersection. A formal parking area is located at the bridge. A short segment of boulder-strewn PFR water flows downstream from the bridge. You'll likely catch very willing small rainbow trout and a few browns by drifting nymphs through the pocketwater. The reach is heavily stocked during May, and the trout are ridiculously easy to catch at that time.

The Flatrock Road bridge crossing marks the lower boundary of the Special Regulation Catch and Release PFR stretch. It extends upstream a good distance to 200 yards downstream of the Cargin Road Bridge. A NYSDEC angling parking lot marked by a large hanging sign is located at the Cargin Road bridge. PFR stretches are also upstream from the bridge.

A couple of miles upstream from Cargin Road, the river flows out of a hydroelectric impoundment and through a gorge area. Impassable to fish, Macomb Dam creates 16-acre Lamica Lake, in Malone, popular with warmwater boat anglers. Plenty of trout fishing opportunities are located south of Malone after you get south of a couple of small dams in the village (Whittelsey Dam in downtown Malone, and a small dam next to the North Country Community College). A long stretch of PFR water exists upstream of Malone along River Road. Access River Road just south of the Franklin County Fairgrounds and Notre Dame Cemetery in Malone.

River Road will lead to the hamlet of Whippleville and County Road 25. Follow County Road 25 south 2 miles at the bridge crossing and a favorite access point for good brown trout fishing (you'll also pass by Cox Road on the right that intersects a short PFR reach). Just after crossing the bridge, the William "Bill" A. King Memorial Park is on the left. You'll likely see fly anglers along the stretch during the annual Hendrickson Hatch Catch and Release Fly Fishing Tournament that takes place in early June.

The Hendrickson hatch that typically appears in mid-May isn't the only macroinvertebrate the river supports. March Browns, Sulphurs, Olives, and other mayflies are present. Stoneflies live along the rocky stretches. You'll want your fly boxes to be stocked with the same patterns you might use around other areas around New York. Bring streamers for the tumbling runs. Caddis patterns are effective when fished over the riffles south of Whippleville when adults appear in swarms.

The Salmon River headwaters near Mountain View Lake can be accessed a few miles upstream from Chasm Falls. The ambitious fly angler can launch a canoe at the Mountain View Lake dam, then paddle upstream into the tiny waters, in search of brook trout. Hornbeck boats (mentioned previously) are perfect for such an outing.

Another option is to access the headwaters downstream from the lake at High Falls of the Big Salmon trail, located off Barnsville Road. Drive 5.3 miles south on County Road 27 from the County Road 27/County Road 25 intersection down at the Chasm Falls area. Turn right on Barnesville Road and drive 1.6 miles to the trailhead. The stream runs through and then borders the Titus Mountain State Forest.

The moderately long footpath leads to a scenic little waterfall that cascades over bedrock. The frothing plunge pool then leads to gentler water. Fish small flies through the runs and riffles with a hope you'll entice a brook trout. Exposed bedrock along the stream near the falls is a nice place to have lunch or munch on an apple.

CHATEAUGAY RIVER

The 72-mile-long Chateaugay River flows south from Chateaugay Lake in Clinton County, passes through the Village of Chateaugay, and then departs the United States

Chateaugay River below the US-11 bridge in the Village of Chateaugay. The stream reach in this area is heavily stocked with small rainbow trout. Brown trout are also stocked in the river. NYSDEC categorizes the stream as both Stocked and Stocked-Extended, depending on the stream reach location.

and continues north into Canada, finally spilling into the St. Lawrence River. The village is located only a dozen miles east on US-11 from the Salmon River in Malone. If on an extended visit to the area, it makes sense to fish both streams since they're so close.

Plenty of PFR water exists on the Chateaugay from upstream in the hamlet of Brainardsville area downstream to the lower reaches. Brainardsville is located on the northernmost edge of the Adirondack Park. The river has both Stocked and Stocked-Extended reaches, marked by signage. NYSDEC stocks around 5,000 brown trout and 2,000 rainbows, spread out from late April into June. The rainbows are planted in the downstream reaches. Anglers frequently catch large holdover browns, with wild fish mixed in.

I'm not sure if the big brown trout my dad and his fishing partner George Kurbaba caught in the Chateaugay River during the late 1950s and 1960s were wild trout or holdover stocked fish. But something about that river—probably the big fish—compelled them to make trips up there on Memorial Day and again on Labor Day weekend.

It was at least a 5-hour drive to the Chateaugay from our home in the Binghamton area. Until I-81 was completed, it must have been an even longer drive. I recall, in 1967, Kurbaba phoned our house, directing me to pick up a couple hundred garden worms down at a golf course leaf pile for their upcoming Labor Day trip, at a couple cents each. They fished bucktails, but the worms were an added insurance policy.

Of course, I expected they would drag me along with them, but it didn't happen. I only heard the stories upon their return home after each outing. Kurbaba kept a 4-pound brown on the 1969 Memorial Day trip; I only was able to drool when he lifted it from the freezer. My time on the river came later, during adult years, fishing in their footsteps while recalling their tales.

I like to think of the Chateaugay in two sections: the stretches above the High Falls, a 120-foot-high waterfall, and the reaches downstream from the falls to the Village of Chateaugay area. To sample PFR water in stretches well upstream from the falls, head for the hamlet of Brainardsville and a formal NYSDEC parking lot and PFR reach at the State Route 24 bridge crossing. Brainardsville is located about 35 miles northwest of the City of Plattsburgh, via State Route 190 (Military Turnpike).

At the State Route 190/State Route 374 intersection, continue on Brainardsville Road (County Road 24). The parking area is located 0.4 mile on County Road 24, marked by a large hanging sign, directly across from the Town of Belmont town hall. The PFR reach is located along both banks, upstream from the bridge, and on the left side downstream from the bridge.

Longer PFR frontage exists upstream from the County Road 24 bridge, about as far upstream to where overhead power lines cross the stream. Lots of woody habitat structure exists on the stretch immediately upstream from the bridge. The stream flows past a dwelling immediately downstream from the bridge but then turns a corner into a nice riffle and run. If fishing this reach, consider making a short drive east to the North Branch of Chazy River, only 8 miles east of Brainardsville on State Route 190 (see page 177).

A few miles downstream, along Healy Road, the river flows over spectacular High Falls. Access to High Falls Park Campground for fishing the stream below and downstream from the falls requires a small fee to enter the facility. The campground accommodates seasonal campers, day campers, and anglers wishing to fish the river that exists in the falls plunge pool. The $5 entrance fee will get you into the river and its interesting runs and riffles. Stairs down a very steep hill lead to the stream below and the falls. Make sure you bring your wading staff, which will come in handy while fishing the stream best suited for streamers and nymphs.

Catskill (Variant) (tied by Mike Stewart) Mike Stewart created his tweak of the classic Catskill wet fly pattern by palmering its orange floss body with furnace hackle. The fly is perfect for attracting rainbow trout that swim in Chateaugay River.

Upper Brainardsville bridge Chateaugay River, upstream from crossing

A couple PFR reaches not far downstream from the High Falls area are two of the most popular with fly anglers. One is located less than 2 miles from the campground at the State Route 11 bridge crossing at the Village of Chateaugay. Take Jerdon Road to Cemetery Road to State Route 11. Parking is available on the west side of the impressive long span, 110-foot-high bridge.

My dad and Kurbaba often described fishing experiences at the "high steel-decked bridge" and their long walk down the steep hill to the stream (the bridge used to be a steel-deck bridge, but it was demolished and completely rebuilt sometime in the 1980s, with it being even higher). A wide yet rocky and steep pathway that a rugged jeep could probably negotiate leads down the long hill to the river below, but don't try it. Once you reach the stream (watch out for plenty of poison ivy along the bank), fish upstream with nymphs and swing small wet flies downstream through the riffles and runs. Bright patterns such as Mike Stewart's Catskill variant wet fly will bring strikes from willing little rainbows stocked by the state fish hatchery that's located right up the road.

The second popular PFR stretch that will get anglers quickly into water is downstream at the Sam Cook Road bridge crossing. If approaching from the previous parking area at the State Route 11 bridge, cross the bridge and take your first left on Chasm Road (County Road 35). In about 3.5 miles down Chasm, you'll pass over the Marble River, a tributary of the Chateaugay River. Ample PFR water exists upstream from the bridge and downstream to its confluence with the Chateaugay River. The Marble River is worthy of a stop on your way to Sam Cook Road. You'll have to park up the road a couple hundred feet at the Simms Road/Chasm Road intersection (parking is difficult directly next to the Marble River bridge).

At the Simms Road/Chasm Road intersection, go left down Simms 0.2 mile to Cook Road. You can park on both the east and west sides of the Chateaugay River bridge crossing, at small parking areas. PFR water is located only on the right bank, looking downstream. It's nice water for both dry fly and subsurface nymph fishing. The river flows north, encountering a couple of island areas. Make sure to keep aware of posted signs once you wander far downstream, but there's more than ample public easement stream frontage. Fishing the Cook Road reach gets close to the United States/Canada border.

Eastern Adirondack Region Waters

The Salmon River and Chateaugay River are two of the better-known fly-fishing destinations in the extreme northern region near Canada, on the fringes of the Adirondacks. Plenty of other less popular and lesser-known smaller trout streams, such as the North Branch of the Chazy River, are located in the region that flow east and empty into Lake Champlain, a large waterbody bordering Vermont. The headwaters of the North Branch are located only a few miles from the upper Chateaugay River. A warmwater fishery, Great Chazy River dumps directly into Lake Champlain (see Warmwater section).

A couple of other Lake Champlain tributaries that are born in the Eastern Adirondacks provide interesting fly-fishing sport. The lower Saranac River at Plattsburgh (located less than 45 minutes from the Chateaugay) and the lower Boquet River at Willsboro a half-hour to its south are streams known for landlocked salmon runs. The West and East Branches of the Ausable River, the most popular fly-fishing streams that are born in the

Lake George, called "Queen of American Lakes," is one of many stillwaters in the Eastern Adirondacks that is inhabited by lake trout and landlocked salmon, as well as a variety of warmwater fish. The picturesque lake is surrounded by beautiful mountains.

Adirondack Mountains High Peaks, send their combined waters into Lake Champlain near Keesville, a few miles south of Plattsburgh. Landlocked salmon also run the lower Ausable River out of Lake Champlain. The extreme southend of Lake Champlain almost touches Lake George, one of New York's most picturesque lakes on the easternmost fringes of the Adirondacks. State-designated Adirondack wilderness areas are in the neighborhood, loaded with remote trout ponds. Schroon River, the outlet of Schroon Lake, also provides fly-fishing opportunities near Lake George.

NORTH BRANCH OF CHAZY RIVER

Flowing westerly through the Ellenburg area, then mostly along US-11 to its confluence with the Great Chazy River at Moores Forks, the North Branch of the Chazy River is categorized as a Stocked-Extended stream. While the Great Chazy River is a warmwater fishery, the North Branch supports trout fishing. Reaches upstream from its junction with the Great Chazy River to Lake Roxanne Road in Ellenburg Depot are typically stocked each spring with over 4,000 brown trout up to 15 inches and a couple thousand 9-inch to 10-inch rainbow trout.

Headwater PFR stretches are located a short distance west of the Village of Chateaugay. If approaching from Chateaugay, drive about 11.2 miles westerly on US-11 to Cashman Road. If approaching from the east, the Cashman Road/US-11 intersection is located about 24 miles west from I-87/US-11 Exit 42 in Champlain. Take Cashman south about 1 mile to State Route 190. A formal NYSDEC parking area marked by a large hanging sign is located at a small parking lot near the State Route 190 bridge crossing intersection. Drop down a steep bank on the upstream side of the bridge to a neat looking ledge rock pool on the left side that often holds small wild trout. Fish downstream from the bridge with small wet flies or skitter dry flies through the riffles and small pools. A 7-foot, 4-weight rod is sufficient along this reach.

North Branch of Chazy River at the Cashman Road reach, at the Town of Ellenburg in Clinton County. The north branch receives ample numbers of both brown trout and rainbow trout during spring stockings.

Another PFR reach at a formal NYSDEC parking lot is located on US-11 just west of Ellenburg Depot. From the Ellenburg Depot Fire Department building on US-11, at a bridge crossing, drive about a mile to the anglers parking lot on the right, marked by a large hanging sign. PFR water runs downstream to Cannon Corners Road through productive riffles and runs that are much wider than the headwater reach, upstream at Cashman Road.

The lower stretches of the section at Cannon Corners Road can be reached by driving 2 miles westerly on US-11 and turning left onto Cannon Corners Road. A formal NYS-DEC angling parking pull-off (not marked by a large hanging sign) is located about 0.3 mile down the road, on the left just after the bridge crossing. A barrier of large stones identifies the parking area along with small signage at the lot. The PFR water exists upstream from the bridge.

If you continue westerly on US-11 about 0.2 mile from the Cannon Corners Road intersection, you'll cross over Graves Brook. PFR water resumes at about that point, on the left side of the stream only for a short distance, looking downstream, before public water resumes. Access to this reach and its riffles and runs is along McDonald Road, 0.3 mile from the Graves Brook Crossing, on the left. Use 8-foot, 3-weight to 4-weight rods in the area, swinging small streamers through the riffles where you might pick up a rainbow trout or two.

Once the stream joins the Great Chazy River and flows downstream into the hamlet of Moores, focus should turn to the river's warmwater species opportunities, which includes everything from rock bass to muskellunge. Moores is located 6.5 miles west of the I-87/State Route 11 intersection at Exit 42 in Champlain (see Warmwater section).

Saranac and Boquet Rivers (Landlocked Salmon Section)

Separated by 30 miles, the mouths of Saranac and Boquet Rivers come alive during October when landlocked salmon migrate out of Lake Champlain on annual spawning

"The Office," a gathering bench on the Saranac River, in Plattsburgh. Anglers solve all kinds of problems sitting in "The Office" at this Saranac River reach, in the heart of a neighborhood.

Mouth of the Saranac River, Plattsburgh. Fishing for lake-run landlocked salmon on the Saranac River is a little different experience than most Salmonfly anglers are accustomed to. It's definitely city fishing.

runs. The Saranac River in the City of Plattsburgh, the northernmost of the two, flows northeasterly 80 miles from the Saranac Lakes region to Lake Champlain. The Boquet is also born in the Adirondack Park, flowing from the Dix Mountain Wilderness, part of the rugged-yet-spectacular high-peaks region. Its inland reaches support a trout fishery along the way to its mouth in the hamlet of Willsboro. The two rivers are completely different types of streams before they approach Lake Champlain; their common feature is the landlock salmon that appear annually in their final miles upstream from the lake.

In some ways, fishing for landlocks on the Saranac reminds me of fishing for steelhead at the mouth of the Genesee River. Both are what I'd call "urban" experiences. The Genesee right smack in the middle of the City of Rochester and the Saranac right in the middle of Plattsburgh. The lowermost Saranac also has limited access points, all within the city limits.

The only lower reach on the Saranac that provides even a remote feeling of fishing outside of the city congestion is downstream at its mouth, along its final couple hundred feet. Even then, a quick glance upstream at a major city bridge will instantly remind the angler he's not fishing in a remote area. However, some mighty nice fish come out of the stream every fall, if you're not bothered by the surrounding atmosphere of city living.

There are more than a couple ways to get to the stretch at the river's mouth. No matter what direction, city driving is required to get to the water. Assuming you're approaching from the south, via I-87, take Exit 38S to Boynton Avenue to Miller Street to Bridge Street to Green Street. A parking area and access is directly next to the river's mouth, off Green Street. Landlocks hang out along the run just downstream from the bridge crossing.

A couple of other stretches are popular, upstream before the impassible Imperial Dam ends the possibility of catching a salmon any farther upstream. However, NYSDEC recently announced the long-anticipated fish ladder construction and rehabilitation of Imperial Dam, proposed more than two decades ago, will soon be underway. One reach is on Pine Street, and the other is off Allen Street. The Pine Street section, next to the Plattsburgh Police Department, is located less than a mile from Green Street. Take Green Street to Peru Street to Broad Street to Pine. Parking is not a problem along the road. Access into the stream is easy.

Rich Redmond is a Saranac River salmon fishing regular who knows how to get into fish. During the fall, he swings traditional Atlantic salmon hairwing flies, or variations of existing patterns. During the spring, he finds minnow or bug patterns effective. Rich uses a heavy wire hook that works well for him and avoids the need for other weight.

The exact pattern isn't as important as getting the fly near a salmon's nose, as is true on the Boquet River at Willsboro where anglers can swing their flies. The best approach to Willsboro and the salmon water via I-87 is off Exit 33 to State Route 22. Drive just over 8 miles east on State Route 22 to the bridge crossing in Willsboro. You can get into the left side of the river downstream from Willsboro dam by taking a left on Mill Street located at the bridge. Drive beyond where the paved road becomes a dirt road. Ample parking is right next to the river.

Access is easy to the water, from both sides of the river. From Mill Street, on the left side of the river, convenient stairs lead down the slope to the water and the runs below

Saranac River landlocked salmon, caught by Rich Redmond, a stream regular. Rich has enjoyed sustained success on the Saranac.

Atlantic Salmon-Style Fly (tied by Rich Redmond) Frequent Saranac River landlocked salmon angler Rich Redmond uses a variety of Salmon-style flies to entice fish. Rich nets mighty nice fish out of the Saranac every fall. He says that during the fall runs out of Lake Champlain, fly size effectiveness can vary. "One day they like streamers, and the next it could be wets." Some of his wet flies are more like small trout flies, something that might be good on an inland brown trout stream.

Boquet River at Willsboro downstream from Willsboro Dam, along Mill Street. Access is very easy on this popular stream reach.

the cascading rapids. The reach is close to 3 miles upstream from Lake Champlain. It's important to remember angling is prohibited from a marked boundary below the dam upstream to State Route 22. During fall runs, the landlocks are quite vulnerable in that stretch directly above the cascades. You'll see them with dorsal fins protruding from the water surface. The salmon tend to not swim above the rapids during the spring when they're also in the river.

Anglers can also sample downstream stretches off Mill Street via a wide grass path that departs the parking area. Yet another option is to locate on the right side of the river by crossing the State Route 22 bridge, then taking a quick left on Gilliland Lane. Two large parking areas are located a short distance down the road, on the left. Convenient stairs lead to the water. Another parking area and boat launch is located just down the road from the Gilliland Lane parking area at a dead end. It's all flat water on that reach. Check out the rustic, very nice Boquet Nature Preserve kiosk, with interesting natural area information, at the boat launch.

During fall runs, when the landlocks are interested in challenging the rapids to get farther upstream, they'll allegedly swim all the way upstream to the impassable falls in the hamlet of Wadhams. PFR easements, along with unofficial access areas, are scattered along river reaches upstream to Wadhams, but be mindful and respectful of private posted land.

SARANAC RIVER (INLAND TROUT SECTION)

The upper and mid-reaches of the Saranac River are heavily stocked with both rainbow trout and brown trout. While it's true the river grows some very nice-size brown trout, many of its stretches are prone to thermal problems during the summer months. Fly anglers either love or dismiss the stream as a trout fly-fishing destination.

The Kent Falls Road reach on upper Saranac River, downstream from the New York State Electric and Gas (NYSEG) facility at the angler parking area. Make sure you have a wading staff while fishing this reach. The Kent Falls Road reach is one of the most popular sections of the river.

The river is big and wide open, poorly shaded in most areas, and flows through impoundments along its path. However, plenty of PFR water exists along many miles of frontage, including two Catch and Release stretches that are heavily stocked with brown trout and rainbow trout. Other pools and runs farther upstream from the Catch and Release stretches, below Union Falls, are also popular.

A good starting point for first-time Saranac River anglers would be at the Catch and Release sections, particularly the upper reach along Silver Lake Road. The lower Catch and Release stretch in Morrisonville is located about 2.5 miles from the State Route 3/ State Route 190 intersection in Plattsburgh. From State Route 3, drive to State Route 22B. A formal NYSDEC angling parking turnout is on the right, at the Sand Road intersection in Morrisonville. A large NYSDEC hanging sign, two picnic tables, and the Millstone Monument (three large, stacked millstones) are situated at the lot, directly next to the river.

The Catch and Release stretch reaches from the Millstone Monument at the State Route 22B/Sand Road/Kent Falls Road intersection upstream to Kent Falls Dam. Anglers interested in fishing this stretch should do so early in the spring, into May. It tends to get warm later in the season but can be quite productive earlier.

A formal angler parking area, courtesy of New York State Electric and Gas (NYSEG), is also located 1.8 miles up Kent Falls Road on the right. Heed the posted warnings of water discharges that can quickly rise along this reach. A wide footpath along the stream bank provides access to the often swift-moving stretch. Make sure you wade with care, and use a wading staff.

Another Catch and Release stretch option is located well upstream from Morrisonville along Silver Lake Road in the hamlet of Clayburg off State Route 3. The North

Branch of the Saranac joins the river at a bridge crossing at Silver Lake Road. A parking turnout is located just after crossing the bridge and about another 0.3 mile up the road. The Catch and Release stretch extends upstream 1.4 miles from a marked boundary 100 yards upstream from the North Branch confluence to Stord Brook. A formal NYSDEC angling parking area marked by a large hanging sign is located 1.4 miles up Silver Lake Road from the lower boundary. A long footpath leads to the river and a very nice riffle and run when the water is at a wadable level.

A good variety of hatches come off the Saranac River, including Hendricksons, various caddis flies, stoneflies, olives, and a few March Browns. Your fly box should also include an assortment of Wooly Buggers, nymphs, and dry flies. A 9-foot, 5-weight rod would be a good choice.

BOQUET RIVER (INLAND TROUT SECTION)

The 14 miles or so of river that flows from Wadhams downstream to the Willsboro Dam is characterized by long, slow-moving pools with areas of intermittent riffles and runs. The wide-open stretches with little canopy shading are vulnerable to thermal heating during summer months to support a self-sustaining inland trout fishery. However, PFR easements that receive annual trout stockings are located both downstream and upstream of Wadhams.

Better trout water is located farther upstream around the Village of Elizabethtown, on the fringes of the Adirondack High Peaks area. If approaching from Wadams, drive 6 miles northeast from the County Road 8/State Route 22 intersection in Wadams. A formal NYSDEC angling parking lot, marked by a large hanging sign, is located on

The Boquet at the Scriver Lane bridge crossing, upstream from the Village of Elizabethtown. The stream along this reach provides pleasant fishing, especially during early fall. It's a great stretch to give your 7-foot, 4-weight rod a workout swinging small wet flies and nymphs through the riffles and runs.

the stream bank. Fish downstream along a nice riffle and run. Additional PFR water is located through the village and upstream.

Most anglers will be approaching the Boquet and Elizabethtown from the south via I-87. The approach will position anglers in the stream's uppermost reaches. Assuming you're driving north on I-87 from more southern areas of New York, take Exit 31 to US-9. (It's the same exit anglers and others take to get to the Ausable River and other areas in the Adirondack High Peaks area.) Keep on US-9 at the State Route 73 intersection just up the road. US-9 will intermittently follow the Boquet 10 miles to Elizabethtown.

Back at the US-9/State Route 73 intersection area, tucked in the woods, the North and South Forks of the Boquet join, creating the main stem. Had you driven north on State Route 73, you would cross the South Fork in 0.2 mile. Shortly up the road, the North Fork comes into view at a small parking turnout next to the road and stream. A footpath leads from the parking turnout to the sparking, tumbling little stream that spells brook trout water. Get out your 7-foot, 3-weight rods and small nymphs. If you net a fish, it will likely be a wild brookie.

Both forks are not stocked, aside from landlocked salmon fry, as part of the Lake Champlain salmon restoration program. However, you might be surprised to net a brown trout or, surprisingly, a small landlocked salmon. Public access isn't a problem as both forks flow out of the New York State Adirondack Wilderness Areas.

NYSDEC conducted brook trout electrofishing studies on both forks in 2019, something that had not been done since 1929. The sampling on 300 feet of the tiny South Fork turned up a dozen brook trout, mostly small 4-inchers to 5-inchers, but a few were almost up to 7 inches. The 20 landlocked salmon were mostly fingerlings, but a few were up to 6 inches. One small wild brown was netted. Access the South Branch at the bridge crossing. This is small water that's best fished with short rods, casting nymphs upstream into the pocketwater or small Elk Hair Caddis patterns. The South Fork is well shaded with excellent habitat structure but lacks significant pools found on the neighboring North Fork.

NYSDEC sampled two sites on the North Fork, one upstream and one downstream at the mouth with the main stem. They turned up small brook trout, fingerling landlocks, and a handful of 6-inchers to 7-inchers. Wild browns were mostly small, but one 9-inch fish was captured. The boulder-strewn brook is larger than the South Fork, with more holding areas.

Anglers desiring to catch larger browns and a few brook trout should head back to US-9 and fish reaches on the way downstream to Elizabethtown. The stream in the lower reaches is dependent on ample brown trout and brook trout stockings. There are about 3,000 browns between 9 to 15 inches along with roughly the same number of brook trout up to 10 inches.

Driving downstream along US-9, the tumbling Boquet runs along Split Rock Falls, a popular swimming area during late summer months. I've never fished that reach, largely because parking in the area is difficult with meager road shoulders and plenty of no-parking signs posted, for safety reasons. My favorite PFR stretch is located a short distance downstream, off Scriver Lane, 3.5 miles north on US-9. A formal NYSDEC angling parking area is located at the one-lane bridge crossing. I came across the reach by accident back in the early 1990s.

During my 20-plus years working for Glens Falls Hospital (located in the Adirondack foothills), I devoted a couple of weeks each summer to treating children in a small town on Lake Champlain. We generally ended the day in late afternoon, affording me time to explore some of the smaller trout streams in Elizabethtown and the surrounding areas.

Wild brook trout inhabit the uppermost reaches, and stocked brookies swim in the lower stretches on the Boquet River.

Atherton #3 Nymph (tied by Mike Valla) In his classic book *The Fly and the Fish* (1951), Atherton promoted tying flies with blends to give artificials "the quality of life."

On one occasion, I happened to have my fishing gear in the vehicle but didn't plan to fish. While driving along US-9, I stopped at Scriver Lane, walked up the stream, and saw a nice-size brown holding in the clear pool. I didn't have waders with me, but wearing work clothing and shoes, I threw out a cast from the stream bank. The beautiful 12-inch brown sucked in an ant pattern I had in my fly box. The water structure where the pool was located has changed dramatically over the years, due to periodic flooding events.

Public easement access is located intermittently all the way downstream to Elizabethtown. If fishing down near Elizabethtown, stop by a small tributary brook simply called "The Branch" that flows through the village. It's stocked with brook trout that are eager to suck in small dry flies fished along the riffles.

WEST BRANCH AUSABLE RIVER

The West Branch of Ausable River is to the Adirondacks what the Beaver Kill is to the Catskills—the crown jewel trout stream of its region. Along its 36 miles of water, born from small brooks in the High Peaks Wilderness near Mount Jo, the river tumbles through one of the most scenic areas in the Adirondacks.

MacIntyre and South Meadow Brooks combine, creating the river just east of Adirondack Loj Road, a few miles south of the resort Village of Lake Placid. From there, the stream flows due north until it veers more northeasterly at State Route 73. It passes next to the Lake Placid Olympic Ski jump, then accepts water from Chubb River and follows River Road (County Road 21) 4 miles to the intersection with State Route 86. After a couple quick turns, the Ausable heads down State Route 86 toward the hamlet of Wilmington, located 9 miles or so downstream.

Most of the fly-fishing activity takes place from the State Route 86/River Road intersection downstream to Wilmington along extensive PFR water. Ample access is not a problem. Like the famous Beaver Kill in the Catskills, the West Branch of the Ausable along State Route 86 flows through a number of named pools and runs that vary from spectacular boulder-laced rapids to gentle flat-water stretches.

From Wilmington, the stream flows under State Route 86 and departs the area, where it traverses more isolated and inaccessible stretches until it reaches Ausable Forks, where it joins the East Branch of the Ausable. Its combined water heads to Lake Champlain, where it ends its journey as one.

Approaching from I-87, two routes will get fly fishers to the Ausable River. One will position anglers for fishing the upper reaches first near Lake Placid before sampling waters downstream along State Route 86 to Wilmington. The other route positions anglers downstream at Wilmington first. Regardless of the fishing starting point preference, from I-87, take Exit 31 to US-9, then on to State Route 73. Driving up State Route 73, you'll notice the brook-like North Fork of the Boquet River next to the road (page 183).

86 Flats, at the State Route 86/River Road intersection bridge crossing. Look for trout sipping Blue-Winged Olives along this reach during early fall. It's a lonely stretch during the first snows in winter.

Monument Falls, with Whiteface Mountain backdrop, is one of the most picturesque sections of the West Branch. It's named for two stone tablets that commemorate the fiftieth and one-hundredth anniversaries of the establishment of the New York State Forest Preserve in 1885. A parking turnout is located at the tablets.

Anglers desiring to fish the upper reaches first should take State Route 73 all the way to the State Route 71/River Road intersection near the ski jump in the Lake Placid area. Take the alternative route by driving 13 miles or so on State Route 73 to the hamlet of Keene. Then go right on State Route 9N along the East Branch of the Ausable 10 miles or so to State Route 86 and the hamlet of Jay. A 5-mile drive on State Route 86 from Jay will get you to Wilmington.

Driving to Wilmington via State Route 9N will provide a good glimpse of the East Branch, a much different stream in several ways, both geologically and in its trout fishing potential. Both the East and West Branches of the Ausable are stocked with large numbers of brown trout.

Brown trout are not the only species that are encountered on the West Branch of the Ausable. The Essex County Fish Hatchery supplements NYSDEC brown trout stockings with rainbows and brook trout. Wild brook trout also inhabit the upper stream reaches. Rainbow and brook trout stockings take place in the Town of North Elba. Anglers after brook trout should head to the uppermost small riffle and runs upstream near Lake Placid, although brook trout are also scattered downstream.

Anglers planning to fish the headwaters near Lake Placid first, before heading downstream along River Road toward Wilmington, should consider making a few casts for brook trout near the State Route 73/River Road (County Road 21) intersection near the ski jump (known as the Ski Jump Pool). Fish the riffles with Elk Hair Caddis or small nymph patterns. To get on classic brown trout water, head north on River Road.

PFR water follows River Road a good distance before it flows in and out of posted water. At first, the stream flows away from the road, but in short time, it again comes into view directly next to the road. The river is laced with small boulders and rocks down the bank from the guardrail. A good place to park is located a short distance down the road, about a half-mile from the State Route 73/River Road intersection on the left at the road shoulder pullover—the access for fishing Red Barn Run. The nice run is named for the large red barn located a couple hundred feet down the road. After leaving Red Barn Run, the stream once again heads a couple thousand feet away from the road, flowing toward the mouth of Chubb River before it eventually swings back into view at the "Iron Bridge," a one-lane bridge that crosses the stream. The expansive road shoulder parking at the bridge crossing will get anglers directly into the stream. PFR water exists on both sides of the river but only for a short distance downstream from the bridge crossing. Be aware of posted property.

Other popular fly-fishing stretches are located downstream, at the upper boundary of a Special Regulations Catch and Release section, one of two Catch and Release reaches on the river. The Catch and Release upper boundary at Holcomb Pond outlet, marked by a NYSDEC large hanging sign, is located about 2 miles from the Iron Bridge on River Road (the lower boundary is 2.2 miles downstream from Monument Falls, on State Route 86). The small parking turnout is directly across the road from the river, at Coty Flats. A small US Army 10th Mountain Division historical monument and bench is located at the turnout. (You would have passed a small parking area on the left side of the road, just upstream from the Catch and Release boundary that anglers also use.)

The River Road/State Route 86 intersection is a mile north of the Catch and Release boundary parking area, at a bridge crossing. Easy parking is available on both sides of the bridge. The stretch at the bridge is called 86 Flats, a long, slow-moving pool that often brings browns to the surface when the hatches are on. It's lonely water during the weeks when fall is about to transform the river into unfishable winter conditions. Late-season Blue-Winged Olives often bring browns to the surface along the State Route 86 bridge crossing reach.

Multiple parking turnouts and streamside parking areas along popular pools and runs are located on State Route 86 from the State Route 86/River Road intersection. Driving north about 0.4 mile toward Wilmington on State Route 86 from the intersection, a road shoulder turnout on the left provides access to the Quarry Hole, a popular pool. A dirt road path leads to the water. (If you were approaching the area from downstream areas near Wilmington, the Quarry Hole parking pull-off is about 0.7 mile south of Monument Falls on State Route 86.)

One of the most popular parking turnouts along State Route 86 is at Monument Falls, named for two stone tablets that commemorate the fiftieth and one-hundredth anniversaries of the establishment of the New York State Forest Preserve in 1885. Whiteface Mountain rises as a backdrop to the falls, making the location popular with photographers. Swift-flowing water plunges through rocks and boulders toward Island Run (named for what else but a mid-stream island) and Shadow Rock Pool.

The parking area to access Shadow Rock Pool is just short of a mile down State Route 86 from Monument Falls. Look for the dome-shaped streamside lot, bordered by small boulders, on the left. Fish high-floating Stimulator and Wulff patterns through the glides and pocketwater and streamers through the deeper pool sections on higher water. It's a good place to relocate after fishing early in the morning during mid-season on Bassett Flats. The parking turnout for Bassett Flats is less than a half-mile down State Route 86 from the Shadow Rock lot.

Reeling in and relocating to other river sections throughout the day during fishless episodes can usually turn luck around. This often amounts to trading early morning fishing on the flats for pocketwater reaches during midday, especially during midseason. Some of the nicest big browns feed early in the day and again in the evening on the flatwater

Bassett Flats, located downstream from Monument Falls, is a popular slow-water reach. One of the more popular fly-fishing sections is Basset Flats, a nice slice of water to fish small dry flies during early morning.

reaches, but those same stretches are dead during afternoon, as is true on many trout streams. Spinner falls on the West Branch flats bring larger fish to the surface in the last light, and very early in the morning, especially later in the season.

Once down as far as Bassett Flats, the lower boundary of the Catch and Release section that started upstream on River Road is not far downstream, about 0.4 mile from the Bassett Flats lot. It's marked by a large hanging NYSDEC sign near the north end of the next riverside parking turnout. The river exits the Catch and Release section and approaches the "Notch," formally known as Wilmington Notch. The now steeper gradient water flows between canyon-like walls where the stream negotiates rocky banks and slams into boulders. The changed geology creates great trout habitat; it also creates dangerous hazards for an uncareful angler who lacks experience fishing such waters. Caution is the word.

Once the river emerges from the Notch, it crashes down the High Falls. It's actually four different falls that cascade down the rocky slope but is collectively called by one name. More of a general tourist attraction, the falls and overlook trails draw visitors to the to the private 22-acre High Falls Nature Park.

The popular NYSDEC Wilmington Notch Campground and Day Use Center, popular with fly fishers who bring tents or campers for an extended experience on the West Branch of the Ausable, is just downstream from High Falls. Anglers enjoy fishing the boulder-laden stream that borders the campground where they can do so, fishing upstream to water that High Falls sends through the stretch.

The campground's location is also convenient for anglers to get quickly into water at the second Catch and Release reach that can be accessed within minutes. Exit the campground and drive north on State Route 86 to the road that enters Whiteface Ski Center. If approaching from the center of Wilmington, the Whiteface Ski Center entrance road is 3 miles south of the State Route 86/State Route 431 intersection. The Catch and Release section starts at the Whiteface Ski Center Bridge and extends downstream to the State

Route 86 bridge crossing at another river feature called "The Flume." Parking is available on State Route 86 next to the road to the Ski Center. The 1.25-mile section is great trout-holding pocketwater, perfect for casting everything from nymphs to heavy-hackled dry flies. Just about every interesting run and pool has a name on that brief mileage—including Fox Farm Stretch, Jenning's Run, and Betters's Pool, among others. You'll be doing some walking back along that reach that's well removed from the road.

The Catch and Release stretch runs behind the Hungry Trout Resort, no doubt one of the most popular lodging facilities frequented by fly fishers. Its fly shop makes staying in one of the 20 streamside units all the more attractive.

Wilmington's Bridge Park and dam located at the State Route 86 bridge crossing is worth stopping by to view the memorial to local fly tier Fran Betters, who passed away at age 90. His Adirondack Sport Shop in Wilmington was a magnet for probably every fly fisher who came to the river. The gigantic, sculptured-steel trout flies at the park overlook give memory to Fran's iconic patterns—Ausable Wulff, Ausable Bomber, and Haystack. They're still effective trout flies to cast on Ausable waters.

Interesting trout water flows downstream from Wilmington, in and out of private waters before it reaches Ausable Forks, although the majority of fly fishers bypass those reaches for the popular pools and runs upstream from the hamlet. PFR water is located off Lenny Preston Road, a couple of miles downstream from the center of Wilmington. A parking turnout on the road provides access to the river public easement stretch.

Usual (tied by Mike Valla) Ridiculously simple in design yet highly effective for enticing trout, the Usual was one of Fran Betters's beloved patterns. Sometimes called the Phillips Usual because Bill Phillips, some were led to believe, had something to do with its creation.

Ausable Wulff (tied by Mike Valla) Ausable Wulff dry flies are synonymous with not only the river but with the pattern's originator, Fran Betters (1931–2009). Betters created the pattern in 1964 after observing some insects inhabiting the Ausable had a slight orange tinge. He also wanted a fly that floated well on the river's rough waters.

Blue-Winged Olive CDC Biot Spinner (tied by René Harrop) It's always a good idea to have ready a supply of Blue-Winged Olive dry flies when that mayfly is on the West Branch. You might encounter Baetis Blue-Winged Olives in both early-mid May and again in the early fall. Corunta species Blue-Winged Olives are on the water during June mornings.

The last time I fished the stretches downstream from Wilmington was in late August of 2009 on Fran Betters's private frontage, on invitation from Derek Muirden and Jan Betters, Fran's wife. Derek was shooting PBS footage for a documentary on Fran. Fran died September 6 of that year. I don't think the documentary ever came to fruition, as far as I know, but Fran is featured in an entire chapter in my book *Tying the Founding Flies* (2015).

Anglers anticipating a first-time session on the West Branch should bring fly boxes loaded with not only Fran Betters's iconic patterns but a selection of dry flies that also float well in heavy pocketwater. While it's not tied with hackle, the Usual dry fly, one of Fran's favorites, floats surprisingly well to fish through pocketwater tailouts. Bring the same small-size dries you'd fish on the flatwater of other trout streams. The same nymphs that produce results on other big trout streams will entice West Branch trout.

You'll want to be ready for the same mayflies that emerge from trout streams in the Catskills. Many of the same hatches come off the West Branch but often a week or so later than the emergence time on more southerly New York streams. Everything from Hendricksons to March Browns to Green Drakes to Sulphurs to Isonychias and later-season Sulphurs and Olives keep the trout feeding and anglers happy. The Green Drake hatch is one of the most anticipated, as well as the Coffin Fly spinners that bring trout to the surface in the evening. I like Bassett Flats during that happening in early June.

I use a 9-foot-3-inch, 5-weight rod for most of my West Branch fishing. A shorter rod works well if targeting pocketwater with short casts. Tippets are generally 5X during mid-season but down to 6X while fishing the flats during early morning late season.

EAST BRANCH AUSABLE RIVER

The East Branch of the Ausable originates from waters that create Upper and Lower Ausable Lakes, deep in the Adirondack Mountains. From the dam on Lower Ausable Lake, the Ausable flows some 4 miles sandwiched between the High Peaks Wilderness

Joe House fishing the Douglas Memorial Park covered bridge reach, in Jay. Completely different from the West Branch, much of the East Branch is slow-moving, almost-dead water. Water downstream in Jay, at the covered bridge, is heavily stocked during early spring.

and the Giant Mountain Wilderness areas to Saint Hubert and the State Route 73 bridge crossing, some 9 miles northeast of I-87 Exit 31. Anglers heading up State Route 73 to the more popular West Branch of the Ausable on the same route will get a first glance of the East Branch at Saint Huberts.

From Saint Huberts, the East Branch heads due north along State Route 73 about 5 miles to the hamlet of Keene, passing by the hamlet of Keene Valley and Johns Brook tributary on the way. At the State Route 73/State Route 9N intersection in Keene, anglers heading to the upper reaches of the West Branch of the Ausable near Lake Placid will continue on State Route 73. Those taking an alternative route to the lower reaches of the West Branch and the hamlet of Wilmington will turn right onto State Route 9N, the same road that follows the East Branch of the Ausable.

Flowing north along State Route 9N, the river passes Upper Jay, then Jay where it intersects State Route 86, the route to Wilmington. The East Branch continues to follow State Route 9N to Ausable Forks, where it joins the West Branch of the Ausable and continues as a main stem all the way to Lake Champlain.

Anglers who venture to the north country to fish and explore the West Branch of the Ausable often make at least a few casts on the East Branch since it flows along the same route to Wilmington and the West Branch. Fishing both, you'll no doubt conclude that the East Branch can't measure up to the West Branch's productivity and water structure variety. However, as is true with the West Branch, the East Branch also receives ample trout stockings.

NYSDEC stocks the stream with several thousand brown trout in the reaches between Keene downstream to the Jay area, along State Route 9N, and a thousand or so brook trout upstream around the Keene reaches. The Essex County Fish Hatchery supplements NYS

Johns Brook, a tributary of the Ausable River's East Branch at Keene Valley. Its junction with the East Branch is popular with anglers. The stream rock structures (shown in the photo) were placed shortly after Hurricane Irene in 2011 ripped through the East Branch at Saint Huberts and Johns Brook. The Adirondack Chapter of Trout Unlimited coordinated the stream-improvement effort after catastrophic flooding caused extensive damage.

trout stockings downstream from Jay with both rainbow trout and brown trout. Essex County also stocks a few hundred rainbows in the Keene area and a couple hundred brook trout in Johns Brook, upstream in Keene Valley. Ample public easement stretches exist along the East Branch from Keene downstream to Ausable Forks. Access is also available upstream in Keene Valley, where the river briefly borders the Giant Mountain Wilderness at Saint Huberts. Streamside public parking areas along the road are also located downstream toward Keene.

Anglers often wonder why the East Branch fishes differently than the West Branch. During the 1930s up into the 1960s, authors such as Ray Bergman and Ernie Schwiebert wrote about their times fishing the East Branch. Geological differences have a lot to do with it, but that aside, the East Branch over the years has taken quite an environmental beating, too, both by human activity and natural disasters.

It's been said that past logging activity impacted shading conditions and gravel removal changed habitat. Silting increased. Even in more recent times the stream has been hit heavy with floods and ice scouring. Hurricane Irene in 2011 ripped through the East Branch at Saint Huberts and Johns Brook. The Adirondack Chapter of Trout Unlimited devoted time and expense to rectifying the damage from the catastrophic flooding.

All that said, some enjoyable fly fishing can be had in the Keene area and downstream toward Jay. The time to enjoy the East Branch downstream from Keene to Jay is best during late April into mid-late May, or very early June before waters warm. Conditions upstream into the Saint Huberts reaches hold on longer. A couple of popular fishing areas downstream from Saint Huberts are at the Johns Brook bridge crossing at Keene Valley and other access areas downstream along State Route 73. Access Johns Brook and it's junction with the East Branch at Point Park, a pleasant streamside public park at the bridge crossing.

A parking area located just over a half-mile down State Route 73 from the Johns Brook bridge crossing is at a cleared area with picnic tables near the stream. Camping isn't allowed, but the location provides good access to the river. The run downstream from the picnic area typically holds brown trout early in the season. Two additional streamside parking areas, separated by a half-mile, are located across the road from Marcy Field, a small airport located a short distance up State Route 73 from the Johns Brook bridge. The lot has a couple of picnic tables, a nice place to have lunch.

You'll likely catch brook trout in Johns Brook and brown trout and occasional rainbows early in the season downstream at the parking area at Marcy Field. A small low-water dam of sorts at the Marcy Field reach keeps a short run of water exiting the structure moving downstream. The stretch upstream from the rocky dam is poor water. The river bottom is entirely sand with little fish-holding structure; it's not worth fishing. In general, the flatwater stretches both upstream and downstream become warm and slow-moving by mid-summer. Johns Brook can also get very low by late summer, but fish still hang out in the hip-boot pocketwater. I use a 7-foot, 4-weight rod fishing the run upstream from the bridge. Bring Elk Hair Caddis dry flies and small nymphs.

You'll cross the East Branch of the Ausable on State Route 73 beyond Marcy Field. The hamlet of Keene and the State Route 73/State Route 9N intersection is just over 2 miles up the road from the bridge crossing. I usually tank up the vehicle at the Stewart's convenient store located on the left as you enter Keene. It's also a good place to grab ice, drinks, or snacks before continuing up State Route 9N.

Once the East Branch hits Keene, the river starts its traverse downstream toward Jay along State Route 9N. The stream runs in and out of PFR stretches that provide public fishing easements on both stream banks. At times, the stream and PFR stretches flow right next to State Route 9N, but parking on the narrow road shoulder creates a challenge. The stretch where Styles Brook joins the river can be good at times, but finding a parking spot can take some effort.

The river approaches Jay about 9 miles from the State Route 9N/State Route 73 intersection back in Keene. You'll see a large streamside parking rest area on the left just before reaching the hamlet, on the left. Again, avoid fishing this reach and the reaches below Jay in summer. The water temperatures can rise too warm for good fishing, and the water levels are low and shallow.

Just past the State Route 73/State Route 86 intersection in Jay, take a right turn on Glen Road just up the road from the rest area. Continue on Glen Road to Covered Bridge Road, located just after a bridge crossing. Parking is available at the Douglas Memorial Park, directly next to the covered bridge. You have a good chance of latching into a hatchery rainbow or brown during early May on the stocked run below the bridge. Fish small streamers through the run. The covered bridge reach is also a popular swimming area, another reason to avoid it during summer.

Working your way downstream toward Ausable Forks access is available just short of 3 miles from the State Route 86/State Route 9N intersection in Jay at a parking turnout and just short of 4 miles at Stickney Bridge Road. PFR water is continuous on both sides of the stream, upstream from the one-lane bridge. Parking is easy on either side of the bridge. The stream flows through an area with scattered small boulders and rocks. In late season, the water levels can be very low. Bring your caddis patterns for fishing this reach during early season.

SCHROON RIVER

From its beginnings at the confluence of small brooks near the hamlet of Underwood, near North Hudson, the Schroon River flows nearly 70 miles south to Warrensburg, where it unites with the mighty Hudson River. Along its way, the river flows into Schroon Lake. The water level of the 9-mile lake is controlled by Starbuckville Dam, near Brant Lake.

Starbuckville Dam, first constructed in the 1800s, was rebuilt in 1965, and again in 2005–2006. Dangerous undercurrents at the old dam were responsible for several drownings at the popular swimming hole. The new dam better regulates lake water levels, something that impacts fly-fishing conditions along the river that resumes its journey to the Hudson.

While NYSDEC stocks some 1,500 brown trout in the Schroon River in Essex County above Schroon Lake (at North Hudson), there's little doubt that the most popular fly-fishing locations on the Schroon River are below the dam, in Warren County. The Starbuckville Dam water discharge attracts fly anglers as well as conventional fishing-tackle enthusiasts, especially during April and May.

Starbuckville Dam is located only a couple miles off I-87, at Exit 25. Swing on to State Route 8 and take your first left onto County Road 20. The dam is located a half-mile up the road. You'll pass Crossroads Sporting Goods Store, where you can pick up supplies and a cup of coffee (it's the same store mentioned in the Pharaoh Lake Wilderness Area section). The dam reach is well stocked by both NYSDEC and the Warren County Fish Hatchery with browns and rainbows, but there's a chance you'll connect with a landlocked salmon that wanders into the river over the dam. Warren County Fish Hatchery typically stocks Starbuckville Dam outflow with 1,500 13-inch rainbows annually.

It's tough to fish Starbuckville when water discharges are high, but casting wooly buggers, streamers, and bucktails out into the flow is easy when water levels are reasonable.

Schroon River at Starbuckville Dam is one of the most popular fly-fishing reaches on the river. Part of its popularity is its easy access to the river. Parking exists at the small dam, at a pleasant picnic table area. (PHOTO VALERIE VALLA)

However, when the fishing is good, there's always competition for the best wading and fly-swinging locations. There are times you'll want to reel-in and head downstream to other popular PFR stretches.

Some nice yet boulder-strewn stream structure will be encountered downstream along Schroon River Road. From Starbuckville Dam, the river continues as slow-moving, often-deep water. A couple of miles downstream from Starbuckville Dam, the stream flows past the Tumblehead Falls reach. Locate there by driving down Schroon River Road south about 3.5 miles or so from Starbuckville Dam (3 miles south from the State Route 8/Schroon River Road intersection).

You'll encounter yellow NYSDEC public fishing signs along the river and a couple of parking turnouts on the road shoulder directly next to the stream. The PFR stretch on the west side of the stream is brief; watch for posted signs. Fish caddis dry flies and Prince Nymphs through the riffles and runs when water levels allow. Streamers and Wooly Buggers work well at other times.

A note of caution: wade carefully, and use a wading staff along the stretch. Stu LaDue, who lives in Saratoga Springs just down I-87 and enjoys fly fishing the Schroon River both at Starbuckville Dam and downstream at the Riverbank reach off Exit 24, makes a good point.

The PFR section downstream below Tumblehead Falls has "man-size boulders" scattered in the river that makes wading very difficult at times. Stu likes the reach a couple miles downstream because the wading is much easier. I first met Stu 20 years ago during my stint on the Saratoga Springs School Board. Stu was a school administrator who prepared PowerPoint presentations for our meetings. Those long meetings were often a cure for insomnia, but Stu's opening screensaver slide of trout flies helped perk me up for the long evenings ahead.

More ample PFR water that's wader friendly is located a short distance downstream, on the east side of the river. Head south on River Road a short distance to the County Road

Stu LaDue on the river downstream near the Riverbank section. Easy river access is available on the east side of the river, along a road that follows the stream. (PHOTO LAURA LADUE)

11 intersection. You'll pass by an old and now closed iron bridge and USGS water gauge station along the way downstream. Hence, the river reach here is sometimes called the "iron bridge stretch." However, the area here is posted on the west side of the river. PFR sections are available on the east side of the river. Brief public water is located upstream from the iron bridge; a long section is located downstream from the iron bridge at what's called the riverbank reach.

Access the east side of the river by crossing the County Road 11 bridge (if you're approaching from the south on I-87, take Exit 24 onto Bolton-Riverbank Road). Take the first left onto East Schoon River Road. At 0.2 mile, you'll encounter a formal Canoe Access and Angling parking area next to the river. NYSDEC signage at the lot notifies anglers the reach is categorized as Stocked-Extended. A path from the lot leads directly to the stream. Drive another half-mile up East Schroon Road to a shoulder turnout that will provide easy access to the river.

The best time to fish the popular Riverbank reach is during May. Warren County Fish Hatchery, located a short distance away in Warrensburg, heavily stocks the Riverbank reach with nearly 2,000 brook trout up to 10 inches in length and 900 or so rainbow trout up to 15 inches in length. Bring Elk Hair Caddis dry flies, small bucktails, and streamers.

In addition to the Riverbank and Starbuckville Dam reaches, trout are stocked both upstream from Schroon Lake and well downstream from Riverbank, in Warrensburg. The river directly upstream from the lake is heavily impacted by sedimentation and silting. A large formal NYSDEC angling parking lot is located on State Route 74 at a bridge crossing located 0.6 mile east from the US-9/State Route 74 intersection, off I-87 Exit 28. The river here is slow and meandering with heavy stream-bottom sediment. The large parking lot itself has substantial sand. Bypass this section and relocate upstream.

A productive fly-fishing pool is located 3 miles north on US-9, from the US-9/State Route 74 intersection, at the Schroon Falls bridge crossing, south of North Hudson. You can park on the north side of the bridge and fish the pool directly upstream from the bridge. You'll encounter all hatchery brown trout here during May. Nymphs and streamers work well. The river is posted on the right side (south side) of the river, downstream from the bridge where short rapids flow. A well-worn footpath access leads to the river from the left side of the river looking downstream (north side of the bridge). This is a popular recreational canoe-launching spot during summer months.

One final Schroon River stream reach worth mentioning is downstream at Warrensburg, off I-87 Exit 23. The Warren County Fish Hatchery typically stocks the Gristmill section with 1,200 9.5-inch rainbows and 120 larger 15-inch rainbows. The section is located downstream from the State Route 418 (River Street) iron bridge crossing. Rapids flow through the stretch, perfect for rainbows.

During my career with Glens Falls Hospital (located a half-hour south), my staff and I annually treated children at Warrensburg Elementary School, usually in early June. The school is located directly across from that reach, so naturally, there were occasions I fished it after work. I never latched into any of the bows during those years but often wished I had given that stretch more attention. But my guess is the river warms too much for it to be worth the bother later in the season.

Pharaoh Lake Wilderness Area

Like the Siamese Ponds Wilderness Area that lies to the west, the 46,282-acre Pharaoh Lake Wilderness Area located in the eastern Adirondacks is also blessed with many trout brooks, lakes, and ponds. Pharaoh Lake, the regions namesake 441-acre water, is completely surrounded by NYS Forest Preserve lands. All the trout ponds are Special Regulation waters that prohibit baitfish angling. Numerous trails throughout the area connect easily accessible ponds to the more remote ponds. Also, as is true with the Siamese Ponds Wilderness, there are often a few different trails that can lead into a given

Adirondack native Bill Altman in his Hornbeck, on Rock Pond. Numerous brook trout ponds dot the Pharaoh Lake Wilderness Area, including Rock Pond.

pond. Study the *National Geographic/Adirondack Mountain Club Illustrated Trails Map #743* and its companion Adirondack Mountain Club's *Eastern Trails* book (5th Edition).

Deciding what trail is best to fly fish a selected water depends on individual circumstances—whether planning for a short day trip or a longer extended backpacking trip, stopping at more than one pond on the trip. Use the same trip preparations that were described for fishing the Siamese Ponds Wilderness Area if trekking into a remote water; again, safety is of paramount importance (see page 146).

PHARAOH LAKE

The easiest trail into Pharaoh Lake is accessed by driving along State Route 8 to the northeast end of Brant Lake. Brant Lake itself is worthy of a cast or two on your way to Pharaoh Lake. You can access Brant Lake via a public boat launch (2.7 miles after Exit 25). While it's not a brook trout pond, the 5-mile-long lake is inhabited by largemouth bass, smallmouth bass, chain pickerel, crappie, rock bass, and yellow perch. NYS stocks the lake with brown and rainbow trout. Fly anglers will have better luck fishing Brant Lake for the warmwater species.

To reach the trailhead into the Pharaoh Lake Wilderness Area, take a left on Palisades Road located 8.1 miles from the I-87 Exit 25. Drive to Beaver Pond Road. You'll eventually see Pharaoh Lake Road. The formal parking area is located 0.4 mile down the dirt road. Use the designated parking area only and be sure to sign in at the NYSDEC kiosk, indicating how long you are planning to be in the wilderness area. Then begin your 3.6-mile hike to the Pharaoh Lake outlet.

The first 1.1 miles is an easy trek along a bumpy, often-muddy dirt road. Vehicles are technically not allowed to use the road, but some disobey the rules and park at the end at a quite large cleared area. I saw a truck back in there on my last hike in. From that point, a narrow trail enters a long, narrow planked bridge that will get you across a beaver flow and back on the trail. Another sign-in kiosk exists at the end of the plank bridge.

The trail is somewhat rocky and bumpy beyond that point, with a slight grade. But it soon levels off for a pleasant walk. You'll eventually reach another small plank bridge that crosses Pharaoh Lake Brook just below one of the largest beaver dams I've ever seen. You'll encounter a sign that indicates it's another 1.3 miles to Pharaoh Lake Outlet. A formal primitive camping site exists to the left of the bridge.

The 1.3 remaining miles follow an expansive beaver flow. The trail continues through mature hemlocks. When you finally arrive at Pharaoh Lake outlet, you'll see another NYSDEC sign-in kiosk and signage that indicates distances to the lean-to shelters and tent sites. One of the best lean-to shelters on the entire lake is #5. Lean-to #6 is also very nice, but #5 is right on what's called "watch rock"—a massive rock shoulder point.

If you plan to reach #5 by continuing to hike along the marked trail, don't let the nearly 4-mile hike so far go to your head. You still have over a half-mile of very rocky hiking to reach lean-to #6 and 1.2 miles to reach #5. But it's worth the effort.

In the event you carried in a floating craft, necessary for fishing Pharaoh Lake as wade fishing is next to impossible, you can paddle up-lake to the tent and lean-to sites. You'll sometimes encounter a "community canoe" beached along the lake. While it's illegal to do so, more than one angler hides a craft back in there, for later use, only for it to be discovered and enjoyed by someone else. A nice canoe was beached at the #5 site the last time I was in. Someone used an old shovel for a paddle; it was left inside the canoe.

I have yet to figure out how to entice the resident lake trout that like the deeper water, particularly down around the middle of the lake. During the fall, lake trout will wander

A 5-mile wilderness trail trek to reach Pharaoh Lake's scenic "Watch Rock" at lean-to #5 is worth the effort, fishing aside. (PHOTO VALERIE VALLA)

in a bit closer to the lake shore but enticing them to strike a streamer is tough. Fly fishers who enjoy catching panfish will find pumpkinseeds right next to shore, sometimes in small schools. They readily strike most any small wet fly.

As nice and picturesque as Pharaoh Lake is to the eyes, if your goal is entirely brook trout fishing, you're much better off sampling some of the smaller reclaimed ponds in the Pharaoh Lake Wilderness Area. Two of my favorites are Rock Pond and Gull Pond. Many good memories surrounding Rock Pond come to mind as I write.

ROCK POND

Rock Pond, adjacent to Putnam Pond (see Warmwater section) is a good brook trout destination for those interested in a day-trip outing or even an overnight lean-to experience. Rock Pond can actually be accessed via an east lake trail leading from Pharaoh Lake outlet to the Grizzle Ocean Trail. Only the very ambitious backpackers would want to hike another 5 miles just to reach Putnam Pond and then nearby Rock Pond via those trails. There's a much easier route to both Rock Pond and Grizzle Ocean, another trout pond in the vicinity.

Take Exit 28 off Interstate 87 to State Route 74. Rock Pond is reached via Putnam Pond State Campground. You won't miss the large NYSDEC Putnam Pond sign hanging on State Route 74 12 miles from the intersection of State Route 74 and State Route 9 just off I-87. Turn right off State Route 74 at the NYS signage and drive a couple of miles along Putts Pond Road to the NYS Putnam Pond Campground. A couple of dollars will get you through the entrance for a day-use permit. However, the campground is fabulous, and I've camped there with family several times over many years. An overnight or weekend stay is even better. Tent sites are very nice.

The Putnam Pond Campground and its namesake pond is the launching area into Rock Pond that's located in close proximity. A couple of trail alternatives will get you back into Rock Pond. Hauling a canoe 2.1 miles over the rocky and rolling trail terrain

Rock Pond, one of several brook trout ponds in the Pharaoh Lake Wilderness Area. A couple of different ways will deliver you to Rock Pond, and the best involves portaging a canoe or small watercraft.

Trail to Rock Pond and other neighboring ponds are marked with trail signs.

is a difficult task for anglers. However, there's an option to paddle across Putnam Pond and portage your craft up over a hill to Rock Pond. Paddle or row your craft to the end of what is called North Pond, a narrow bay of Putnam Pond.

Portaging a short distance into Rock Pond via the short portage after paddling to the end of North Pond is the best for fly fishers seeking a day trip and an easier route into Rock Pond. However, keep an eye on updated weather forecasts if taking that option. My brook trout fishing buddy Bill Altman and I found that out during what began as a pleasant early spring outing.

We both rowed lightweight Hornbeck boats to the portage trail at the end of North Pond during a beautiful morning. Bill soon got into a handsome brook trout on Rock Pond. I was still rowing my Hornbeck trolling streamer flies, tight to the shoreline—the usual springtime fishing tactic because the brook trout are closer to shore that time of year. But after landing the fish, he abruptly pointed to the darkening sky. The cold front was arriving sooner than we thought, and waves picked up on the earlier calm pond water surface. We quickly made a decision to get the heck back to Putnam Pond and the boat launch.

Mickey Finn (tied by Mike Valla) Classic Mickey Finn bucktails are effective flies to either cast or troll along the banks of Rock Pond. Popularized by John Alden Knight (1890–1966), the colorful pattern has accounted for many brook trout brought to the net. Mickey Finn bucktails, still effective for enticing brook trout, go back to the 1930s during the time it was originally called the Assassin by Knight and his fishing companion, Frank Cooper. A Toronto, Canada, newspaper writer soon after named it Mickey Finn.

After the portage back to North Pond, the wind was blowing hard, creating white caps—not good for our lightweight Hornbecks. Bill was yelling from his boat for me to hug the shoreline, and as soon as we turned the corner out of the narrow North Pond bay into Putnam Pond, I rowed as hard as arms would allow, crashing my craft head-on into the waves. There was panic in Bill's voice that I might get broadside to the now-crashing waves and flip my boat. I never rowed so hard, and we both made it back to safety at the boat launch. Such can be the case fishing in the Adirondacks. Hunkering down in a nearby lean-to might have been a better option that day. A lean-to shelter exists near the portage route.

If you decide to trek into Rock Pond via the trail instead of paddling to North Pond and portaging, the easiest hiking route begins near the Putnam Pond boat launch. Walk across the bridge at the pond's dam and interesting spillway outlet. You'll encounter signage and eventually reach the trailhead near campground sites #38 and #39. You'll reach Rock Pond after hiking a little over 2 miles. Signage along the trail will lead you to Rock Pond.

As mentioned, wade fishing is tough not only on Rock Pond but on most all Adirondack brook trout ponds. We usually bolt our Hornbecks to metal-frame backpacks if trekking long distances along trails. It's not too hard to hike the rocky trail employing that technique because your hands are free as you negotiate the rolling terrain with a walking stick on the way into a pond. An inflatable craft or float tube is also an option but not nearly as effective as fishing out of a canoe or Hornbeck boat. Whatever the method of choice to fish Rock Pond, bring Mickey Finn bucktail flies to entice the brook trout.

GRIZZLE OCEAN

NYSDEC biologists believe the little pond still has characteristics necessary to support a more vibrant trout population.

The biological survey conducted by the Bureau of Fisheries in 2019 turned up brook trout ranging in size from 7 inches to almost 15 inches. Compared with surveys going back to 1984, this points to a "steady deterioration" in size and numbers. Greater numbers of brook trout ranging from 8 inches to 18 inches turned up in sampling nets a few decades ago.

Despite those findings, the little pond has great water chemistry and is a prime candidate for reclamation. Non-native golden shiners that inhabit the pond have impacted brook trout populations. As it now stands, the management recommendation is to treat the pond with rotenone, then restock it with brook trout. The pond is still worthy of a fly angler's cast now, by accessing it at the Putnam Pond Campground.

There are two ways to get to the pond from the campground area. A trailhead exists next to a parking area at the campground. Portaging a canoe 2.1 miles from Putnam Pond

Grizzle Ocean, in the Pharaoh Lake Wilderness Area Grizzle Ocean is hardly an ocean-size pond; it's all of 22 acres in size with a depth of 36 feet. While brook trout inhabit the pond (it's stocked every fall with hybrid fingerlings), populations have suffered over the years according to NYSDEC fisheries biologists who conducted sampling studies a couple of years ago. (PHOTO VALERIE VALLA)

Campground to the lean-to shelter at Grizzle Ocean isn't the issue; it's the rolling terrain trail, which is very rocky and cumbersome to negotiate. The series of narrow-planked bridges will easily get you across a few drainages that cross the trail among the nice hemlock stands, so that isn't a problem either. Trekking the entire trail from the parking area to the pond is a nice yet bumpy hike but not very conducive to hauling in watercraft.

Adequate signage along the way will keep you heading the correct direction on the trails, especially when encountering intersecting trails to other locations, such as Clear

Narrow-planked bridges along the trail to Grizzle Pond

Gull Pond, located near the east shore of Schroon Lake, is one of the easiest brook trout ponds to access. Anglers can easily portage a canoe from the formal NYSDEC parking area to the water.

Pond and Rock Pond and even distant Pharaoh Lake. Approximately 0.9 mile from the parking area, the trail intersects a short portage trail that originates at the south end of Putnam Pond, the much better option for getting watercraft into Grizzle Ocean.

Paddling a craft from the boat launch area at Putnam Pond to its south end then portaging a very short distance to the main trail will cut off half of the trail-hiking miles to Grizzle Ocean. You'll still have a bumpy trail remaining on your portage journey to the lean-to, but that option is much better than the alternative.

The lean-to is very nice, situated a hundred or so feet from the pond's shore. Shortly after ice-out, in spring, brook trout come in close to shore. It's somewhat possible to wade directly out into the pond in the area just down the slope from the lean-to. The area has a rocky bottom, allowing the angler to make casts without the need for a watercraft.

However, unless you have a canoe that can be rowed along the full extent of the shoreline, your success in enticing brook trout will be limited. The same holds true if sampling Grizzle Ocean during the fall season. Use the same fly patterns that are effective in other brook trout ponds if trolling out of a canoe—a size 10 Mickey Finn bucktail is my pattern of choice. A floating line with a short sinking-tip length works well.

GULL POND

Anglers not desiring a laborious hike into the most remote Adirondack area brook trout ponds should try Gull Pond. It's very easy to get to. Take Exit 28 off Interstate 87 to US-9/State Route 74, the same exit that will get you to Rock Pond and Grizzle Ocean (described in the previous section). Instead of heading east on State Route 74, go south of US-9 a little less than a mile, then a left on Alder Meadow Road. Follow Alder Meadow Road about 2 miles to a right turn on Adirondack Road. A formal NYSDEC parking lot and Gull Pond trailhead, marked by a large hanging sign, is less than 2 miles down the road. Make sure that you sign in at the NYSDEC kiosk at the trailhead. You'll encounter signage alerting visitors that camping is not allowed. Gull Pond is a day-trip destination.

The half-mile trail to the pond is often wet and rocky, but narrow plank bridges will easily get you over the worst areas. It's not very difficult to portage in a canoe. You'll need a watercraft to fish the pond effectively. Gull Pond has awesome views from the rocky outcrop at the trail's end, especially during the fall season.

Trolling up and down the shoreline with colorful bucktails will interest the brook trout, if they're in the mood. I've had blank days there, as well as successful outings.

LOST POND

While driving along Putts Road on your way to Putnam Pond Campground, you'll notice a trailhead sign that leads to Lost Pond, another trout pond in the Pharaoh Lake Wilderness Area. The trailhead is located on the left side of the road, a little over 3 miles from the State Route 74 intersection.

The pond is located about 1.4 miles from the trailhead. It's not an overly difficult trek to the pond. A plank bridge, located about a mile from the trailhead, will easily get you over a small stream. Unfortunately, there are no lean-to shelters, but a couple of formal campsites are located at the pond. Lost Pond is also known for rainbow trout NYSDEC stocks annually.

CLEAR POND

Clear Pond is located in the same vicinity as Rock Pond, Little Rock Pond, and Putnam Pond. You can trek to the pond, and its lean-to shelter, by following the same trail that leads to Little Rock Pond and Rock Pond (see Rock Pond section). Follow the signage that begins at the boat launch area and at the campsite #38 and #39 area trailhead. However, as is the case with fishing Rock Pond, you're better off paddling a watercraft west across Putnam Pond to a trailhead that will lead to the pond and lean-to after a short 0.6-mile portage.

OTHER BROOK TROUT PONDS IN PHARAOH LAKE WILDERNESS AREA

- Burge Pond (Schroon Township)
- Cotters Pond (Schroon Township)
- Crab Pond (Schroon Township)
- Goose Pond (Schroon Township)
- Lilypad Pond (Ticonderoga Township)
- Spectacle Pond (Schroon Township)
- Springhill Pond (Ticonderoga Township)
- Whortleberry Pond (Schroon Township)

Lake George Wild Forest

Part of the Adirondack Forest Preserve, 72,508-acre Lake George Wild Forest lies to the south of the Pharaoh Lake Wilderness Area. It's considered one of the most popular areas in Adirondack Park because of its proximity to the resort Village of Lake George and other popular vacation hamlets along the west shore of Lake George. Numerous hiking trails run through the area. It's also dotted with brook trout ponds.

Duell Hill Road and Grassville Road, off State Route 8 on the south east shore of Brant Lake, will get to trailheads that lead to Island Pond, Long Pond, Round Pond, and Buttermilk Pond. You'll pass these roads, on the left, along the same route directions provided for Pharaoh Lake Wilderness Area trailhead, located at the north end of the lake. Study the *National Geographic/Adirondack Mountain Club Illustrated Trails Map #743* and its companion Adirondack Mountain Club's *Eastern Trails* book (5th Edition) for directions to these ponds, although some are difficult to access. By far the easiest trout pond to reach in the Lake George Wild Forest is Jabe Pond, one of my very favorite brook trout and rainbow trout ponds in the area.

Rob Streeter with a lake trout, on Lake George. Rob catches lakers on flies during first light.
(PHOTO ROB STREETER)

JABE POND

The nice thing about Jabe Pond, besides the brook trout that the Warren County Fish Hatchery typically stocks, is you can drive almost up to the pond's shore. Regular canoes are an easy quick portage from a formal NYSDEC parking area to the water. Within minutes, you can rig up and start casting without having to endure a long hike carrying a watercraft. Boat motors are allowed if rated 10 horsepower or less. The 146-acre pond, with 3 miles of shoreline, is named for Jabez Patchin, one of the early settlers that was said to have built a cabin on the site. For that reason, it's often called Jabez Pond.

Jabe Pond is easy to reach. Approaching from areas south, take I-87 Exit 24 to County Road 11 to State Route 9N. Follow State Route 9N 15.7 miles to Split Rock Road in the hamlet of Hague. In less than 2 miles, macadam-surfaced Split Rock Road joins Jabe

Jabe Pond, a Special Regulations artificial-lure-only water, is one of the easier Adirondack trout ponds to access in the Lake George Wild Forest Area. (PHOTO VALERIE VALLA)

Pond Road (Battle Hill Spur), a gravel road that's not always maintained, but lately, a local hunting club has added crushed stone to improve the surface and driving conditions. The total distance to the NYSDEC pond parking area from the 9N/Split Rock Road intersection is 2.5 miles. You might run into potholes along the bumpy road. A four-wheel drive vehicle is best. I've driven both four-wheel drive sedans and a Jeep up there, but road conditions can be iffy. Primitive tent-site camping is allowed around the pond at specific designated areas, but be sure to read the regulations that are posted at the parking area. Camping isn't allowed on the islands.

Jabe Pond Road will deliver you to the narrower and shallow northeast end of the pond. The wider south end, dotted with a couple islands, has the deeper 40-foot to 75-foot water.

May into June is a good time to fish the pond, and again in the fall. Troll or cast small streamers along the shorelines.

Fish will rise to hatches; the most anticipated is the annual *Hexagenia* emergence that usually takes place the third week to the end of June. You'll encounter other fly fishers on the pond during the Hex hatch, for sure. Bring large dry flies as well as *Hexagenia* nymph or emerger patterns. As is true on Thirteenth Lake during that same hatch, the fish don't seem too picky about dry fly pattern choice.

When light begins fading away, I use the same Big Fish dry fly, created by Ralph Graves, that I cast on Thirteenth Lake for the same hatch, largely because I can spot it easily on the water (see Thirteenth Lake section).

LAKE GEORGE (LANDLOCK SALMON AND LAKE TROUT)

The 32-mile-long, 187-foot-deep lake tucked over on the southeast edge of the Adirondacks has been called the "Queen of American Lakes." During summer, the resort Village of Lake George attracts thousands of tourists, seasonal homeowners, and recreationists.

Boaters, kayakers, and swimmers enjoy its waters and children splash at the village's NYS-operated, public Million Dollar Beach. Grills fire up and picnickers enjoy the scenery. Docked over to the left of the beach along West Brook, when it's not out on a shoreline cruise with tourists, is the popular *Lac du Saint Sacrement*. By the end of summer, the crowds leave Million Dollar Beach. Other visitors begin poking their way into the area in early fall—landlocked salmon that are attracted to the flow of West Brook out into the lake. The landlocks will also show up in the same area during mid-April, along with lake trout that wander in closer to shore. Fly anglers targeting landlocks are sometimes surprised to net a nice laker.

When I joined nearby Glens Falls Hospital, in the late 1980s, one of the first items on my list was to sample Million Dollar Beach and the landlocked salmon that a fellow hospital practitioner alerted me to. Fly anglers got into fish, but it was tough going, with a lot of blank days. Through the 1990s into the mid-2000s, the prospects of hooking into a landlocked salmon not only at that location but throughout Lake George were dim. Conventional tackle anglers out on the lake also experienced decline. Plenty of salmon were stocked, but they seemed to just vanish.

However, prospects began to turn around a few years later. Dan Wanczyk ran into me at one of the fly-fishing shows, and I asked him about Million Dollar Beach and the landlocked salmon. To my surprise, Dan mentioned that NYSDEC experimented with a different landlocked strain, the Sebago strain from Maine. It wasn't until recent years that conventional tackle lake anglers noticed an uptick in catch rates. Once again, I found myself fishing Million Dollar Beach, this time with Dan, since the location is only an hour drive from my home.

Dan Wanczyk fishing the mouth of West Brook, on Lake George. Landlocked salmon cruise the mouth of West Brook, located at the south end of the lake, during April. Anglers also have a chance of enticing a lake trout in the same location.

You'll sometimes see the salmon rolling on the water surface very early in the morning or late in the afternoon into evening. Wading is very easy along the sandbar at the mouth of the stream. You'll rarely have to wade more than knee-deep, positioned on the sandbar, then casting into the deeper water where the fish hang out and cruise. Fishing success is far from guaranteed; you might get into a salmon one day and the next draw a blank. It could happen in less than an hour, hours later, or not at all when the fish are not yet cooperative or interested. Avoid days with extremely placid water and full sunshine. A slight chop on the water is favorable, something I learned many years ago on Cayuga Lake off of Salmon Creek.

Dan, who lives only a few minutes away in the Glens Falls area, fishes the lake not far off the mouth of the brook with a Guideline LPXe 13-foot, 7-to-8-weight two-handed salmon rod, which provides effortless casting. He uses a 465-grain, 34-foot Spey floating line and a Rio 500-grain skagit max for sinking tips. I use an Orvis 9-foot, 7-weight rod with a floating line and various sinking tips. We both use featherwing fly patterns, including classic Grey Ghost and the Green Ghost streamers.

Make sure your tippet has the strength to withstand the attack once a salmon intercepts the fly. On one recent occasion, after patiently casting for a few hours, my fly was wacked, and in seconds, the fish broke off from an undersized tippet. I now use 8-pound Maxima. I assumed the fish was a salmon until two days later when I received an email photo from Dan. "Is this your fly, Mike?" Dan asked. "A fellow caught a 5- or 6-pound laker today, and this fly was in its jaw." Yup—my fly, my fish that broke off. Odd things can happen fly fishing.

Like the landlocked salmon, lake trout are also on the hunt for spawning rainbow smelt that frequent the mouths of streams that flow into Lake George. Rob Streeter targets the lake trout off the mouth of West Brook using a different tactic by fly casting from a boat in darkness. Inhabitants of deep, dark waters, lakers shun sunlight and bright conditions

Laker Taker (tied by Rob Streeter) Aptly named Laker Taker, Bob Steeter's purple rabbit strip fly attracts lake trout that frequent Lake George, particularly during early spring on the lake's south end.

Lake George landlocked salmon caught off the mouth of West Brook are beautiful fish. (PHOTO DAN WANCZYK)

in shallower water than they might wander into during the smelt spawning runs. Bundled up for the occasion and with headlamp secured, he's had sustained success with lakers on Lake George, arriving on the scene in darkness. Rob finds that getting into lakers requires very early morning fishing, before 7:30 a.m. He prefers a double rabbit strip and purple pattern he created and which he calls the Laker Taker.

To reach the mouth of West Brook, take I-87 Exit 22 to a left on US-9. Drive about a half-mile to right on Fort George Road (just past the Stewart's convenience store). Follow Fort George Road to Beach Road, then take a left to parallel park on Elizabeth Little Boulevard at the lake. A popular public boat launch is also within sight of West Brook inflow, located a short distance down the shoreline.

Because netting one of the landlocks off the shore at Million Dollar Beach is hit or miss, and episodic, the best approach would be to combine an outing when planning to fish other nearby streams or ponds. Schroon River is not far away, as well as other waters described earlier. It's a good place to head during April or during fall months when area rivers are blown out during highwater conditions.

Green Ghost (tied by Mike Valla) A variety of streamers, both classic and contemporary, are effective for catching landlocked salmon at the south end of Lake George during April, and again in the fall. A classic Green Ghost, originated by Bert Quimby from South Windham, Maine, is a heritage landlocked Salmonfly first fished on Maine lakes.

Male Dace (tied by Mike Valla) Originated by Lew Oatman (1902–1958), the so-called father of baitfish fly imitations, his Male Dace is another splendid choice for landlocked salmon hanging off West Brook during spring and fall.

Mettawee River

Straddling two states, and two New York regions, the Mettawee River is a charming trout stream that provides great fly-fishing opportunities from its Vermont headwaters near Dorset all the way into New York. All 17 miles of its Vermont water is a wild trout fishery supporting brook, rainbow, and brown trout. NYSDEC stocks trout along several reaches downstream. From Granville to the Vermont border, the stream is categorized as Stocked-Extended.

The Mettawee cuts across New York for some 20 miles, give or take, before eventually emptying into Lake Champlain near Whitehall, a village near the extreme southeast border of the Adirondack Park. The lowermost New York section where it approaches Whitehall is a warm-water fishery. The upper New York public fishing stretches, in the Granville area, are inhabited by stocked rainbow and brown trout, with some holdovers, and a few wild fish. Given my experiences fishing the stream throughout its length, over many years, I can easily give the Mettawee a nod; it's a great trout-fishing destination.

The Vermont Mettawee hasn't received the same attention, or respect, given to its famous neighbor, the Batten Kill (a stream that also straddles both states). True, it's a smaller stream and miles of it flow well away from roads and access points. Unlike the Batten Kill, the Mettawee hasn't been the focus of major books or other profile-raising fanfare. No cane rods or exquisitely machined fly reels have been named Mettawee. Major fly-fishing personalities haven't hitched their fame to the stream. Yet the Mettawee provides plenty for fly fishers willing to put time into exploring and understanding the stream in all its pleasant variety.

The Mettawee, home to healthy stream-bred trout in the Vermont reaches, flows through some of the nicest countryside you'll ever hope to visit—in both states. It all begins in its brook-trout-filled headwaters. The little stream is born on the southern slopes of Dorset Mountain in Vermont, not far from the Batten Kill, near Manchester—home of the Orvis Company. It tumbles swiftly down the mountainside, skirting the base of its namesake 2,800-foot mountain, the Mettawee.

"The brook trout are not big in the extreme headwaters, but there's plenty of them," Chris Alexopoulos, a staffer with the US Forest Service, told me a few years ago. He

Mettawee River upstream in Vermont, 2 miles from the New York border. When planning an outing on the New York Mettawee River mileage, consider purchasing a one-day Vermont license. Very good Mettawee water flows just over the state borderline in Vermont. NYSDEC categorizes the Mettawee as Stocked-Extended.

did some electrofishing along the tiny stream tucked in the woods near the base of the Mettawee. It's rare to find anglers near the Mettawee's source.

After leaving the Pawlet area in Vermont, well downstream from the river's source, the stream pushes on for another 7 or so miles to the New York border. The stretch along River Road, less than 2 miles from the New York border as the crow flies, is one of my favorite Mettawee areas. It's located so close to the New York State border that anglers visiting the Mettawee should consider purchasing at least a one-day Vermont fishing license. From the New York/Vermont border in West Pawlett (off County Road 29 or Town Highway 19, depending on the approach), drive about 2 miles to River Road along Vermont County Road 153. Take a right on River Road 0.7 mile to the Betts Road bridge crossing and a couple parking turnouts along the stream.

You can fish a mile from the bridge upstream or downstream. During the early-season high water, bucktails, fished slow and deep, can bring strikes. During later spring and early fall, I enjoy fishing upstream from the bridge, where the secluded Mettawee flows along a mountain base well removed from the road. I like to twitch a caddisfly dry in the small pools and dead-drift Atherton Hare's Ear Nymphs in the pocketwater.

Every year, the River Road section gives up some fine, 16-plus-inch brown trout to persistent anglers who realize that the Mettawee can be a tough river that is not always willing to surrender its trophies. This wild trout fishery often discourages anglers who expect to land a trout during every outing. But the stream-bred trout are there, and netting one of them is an accomplishment. The chances of netting trout are much better in New York because the stream is stocked with hatchery fish.

Leaving the River Road stretch in Vermont behind, the Mettawee crosses into the Village of Granville, New York, after flowing over impassible (and inaccessible) Button Falls, which keeps New York's stocked trout out of Vermont. The Mettawee picks up additional water from the Indian River, a meandering Vermont-born tributary. Fewer than 20 miles later, well beyond its impressive Class IV and V whitewater rapids sections around North Granville, the Mettawee dumps into the Champlain Canal and then finally into Lake Champlain south of the village of Whitehall.

The most popular New York Mettawee PFR trout water is located in the Middle Granville, Truthville, and North Granville areas, where some 8,000 trout are stocked annually. The best way to reach these waters, and the formal NYSDEC fishing access parking areas, is to use State Route 22 at the Village of Granville, your gateway route to miles of stocked-trout public-fishing waters. Back in West Pawlett, at the Vermont border, cross into New York and take County Road 22 to State Route 29, then north a couple of miles to Granville.

Granville is often referred to as the "Colored Slate Capital of the World." Slate quarries, scattered around the area, mine green, gray, gray-black, purple, and red slates. In fact, the only working red-slate quarry in the world is located here. Many rooftops, along with other structures, display the colored slates the town is famous for. If the fishing is slow, or if you have time to do so, stop in at the Slate Valley Museum in Granville. Displays tell the story of mid-1800s immigrants, arriving first from Wales and then from elsewhere, who came to the region with skills that helped transform the area into the home of a booming industry that still persists.

The slate industry is apparent as you drive westerly along State Route 22 in route to several NYSDEC stream access parking lots scattered along the river. One formal NYSDEC angler parking lot is located not far from where State Route 22 merges with State Route 22-A at Middle Granville. Look for a large red Bobcat farm equipment sign on your left 1 mile north of State Route 2-A; just beyond the sign and slate quarry tailings, the large parking lot comes into view on your right. You won't miss the large NYSDEC sign.

A footpath easement leads from the lot to the low-gradient Mettawee stretches. A pleasant, grassy streamside path goes upstream, providing easy access to the riffles and

The Truthville reach at Middleton Road holds nice trout in early spring. Fish streamers through the runs and small pools. (PHOTO VALERIE VALLA)

Mettawee Falls, on the lower river, inhabits both trout and warmwater species. Anglers never know what fish species are on the line once they hook up. It could be a stocked trout or even a big bass. (PHOTO VALERIE VALLA)

pools. This section is best fished during the first couple weeks of May, about the time the Hendrickson hatch begins.

Other formal access points are located a short distance downstream from the Middle Granville NYSDEC parking lot. Drive another 1.5 miles north on State Route 22A and then veer left onto County Road 21 (you'll see Hilltop Slate on the left, where County Road 21 merges into State Route 22A). In less than a half-mile, after the road crosses over the Mettawee, look for a small parking area on your left next to the bridge, on De Kalb Road. Because the New York Mettawee stretches are stocked, it's common to see local bait casters in action on the river for several days after the hatchery truck has made its annual appearance. They tend to fish from the banks close to the public angler-access parking areas.

A NYSDEC fishing parking lot in Truthville also provides easy access to the river. My largest holdover brown came out of this water several years ago during a late-May evening caddisfly flight—it's a stretch that sometimes prompts fish to rise at dusk. A 3.5-mile drive from the De Kalb Road fishing access parking lot gets you to the site: turn left out of the De Kalb Road parking lot, drive 2 miles to the end of De Kalb Road, and turn left onto Truthville Road. Drive just over a mile on Truthville Road to Middleton Road and the County Road 12 bridge that spans the Mettawee. The Truthville NYSDEC angler parking lot is located just 0.2 mile upstream from the bridge, on Middleton Road. You can also park at the bridge and walk down a steep trail to fish the pocketwater and pools downstream from the bridge.

I like to skitter caddisfly dry patterns over the riffles and runs in this area. Elk Hair Caddis patterns work well, but I also like caddisfly dry flies that have hackle in front of the wing, to aid in skittering the fly across the water. Hendricksons emerge in early May. Small bucktails and streamers work well in this section when bugs are not in sight.

There's a final place anglers should visit when fishing the lower Mettawee River. Mettawee Falls plunges out of a gorge-like setting into a large, deep, swirling pool. You might run into a big rainbow, brown, or smallmouth bass. There's also a good chance you won't net a single fish. You're more likely to run into bait anglers than fly fishers at Mettawee Falls. Expect swimmers and other recreationalists if you visit during the hot summer months. I most enjoy admiring Mettawee Falls in early May, about the time when the first signs of spring are evident in the shrubbery along the river. A massive rock slab dips into the pool, offering a great place to sit just after sunrise and have a cup of coffee while enjoying the scenery. For me, the place is more of a scenic destination than a fly-fishing destination.

Reach Mettawee Falls by taking State Route 22 to the North Granville area from the State Route 22/State Route 22A in Middle Granville. In about 4.5 miles, watch for the large, white Calvary Baptist Church building on your right at Sheehan Road. Turn right onto Sheehan and drive 0.2 mile to Upper Turnpike Road, and then turn left. The NYS-DEC angler parking lot is 1 mile down Upper Turnpike Road (a NYSDEC angler parking sign on Upper Turnpike Road marks the location). A path leads down the hill to the falls.

In areas downstream from Mettawee Falls, all the way to the river's mouth at the Champlain Canal in Whitehall, the now turbid Mettawee flows at a low gradient, transforming into a warmwater fishery. By the time the Mettawee reaches Whitehall, the once-crystalline, cold waters found in the headwaters are long gone. By summer, most of the New York Mettawee warms too much for trout. Trout fishing can turn marginal in many of the stretches that provided good sport during May and early June.

Capital Region

Straddling both Vermont and New York, Batten Kill is no doubt one of the better known trout waters that flow through the Capital Region, but there are many other lesser known trout creeks, brooks, and ponds in the area. As is the case with all New York State regions, depending on which agency you reference, boundaries of the Capital Region vary. I've limited its extent to just south of Lake George, straddling the Hudson River that flows south through Albany, New York, the state's capital, into the mid and lower Hudson River valley. It's bordered on the east by Vermont, running west into Central New York and the fringes of the Catskill Mountain Region.

On the east side of the Hudson River, the region's waters include well-known trout rivers, such as the Batten Kill, as well as smaller, lightly fished, trout-filled creeks and brooks. Like the Batten Kill, a few of the streams originate in Vermont then traverse across state lines, creating, in some instances, much different fisheries. Habitats change, as well as state fishing regulations.

Springheads along the Taconic Mountains of Massachusetts, a range that runs north-south along the New York border, also sends water into New York, creating coldwater flows that support trout, such as Kinderhook Creek. Some streams closer to Albany and the Hudson River are born on the high-elevation, rocky, Adirondack-like Rensselaer Plateau, New York's fifth largest forest. The National Audubon Society considers the Plateau an Important Bird Area. Dairy farms are scattered in the lowlands.

Batten Kill in winter at the Eagleville Bridge reach, downstream from Shushan. Historic Batten Kill is one of the best-known trout rivers in the Capital Region. (PHOTO VALERIE VALLA)

On the west side of the Hudson River, the mighty Mohawk River traverses regions to the west and ends its journey at the Hudson River near Albany (see Warmwater section). Other smaller trout waters on the west side of the river, like Catskill Creek, originate from areas that are near the fringes of the Catskill Mountains Region. Farmland streams, such as Schenevus Creek, flow west, away from the Hudson, and end up in the Susquehanna River in the Central New York Region.

Trout fishing aside, plenty of small warmwater ponds and lakes provide fishing opportunities for bass, tiger muskellunge, and northern pike. Anglers often seek out stillwaters and target those species during late season when trout streams warm. All in all, the Capital Region is a great area to give your fly rod a workout, no matter what season finds you seeking fishing opportunities.

Batten Kill

In his 1993 book *The Battenkill*, Vermont fly-fishing author John Merwin (1946–2013) insisted that this famous river is "among the—if not the most—technically difficult fly-fishing streams in America."

I agree. I've experienced more frustration—angling and otherwise—during my over four decades of fishing the New York stretch of the Batten Kill (aka Battenkill) than on any other trout stream in the state. Other regulars feel the same way, but the lure of the stream, which flows through some of the most charming country in New York, is enough to keep some anglers satisfied.

Arising in East Dorset, Vermont, the celebrated Batten Kill flows southwesterly through Manchester and then Arlington before heading west into New York, leaving 28 of the river's 59.4 miles behind. The stream pushes into the little hamlet of Shushan, where it picks up Camden Creek before turning north and passing near Salem, where it gathers Black Creek and White Creek, both trout streams. The Batten Kill widens and maintains its low-gradient flow through East Greenwich, where it again changes direction, heading south toward Battenville and then west to Greenwich, before it finally dumps into the Hudson River near Schuylerville.

Trout inhabit nearly all of New York's share of the Batten Kill as it winds and turns after clearing the Vermont border, a fact that may surprise nonregulars, who may be more familiar with the famous Vermont section. Those new to the New York stretch of the river may also be surprised to learn that it, like the Vermont reach, carries an impressive angling legacy that included iconic fly-fishing figures such as John Atherton (1900–1952), Lew Oatman (1902–1958), and Lee Wulff (1905–1991). Atherton was largely attached to the Vermont section around Arlington. Lew Oatman and Lee Wulff are more associated with New York reaches around the hamlet of Shushan. Extensive chapters on these individuals are found in my book *The Founding Flies* (2013).

Besides his craft as a well-known illustrator, Atherton is known for his classic Atherton series fly patterns. While the New York Batten Kill's angling heritage is as important as that of the Vermont stretch, fishery management practices differ greatly between the two states: New York stocks fish, while Vermont has abandoned the practice. However, the Batten Kill displays fickleness in both states; it can be extremely challenging.

The first 4 miles in New York's Batten Kill from the Vermont border on State Route 313 down to the quaint Eagleville Covered Bridge is regulated as year-round Catch and Release water. This is by far the most popular fly-fishing section on the river but also the most popular mileage among recreational kayak, canoe, and inner-tube enthusiasts. The multiple-use concept is alive and well on the river—a bit *too* alive and well for many fly fishers, including this one.

I first fished the Batten Kill in May 1978, during the time my wife Valerie and I were still living in Ithaca, in the Finger Lakes region. Val's parents live near Schuylerville, only a half-hour drive to the stream. During the times we visited her parents, I always headed to the river, to throw a few casts in between family obligations. In 1988, we moved to Saratoga Springs when I joined the staff at nearby Glens Falls Hospital. The move allowed much more time for me to fish and understand not only the Batten Kill but other area waters, especially in the Adirondacks.

During the early to late 1970s, fishing was rarely interrupted by recreational floaters. A canoe would float by now and then, with a friendly wave as they drifted by. That all changed when the first commercial inner-tube establishments colonized the stream. The "industry" grew, expanding into Vermont. Then came the kayak and canoe renters. Today, a Vermont canoe-rental company is involved, as well as a newly established Vermont tube-rental outfitter. It's become insane.

Batten Kill reach at the Pooks stretch located at the County Road 64 bridge crossing in Shushan. Farmers who own property along the Pooks reach have always allowed fishing on their river frontage. The reach is named for Charles "Pook" Gilchrist, who owned land next to the stream. (PHOTO VALERIE VALLA)

The "theme park" atmosphere on the Special Regulation No-Kill stretch. Recreational kayakers and tubers during summer floating the Special Regulation stretch, at the Spring Hole pool in Shushan. The small parking area next to the water at Buffum's Bridge is frequently crowded with vehicles from recreational swimmers, tubers, and other watercraft enthusiasts. Commercial canoe and tube rental establishments use the fishing access lot as a ferrying point.

During the hot summer months, the State Route 313 rest stop turnout, located only a short distance from the Vermont border along the Catch and Release stretch, swarms with swimmers and floaters. The only way I can describe just how bad it has become is to liken the river to a theme park. Commercial canoe- and tube-rental businesses cart dozens of floaters to the convenient put-in at the rest stop, creating much angst among anglers. Some anglers never return.

There was one occasion on a weekday morning in late May, during the time I owned a fishing cabin in Shushan that was walking distance to the river, that a bunch of drunken floaters slammed into me while I was fishing during a caddis hatch. I wasn't too happy, either, when a McKenzie drift boat came through, asking me to "get out of the stream" because "there isn't enough water for us to get around you." Hello? Shared use, sure. But this isn't respectful multiple use of a resource.

Some Batten Kill anglers have learned to fish the Catch and Release section very early in the morning, late in the evening, or even off-season during early and late winter to dodge the commotion. Trout can be taken during the winter if the weather cooperates. Hardy and optimistic fly fishers have an opportunity to escape winter's cabin fever by stepping into the Batten Kill's trout wintering holes.

This activity was once limited to the Catch and Release year-round fishing regulations. With NYSDEC's changed regulations, winter Catch and Release fishing is allowed on the entire New York section. If the planets align themselves, there is always the possibility of taking a fine Batten Kill brown trout in atypical circumstances. My friend, Teddy Patlen, stumbled upon such a day on January 1, 2011. Ted routinely makes an annual trip to the Batten Kill around January 1 to visit our mutual fly-fishing friend (and my Cambridge neighbor) Adriano Manocchia. The weather was unusual—bright sunshine, no wind, and ambient temperatures above freezing, maybe 40 degrees. Fly fishing was worth a try.

The location was a gentle pool on the Catch and Release stretch. Adriano was using a sinking-tip line, fishing an olive Matuka; Ted selected a black leech pattern, fished on a floating line and long leader with split shot. Fishing midday for only a few hours, they both got into fish. Patlen lost his, but Manocchia landed and photographed a husky brown trout. Ted was convinced that the Catch and Release stretch on the Batten Kill had winter-fishing potential. He was right. Scott Sztorc, one of the Batten Kill's most knowledgeable guides, has enjoyed his best winter fishing after an unexpected rain that brings the water temperature up a few degrees. He likes to fish leech patterns, or streamers during winter months.

Winter aside, one of my favorite Catch and Release stretches, during early spring and early fall, is the Grocery Pool and the glide below it. I like to slip into the river here very early in the morning, before the flotillas begin, and later in the evening. Just past the State Route 313 rest stop, you'll see a large white house on the road. The Grocery Pool, named for the old red grocery store that existed nearby in the 1800s, is located several hundred feet behind the large white house and field along the road. Park at the State Route 313 rest stop turnout and walk downstream along a river path or park at the State Route 313 bridge, located a mile or so from the Vermont border, and fish upstream to the pool. Before heading down to the Grocery Pool, try Dutchman's Hole, located just upstream from the rest area. A small bridge spans the river, marking the pool and the glide below it. It's best known for the then-state-record 32-inch, 12.25-pound brown trout that area resident 17-year-old Roy Brown took on May 11, 1923. Brown also took a 6-pounder out of Dutchman's in 1942. The mounted fish, what remains of it, is located at the covered bridge museum in Shushan.

I've not repeated Brown's accomplishments on Dutchman's, but I've netted some big browns out of the Grocery Pool, a hemlock-shaded, ledge-rock hole at the base of a steep mountain, well away from the main road. The pool is known for large trout. I twice hooked and lost a big brown I named "Tethys" (after the Greek Titan goddess of fresh water). I finally netted the fish on an old Catskill-style dry fly called the Firehole No. 1 after pursuing the trout for a good month, before sunrise on some days and until

Tethys, the big brown that occupied my attention for a month on Grocery Pool

last light on others. I've taken some nice fish casting and skittering dry flies along the heavily shaded hemlock banks downstream from the Grocery Pool, working my way down to the State Route 313 bridge.

The Sucker Hole, a popular pool located a half-mile or so downstream from the State Route 313 bridge, is reached via Hickory Hill Road (gravel), located kitty-corner to the bridge. There's one small parking turnout marked by a fishing access sign on the south side of Hickory Hill Road next to the river. The deep pool and the run hold fine fish. It's a popular winter fishing area.

Leaving the Sucker Hole behind, continue down Hickory Hill Road a short distance to a small bridge that spans Camden Creek, a Batten Kill tributary. Public Fishing Rights extend both above and below the bridge in the typically crystal-clear stream that has received recent Adirondack Chapter of Trout Unlimited habitat improvement work. I've had great fun fishing upstream with my 7-foot, 4-weight cane rod, catching the wild brookies on dries. However, the creek's mouth, where it pours into the Batten Kill, has always been a favorite spot, located within walking distance of a fishing cabin I once owned 5 minutes away on Perry Hill Road. I call the stretch Camden Creek Run. It's relatively secluded and well-shaded by overhanging hemlocks.

While it's best to avoid Camden Creek Run on the Batten Kill during hot summer days because of heavy inner tube and kayak traffic, fishing can be good in early May and again beginning in September. I've encountered everything from unbelievable swarms of American Grannom caddisfly flights and heavy Hendrickson flotillas in May to Trico dances in August. However, I've done best here by swinging small bucktails fished across and downstream through the moderate flowing current. A classic Batten Kill bucktail called the Shushan Postmaster works well. Lew Oatman created the fly many years ago for the town's beloved postmaster, Al Prindle.

Oatman, who was born and raised on the Batten Kill in Greenwich, and who later acquired a summer place on Roberson Road in Shushan, is considered the father of baitfish fly imitations. His former house is within walking distance of the next important pool, the Spring Hole, within sight of Camden Creek Run. The deep pool is located upstream from the County Road 61 bridge (locally called Buffum's Bridge). The pool derives its name from numerous coldwater spring seepages that provide thermal refuge for both brown and brook trout.

Driving west to the end of Hickory Hill Road and turning south (left) onto Camden Valley Road will deliver you to a small parking lot next to the Spring Hole. You can also get to the parking area by driving west on State Route 313 a mile or so beyond the State Route 313 bridge to the junction with County Road 61. Turn right to reach Buffum's Bridge in less than a half-mile. The old historic Buffum's Bridge was taken down a couple of years ago and replaced with a modern structure. Locals still call the new bridge Buffum's. A popular gathering place called the Tackle Box, once frequented by anglers, including Lew Oatman, was located on the bank at Buffum's Bridge. The small cabin that housed it is still there, now owned by friendly fly angler Dave Fuller, although it's no longer a tackle shop. Lee Wulff lived in Shushan from 1941 to 1962 and once jumped off Buffum's Bridge with his waders on to prove that he wouldn't drown wearing them.

Expect a lot of company at the Spring Hole, one of the most popular fly-fishing pools on the New York Batten Kill. The banks and parking lot are also heavily used by recreational kayakers, tubers, and swimmers. A Vermont canoe-renting outfit often parks at the bridge-side angling access lot, ferrying clients. Fishing here during the summer requires getting into the river at daybreak and getting back out by early morning. Avoid it altogether on summer weekends, especially holiday weekends. Go play golf, fish another brook in the area, or clean out your garage.

Fly fishers head to the Spring Hole and the run below Buffum's Bridge when the Hendrickson mayfly hatches begin during late April or early May. However, I've had more action during the Hendrickson evening spinner fall at the Spring Hole, as well as on many other Batten Kill stretches, than during the actual hatch in the afternoon. A size 14 Rusty Spinner is a favorite local pattern. Many times on the Batten Kill, I've watched dense Hendrickson hatches in which hundreds of duns floating on the surface were ignored by the trout.

An equally peculiar situation occurs during late August and early September, when (size 18) cinnamon flying ants briefly appear on the water. I encountered hundreds of the ants below Buffum's Bridge a few years ago. The same stretch of water that produced no rises during Hendrickson dun emergences brought multiple consistent risers to the ants. The fishing was fantastic. My theory is that if the trout are hungry and want to eat, they have to rise to the ants. But during a Hendrickson hatch, they can feast on nymphs and emergers below the surface. The ant flights last only a week or two and are difficult to anticipate or predict.

In general, Batten Kill hatches are not as dense as those on Catskill region streams to the southwest. In *The Battenkill*, Merwin succinctly summarized the reasons. The Batten Kill is a slow-moving, relatively low-gradient stream with a homogeneous bottom substrate aside from a few mucky and sandy area. Grapefruit-size and smaller stones abound, with a few larger rocks located here and there. Fast-water-loving clinging mayfly species, such as March Browns and Quill Gordons, are generally absent or uncommon, although I've seen a few Quill Gordons hatch on the lower river during April.

The two consistent mayfly hatches are Hendricksons from April into May and tiny *Tricorythodes* from mid-July into September. Blue-Winged Olives, Little Black Stonefly, and Little Brown Stonefly are on the water during early Hendrickson hatches. I was surprised to also encounter a large Golden Stonefly (*Paragnetina*) during late April at the Rexleigh Bridge crossing.

I've encountered hatches of Blue Quills (*Paraleptophlebia adoptiva*) during early May. Cream Cahills (*Maccaffertium* spp.) emerge on some lower Greenwich area reaches as early as the end of May into June and big Yellow Drakes (*Ephemera varia*) in mid-June, downriver. Sulphurs begin to show on some stretches during late May and June. While not as prolific as the notably hatch that occurs on Catskill area waters, Green Drakes emerge on some sections for a brief time during late May or early June. The imago stage of the bug, called coffin flies, can be encountered around the East Greenwich area as early as the third or fourth week of May.

Golden Drakes (*Anthopotamus distinctus*) emerge on the lower river flats in early July but often in limited numbers. Blue-Winged Olives of various genera continue to hatch any time from July into October.

I always look forward to scouting for hatches of tiny *Pseudocloeon* Olives that can bring fish to the surface from late September into October. The October Caddis, often called the Great Brown Autumn Sedge (*Pycnopsyche* sp.), appears at about the same time, usually in the early morning or late in the evening, but not in swarms.

The river has additional Catch and Release stretches downstream from the Spring Hole. To reach them, drive back up County Road 61 to State Route 313 and turn southwest (right). About a quarter-mile down State Route 313, a NYSDEC large hanging sign marks an angler parking turnout. A footpath along Murray Hollow Brook leads to the river and a deep pool. Years ago, Murray Hollow Brook was stocked with brook trout. Incidentally, before his death Lew Oatman briefly lived in the yellow house at the corner of Murray Hollow Road and State Route 313, after he vacated a dwelling on Roberson Road, located on the opposite side of the river.

I used to fish this area extensively 30 years ago, but lately, I've passed it by, favoring instead a beautiful dry-fly stretch located a bit farther downstream: park at a turnout at the end of the guardrail a half-mile down State Route 313 from the parking area just described. The stretch that I enjoy fishing at dusk is located several hundred feet downstream from this turnout. The relatively shallow and placid glide is easy to wade and perfect for fishing small flies over risers. The Catch and Release section ends at the Eagleville Covered Bridge, some distance below Wulff's Beat, the next popular piece of water if you continue to fish downstream. Lee Wulff once lived in the red-roof home along the river bank, a short distance upstream from the covered bridge.

While the Batten Kill's Catch and Release water is the most popular, fly anglers shouldn't ignore other stretches downstream. Pook's Bridge, located on County Road 64 in Shushan and named for Charles "Pook" Gilchrist, who owned land next to the stream, can be productive both upstream and downstream from the bridge. The Georgi on the Battenkill Museum and Park grounds, located on Adam Lane off County Road 61, in the tiny hamlet of Shushan next to Yushak's Market, is another nice spot. While you're down that way, grab a sandwich at the small market.

The lower end of the river along the Georgi grounds flows under a high County Road 61 iron bridge, next to a historic covered bridge that now serves as a museum that houses farming artifacts. Roy Brown's mounted 32-inch brown trout caught in 1923 is on the wall. A new County Road 61 bridge was finally opened this year, now enabling anglers and others to avoid detours to the area.

Remote stretches of the river, downstream from the bridge all the way to Rexleigh, are largely inaccessible unless you float through or walk along the occasionally used railroad tracks that follow the stream (use caution if walking along the tracks). Few anglers fish the 3-plus miles of remote river that lead from the Georgi stretch to the Rexleigh covered bridge, but this isolated stretch produces some of the Batten Kill's largest brown trout.

Not being a float angler, I access the water by parking at the formal (NYSDEC) parking turnout on Rexleigh Road next to the historic red covered bridge; reach Rexleigh Road by taking County Road 61 west to State Route 22 and turning north (left) a few miles from Shushan. On low water, you can also get into the upstream part of that section at the old covered-bridge museum, located at the County Road 61/County Road 64A intersection and bridge crossing, a few hundred feet from Yushak's, just downstream from the lower end of Georgi. Drive down the gravel road next to the now old "museum" bridge that's right next to the modern County Road 61 bridge recently constructed. You'll want to fish the beautiful pool at the old covered bridge. Park at the museum area. A footpath leads down to the run and pool once favored and fished by Lew Oatman. A NYSDEC sign marks the area as a Wild Trout reach, although NYS stocks the stream just upstream at the Georgi grounds. After fishing that stretch, drive downstream to the Rexleigh covered bridge.

A 20-minute walk upstream from the parking turnout near the Rexleigh Bridge leads to the lowermost railroad trestle. Almost all the water on the way upstream to the trestle crossing, aside from the deep pool located at the covered bridge, is low-gradient, shallow, troutless water, although the deep pools at the covered bridge itself harbor stocked brown trout. The river narrows at the trestles, providing some fish-holding water. On your way up to the first trestle pool, you'll pass by a striking dilapidated, historic white marble mill. The old Baxterville mill, destroyed by fire in the early 1990s, dates back to Revolutionary times. The Batten Kill Conservancy is exploring options to "preserve, secure, and enhance the iconic site as an important public asset."

The Rexleigh area between the covered bridge and the next downstream river crossing is heavily stocked and heavily fished by bait-and-lure casters, especially in May.

About a mile downstream from the Rexleigh covered bridge, the river flows under the State Route 22 bridge. You can park at a NYSDEC lot next to the bridge. I prefer to fish upstream from the bridge to target fish that hold in the shaded areas along the north bank. Swinging small wet flies or bouncing caddisfly dry flies through and along the riffles is effective. Wading is easy upstream from the bridge, a perfect spot to introduce a youngster to the sport. Significant numbers of *Apotomanthus* nymphs inhabit the stream riffle substrate at the bridge crossing. During fall, swing dark-amber-colored nymphs—such as Dave Whitlock's Red Fox Squirrel-Hair Nymph—through the riffles.

The Batten Kill continues downstream toward Greenwich, following State Route 29. White Creek, a Batten Kill tributary not far from the State Route 22/State Route 29 intersection, is worth fishing. From State Route 22, follow Hanks Road north a half-mile to Cemetery Road and turn east (right); go about a half-mile to Evergreen Cemetery, park along the road, and walk south to the creek.

On the lower Batten Kill, miles of water remain seldom fished but have produced some huge fish. On April 8, 2011, Shushan angler J. T. Trainor took a 29.5-inch, 9-pound brown on a Rapala. During my early years on the Batten Kill, I frequented a reach of the lower river that I named Adams Pool, in honor of Bill Adams, the fly angler who showed me the area in 1978. It's located next to a turnout on the left side of the road 5 miles west of the State Route 22/State Route 29 intersection. During one session, the Adams Pool gave up a 19-inch wild brown that sucked in a dry fly I call the Batten Kill Badger. The glide above the pool used to be great during late May, when trout rose persistently in the evenings. I'm not sure how well it now fishes.

Areas downstream toward Greenwich also hold trout. Pools and runs upstream and downstream from the County Road 61 bridge crossing (off State Route 29) are popular with fly fishers, especially during the Hendrickson hatch. While in that area, try the section off Skellie Road. At the State Route 29/County Road 61 intersection, cross the bridge and take the first left onto Skellie Road. About 1.7 miles up Skellie, the river flows right next to the road. The long, slow-moving pool holds a good number of brown trout that can be taken by casting from the road shoulder.

The best time to fish the Skellie Road section is during late May into June, right after daybreak. Cast small dry flies to the sipping rises. The pattern doesn't seem to matter (I use size 16 and 18 Elk Hair Caddis patterns.) Also get down into the stream and fish downstream through the runs and pools.

A Greenwich location that provides easy access to the river is at the Town of Greenwich Batten Kill Riverside Park on State Route 29 just north of the village. The slow-flowing river along this reach holds trout next to the far bank that sometimes show themselves during evening. Mid-May is a good time to fish this reach. A floating craft can be useful when targeting rising brown trout. The fish hold along the slow moving long flat just downstream from the park. Plenty of Sulphurs and Cream Cahills emerge at the same time, as early as late May in some years, along the stretch. Golden Drakes (*Anthopotamus distinctus*) emerge in early July, but by then, the stream reach is very low, and the water temperatures are too high in that area. The park closes at sunset, sometimes just when you'll encounter a rising fish, but with a little effort you can access the water by walking along the fence that borders the park. It's usually thick with brush and growth but worth the effort to fish a little beyond the time the park closes. Anglers have caught nice brown trout fishing out of a canoe, just downstream from the park.

Downstream in the Greenwich area, a pool repulsively called the Sewer Hole off Mill Street in Greenwich, also holds a few wild trout. I now refer to it as "Norman's Sewer Hole." Rich Norman, a local area resident until recently, always liked that stream reach. It's best fished during early and late season. Park near the small Town of Greenwich Pump Station structure at the end of Mill Street. A footpath leads to the water. The footpath serves as a public canoe-launch site. Blue Quills emerge along the reach during spring, but trout rises are often not in sight. Sulphurs also come off that stretch but usually not in significant numbers.

For some time, I've scratched my head wondering why the Sewer Hole harbors wild trout. They don't show easily as surface feeders, but they are present. You won't get into them during summer because that area of the Batten Kill warms significantly. My theory is that some natural spawning occurs in a pair of tiny tributaries that flow through private lands (one called Fly Creek). During the early 1960s Fly Creek was stocked with brown trout.

I've scouted a couple non-posted sections on Fly Creek for spawning redds that flow a few minutes from my home, but so far, I haven't discovered any. The small waters join and spill into the stream near the old Greenwich & Johnsonville Railway crossing at the Sewer Hole reach. All that remains of the railway are the corroded, dilapidated, concrete trestle support structures at the slow-moving Sewer Hole and its run. The Batten Kill departs the Sewer Hole and flows about 3 miles downstream to Middle Falls, a hamlet in the Town of Greenwich. A formal picnic and canoe launch parking area, sponsored by the Batten Kill Conservancy Corridor Connection Project, is located at the State Route 29 bridge crossing at the impassable namesake waterfall. The river reach here is wide open, very slow moving and unappealing. A more interesting fly-fishing section is located downstream from the falls, accessed at the Dahowa Hydro Fishing Area Access site, open to the public. It's easily reached by taking County Road 53 (located within sight of the bridge crossing) 0.7 mile to a small parking area next to the railroad tracks. A long path leads to the river and railroad crossing. The river in this area is wide flatwater, aside from riffle structure located several hundred feet upstream, across from the Battenkill Country Club golf course near the falls. Three miles or so downstream from the Dahowa stretch railroad crossing, after flowing over a couple of dams, the Batten Kill completes its long journey, emptying into the Hudson River not far from the Hollingsworth & Vose facility on County Road 113. From the Conservancy Corridor Connection Project parking lot in Middle Falls, drive 2.4 miles east on State Route 29 toward Schuyerville. At the flashing yellow light, turn right on County Road 113 and drive 1.5 miles to a recreational user parking area at the bridge crossing, next to the Hollingsworth & Vose facility. Bass fishing can be good where the rapids at the bridge enter slower water.

Along many of its reaches, the New York Batten Kill mileage is home to a healthy wild trout population. Vermont's Batten Kill management relies on habitat improvement and no stocking. New York stocks much of the river, relying somewhat on the wishes of various angling organizations, but data collected in the last electrofishing survey seems to point to a less-than-favorable cost-benefit equation. Oddly, many of the stocked fish don't hold over well, while the wild fish appear to thrive. This seems to be the case not only in the Catch and Release section but also the entire river. NYSDEC recently decided to no longer stock the Catch and Release section.

Ongoing habitat improvement activities on both the Vermont and New York stream reaches has benefitted trout populations. Collaborative efforts between several conservation groups, state and federal agencies, and volunteers have already shown positive results.

A 2009 NYSDEC electrofishing survey on the Batten Kill, including the 4-mile Catch and Release section that was heavily stocked with 2-year-old brown trout, turned up 80 wild trout but no hatchery fish (identifiable by fin clips). While changing fisheries management plans are always contentious, it was prudent to rethink stocking trout in the Catch and Release reach. Data and results from Vermont's ongoing Batten Kill Habitat-improvement projects have proved more than encouraging. Fortunately, the Batten Kill Watershed Alliance, along with other conservation partners, such as the Adirondack Chapter of Trout Unlimited, has been working hard on a variety of habitat improvement at various location on New York's reaches, both inside and outside the Catch and Release boundaries.

Anglers sampling New York's section of the Batten Kill, especially its upper stretches near the New York/Vermont border, should consider obtaining at least a one-day Vermont fishing license. Several wild trout reaches located just a short drive from the New York State/Vermont border are good alternatives during times when downstream river reaches are overwhelmed by tubers and recreational floaters. Licenses can be obtained at Wayside Country Store, conveniently located about 3 miles from the State border line, on Vermont State Route 313.

Ample public water is accessible along the 6.7 State Route 313 miles between the State Line and Vermont State Route 7A/State Route 313 intersection in Arlington. A formal fishing access parking lot is located just a mile beyond the State line. Road shoulder turnouts also provide quick access to the river.

Incidentally, on your drive toward Arlington you'll pass by a historic red covered bridge (on Covered Bridge Road). Illustrator Norman Rockwell's former home and studio is located just beyond the bridge crossing, marked by signage at the large white house. John Atherton's former contemporary-style home is located on the right side of State Route 313, 0.2 mile east of Wayside Country Store. Atherton and Rockwell, *Saturday Evening Post* cover illustrators, were friends even though Rockwell wasn't into fishing. Productive water is available off River Road, about half a mile before reaching the

Keelan House stream reach, located about 6.9 miles west of the Vermont/New York border, off River Road in Arlington. Hiking and fishing are allowed along the privately owned stream frontage. Access is made possible by Don Keelan who operated a bed-and-breakfast on the property. A trail beginning at River Road leads to the stream.

Winter fishing above the State Route 313 bridge, along the Catch and Release stretch. Trout can be enticed all winter, provided weather conditions are favorable enough. Fish the slow-moving, deep pools with Matuka style patterns. (PHOTO VALERIE VALLA)

CDC Grannom Pupa (tied by Tom Baltz) Blizzards of Grannom flights come off the river above the Spring Hole every May. The browns typically feed underwater, on pupas. Tom Baltz's well-tied Grannom Pupa is exactly the type of fly that will elicit strikes. Tom uses a 50-50 blend of gray squirrel and CDC clippings with Ice dub for the thorax. The body is tied with darker hair from a hare's mask dyed chartreuse, ribbed with chartreuse UTC Ultra Wire. An interesting feature are pheasant tail fiber "swimmers," two on each side.

Cinnamon Ant (tied by Mike Valla) Local Batten Kill fly anglers, including this author, wait impatiently for the annual ant flights that occur on humid days during the first part of September. Pools that seemed fishless all season long all of a sudden came alive with trout sipping in the ant.

Shushan Postmaster (tied by Mike Valla) Lew Oatman (1902–1958) tied this attractor pattern in honor of Al Prindle, the colorful postmaster in the tiny community of Shushan, located on the Batten Kill.

Atherton #1 (tied by Mike Valla) Illustrator John Atherton (1900–1952) lived on the banks of the Batten Kill and developed his now-classic series of dry flies. His Atherton #1 still takes fish on the river. Atherton tied a range of patterns, from nymphs to wet flies to dry flies. However, he's best remembered for his dry fly patterns tied with fur and hackle blends that, in his opinion, better exhibit lifelike qualities. His ideas were drawn from artists such as Renoir, Monet, and others from the impressionistic school of art. The #1 is his lightest in the series.

Vermont State Route 7A/State Route 313 intersection in Arlington. You'll see a metal gate, with a small "Keelan House" sign attached, on the left side of the road after making a turn onto River Road, just before the bridge crossing. Trails that cross quaint foot bridges lead to the river. Popular with both dog walkers and anglers, signage clearly indicates hiking and fishing are allowed on the private land owned by Arlington resident Don Keelan, an active community member. Keelan once operated a bed-and-breakfast on the property where he still resides.

The Hill Farm Riverside Conservation stream reach, accessed off Hill Farm Road a few miles north of Arlington via Vermont State Route 7A, is one of the more popular stretches during May hatches and again in late summer into September when Tricos are on the water. You won't run into the craziness of recreational tubers and floaters on that reach, making it a good location during summer Trico season. Park at the road shoulder just past the bridge crossing. Walk the wide, grassy maintained trail that starts directly across from the parking turnout about 1,300 feet to a riffle section and series of slow-moving pools. The trail at the point closely hugs the stream, providing very easy access. Look for a large willow tree where a path (sometimes hidden by vegetation) leads to the riffle.

Dead Lake

Within sight of Lake Lauderdale (see Warmwater section) is a little roadside trout pond named Dead Lake, located just over the hill from Shushan. It was once frequented by the iconic fly angler Lee Wulff (1905–1991), who lived in Shushan at the time, and the illustrious Al Prindle—the hamlet of Shushan's postmaster. Back in the 1950s, streamer fly tier Lew Oatman named the now-famous Shushan Postmaster bucktail after Prindle (all of this neat history is found in my book *Tying the Founding Flies*, in the Oatman chapter).

Anyway, during an outing on Dead Lake, Wulff learned firsthand Prindle's fear of snakes. They were bass fishing when Wulff hooked a water snake on a streamer fly. As Wulff told the story, that's when Prindle threatened to jump out of the boat if Wulff reeled it in any closer. And Prindle couldn't swim.

I've never seen a water snake swimming around the little "lake," which is more of a tiny, round pond. And I've never netted a bass while fly fishing that water. Dead Lake is a Special Regulations trout pond, and baitfish are not allowed. However, I've noticed a few pumpkinseeds along the shoreline of the 10-acre pond while launching my Hornbeck. The best way to fish Dead Lake is via a floating craft.

You'll have no problem getting a canoe, boat, or float tube into the water. Parking is available at the shoreline located at the intersection of State Route 22 and County Road 61, about 5 miles north of the Village of Cambridge, just beyond the entrance to Lake Lauderdale.

Dead Lake, a tiny pond near Shushan, New York, is a Special Regulations water. Baitfish are not allowed. About 500 brown trout are stocked annually. Canoe launching is easy at the small parking area next to the lake.

Dead Lake is stocked with around 400 brook trout and a couple hundred brown trout. I've netted browns by trolling small streamers out of my Hornbeck. However, you can also cast and strip flies out of a canoe or other craft.

I've often wondered what the little pond might have looked like back in Prindle and Wulff's years—no doubt more esthetic than today. The only drawback to fishing Dead Lake are the dwellings that line the north shoreline. Of course, it's so close to the roads you'll also see and hear vehicles that pass by. I fished it often during times the Batten Kill was in craziness mode with all the recreational floaters clogging up the river, or when I happened to be over on Lake Lauderdale the same day. Both waters were minutes from my fishing cabin in Shushan. Today, I routinely fish both ponds located a short drive from our home in the Town of Cambridge.

Little Hoosic River

A major tributary of the Hoosic River, the Little Hoosic River—really a small creek—is born on the west slopes of the Taconic Mountains above Cherry Plain in Rensselaer County, New York. It flows north some 18 miles through the State Route 22 corridor, passing through the towns of Berlin and Petersburgh before it dumps into the Hoosic River at North Petersburgh. Dill Creek—really a small brook—flowing from the forested Rensselaer Plateau to the west, is a significant tributary of the Little Hoosic.

Dill Creek and the Little Hoosic are managed as wild trout fisheries. In the early 1970s, the Rensselaer County Conservation Alliance annually stocked some 8,000 trout in the watershed, but today, virtually all of the resident rainbows and browns, and even a few brookies, are wild.

Many fly anglers remember the Little Hoosic for the fish they never caught. It's that kind of stream. Even some bait-casting old-timers acknowledge that the fish—some occasionally reaching 20-plus inches—are present but that catching them is a challenge. My typical success has been with the small, frisky wild trout.

Public Fishing Rights (PFR) stretches on Dill Creek and the Little Hoosic River provide ample access. Yet some sections are more conducive to fly angling than others. The headwaters in the Berlin area are narrow and very brushy and better suited to bait fishing. The better fly water is located from just south of Petersburgh to the confluence with the Hoosic River.

A good strategy is to begin a fishing day on the lowermost Little Hoosic PFR reach that's accessible several hundred feet from the intersection of State Route 22 and State Route 346 at North Petersburgh, just upstream from the confluence with the Hoosic River. It was once easier to access the water at the State Route 346 bridge by parking on the road shoulder—about enough room for one vehicle.

A few years ago, the tight parking area vanished when the bridge was refurbished. Private property on the far side of the bridge doesn't allow for parking. I usually park back down near the State Route 22/State Route 346 intersection and walk to the bridge crossing and the path that leads into the stream.

There's about a mile of mostly secluded fishing in the section upstream from the bridge that provides good trout habitat among the logjams and undercut banks. An old yellow-bodied, red-throated bucktail pattern called the Shushan Postmaster has produced well, fished through the sycamore tree deadfalls along the stream banks. Bypass the flat, shallow dead water you'll eventually encounter and continue upstream. There's a lovely boulder-strewn and shaded deeper section that can harbor some mighty nice trout.

Little Hoosic, at the lower reach, a short distance upstream from the State Route 346 bridge crossing. Juvenile rainbows willingly strike small, colorful flies fished through the small runs and pools.

Leaving behind what I call "sycamore grove," from the State Route 22/State Route 346E intersection, drive 4 miles south on State Route 22 to the Dill Creek tributary bridge crossing. One stretch worth fishing on the way to the Dill Creek crossing is located at Prosser Hollow Road. Prosser Hollow Road is located off State Route 22 about 3 miles south of the State Route 22/State Route 346 intersection. The stream in that location is not formally a PFR stretch, yet many have had no issues fishing there.

Dill Creek is somewhat of a trickle by late summer, but small wild brook and rainbows can be seen darting through the few small pools that remain. The best location to fish the brook upstream from the bridge crossing is located about 0.6 mile up Dill Brook Road. You can park either at the small shoulder turnout on the left side of the road or a few hundred feet up the road at the intersection with Potter Hill Road.

Dill Creek dumps into the Little Hoosic at a point several hundred feet downstream from the State Route 22 bridge. There's some interesting boulder habitat at the base of the mountainside near the confluence of Dill Creek and the Little Hoosic. One October I came across a trout, in excess of 20 inches, that darted out from under a midstream lifeless water. After being startled by that big fish, I now consider the Little Hoosic a stream that I most remember for the elusive large trout I've seen but have yet to catch.

As you continue driving south on State Route 22, additional PFR stretches occur in the Petersburgh village area. I've never liked fishing around the village and usually instead opt to head to a formal NYSDEC angler parking turnout located about 3 miles south of the Dill Creek bridge. It's well-marked by a NYSDEC sign on the left side of State Route 22. Small trout can often be spotted upstream from a dilapidated bridge that crosses the stream. My fly of choice is, again, a Shushan Postmaster bucktail fished downstream through the riffles.

Fishing the main stem of the Hoosic River is a whole different ball game when compared to the Little Hoosic River. The 76-mile-long "big Hoosic," begins in Massachusetts, then flows through a section of Vermont before it hits New York State a short distance upstream from North Petersburgh. The Little Hoosic joins the Hoosic River several hundred feet downstream from the State Route 346 bridge at North Petersburgh. PFR water is available on the Little Hoosic all the way downstream to its confluence with the river.

The slow-moving river at the confluence is popular with bait anglers who frequently prop their rods up on forked sticks along the bank. Many sections are better fished with bait or lures than flies. Its appearance is more likened to a bass river. Most trout anglers would find it hard to believe that some nice wild rainbows would come out of the river.

Other Hoosic River PFR reaches are located a short distance upstream from the Little Hoosic River confluence. One is off Indian Massacre Road at the Onaaktokok fishing access site. Drive 0.2 mile past the Little Hoosic River bridge crossing on State Route 346 to a left turn on County Road 95, then a right turn onto Indian Massacre Road at the Hoosic River bridge crossing. In 0.2 mile, you'll see the large NYSDEC hanging sign at the fishing access parking lot. A footpath leads down from the lot over a slope to the river. For years, signage marking the access lot was missing. In addition, yellow NYSDEC PFR signage is nailed to trees along the stream in that area. The deep, slow-moving pool is best fished with weighted Matuka-style streamers, although on occasion you might notice fish rising along that reach just before dark during spring or fall.

Access areas are also located on State Route 346 within a mile or so past the State Route 346/County Road 95 intersection, toward Pownal, Vermont. A deep strewn-boulder pool is located 1.1 miles from the intersection. Carefully walk across the railroad tracks, then down the footpath to the river. The very fishy-looking water requires weighted streamers or conehead patterns. You'll reach the Vermont State Line in about a mile past this location, at a bridge crossing.

Another Hoosic River stretch worth fishing, along with an interesting small tributary, is located just over 3 miles downstream from the Hoosic River/Little Hoosic river confluence, at the State Route 7/State Route 22 intersection. It's near the State Route 7 bridge crossing down the road from Stewart's convenience store. A parking turnout is located at the bridge crossing. Brown trout and rainbows inhabit this stream reach. As is true elsewhere on Hoosic River, you'll likely experience plenty of blank days before hooking into one on this hit-or-miss river.

Shingle Hollow Creek, more of a small tumbling brook, runs parallel to State Route 7. It pours into Hoosic River a couple hundred feet downstream from the State Route 7 bridge crossing, next to State Route 22 at the intersection. The brook passes through a concrete box culvert directly under State Route 22, then exits into the Hoosic. It's better to sample the brook for small trout at a large parking turnout 0.7 mile west of the State Route 7 bridge crossing intersection. You'll see an informational NYSDEC Tibbets State Forest informational kiosk at the lot. A short path at the west end of the lot will quickly get you into the little brook.

NYSDEC sampled the river years ago and found rainbows far downstream, even downstream from the Eagle Bridge section, on State Route 67. The rainbows and a scattering of brown trout tend to hangout in stretches where some degree of thermal refuge can be found. The low-gradient river warms significantly through the New York sections. Thermal refuge is found at locations where cold tributaries enter the stream. The Owl Kill weds the river at Eagle Bridge and provides some refuge. Smaller tributaries that enter the river help, too.

The Eagle Bridge reach is a popular fly-fishing location and one of my favorite stretches because it's located only a couple of miles from my home in the Village of Cambridge. From the center of the Village of Cambridge, take State Route 22 south a

Hoosic River, at Buskirk Covered Bridge, off Washington County Road 59. The best time to fish the Hoosic River is during May and again in late September into November. Wild rainbows and brown trout inhabit the river, usually in stretches where small brooks or creeks enter the water. (PHOTO VALERIE VALLA)

little over 5 miles to the State Route 67 intersection (next to Benson's Restaurant). Take a right on State Route 67 to the bridge crossing. You can park on the road shoulder next to the bridge. Fish your favorite streamers, muddlers, and woolly bugger patterns through the riffle downstream from the bridge. When water levels allow, the stretches upstream from the bridge near the railroad trestle can produce rainbows.

A couple formal NYSDEC fishing access areas are located just a couple of miles downstream from the Eagle Bridge crossing. A large NYSDEC hanging sign on State Route 67 marks the location. Drive west on State Route 67 a half-mile or so to a gravel access road that leads to the streamside parking area. The parking area comes with a handy canoe launch. The river here is slow-moving, but depending on water level, there's a riffle/run stretch upstream a couple hundred feet. This reach is best during lower-water conditions. During late evening, or early in the morning, you might spot a rising trout.

Another NYSDEC formal parking area is located at the quaint Buskirk covered bridge, on the Buskirk-West Hoosic Road (County Road 103). A drive of 1.5 miles or so west on State Route 67 from the last formal access lot will get you to the right turn on County Road 103. The parking lot, also marked by a large NYSDEC hanging sign, is at the bridge. You'll no doubt drop your jaw, thinking this is just some more carp water. It's unesthetic, in trout-fishing terms. Bait anglers often sit at the stream bank, hoping for a catch. A couple hundred feet downstream from the bridge, a tongue of water from Whipple Brook and its cooler water enters the river. The river tends to get very shallow on that reach, but during a rain event, Whipple Brook provides enhanced water flow into the river. Again, like other areas on the Hoosic, anglers shouldn't expect action at all times; you'll have plenty of blank days. The Hoosic, for sure, is a "hit or miss" river in the area.

The best time to fish the Hoosic River is during early to mid-May and again when the river cools in late September into October and November. During early June and early

Wild rainbow trout inhabit the Hoosic River and its major tributary, the Little Hoosic River.

September, you might see a fish rise just before dark. I have netted fish at other times, but I have the luxury and advantage of living 5 minutes from the Buskirk covered bridge and can pick and choose when to fish, based on conditions that might provide potential for a successful outing. If the Hoosic or Little Hoosic rivers are not productive on an outing, the Walloomsac River, a major tributary of the Hoosic, is just around the corner.

Walloomsac River

"There they are boys! We beat them today, or Molly Stark sleeps a widow tonight!" And with that somewhat grandiloquent declaration, Brigadier General John Stark (1728–1822) launched the American Revolution's Battle of Bennington on August 16, 1777. Stark and his 2,000 militiamen, a force that included members of the Green Mountain Boys, were victorious over British forces. Molly Stark slept just fine that night.

Opened in 1891, the 306-foot Bennington Battle Monument rises high above the town of Bennington, Vermont. A bronze marker engraved with Stark's words is located at the towering obelisk's base, reminding tourists of the historic encounter. However, the battle wasn't fought in Bennington at all but rather on a promontory overlooking the Walloomsac River, a few miles across the state line, in Walloomsac, New York. Like the Mettawee and Batten Kill Rivers, the Walloomsac straddles both states. Anglers interested in sampling New York's mileage should consider purchasing a 1-day or longer Vermont fishing license since interesting reaches are found just across the state line.

The 16.8-mile-long Walloomsac begins where South Stream and Jewett Brook join just south of Bennington. A dendritic complex of other area streams that drain much of south-central portions of Bennington County contributes to its hydrology. After departing the Bennington area, the river soon crosses into New York and enters Hoosic Junction, where it dumps into the Hoosic River.

New York's section of the Walloomsac relies on hatchery brown trout. A little over 3,000 browns are stocked annually by NYSDEC. Rainbow trout are also stocked from time to time. Wild brown trout and brook trout persist in the Walloomsac's headwater

Walloomsac River, a couple of miles across the New York border, at Henry Covered Bridge (PHOTO VALERIE VALLA)

tributaries, yet the Vermont stocks even some of these little streams. Fish are reared at the Bennington Fish Culture Station, located 2 miles from downtown Bennington on South Stream Road (it's a nice place to visit if you're in the area). The largest stocked fish, both brown trout and rainbows, are found in the Special Regulations "trophy trout" stretch that runs from the New York border upstream to the former Vermont Tissue Plant Dam at Murphy Road in Bennington. A thousand 2-year-old trout, rainbows, and browns are stocked in May at several release points along the river.

The rainbows are triploid fish, meaning that they have three of each chromosome, unlike natural fish, which have two of each chromosome. Two-year-old triploid rainbows tend to grow faster than diploid fish because they are sterile (no energy spent on reproduction). The brown trout stocked in the Special Regulations section are regular diploid fish. Diploid rainbows and browns are also stocked upstream from the impassible dam at the upper boundary of the trophy section. Because the stocking release dates are well-publicized, the trophy section gets hammered by local bait anglers during early May, especially downstream of the dam at the former Vermont Tissue Plant and a couple of miles downstream at the historic Henry Covered Bridge, a red-painted quintessential Vermont covered bridge located at the intersection of River Road, Murphy Road, and Harrington Road.

While it wasn't always the case before the water quality on this area of the river improved, there's some decent New York water upstream from the Edward Cottrell Bridge. For many years, the Bennington Wastewater Treatment Plant (WWTP) had an adverse impact on the lower Walloomsac's water quality. The affected stretches included not only what is now designated as the Vermont trophy Special Regulation section but also most of the New York water.

Stream studies conducted in 1984 pointed out the effects of sewage, such as persistent odor and river-bottom substrate covered with algae. Midges and worms made up 90 percent of the aquatic macroinvertebrate population in the river. However, water quality improved once the WWTP was upgraded in 1985. Subsequent surveys have shown the river to be essentially unaffected, based on macroinvertebrate and water-quality sampling.

The low-gradient, slow-moving river below the Henry Bridge is largely inaccessible from the point where it turns away from River Road, unless you're inclined to float it. However, the riffle where tiny Cold Spring Brook empties into the river, a few miles downstream from the Henry Bridge, is a nice easy-access location. From the Henry Bridge, drive 2 miles north along Harrington Road to a turnout on the left side of the road just before Harrington joins State Route 67.

I've always called this section Cold Spring Brook Run. It's located only a mile upstream from the New York border. In recent years, the landowner has posted the frontage against hunting, but you can get into the river at the small bridge crossing over the brook where it enters the river. Incidentally Cold Spring Brook itself, a trickle, is almost entirely inaccessible aside from a couple of stretches upstream a few miles along Rollin Road, where anglers can get into the water at the small bridges. The stream holds a few brook trout and small brown trout.

The Cottrell Bridge access site in New York is located 3 miles east from the State Route 67/State Route 22 intersection in North Hoosic. Parking space for a couple vehicles is located directly next to the stream, at the bridge. The railroad trestle runs upstream from the bridge produces fish early in the season but falls off by summer. Bait casters typically set up shop at the parking area just after fish stockings in April. Another popular reach is located another mile downstream from the Cottrell Bridge, at Caretaker Bridge along Caretaker Road. (The one-way Caretaker Road is located 2.3 miles east of the State Route 67/State Route 22 intersection.)

General Stark and his army battled high on the hill above the Caretaker Road stretch. Fishing is allowed along the NYS Bennington battlefield park river frontage downstream from the bridge. The run upstream at the railroad trestle crossing also produces trout, all hatchery fish. Your fly boxes should be filled with a variety of dry flies along with streamers and bucktails when fishing the Caretaker Road reach.

The hatchery browns that generally are stocked directly off the bridge are not too fussy. The predominate hatches on the Walloomsac are Sulphurs and caddis, although Hendricksons and Tricos come off the river, too, along with a few other mayfly hatches. An 8-foot, 4-weight to 5-weight rod will get your flies out in front of a trout's nose.

If fishing success is less than anticipated on the New York Walloomsac water, and at least a 1-day or longer Vermont license was purchased, head back across the state border to one of the tributaries. Wild brook trout inhabit the small water. An area worth a few casts in the Woodford Hollow area is located approximately 4 miles east of dead-center Bennington.

Take State Route 9 east to the intersection with Harbour Road, on the left. A small turnout is located about 0.1 mile up Harbour Road, on the left, at a bridge that crosses City Stream. City Stream dumps into Bolles Brook at this point, creating the Roaring Branch (some maps call it Walloomsac Brook in this area). Access to the junction of both streams is easy. You'll no doubt pick up some colorful wild brookies and sometimes even a small wild brown trout. For years, I had assumed that the brook trout I caught in this area were all wild fish. However, this area is also stocked with hatchery fish. City Stream is stocked too, but it can be difficult to get a decent nymph drift in the tumbling pocketwater.

Rather than trying City Stream, your time is better spent on the Roaring Branch drifting small flies through the riffles and runs. However, a beautiful area to fish is in the upper reaches of Bolles Brook located within Green Mountain National Forest. You can reach it by driving 2 miles up Harbour Road. The pavement ends at a rather large "NO PARKING" sign. Drive beyond the sign, where the road enters the national forest and public access.

The Caretaker Road reach, downstream from the bridge crossing, is productive during May. Parking and access are easy. (PHOTO VALERIE VALLA)

The gravel road that enters the national forests at this point is better suited for off-road vehicles, but if you take it slow, cars with reasonable clearance can continue on another half-mile to a road gate and a turnout for parking. The gate is there to protect the fragility of the gravel road from that point onward. Bolles Brook is located a couple of hundred feet away. Within sight of the gate, some beautiful small pools and runs in the forest stream hold wild little brook trout. In the spring, I fish it wearing hip boots; during the summer, it's a great wet-wade brook.

Upper stretches of Bolles Brook hold not only wild brookies but also much in the way of history and folklore. The Glastenbury ghost town, located along Bolles Brook about 2 miles upstream from the road gate, is renowned for giving some hikers (and anglers) the heebie-jeebies. During the 1800s, the area supported a thriving charcoal-making industry until the mountains were eventually depleted of hardwood timber. What turned out to be an ill-fated resort designed to attract vacationers to the salubrious Green Mountains sprung up here in the late 1800s, but it quickly vanished when Bolles Brook flooded and wiped out the rail lines that led to the community.

The Glastenbury area is now known for mysterious murders and disappearances, as well as for its historical intrigue. If fish aren't hitting along Bolles Brook, a hike up the gravel road takes curious anglers to the location of a once-thriving community. Few hints of its existence are now apparent, aside from a few old cellar holes buried here and there; its buildings and structures were swallowed up long ago by the forest.

The Walloomsac River and its tributaries, both in New York and across the state line in Vermont, can provide fly anglers with a wide range of experiences. Walloomsac fishing, as well as the rich history of the historic battlefield in Walloomsac to the remote Glastenbury ghost town, provides ample reason for anglers to wet a line in waters that flow in one of the nicest areas of both states.

Black River

I couldn't recall a summer in New York that was as hot and humid as one a couple of years ago. By August, many of the larger trout streams were warming, sending trout into thermal refuge. One morning I decided that the respite for my itchy rod hand might best be a small, cold brook trout stream that flows through the Capital District Wildlife Management Area (WMA), a nearly 4,000-acre parcel acquired piecemeal by the state between 1928 and 1941.

Plenty of such waters flow hidden in the hollows of my usual Catskills-region haunts, but I had time constraints, so I needed a stream located relatively a short distance from my home. The headwaters of the Black River in Rensselaer County quickly came to mind. The stream provides pleasant fishing in relative isolation as it flows southerly off the Rensselaer Plateau, eventually dumping into Black River Pond at 175-acre Cherry Plain State Park, located just west of Cherry Plain along State Route 22.

If approaching from the north, from the Little Hoosic River/Dill Brook area, drive about 11 miles south on State Route 22 from the State Route 22/State Route 2 intersection in Petersburgh. Turn right onto CCC Dam Road, located just beyond the Atlantic Equipment Corporation building. (You'll see a large Capital District Management Area sign on the corner.) If approaching from the south, drive about 4.5 miles north on State Route 22 from Stephentown to CCC Dam Road.

A 2.5-mile drive up the road from the State Route 22 intersection will deliver you to Cherry Plain State Park. You'll pass over the headwaters of Kinderhook Creek about 0.3 mile from the intersection, a popular trout stream.

Prior to World War II, the Civilian Conservation Corps (CCC) constructed the dam that formed Black River Pond, which, along with the state park, sits within the much

Black River is a small brook that inhabits small, wild brook trout. It's a perfect place for anglers to cast short rods with tiny flies. The fish are not large, some "French Fry size," but they're wild.

Small brook trout inhabit Black River.

larger WMA. I'd been wanting to try my new 6-foot, 9-inch Becker cane rod on small brook trout, and for that reason alone, Black River seemed a good option. My fly would be a Little Green Stone dry, in sizes 16 and 18, an effective pattern on similar brook trout streams found in the Catskills.

The Black River is a trickle by late summer, and mostly shallow, but the water is always plenty cold. Better yet, the stream is well shaded by stands of black cherry, yellow birch, hemlock, red oak, and red spruce. It's a place worthy of both anglers and naturalists. (The stream actually looks black, hence its name.) Small waterfalls are visited more by hikers than by anglers, thanks to a well-marked trail leading to the stream from the state park. However, there are better access options for anglers.

You can park along Miller Road (gravel) just beyond the entrance to the state park. The stream flows directly alongside Miller Road at that point but quickly enters a forested area just upstream. You can fish your way upstream for a little over a mile, through small boulders and rocks, until you are greeted by a scenic waterfall. Another choice is to drive north about 0.3 mile and park along the road where a cable cordons off access to a small plot of ancient cemetery headstones under the tree canopy. Head down the slope over an old, moss-covered stone wall to the water and fish upstream a shorter distance to the waterfall.

Another option is to drive a half-mile up Miller Road beyond the park entrance to the intersection with Jiggs Highway, an informal WMA gravel road (despite its "highway" designation). There's a small parking area and a trailhead marked by blue signs that lead to the waterfall and other upstream stretches after a 5-minute trek. Brook trout also inhabit the stream upstream from the waterfall.

This small stream and its dainty wild trout are great fun on a summer day. Considering the habitat, my first catch from the Black River didn't surprise me: a 1.5-inch brookie ate my size 18 Little Green Stonefly, which was as big as the little trout's head. My fishing buddy Ed Ostapczuk, a fellow Catskills-area brook trout enthusiast, calls diminutive fish like my 1.5-inch specimen "pizza-pie length," but worry not—Ed doesn't keep trout for his pizzas. However, you can catch what Ed calls "French-fry" size and "dollar-bill" size brook trout in this splendid little stream.

Kinderhook Creek

If streams like the Black River or Little Hoosic River didn't produce and you're in the area, head over to nearby Kinderhook Creek near Stephentown. From its headwaters near the Massachusetts border, Kinderhook Creek, a significant fly-fishing destination, cuts through both Rensselaer and Columbia Counties on its 49-mile journey. The creek's waters eventually end up in the Hudson River.

While Kinderhook Creek receives substantial stockings of both rainbow and brown trout, the majority of its extensive continuous PFR mileage is categorized by NYSDEC as Stocked-Extended. Small, wild brook trout are found in its headwaters, and its lower reaches produce some very large holdover brown trout. Some 17,000 rainbows and nearly 2,000 brown trout are stocked along the stream. Access, for the most part, is very easy. Formal NYSDEC parking areas are scattered throughout its mileage. Much of the stream flows well away from roads, providing solitude for anglers desiring that kind of experience.

The easiest access to the headwaters is located off CCC Dam Road, using the same road directions that were described for fishing Black River. The little stream meanders through areas that become brushy during summer but is easy to fish in early and late seasons. Most of the PFR water is located downstream from the bridge although a short section exists upstream. Better fly-fishing water is located downstream on Garfield Road just west of the Village of Stephentown.

At the State Route 22/State Route 43 intersection in Stephentown, drive west on State Route 43 a little less than a mile to a slight left onto Garfield Road. A formal NYSDEC parking lot marked by a large hanging sign is on the left, in a little less than 2 miles. The small parking area, located next to the Roaring Mill Brook bridge crossing, is about 0.6 mile past the Stephentown Federated Church.

You'll be greeted by signage at the start of a footpath that indicates this reach is in Stocked-Extended waters. The section downstream from where Roaring Mill Brook enters the creek is a good place to start fishing. PFR water exists upstream from the junction along the left bank, looking downstream, and both sides of the creek downstream, aside from a short gap on the right bank. Look for the yellow NYSDEC public fishing signage along the creek. Nice riffle structure is located upstream from the junction pool.

From the Garfield Road reach, the stream flows along continuous PFR water along both banks, for several miles. Much of it is through isolated areas that can be accessed at bridge crossings and formal parking areas. Another formal NYSDEC parking lot not far downstream from the Garfield lot is only a couple of miles away. From the Roaring Mill Brook parking lot on Garfield, drive 1.1 miles southwest to a left onto Gentile Road and then a left onto Goold Road. The parking area is at the green-painted truss bridge crossing on Goold.

While the Goold Road bridge crossing site makes for quick and easy access into the stream, the same can't be said about getting into the creek at the next downstream bridge at Bert Hager Road. Continue on Goold for 0.2 mile to the intersection at Stephentown Road. Take a right turn on Stephentown Road and continue just over a mile to Bert Hager Road. The single-lane truss bridge is 0.1 mile down the gravel dead-end road. A NYSDEC large hanging sign is located at the bridge. The stream section upstream from the bridge is very nice, a perfect stretch to cast both dry flies and nymphs. It's a very picturesque stream reach that's one of my favorites on the Kinderhook.

The problem at the Bert Hager bridge is there's little room on the road shoulder to park next to the bridge, even with the standard 33-foot road shoulder right-of-way set back a

Bill Newcomb fords Kinderhook's Goold Road reach, downstream a few miles from Stephentown. Kinderhook is heavily stocked with rainbow trout and brown trout.

distance from the center line of the road. The adjacent landowner has made it clear with no parking signs to keep clear of his property. An alternative is to park somewhere up on Stephentown Road and walk to the bridge or try to squeeze in closer. Or have a buddy drop you off at the stretch.

Anglers can once again find easy and direct entry into the stream at the next bridge crossing downstream at Adams Crossing Road. From the Bert Hager Road intersection, continue west on Stephentown Road 2.7 miles then take a right onto Adams Crossing Road. The bridge crossing and parking area is just down the road, marked by a NYSDEC large hanging sign. Park at the small lot or on the road shoulder. Fish small streamers through the riffles and runs on that reach.

Continuing along Adams Crossing Road from the parking area a short distance will get you to a bridge crossing next to US-20. At this point, Wyomanock Creek joins the Kinderhook. With addition of water from the Wyomanock, the Kinderhook continues flowing downstream as a larger creek. Parking is not an issue. It's available at a long parking area on US-20, just east of the bridge, at streamside.

Your fly box arsenal should also include larger streamers when fishing from the Wyomanock junction downstream in the now larger creek that flows during spring. Ample and continuous PFR water continues downstream all the way to the East Nassau area, off State Route 66. Pick up State Route 66 just a couple miles west on US-20 (you'll pass by Lebanon Valley Speedway on the way). Take a right on State Route 66 and drive to Tayer Road. The formal NYSDEC parking area at Tayer Road provides easy stream access near a residence. You'll notice more presence of dwellings along the stream in this area.

After sampling the Tayer Road reach, get back onto US-20 and drive another couple of miles to two additional formal NYSDEC access sites at the US-20 bridge crossings. The first one is at a parking area marked by a NYSDEC large hanging "Bridge 2 fishing access" sign. The "Old Route 20" once crossed the Kinderhook here (you'll notice

Martinez Black (tied by Mike Valla) Donald Skillman Martinez (1903–1955) was influenced by the so-called early Catskill School of fly tiers, but he made his mark in the West, particularly in West Yellowstone. Martinez is most associated with the famous Woolly Worm, a simple pattern he didn't create but helped popularize. However, his Martinez Black has found its way back into fly boxes of New York fly fishers, such as Ed Ostapczuk, who has enjoyed much success with the old classic.

Gold Opossum (tied by Mike Valla) The Gold Opossum, and its sister, Silver Opossum (varied only by their flashy tinsel bodies), are effective on most any trout stream. Its opossum guard hair and underfur wing gives motion to the fly as it swings through stream currents.

Hendo Hammer (tied by John Collins) John's unique Hendo Hammer is suggestive of a Hendrickson attempting to shed its nymphal shuck. Its Turkey Biot dyed Hendrickson Pink abdomen and its thorax created with urine-burned fox fur is an interesting combination.

remnants of the old road on the downstream side of the bridge while locating the footpath that leads down to the water).

The "Bridge 1 fishing access" is located about 0.6 mile west of Bridge 1. Cast streamers and bucktails through the riffle and run upstream from the bridge. You'll likely pick up a rainbow or two during early May along that reach. Good patterns would include Mickey Finn, Shushan Postmaster, and Gold Opossum. You'll want to carry Hendrickson patterns and caddis pupae flies in your boxes.

To reach other stretches downstream from Bridge 1, get back onto State Route 66 near the bridge and continue following the creek downstream about 3 miles to a bridge crossing. Official NYSDEC public fishing signage is along that reach, but make sure that you don't wander into private property beyond the public-fishing easement. Park on the road shoulder next to the bridge, on the downstream side. You'll likely spot posted signs near the upstream side of the bridge. Some nice riffles and runs are located upstream from the bridge. A nice pool that makes for nice fall fishing is located directly downstream from the bridge.

Poesten Kill/Quaken Kill

The Poesten Kill and its major tributary Quaken Kill (aka Poestenkill and Quakenkill) have limited PFR water, but anglers sometime locate unofficial yet unposted sections along its length. The NYSDEC formal parking lot located at the hamlet of Poestenkill is

Quaken Kill at the formal NYSDEC parking lot, off Garfield Road

used to access both streams. Poestenkill is located about 15 miles northeast of Stephentown and about 7 miles southwest of the City of Troy.

The streamside parking area is off Garfield Road. If approaching from Poestenkill, take State Route 355 a little less than a mile to Garfield Road. A Quaken Kill streamside parking area is about 0.7 mile down Garfield. A footpath follows the Quaken Kill a few hundred feet downstream to its confluence with the Poesten Kill, but you'll want to drift flies through the couple Quaken Kill riffles and runs on your way downstream to the junction pool. NYSDEC doesn't stock the Quaken Kill, but it inhabits wild brown trout.

However, the Poesten Kill receives a few thousand stocked brown trout, typically during April, and some of the stocked fish likely make their way into the smaller Quaken Kill. Junction pool, popular with bait and conventional tackle anglers, usually holds fish during spring.

Kayaderosseras Creek

Kayaderosseras Creek, locally called Kaydeross Creek, is a small stream that flows southerly from its origins in the Kayaderosseras Range in Saratoga County. The creek once provided hydrologic energy for some two dozen mills as it flowed to its terminus at Saratoga Lake, a warmwater fishery. The mill industry, which peaked in the late 1800s, is all but gone, along with the industrial-age character of the stream.

The Cottrell Paper Company, in Rock City Falls, is the only mill still in existence on the creek, and its dams are still in place. They provide prime habitat for lunker brown trout in their plunge pools. The well-known Cottrell Pool above a small dam, just upstream from the operational part of the mill, serves as a magnet for early-season bait-fishing enthusiasts after trout have been stocked.

A collaborative habitat-improvement project was completed in 2013, a couple hundred feet downstream from the mill dam adjacent to a small park-like facility along the stream.

Cottrell Mill stretch below the popular dam. Kayaderosseras Creek is one of the most popular trout waters in Saratoga County. The Cottrell Pool above the old mill dam is the most popular with bait casters. Fly fishers can find better water a couple of miles upstream in Middle Grove.

Fly anglers are better served by exploring other sections of the stream, away from the bait crowds that frequent the roadside pools.

NYSDEC has mapped the public-access areas along the Kaydeross, breaking the creek into four sections: the South Corinth and Porter Corners areas near the headwaters, the middle Rock City Falls section, and the lower Milton Center–Ballston Spa section. My favorite fly-fishing stretches are in the upper and middle sections, from Porter Corners downstream to the riffles above and just below Rock City Falls.

The NYSDEC Porter Corners fishing access parking lot, on Bockes Road, lies along the creek some 8 driving miles upstream from the Cottrell mill. Fly anglers routinely avoid the small water of the upper creek because saplings and brush anchor its banks, and such structure offers water-cooling shade and good trout habitat, yet it causes a casting nightmare for fly fishers.

Stream-bred brook trout, the jewels of the Kaydeross, can often be seen darting in the low waters of late summer. Years ago, when we lived in nearby Saratoga Springs, I purchased a small vacant lot along one of the small tributaries near Porter Corners. The non-buildable lot on Coy Road near Porter Corners went up for sale at the county auction. The $600 was worth the price. I never fished the water but only stopped by to observe the small brook trout. The creek in the small water is best fished with small nymphs cast carefully downstream and drifted along the undercut banks and through small pools. Expect frustrating fishing yet relative solitude in the upper sections.

Downstream from Porter Corners, 4 miles south on North Creek Road from the Porter Corners Road/North Creek Road intersection, there's a small informal road shoulder parking spot and a footpath that leads to a section of the creek at Middle Grove. (If approaching from the hamlet of Middle Grove downstream, it's located just short of a mile from the intersection of Middle Grove Road/North Creek Road, on the left.) It's best to fish upstream from this point on the creek, skipping caddisfly dry flies along the riffles in the spring and floating ant patterns in the small tailout pools during early fall.

Continuing south, North Creek Road ends at Middle Grove Road just short of a mile. A quick right turn and a half-mile drive leads to South Creek Road. The Kaydeross follows the road tightly and offers several formal parking areas for the next mile or so. There are some nice pools along the road, along with a few very low-gradient, silted stretches of water that have always seemed lifeless.

The unfortunate malady of the South Creek Road stretch is the enormous amount of littering along its banks. However, collaborative efforts between Trout Unlimited, the Saratoga County Soil and Water Conservation District, and others have made great progress in stabilizing the stream bank itself. South Creek Road soon ends at State Route 29, and a quick left turn leads back to the Cottrell stretch at Rock City Falls.

Plenty of PFR water flows downstream from the Cottrell Mill area all the way downstream to the Village of Ballston Spa. One formal NYSDEC parking area is located a short distance downstream from the hamlet of Rock City Falls. At the intersection of Rock City Falls Road and State Route 29 (just beyond the Cottrell area), drive just short of a mile down Rock City Falls Road to a bridge crossing and parking area. The browns are typically all hatchery fish not only along this reach but also downstream at another formal NYSDEC parking area in Milton. From the previous parking area, continue south on Rock City Falls Road about a half-mile, and bear left at the road fork. The parking lot is next to the bridge crossing at the intersection of Middleline Road and Geyser Road (County Road 43).

During the 20 years we lived in Saratoga Springs, and again in more recent years in Ballston Spa where my wife Valerie taught school, I never enjoyed fishing the creek that was within walking distance to our home in the village, or along the reaches not far upstream in Milton. Although the stream is open year-round, fishing is best in early spring and early fall. More than 13,000 brown trout are typically stocked during April and May.

Schenevus Creek

The headwaters of Schenevus Creek, located in the East Worcester area, is located at the extreme western fringes of the Capital District, in a transitional area with other regions. Some would categorize the little creek that flows nearly 30 miles westerly through agricultural lands, before it connects with the Susquehanna River not far from the City of Oneonta, as a fringe Central Region stream. An hour drive due south from its waters will put anglers in the Catskill Region. However, since the creek receives attention from the Clearwater Chapter of Trout Unlimited, based in the heart of the Capital Region, it's discussed here.

Schenevus Creek, and its main tributary Elk Creek (aka Elk Brook) in Otsego County are categorized as Stocked. Between the two, several thousand 9-inch to 15-inch brown trout are stocked along its PFR reaches. NYSDEC reports wild brook inhabit areas upstream from the Town of Worcester.

East Worcester Reach: The reach in East Worcester, located off State Route 7, is small water at the formal NYSDEC parking located on South Hill Road just beyond the railroad tracks crossing along farm fields. The tiny, hip-boot water flows through pasturelands. You'll want to use a short 7-foot rod and small wet flies along this stretch. Relocate downstream where wider water with deeper pools is found.

South Hill Road Reach: The PFR stream reach located downstream in Worcester, located by taking State Route 7 to South Hill Road and road shoulder parking marked

Schenevus Creek at Leonard Road reach. The headwaters of Schenevus Creek begin in the western fringes of the Capital Region, on the doorstep of the Catskill Region. The stream is popular with the City of Albany area fly fishers. (PHOTO VALERIE VALLA)

Schenevus Creek directly upstream from its junction with Elk Creek

by a large hanging NYSDEC sign, is wider than upstream, but still small water with some riffle structure.

Stevens Road Reach: A formal NYSDEC parking lot marked by a large hanging sign is located at the Stevens Road bridge crossing, in Schenevus, a little over 4 miles west of Worcester. Take Country Route 56 off State Route 7 to Stevens Road. A deep pool upstream from the bridge is favored by early season bait-and-lure anglers. The pool on the downstream side of the bridge flows slowly a few hundred feet to a run. Better fly-fishing water is located downstream at the Elk Creek and Leonard Road areas.

Elk Creek Crossing Reach: You won't miss the formal NYSDEC parking area marked by a large hanging sign next to State Route 7. It's located about 6 miles west of Worcester at the Elk Brook bridge crossing. A convenient ladder stile at the parking lot will get anglers over the farmland fence to the stream. The stretch upstream flows through wide-open pasture. Fish downstream from the creek's junction with Elk Brook and try the small Elk Brook itself.

While I enjoy fishing the Elk Brook section downstream from the confluence of both streams, my favorite stretch is located just a few miles west, off State Route 7 and Leonard Road. From the Elk Creek parking area, drive 4.2 miles west on State Route 7 to Leonard Road. A NYSDEC public fishing access sign is located at the intersection. However, the access parking area is located a half-mile down Leonard Road, at the intersection with Heaney Road, at a bridge crossing. Nice fly-fishing water is located both upstream and downstream from the bridge to the railroad crossing. The tailout run from the pool on the downstream side of the bridge is productive during May.

Charlotte Creek

Located not far from Schenevus Creek, nearby Charlotte Creek flows nearly 30 miles to the Susquehanna River near Oneonta. Like Schenevus Creek, Charlotte Creek is located on the extreme western fringes of the Capital region, perhaps more aptly defined as a central region creek. However, the creek is located in Delaware County, bordering Otsego County. The Catskill region is just south of Charlotte Creek.

Anglers sampling one creek routinely relocate to the other. From Schenevus, take County Road 56 to County Road 41 to County Road 9. A formal NYSDEC parking lot is located on County Road 9 in Fergusonville along a farm field. PFR water exists upstream

Charlotte Creek at the Olive Branch Road reach. Anglers who fish Schenevus Creek often head over to Charlotte Creek since it's in the general area. Like Schenevus Creek, Charlotte Creek is on the doorstep of the Catskill Region. (PHOTO VALERIE VALLA)

from the bridge crossing categorized as Stocked by NYSDEC. Access is also located about 0.6 mile downstream from the parking lot, off County Road 9 at the Keyser Brook crossing. A short trek down formal PFR Keyser Brook will get you to the Creek.

If you're after trout it's best to locate upstream from the hamlet of Davenport, off State Route 23, and around the Fergusonville/Simpsonville areas, although PFR stretches also flow downstream not far upstream from the Susquehanna River. Informal access stretches are also located at bridge crossings upstream from the Olive Branch Road reach.

While not posted, some of the bridge crossing reaches are best approached by first seeking permission from private landowners. Some of the headwater reaches inhabit wild brook trout and a few wild brown trout. Among other stretches, the bridge crossing off Johnson Road in Simpsonville provides access. Park at the area next to the bridge where an old bridge once crossed the stream. The run along the bridge on the upstream side often holds trout.

Charlotte Creek is pleasant water best fished with a 7.5-foot, 4-weight rod. Cast small dry flies upstream into shaded riffles and small nymphs wherever pocketwater can be located. It's best fished during May and early June.

Catskill Region

Of all the regions in New York, the Catskill area is considered the crown jewel fly-fishing destination. Its waters are many and the variety not few. From the tiniest brooks, some not even named, to the famous rivers that have played a key role in our fly-fishing history, to tailrace waters below several reservoirs, there's something for every fly fisher to enjoy. For well over a century, the rich Catskill region fly-fishing literature alone has steered many to its waters that flow through its mountains and rolling hill valleys.

It's not surprising that fisheries biologist and former Deputy Commissioner of the NYS Conservation Department Cecil Heacox called the region "the Charmed Circle." In *Tying Catskill-Style Dry Flies* (2009), I told the story how Heacox's March and April 1969 two-part *Outdoor Life* magazine article titled "The Charmed Circle of the Catskills" sent me on an adventure to the Beaver Kill and Willowemoc Creek. I was only 15 when I took that solo bus trip in that year from my home in Binghamton to Roscoe, captivated by Heacox's story, in search of trout on the Beaver Kill and "Willow." Other fly fishers, like my good friend Ed Ostapczuk, fell under the same spell when he read Heacox's words. Ed, who fishes Catskill streams 180-days-plus a year, has been a resident near his beloved Esopus Creek for many years. While my adventures and interests in many other waters around the state expanded in the ensuing years, Catskill streams will always remain my favorites.

Upper Esopus Creek, known for its resident wild rainbow trout and *Isonychia* hatches, is surrounded by Catskill hills and mountains as it makes its way to Ashokan Reservoir. Its upper reaches are both intimate and peaceful. (PHOTO VALERIE VALLA)

Catskill Creek

Traversing three counties—Schoharie, Albany, and Greene—Catskill Creek provides angling for both wild and stocked brown trout. The creek flows nearly 40 miles from its headwaters in Schoharie County to the Hudson River at the Village of Catskill. The lower 16 miles is considered a warmwater bass fishery. Its major tributary, Tenmile Creek, also has significant PFR water with plenty of access.

Fly fishers targeting wild trout populations should focus activity on the upper stream reach above the hamlet of Preston Hollow in the southwestern corner of Albany County. Stream reaches downstream from Preston Hollow, into Greene County, are stocked. NYS-DEC categorized Catskill Creek as Stocked-Extended from the mouth of Basic Creek in Freehold upstream to the confluence with Fox Creek in Preston Hollow.

Most of the small yet wild trout inhabit the stream roughly from the Bayard Elsbree Memorial Park area (just north of Preston Hollow on State Route 145) upstream to the Livingstonville reach in Schoharie County. The creek in this area is mostly small, 10-foot-wide water. It's small pools and runs are easily fished with hip boots and short 7-foot, 4-weight rods. PFR mileage exists for a significant distance both upstream and downstream from the park.

Elsbree Memorial Park is a nice streamside park that provides quick access into the little creek. You'll encounter a few *Isonychia* shucks along the shoreline rocks during early June. Nymphs drifted through the runs during that part of the season would be a good choice. Cast Elk Hair Caddis dry flies into the pocketwater if fishing upstream.

A couple of other stream access points are located a short drive upstream from Elsbree Memorial Park. The CCC Camp Road reach is located about 2.6 miles upstream from Elsbree Memorial Park, in Schoharie County along State Route 145. The creek's PFR mileage between Elsbree Memorial Park and CCC Camp Road crossing parallels State Route 145 but is set back far from the road.

Catskill Creek at Bayard Elsbree Memorial Park reach at Preston Hollow. The upper reaches of Catskill Creek inhabit trout while the extreme lower sections transition into bass water. (PHOTO VALERIE VALLA)

You'll notice the long ridgeline off to the left as you're driving to CCC Camp Road. The stream runs intermittently along the base of the hill in a relatively isolated area but reappears upstream at the CCC Camp Road bridge crossing. Park along the large streamside road turnout at the bridge. Try the runs and riffles that flow downstream from the bridge. The creek experienced bankside damage from a couple of floods. Large rocks and boulders were placed along the stream bank at this location and others. This reach also benefitted the NYS Trees for Tribs program.

Another easy access site is located a short distance upstream in the Livingstonville area at Broome Community Park, located on State Route 145 across from County Road 19A (Hauverville Road). The park is set back behind the Broome Fire Department buildings. A small pavilion and picnic tables are located behind the buildings. Walk to the far end of the large, mowed field to the creek. A small pool worthy of a few casts exists at the entrance to the creek from the field.

Anglers who prefer a better chance of catching fish can try the stocked stream reaches downstream from Preston Hollow. NYSDEC stocks several thousand 9-inch to 15-inch brown trout during April and May in the Towns of Rensselaerville and Cairo, in Greene County. One stocked stretch near the Albany County/Greene County line is located across from Burkhardt Road, 1.6 miles south of Elsbree Memorial Park at a State Route 145 bridge crossing. The large parking lot at the bridge is marked by a large NYSDEC hanging sign. Signage at the lot reminds anglers that the reach is stocked. Parking along the large turnout and access to the now-wider creek is also available at the bridge crossing a half-mile downstream from this point at the intersection of State Route 145 and State Route 81. The bridge crossing a few miles downstream in the Oak Hill area at Brandon Memorial Park (off County Road 22 and Clay Hill Road) is also popular.

A mile or so downstream from Brandon Memorial Park Catskill Creek picks up Tenmile Creek. A formal Tenmile Creek NYSDEC parking area marked by a large hanging sign is located on Saybrook Valley Road, just a short distance from its intersection with State Route 81, not far from the Durham Town Clerk Office. Catskill Creek in this area is wide open and tends to warm later in the season.

Esopus Creek

Esopus Creek arises in one of the most picturesque areas of the Catskill Mountains, a region once admired by the famous naturalist John Burroughs (1837–1921). From its headwaters at Winnisook Lake, near the 4,200-foot Slide Mountain—the Catskill's highest peak—Esopus Creek begins its 26-mile journey to the Ashokan Reservoir.

The stream flows in a quick decent, from 2,600 feet of elevation at Winnisook Lake to 630 feet at the reservoir. From its origin, the Esopus cascades down a steep gradient that provides the creek with well-oxygenated riffles and fast-moving pocketwater, optimum conditions for sustaining trout populations—especially wild rainbows. The character of the creek changes as it traverses downward from its forested heights, eventually reaching scattered development along State Route 28.

From its source at Winnisook Lake, the creek flows north, in a peculiar clockwise arc, passing through Big Indian and Shandaken, then redirects itself southeasterly, flowing through Allaben, Phoenicia, Mount Tremper, and Boiceville, where it enters the Ashokan. The Esopus realizes its dramatic transformation at Allaben.

At exactly 9:01 a.m. on Saturday, February 9, 1924, the Esopus Creek was about to change forever. There was a "subdued roaring" when the waters from Schoharie Reservoir

Lower Esopus Creek below Five Arch Bridge. The bridge itself was made famous in fly-fishing literature when Arnold Gingrich described in his *The Well-Tempered Angler* (1965) how he took a nasty spill into the water at one of the bridge's arches. This historic bridge is in the process of being replaced with a new structure.

(created by the construction of Gilboa Dam) came crashing through an 18-mile under-mountain tunnel, about to empty into Esopus Creek at Allaben. The February 10, 1924, *New York Times* article, which announced the historic event that occurred the day before, was written with a sense of excitement. After the waters of the Schoharie combined with the Esopus at Allaben, it took just 5 hours for the Ashokan to welcome its collective flow. "In forty-eight hours," the story continued, "they [the combined waters] will be drawn from faucets and taps in New York City." The Esopus Creek would never be the same.

Schoharie water exiting from "the Portal," as it is called, completely changed the creek's hydrology, in mostly a positive way, for its final 12 miles before vanishing into the Ashokan. Most Esopus anglers consider the inflow from the Portal as both a blessing and a curse. Thermal stratification occurring in Schoharie Reservoir sends cold water through the tunnel, cooling the Esopus downstream from the Portal. The curse is that the inflow adds turbidity to the stream, which is upsetting to some fly anglers. Yet it's a fair trade when considering the thermal lowering that the *usually* cold water brings to the Esopus during hot summer months. If not for the inflow of cold water at the Portal, the creek would have never realized the trout fishing that has been enjoyed by anglers for many decades.

The roaring sound first heard from the dark tunnel in 1924 could just as well have been an audible invitation for all anglers to come fish the Esopus. And come they did—giving a lifetime of fishing enjoyment for anglers from all walks of life. Arnold Gingrich, the founding editor of *Esquire,* wrote the Esopus was where he "spent the most miserably happy years" of his life. Yet fly fishers who waded the Esopus's waters long before Gingrich could only dream about the changes that would come to the fishery.

Some 50 years before Gingrich wrote those words in his *The Well-Tempered Angler* (1965) Theodore Gordon, in his May 31, 1913, *Forest and Stream* "notes," praised the creek's potential for someday affording "the finest trout fishing in America." With a clairvoyant's facility, Gordon predicted that once the Ashokan reservoir was constructed, trout "will be stocked naturally from the Esopus with the rainbow and European trout of good size and quality." Gordon's predictions proved true; the Esopus soon became one of the most—if not "THE most"—healthy, self-sustaining wild rainbow trout fisheries in the Northeast. Others also echoed Gordon's predictions and were able to experience what Gordon never lived long enough to witness.

Important historical fly anglers and authors such as George M. L. LaBranche, George Parker Holden, Larry Koller, Ray Ovington, Cecil Heacox, and A. J. McClane (among many others) all had something to say about their experiences on the Esopus. Preston Jennings's *Book of Trout Flies* (1935), a classic volume that served as the foundation for Ernie Schwiebert's *Matching the Hatch* (1955) and Art Flick's *Streamside Guide*, sang the virtues of the Esopus's *Isonychia bicolor* (Slate Drake) mayfly emergence—still considered the creek's premier hatch.

Besides all the important authors who frequented the Esopus, the area's past resident fly tier, Ray Smith, is also fondly remembered. Ray Smith, once a member of the "Catskill School" of fly tiers, crafted his flies on the banks of the Esopus at Phoenicia and Mount Tremper. Smith tied trout flies for eager Esopus anglers from the 1930s until his death in the 1970s. The extensive list of notable fly-fishing writers and anglers who admired, studied, and fished the Esopus demonstrates its importance as both a precious fly-fishing destination and a fly-fishing landmark.

Ed Ostapczuk knows every riffle, every pool, and every stretch of water on Esopus Creek, from its upstream sections at Big Indian to its mouth at the Chimney Hole at the Ashokan. Ed waits in restless anticipation when *Isonychia* mayfly nymphs are due to start emerging—first in late May or early June, then again in late August into September or even October. Swimming and wiggling like little minnows on their way to streambank rocks, where they'll crawl up and emerge as adults leaving behind their nymphal shucks, it's an annual Esopus entomological event. In some years, hundreds or even thousands of *Isonychia* shucks will cover exposed streambank rocks along the creek.

The large Ashokan-reared rainbows that are after them are on Ed's mind. When a good Esopus Iso hatch happens, he's right on the 'bows, casting flies such as Haystacks, Iso Spunduns, Parachute Mahogany Duns, and Hairwing Royal Coachmans off his Thramer Payne 102 cane rod. Yet, he'd be the first to tell prospective Esopus first-timers, looking for wild rainbows, that the stream fishes in cycles—some years might be good or even incredible; others might rank as abysmal.

Depending on the time of the season and water conditions, an angler new to the system might plan to sample the very lowest extent of the river first then fish waters upstream to Phoenicia. The latter part of the day can be devoted to exploring a few of the upstream stretches above the hamlet. The section below Five Arch Bridge, to the mouth of the Ashokan at the Chimney Hole pool, has some nice riffles, runs, and pools and potential for some nice fish. It's a good place to start.

Beginning at Phoenicia, loop out of the hamlet onto State Route 28 and head east approximately 6.5 miles along the highway to the Boiceville area. Take a right on State Route 28A and drive 0.4 mile (passing over Five Arch Bridge) to a gravel road on the left that leads to the Ashokan Rail Trail (ART), a relatively new 11.5-mile recreational trail that was opened a few years ago. As a result, you'll often see more trail hikers than anglers back near the parking areas. However, ample angling parking is located at the end of the entry road. In years past, fly fishers desiring to fish this Esopus reach had to park on the State Route 28A road shoulder's meager room for vehicles.

The Ashokan Reservoir is part of New York City's water supply; a DEP permit is required to fish the Esopus from Five Arch Bridge (scheduled to be demolished and replaced) downstream to the reservoir. There's just short of a mile's worth of good water between the Five Arch Bridge and Chimney Hole at the Ashokan, well worth the trouble of acquiring a New York City Watershed Recreation Access Permit. The permit is easily applied for online (it's free of charge). It's unlikely that you'll be checked by DEP patrols every time you fish that part of the Esopus, but they do check anglers who park at the lot and along the stream itself. In May 2011, two DEP officers checked Ed Ostapczuk and me for fishing licenses and access permits shortly after we crawled out of the stream below the Five Arch Bridge.

Fish the pocketwater just below "Five Arches," as it's sometimes called, as well as the famous Big Bend Pool (Arnold Gingrich's favorite) just downstream. The Trestle Pool area comes next, (although the former "old" dilapidated railroad trestle itself was washed away with Hurricane Irene several years ago) and finally the expansive Chimney Hole, where there's a chance you could land a trout as well as big bass in the deep water. Many large, reservoir-reared trout have been taken from the large pool, including a 19-pound brown trout caught by T. F. Spenser in 1923. The monster brown held the state record for 31 years. If you choose to fish as far downstream as the Chimney Hole, it's best to ford the creek (water depth permitting) just below the Trestle Pool. You'll get a better line drift from that side of the creek (which is really more of a river in the downstream areas).

While a DEP permit is required to try for the rainbows and browns in the historic pools and runs below Five Arch Bridge, areas upstream from that point do not require DEP permissions. Additional interesting water can be found as you head back toward Phoenicia, a few miles upstream, near Mount Tremper. Back on State Route 28, now traveling westerly, you'll drive about 2.3 miles then bear right on to Route 212 into the Mount Tremper area. In another 0.6 mile, you'll turn left over the bridge, putting you on "Old Route 28," a road that will eventually run right along the stream and lead right back to Phoenicia. The bridge passes over a very important Esopus Creek tributary, the

Typical Esopus Creek "Silver Bullet" wild rainbow that ate a Hairwing Royal Coachman. While most contemporary fly fishers would consider classic Hairwing Royal Coachman dry flies too stale to be effective fish catchers, given the abundance of good modern patterns, the classic fly interests Esopus rainbows, including fish larger than silver bullets. Long-time Esopus angler and local resident Ed Ostapczuk fishes it during *Isonychia* emergences.

Beaver Kill (not to be confused with "the" famous Beaverkill River flowing through the lower Catskills). The stream inhabits both rainbows and brown trout.

There's not much of a shoulder along Old Route 28; it's best to locate one of the turnout areas, park, then explore and fish upstream or downstream from those points. A formal NYSDEC angling parking sign will be found about 2.3 miles after crossing over the bridge just mentioned. Mother's Pool, a very famous slice of Esopus water, will come within view after driving another half-mile or so beyond the NYSDEC public fishing parking area. It was named, years ago, for Esopus area fly tier Ray Smith's mother.

Mother's Pool gained notoriety back on Friday afternoon, April 29, 1955, when Lawrence Decker (a veteran minnow fisher) landed his 30¾-inch, 10-pound brown trout before an audience of perhaps a hundred people on the bank. The crowd had gathered to witness the outcome of Decker playing what appeared to be a very large fish. Mother's Pool is best fished from the far side of the river. Park at the NYSDEC parking turnout, cross the creek above Mother's, wade downstream, and fish back up into the pool. One word of caution: use a wading staff on the creek. Arnold Gingrich called wading the Esopus "manslaughter"; Theodore Gordon called it "murderous."

Upstream from Mother's you'll encounter a boulder stretch called Elmer's Bend. The stream comes tumbling down from upstream and then hugs the road. Esopus fly-fishing regulars fish this stretch during periods of low water. Elmer's deep, rock-strewn pocketwater holds large trout, but normally only the bait guys seem to get into them. Wait for low summer/autumn flows to have a good chance with the fly rod. After passing Elmer's bend, you'll be back in Phoenicia within seconds. If you're ready for lunch, try Brios along the business strip; they make a good Rueben sandwich. Then explore the Esopus above the hamlet.

Swing up out of Phoenicia to State Route 28. Then turn right, drive westerly along Route 28 0.6 mile. Then take a left on Woodland Valley Road. After crossing the bridge over the Esopus that will come into view in 0.2 mile, you'll find ample parking on both sides of the road. The stream can be sampled here, both upstream and downstream. However, a better choice would be to take a right turn, just after crossing the bridge, and then another quick right onto Herdman Road. In 0.1 mile, there's a couple of parking area turnouts. (You'll notice Woodland Valley Creek tributary entering the Esopus.)

The stream is easily reached down the bank. Fish upstream along some nice runs and small pools. It's generally a nice section of the stream to enjoy except during midday during hot summer months. During that time of the year, you'll likely encounter the "rubber hatch," dozens of summer visitors floating lazily down the stream in their inner tubes, sporting orange life vests. Esopus regulars have learned to live with the tubing activity by adjusting their fishing plans to avoid what they consider a nuisance. Many hold the belief that the concept of recreational multiple use requires compromises.

A local inner-tube rental establishment transports busloads of summer water lovers to a launching point a couple of miles upstream from this area. I've fished this section of the stream during the "rubber hatch" and was still able to take small rainbows fishing Elk Hair Caddis patterns upstream, along the left bank, in a channel that could not be navigated by the tubers. However, it was not pleasant fishing, with all the festive noise from tubers floating along. At times, there seems to be no end to the "theme park" flotilla passing by on their way downstream to the Phoenicia area. Esopus regulars stay out of this section of the creek during the heat of the day. Fish this section either early in the morning or during the evening. Or avoid this area altogether during summer months. One option is to fish Woodland Valley Creek once the recreational tubers appear in the area.

Woodland Valley Stream, an important Esopus tributary. Woodland Valley Stream is a nice little creek that flows near Phoenicia. Fly fishers have access to both formal PFR water and sections where a landowner posts his land as allowing fly fishing.

WOODLAND VALLEY STREAM

Woodland Valley Stream is a lovely little stream that flows mostly through private property but can be fished at a couple locations. A formal NYSDEC angling access area, marked by a large hanging sign, is located a short drive upstream from the Herdman Road/Woodland Valley Road intersection, at a bridge crossing. Fish nymphs and wet flies through the pocketwater. Elk Hair dry flies are also effective when the water levels are lower. As you continue driving upstream along Woodland Valley Road, you'll encounter stream reaches that are private but posted as access for fly-fishing-only.

A good way to avoid all the recreational floaters is to fish the Esopus at locations upstream from where tubers typically enter the creek. To reach the upstream sections of the Esopus, return to State Route 28, taking a left as you exit Woodland Valley Road. Continuing westerly on State Route 28, a formal NYSDEC parking area will come into view on the left, near the cemetery. This is where the busloads of tubers put into the creek to begin their downstream journey. In another mile, you'll come upon the Portal. Those new to the Esopus will immediately notice a line of demarcation where the waters from the Schoharie crash into the Esopus.

To reach stretches upstream from the Portal, drive along State Route 28 another 1.5 miles and take a right on County Road 42, then a left on County Road 47. In 3 miles, two consecutive NYSDEC fishing access areas will come into view on your left, affording easy access to the creek. I fished that stretch last season. The fishing was far from phenomenal, but I did pick up a couple of highly colored, small wild browns and one small wild rainbow fishing a size 14 Elk Hair Caddis along the riffles. Departing the area, County Road 47 will eventually take the angler back onto State Route 28, but sections of the Esopus upstream from that point to its headwaters are almost entirely private and posted.

As far as gear, I fish a 9-foot, 5-weight rod on most all of the Esopus, aside from the tributaries, such as Woodland Valley Creek, where I like my 7-foot, 4-weight Becker cane. During the very early and late parts of the season, streamers can bring results. Once the hatches begin, the fun starts, especially during the *Isonychia* hatch. You'll want a supply of Tony Cocozza's Spun Duns, *Isonychia* nymphs, Lead-wing Coachman wet flies, and Hairwing Royal Coachman dry flies. Both Ed Ostapczuk and I have taken rainbows on the classic Hairwing Royal Coachman dry fly, including sizeable fish. Bring Sulphur and Blue-Winged Olive patterns. I've taken some nice rainbows on Blue-Winged Olives when those bugs are on the water. During the very late November season, Ed fishes a Yellow Madonna streamer. He's landed some dandy-size browns on the fly. The pattern, featured with Ed in my *Favorite Flies for the Catskills* book, is tied with yellow rabbit strip wing, gold tinsel body, and a clipped deer hair head.

Anglers requiring advice or gear can visit two fly shop located in Phoenicia. One is the Esopus Creel, located on State Route 28, owned and operated by Todd Spire. The

Beaver Kill Esopus tributary, at Mount Tremper. The stream that shares the same name as the historic Beaver Kill inhabits both brown trout and small rainbows. (PHOTO VALERIE VALLA)

Iso Spun-Dun (tied by Tony Cocozza) Todd Spire, Esopus fly-fishing guide and owner of the Esopus Creel fly shop located on State Route 28 in Phoencia, stocks this important Esopus pattern in his shop bins. Tied by Esopus regular Tony Cocozza, this dry fly is a must-have when fishing the stream.

Blue-Winged Olive CDC Biot Emerger (tied by René Harrop) A few different Blue-Winged Olive species emerge on the Esopus throughout the fishing season, spring into fall. Anglers heading for the Esopus should have a supply of the little dry flies in their fly boxes.

other, Catskill Outfitters, is located along the heart of the Phoenicia strip, on Church Street. Both shops can also advise you what hatches are currently on the water and what patterns would be most effective to fish on the Esopus or area tributaries.

While fishing the Esopus, if time allows, tributaries besides Woodland Valley Creek can provide good fishing, especially during periods when the Esopus is not producing. Stony Clove Creek, a small brook that crosses Main Street in Phoenicia at the State Route 214 intersection is worth fishing. The tiny Rochester Hollow brook is nice during the heat of summer.

The previously mentioned Beaver Kill at Mount Tremper is also loaded with small rainbows. Sizeable browns also inhabit the stream. On one occasion several years ago, I was checking out the Beaver Kill on a crisp autumn day with then-teenager Michael Arnold, a local fly-fishing enthusiast. During that banner day, I witnessed him land no fewer than 20 small-yet-beautiful wild rainbows. An 18-inch wild brown topped off that morning.

Other small tributaries that directly feed the Ashokan Reservoir are also in the area, such as Traver Hollow Brook, Bush Kill, Kanape Brook, South Hollow Brook, and Rondout Creek are not far away from the Esopus.

Traver Hollow Brook/Kanape Brook/Bush Kill

Small creeks and brooks that contribute water to the Ashokan Reservoir are not far from the Esopus Creek; they provide good fishing, especially when conditions might be unfavorable on the larger streams, such as the Esopus. You'll mostly encounter small wild browns and brook trout along the stream reaches, especially in their headwaters.

To access the upper reaches of Traver Hollow where it flows through a section of NYS Forest Preserve lands, cross the Five Arch Bridge over the Esopus at the State Route 28/State Route 28A intersection. In about a mile, turn right onto Traver Hollow Road. In less than a mile, bear left onto Bradkin Road. In less than a half-mile, Bradkin Road crosses the stream. You'll encounter NYSDEC Forest Preserve signs along the brook a short distance after the bridge crossing. A convenient place to park next to the stream is located just up the road. The water inhabits small brown trout that can be enticed by casting nymphs upstream into the little pools.

Other small tributaries, such as Bush Kill and Kanape Brook, are located off County Road 42, a short drive from Traver Hollow Road/State Route 28A intersection. Continue south on State Route 28A to County Road 42. You'll find easy access to the Bush Kill Creek and Kanape Brook by parking at the official NYSDEC Kanape Brook parking lot on County Road 42 (Watson Hollow Road), marked by a large hanging sign. The parking area, that serves mostly hikers heading up the Ashokan High Point trail along the Kanape Brook, is located about 4.2 miles south on Watson Hollow Road. The Bush Kill will appear on the left of County Road 42 (Watson Hollow Road) flowing downstream

Fluffy Nymphy Emerger Thingy (tied by Ted Patlen) When my good friend Teddy Patlen first handed me this fly, and I asked its name, I thought he evolved into some kind of crazy person, but that's our Ted. It was one of the most bizarre discussions I ever had concerning a trout fly, so bizarre that I included it in *Favorite Flies for the Catskills* (2020).

Upper Bush Kill is a small stream that contributes water to the Ashokan Reservoir. The small tributaries that feed Ashokan Reservoir inhabit colorful wild brown trout. (PHOTO VALERIE VALLA)

through private posted property until a point you'll notice NYS Forest lands signage along the creek 3.6 miles upstream from the State Route 28A intersection.

The parking lot is a good launching point to fish the Kanape as well as the Bush Kill stretch that runs downstream the half-mile or so distance along NYS Forest lands before it flows through private areas. A footpath across the road from the parking lot leads directly to a quaint bridge that crosses the Bush Kill.

Small nymphs fished in tandem with a dropper fly will entice the small-yet-colorful little wild browns. During summer, Elk Hair Caddis-style dry flies will interest the little fish, too. The Bush Kill experiences good early-season Quill Gordon (*Epeorus pleuralis*) hatches. Ted Patlen's oddly named dark dun-shaded Fluffy Nymphy Emerger Thingy would be a good choice during April.

I love fishing Kanape Brook and the upper Bush Kill with my 6-foot, 9-inch Becker on these little streams during the heat of the summer. Hip boots, thigh-high boots, or even wet-wading will serve you well during late summer. I ran into Ed Ostapczuk at the Kanape parking lot during one of those hot and humid summers New York is known for. We were both dripping with sweat. My intention was to fish the Bush Kill, but Ed turned me on to trying the Kanape, too. It's such a nice place.

If in the area of Bush Kill and Kanape, or just wandering for something other than larger rivers like the Esopus, it makes sense to continue down Watson Hollow Road to Rondout Creek.

Rondout Creek

In his 1887 "A Bed of Boughs," essayist and naturalist John Burroughs wrote, "If there ever was a stream cradled in the rocks, detained lovingly by them, held and fondled in a rocky lap or tossed in rocky arms, that stream is the Rondout." While not a major

Rondout Creek at the Trailer Field access area. Historic Rondout Creek has experienced issues with overuse, not by anglers but by other users of the resource, from swimmers to day-users to campers. However, it's still a beautiful little Catskill stream that can please the fly angler with its small but colorful trout.

fly-fishing creek, Rondout Creek is truly one of the quintessential Catskill streams. You'll want to locate well upstream from the Rondout Reservoir, in the headwaters, where the creek flows through NYS Forest lands that provide fishing access. Much of the lower river directly upstream from the reservoir is posted.

Located only a few miles south on County Road 42 from the Ashokan Reservoir area, and the tributaries discussed previously, Rondout Creek deserves a visit while fishing the lower Esopus watershed and its nearby tributaries that dump water into the Ashokan. As you drive south 7 miles or so from the State Route 28A/County Road 42 intersection back near the Ashohkan, and south of the NYSDEC Kanape Brook parking area 3 miles, you'll encounter a small pond on the right side of the road called Peekamoose Lake.

Water that departs Peekamoose Lake combines with the headwaters of Rondout Creek that approaches from the Slide Mountain area. The stream then heads along County Road 42 (now called Peekamoose Road), first through private lands before it soon intersects NYS Sundown Wild Forest. Watch for the NYSDEC forest lands signage along the road that you'll eventually encounter next to the stream in about a mile downstream from the outlet of Peekamoose Lake. Don't attempt to park along the narrow road that lacks shoulders. Park at one of the official NYSDEC parking lots located along Peekamoose Road that provides access to the creek.

Three small parking areas, separated by about a mile each, are located downstream from Peekamoose Lake outlet. Additional and more frequent parking turnouts are available once Peekamoose Road arrives at a main parking and camping area called Trailer Field, marked by a NYSDEC hanging sign next to a bridge crossing.

After the bridge crossing, you'll find plenty of places to park, especially at the larger "Upper Field," "Middle Field," and "Lower Field" lots marked by large hanging NYSDEC signs. During summer, you'll also encounter lots of hikers and campers along the Peekamoose Valley corridor. The valley attracts large numbers of seasonal campers. Some 89 camping sites are available. Reservations can be obtained online. Day-users are also required to pay a $10 fee. I recently learned from a NYSDEC official that formal plans are in the works to wave the fee for anglers.

The day usage limits were sorely needed to help stop the overuse of the beautiful stream and natural area. In recent years, the famous, if not infamous, "Blue Hole" swimming hole just up the road from the Trailer Field parking area was so trashed up something had to be done. The crowds of sometimes rowdy swimmers left the place in such a mess that John Burroughs would have shaken his head in disbelief. Many of us did just that. Keep from fishing the stream on weekends to avoid the highest numbers of visitors, but during the summer, it's always a popular location for recreational hikers, day-users, and campers.

Rusty Chuck Caddis (tied by Mike Valla) A spinoff of Eric Leiser's regular Chuck caddis, Rusty Chuck Caddis is an equally easy fly to tie. Leiser favored woodchuck hair for both streamers and dry flies such as his Chuck Caddis.

Fish caddis dry fly patterns, such as small-size Rusty Chuck Caddis, along the little runs and pools that flow through state land. A 7-foot, 4-weight rod is a good choice along the creek's upper reaches. The little creek is loaded with small wild brook trout in its upper stretches. A few wild brown trout, mostly small, inhabit the upper stream.

If you're after larger hatchery brown trout, along with wild browns, fish the access areas available below the Rondout Reservoir dam off State Route 55. Peekamoose Road (County Road 42) intersects State Route 55 about 7 miles south of the NYS lands. NYS-DEC stocks around 1,800 yearling 9-inch to 10-inch browns and a few hundred 2-year 12-inch to 15-inch fish. The best water, and the stream reach that's stocked, is between the dam and Honk Lake.

During 2018–2019, NYSDEC experimented stocking the reach with a hybrid strain of brown trout. Data collected showed the hybrid strain had higher summer survival rates than the domestic brown trout strain. Another encouraging finding was the abundance of wild brown trout.

Lower Rondout Creek Tributaries

Flowing into Rondout Creek well downstream of the reservoir Vernooy Kill, a small tributary that flows through Vernooy Kill State Forest, is categorized as Stocked. It receives only a handful of hatchery brown trout. Rochester Creek is categorized as Wild-Quality. Sandburg Creek and Beer Kill, categorized as Stocked, are not far away. From its confluence with Sandburg Creek upstream to the West Branch the Beer Kill is categorized as Stocked. However, from its confluence with the main branch upstream to Windsor Lake the West, Branch is categorized as Wild-Quality.

Neversink River

One of the principal Catskill rivers, the Neversink is steeped in fly-fishing history.

In *Tying Catskill-Style Dry Flies* (2009) a good synopsis of the river's past was described. Mention was made of the illustrious fly-fishing and fly-tying personalities

Neversink River downstream from Neversink Reservoir dam at BWS Road Bridge Crossing. Fall is a great time to sample its pools in solitude. Neversink River is no doubt one of the most popular trout in the Catskills in New York. The big brown trout that swim in waters downstream from the dam are taken annually on both dry flies and streamers. Public water is very limited upstream from the reservoir. (PHOTO VALERIE VALLA)

who cast their lines on the stream well before the river was dammed to create a reservoir that contributed water to New York City's growing needs.

Anglers and tiers such a Theodore Gordon, Herm Christian, Roy Steenrod, and Rube Cross waded its stretches. Ed Hewitt, who almost defined the Neversink, was there experimenting with habitat improvements on his frontage. His stream reach was later inundated when the dam was constructed in 1954. Hewitt's frequent angling companion, artist John Atherton, fished Hewitt's large-hackled skater dry flies along the plank-dam pools on Hewitt's Big Bend Club reach.

After the dam was built, the river evolved into two different fisheries: the tailrace below the dam and the upper river and its two branches, where today there are stretches that can still remind fly fishers what it must have been like during Hewitt's time. Anglers adapted, and other personalities took over where Hewitt left off. Lenny Wright, author of *Fishing the Dry Fly Like a Living Insect* (1972), stepped in with his valiant effort to establish big hybrid brook trout on his waters upstream from the reservoir at the hamlet of Claryville, where the two branches join. His Fluttering Caddis pattern is still fished on the stream today.

NEVERSINK RIVER ABOVE THE RESERVOIR

Aside from just a couple short stream reaches, one at Claryville, the entire 7 miles of Neversink River upstream from the reservoir is private property with no access. One official NYSDEC parking area is located at Claryville off County Road 19 (2 miles south from the County Road 19/County Road 47 and West Branch Road/Frost Valley Road intersections) near where the East and West Branches join. The public access reach is short. The only additional public water, also short sections, are located far upstream on the East Branch and West Branch headwaters, on New York State Forest lands.

The NYS Forest lands access on the short public East Branch reach is located about 6 miles or so north on Claryville Road/Denning Road from the County Road 19/County Road 47 intersection in Claryville. The formal NYSDEC lot, marked by signage at a small bridge, is located 1.9 miles north of New Road Hill bridge that you'll pass on the way. Wild brook trout inhabit the stream. It's a good late-summer location.

Limited access is also available on the East Branch of the Neversink headwaters, located at the NYSDEC Biscuit Brook trailhead parking area, marked by a large hanging sign. The reach that flows through NYS Forest is located about 8 miles or so north of Claryville, on County Road 47. (If approaching from the north near Esopus Creek country, the lot is located about 13 miles south of the State Route 28/County Road 47 intersection in Big Indian.) This is small water that inhabits small fish. It's best fished during summer when brook trout are more willing to strike flies. While fishing this reach, make sure you don't wander into property owned by Frost Valley YMCA or other private property.

I use my 7-foot, 4-weight and 6-foot, 3-weight rods on the upper Neversink branches. Ed Ostapczuk's Elk Hair Stonefly (EHSF) is so effective that I rarely fish any other fly during summer. Ed has caught dozens of small brook trout, during the summer, on his EHSF. Small nymphs work well, too.

Anglers fishing the meager public frontage on the upper Neversink branches who still desire small-water fishing can head over to upper Willowemoc Creek and its ample PFR stretches. A 15-minute drive or so from Claryville will get you over the mountain to that watershed and the creek. A shortcut road of sorts in located by taking a right on Hunter Road, 2 miles south of Claryville on County Road 19 (Claryville Road). Follow Hunter Road over the mountain to Willowemoc Road (see Willowemoc Creek page 264 for more details on that stream).

Otherwise, to get on the tailrace water of the Neversink below the reservoir, take Claryville Road 5 miles south or so to State Route 55, then go right 4 miles or so to the reservoir dam and Hasbrouck Road that will lead down the river from below the dam.

Upper Neversink River at Claryville. The short Claryville stretch is one of only a couple public access reaches on the upper river. (PHOTO VALERIE VALLA)

NEVERSINK RIVER BELOW THE RESERVOIR

The river that flows as a tailrace below the dam is everything the upper Neversink isn't. Significant PFR mileage water, easy access, big brown trout (both wild and hatchery fish), and long, deep pools that harbor both wild and hatchery large brown trout and interesting hatches.

Of course, both the upper river and lower tailrace water are cold-flowing, and big browns that sometimes wandered up from the reservoir are netted as far up as the two branches are caught. Access available on the lower river available makes it much more popular with fly anglers who can enjoy the most-popular public water that flows inter-mittently between the dam and the hamlet of Woodbourne.

Three easy access points are located within a few miles of each other, beginning with the uppermost Department of Environmental Protection (DEP) section just downstream from the dam at the BWS bridge crossing. From State Route 55 on the east side of the dam, drive south less than a mile to the bridge crossing. Anglers and others are not allowed to fish upstream from the bridge, directly below the dam, but New York City DEP allows fishing downstream from the access point, by permit. There isn't a formal parking lot, but anglers can squeeze in a vehicle by carefully parking near the bridge on Hasbrouck Road. Trekking down the somewhat steep hill on the east side of the bridge will get anglers into the water.

Other access areas on PFR water are located a couple of miles downstream from BWS Road. If approaching from the dam area, cross the bridge and go left onto Devine Road. Take Devine Road straight onto Dreyer Road and then to the Hasbrouck Road bridge crossing parking turnout on Lippman Road at the bridge. (You can also park on the opposite side of the bridge, across from Park Garden Estates on the road shoulder.)

The long pool downstream from the bridge is where I keep my eyes peeled for signs of dimpling trout along the flat-water pool that runs a distance downstream before hitting a nice run. Water upstream from the bridge that has more structure is also good.

A formal NYSDEC parking area is located a half-mile downstream from the Has-brouck Road bridge crossing. I call it the "gravel pit reach." From Lippman Road at the

Ed Ostapczuk netted this 20-inch Neversink Brown on a Black Conehead Woolly Bugger. (PHOTO ED OSTAPCZUK)

Black Conehead Woolly Bugger (tied by Mike Valla) Ed Ostapczuk's pattern is more often tied with a red butt tag that he calls Red-Butt Conehead Wolly Bugger. So effective in taking large Neversink brown trout, it's doubtful Ed would enter the Neversink without a supply in his box. Those of us who are fortunate to receive Ed's seemingly daily Catskill rivers fishing outings reports figured out long ago just how effective Ed's conehead is for bringing big brown trout to his net.

Sulphur CDC Parachute (tied by Mike Konecni) Mike Konecni, a staff member of the Dette Flies shop in Livingston Manor, loves his own Sulphur CDC Parachute when the sulphur mayflies emerge on the Neversink River.

Adams Streamer (tied by Seth Cavarretta) Catskill region resident and fly fisher Seth Cavarretta ties a variety of beautiful flies for Catskill streams, including some of the most awesome Catskill-style dry flies. A spinoff of sorts from the classic Adams dry fly, it borrows features from it, such as the mixed brown hackle. He likes this streamer when on the Neversink.

bridge, drive about a half-mile south on what is now named Hasbrouck Drive. A NYS-DEC large hanging sign is on the left side of Hasbrouck Drive at a gravel road. The gravel road continues a short distance to the streambank, where the river runs around an island of sorts downstream. I usually cast streamers next to the east stream bank, working my way downstream. Yet another formal NYSDEC parking area, marked by a large hanging sign, is located directly on Hasbrouck Drive a half-mile south of the gravel road access area. The pools here are large and deep.

A variety of hatches make their appearance on the Neversink. Your fly box should include flies that can be fished slow and deep during early spring and when water levels are running high. Ed Ostapczuk's boxes never leave his truck if they don't carry a supply of Black Conehead Woolly Bugger patterns that get down to the fish, or his beloved Black Leach during times the water levels accommodate that pattern. Ed has taken some mighty big Neversink browns on the conehead pattern. His leach that he first conceived tying for Thirteenth Lake in the Adirondacks has produced for him, too. Seth Cavarretta likes to fish his Adams Streamer on the Neversink River. However, the Neversink isn't all about big streamers that work well. Ed took a nice brown last season fishing a Hendrickson Comparadun.

Your boxes should carry a full complement of dry fly patterns—caddis, Hendricksons, Sulphurs, and other common Catskill mayfly patterns. Neversink enthusiast Mike

Konecni, who works at the Dette Flies shop in nearby Livingston Manor, loves to fish his Sulphur CDC Parachute pattern that also finds effective during the fall when Pale Evening Duns (*Leucrocuta hebe*) are on the water. Be sure to carry Olives tied in small sizes for the browns that dimple on the long, flat pools when that bug is on the water.

I use only one fly rod for all of my Neversink River fishing on the tailwaters below the dam, a 9.5-foot, 5-weight *Catskill Research* model. You'll generally want the extra length rod on the big pools.

Willowemoc Creek

It might be argued that Willowemoc Creek holds as much significance in the history of American fly fishing as the celebrated Beaver Kill, the water it weds after its 27-mile journey through a lovely valley in the Catskill Mountains in New York. In his influential 1864 work, *The American Angler's Book*, Thaddeus Norris (1811–1877) described fishing the stream with Grannoms and Jenny Spinners, two old British patterns. Anglers who followed Norris also wrote compellingly about the creek.

Theodore Gordon, who learned to tie flies from Norris's book, wrote about the Willowemoc in the late nineteenth and early twentieth centuries. George M. L. La Branche (1875–1961), in *The Dry Fly and Fast Water* (1914), described his first experience fishing a floating fly, an event that occurred on the upper Willowemoc a dozen or so miles upstream from the creek's junction with the Beaver Kill in Roscoe.

"Upper Willow," as it is informally called, is generally defined as water upstream from Livingston Manor; "Lower Willow" runs downstream from "the Manor" to the Beaver Kill. The oft-ultra-clear upper creek, rife with aquatic invertebrates, provides plenty of forage for its stocked brown trout, wild brown trout, and wild brook trout.

UPPER WILLOWEMOC CREEK

The upper creek offers the quintessential Catskill fly-fishing experience. I love fishing my 7.5-foot, 4-weight along most of the stream, reserving shorter, lighter rods for the upper

Mongaup Creek, a tributary of the Willowemoc. If sampling Willowemoc Creek, anglers should consider fishing the little Mongaup Creek. More of a brook, the stream inhabits trout that will please any fly fisher. Dropped into pools and runs, beadhead flies work well. (PHOTO VALERIE VALLA)

Willowemoc Creek, upstream from DeBruce. Willowwemoc, a quintessential Catskill stream, is steeped in fly-fishing history. Ample public fishing easement water provides some of the best trout fishing in New York.

reaches. Classic Catskill patterns still perform well on the stream. The upper creek runs in and out of private land, but ample public mileage is accessible via multiple formal state parking turnouts along County Roads 81 and 82, which follow the creek from Livingston Manor upstream to its headwaters.

I like to think of Upper Willow in three sections: the lower 6 miles between and the hamlet of Willowemoc and DeBruce; the middle 4-mile stretch between DeBruce and the hamlet of Willowemoc; and the uppermost trickles between Willowemoc and the creek's origins in a tract of state land called the Big Indian Wilderness. Some of my most cherished memories stem from experiences fly fishing the section from Livingston Manor to DeBruce.

Three state parking areas are located along County Road 81, which follows the stream between Livingston Manor and DeBruce. You'll be in the company of other anglers during May and June, when Hendricksons, March Browns, and various caddisflies bring fish to the surface. However, the parking turnout at the old DeBruce Road, 1.5 miles upstream from the intersection of County Road 81 and State Route 17, is not directly on the stream; the creek is accessed via a footpath down a steep hill. The walk deters some anglers from fishing that section, which holds some fine browns and a few brook trout.

As you approach the hamlet of DeBruce, 4 miles upstream, you'll encounter posted signs marking the DeBruce Fly Fishing Club's private waters. I snuck onto those waters as a teenager back in 1971, and was met by the caretaker, who chambered a round in a .30-30 Winchester rifle and yelled at me to leave. When I became a club member 40 years later, I recounted the incident to fellow members; we all had a good laugh. There's no fear of being shot today, but the water is still patrolled. The club stocks its 5 miles of water with brown trout, but these big trout don't know the property boundaries.

Mongaup Creek, a small tributary filled with brook trout and brown trout, joins the Willowemoc on DeBruce Club water. The Junction Pool is off-limits, but Mongaup is accessible upstream to Camp DeBruce, the state's conservation education camp, and the Catskill State Fish Hatchery; there's plenty of public water along Mongaup Road, which follows the little brook. John Bonasera likes to plop his Catskill Cannonball beadhead nymph in its small pools and runs.

Departing DeBruce and driving along County Road 82, toward the hamlet of Willowemoc, you'll find additional public parking areas for fishing. There's also a nice parking area in Willowemoc, at the bridge. You'll catch browns, but brookies are increasingly common. I like to drift wet flies at the pool heads, but the fish are not overly selective.

The creek becomes quite small upstream from Willowemoc, but it is filled with wild brook trout as it flows through the Willowemoc Wild Forest. Be sure to sample the isolated headwaters along Flugertown Road and also Fir Brook, a tributary, located about a mile up the road from the Willowemoc bridge parking area. John Checchia's Little Green Stonefly was designed for the shaded upper stretches.

LOWER WILLOWEMOC CREEK

The lower Willow that flows downstream from Livingston Manor to its confluence with the Beaver Kill is popular largely because of the significant amount of easy-to-access PFR stretches. While in Livingston Manor, you'll want to stop in the Dette Flies shop located on Main Street, just off Old Route 17. The shop posts current fly hatches in progress on the area streams, as well as stream conditions and where to fish. Favorite sections include the Special Regulation reaches available on the lower Willowemoc. The Special Regulation sections draw numbers of fly fishers to those stretches (check the NYSDEC online maps for descriptions of those reaches).

A popular stretch is located very close to Livingston Manor, on Covered Bridge Road. From the Old Route 17/Main Street intersection in Livingston Manor, drive about a mile east to Covered Bridge Road Pass through the quaint covered bridge then access the

Dette Flies shop co-owner Joe Fox on the Covered Bridge stretch in Livingston Manor. The town park along the stream is a great place to take a lunch break.

stream at a town park. It's a nice stretch that flows next to a pavilion that's convenient for a streamside lunch.

After sampling the creek at the covered bridge area, drive 0.6 mile past the park to Hazel Road. Bear right, and continue 2.8 miles to a formal NYSDEC angling parking lot located at streamside. You'll notice signage that alerts anglers that the section is part of the creek's Special Regulations artificial-lures-only area. It's always been a favorite of mine, especially during Hendrickson hatch time.

Other access points are located downstream along Hazel Road. Another formal NYSDEC parking area is located 0.7 mile down Hazel Road at the intersection with Wegman Road. It's next to J&S Creekside Cabins, a convenient stretch for those staying at the facility. Just 0.3 mile downstream from Wegman Road, the historic Hazel Bridge Pool is located at a bridge crossing next to a formal NYSDEC streamside parking area. Once you cross the bridge, you'll end back up on Old Route 17. The old Harry and Elsie Darbee fly shop (painted green) is at the intersection.

Catskill Cannonball (tied by John Bonasera)
"Catskill John" Bonasera, from Yardley, Pennsylvania, loves his little beadhead, especially when fishing small waters like Mongaup Creek. John crafts his "Cannonball" with Hare's ear over .015 lead (substitute) wire wraps. Its handsome wingcase is formed with golden pheasant center tail fibers coated with thick Loon UV Clear Fly Finish.

Brown Bivisible (tied by Ron Frost) Ron "Ronbo" Frost, who owns a great little place near the Catskill region Village of Walton, complete with a small trout pond, likes to fish a classic Brown Bivisible on local Catskill streams. It's an old pattern originated by Edward Ringwood Hewitt (1866–1957), and its "bivisible" name was derived from Hewitt's belief it was visible to both fish and angler.

Little Green Stonefly (tied by John Checchia)
"Hardware John" Checchia, who owns a hardware store in Livingston Manor a short walk down Main Street from the Dette Flies shop, loves his Little Green Stonefly for after-work-hours evening fishing on Willowemoc and other local waters.

Wemoc Adams (tied by Mike Valla) A tweaked version of the famous Adams dry fly, I never claimed the Wemoc Adams as a totally different pattern. Created many years ago, I decided to rib the body with fine gold wire to keep muskrat dubbing in place and use cree for hackle for the collar.

From that point, you can drive east on Old Route 17 back toward Livingston Manor and fish the reach that flows along the Catskill Fly Fishing Museum. The stretch, located a few miles downstream from Livingston Manor on Old Route 17, is enjoyed by many. Parking is available directly next to the creek at both a formal NYSDEC parking area and at the museum's entrance.

Another option is to head west along Old Route 17 toward the Village of Roscoe. In about a mile from the Hazel Road intersection, you'll pass by Buck Eddy, a storied pool and run that can provide good fishing. From there, the stream passes under the "new" Route 17 bridge. During my teen years, in the very early 1970s, the section that's relatively isolated was always my favorite. The stretch flows along the highway, away from convenient access in its midsection area.

The creek flows past what we always called "the Wall Pool," or Winnie's Wall, something that I described in my *Tying Catskill-Style Dry Flies* book (2009). It's where Catskill fly-tier Walt Dette found me fishing alone on a day's solo fishing adventure, in 1969. Winnie had suggested I fish that pool when I stopped in the shop, after taking a trip alone that morning from my home in Binghamton, located 65 miles to the west. Winnie sent Walt out looking for me in the evening, for fear I'd miss my bus back home. I have many good memories of fishing the pool late into the night back in those years, with Gary Clark, who is Walt's grandson, Mary Dette Clark's son, and Joe Fox's uncle. We landed some sizeable brown trout near the wall, an old railroad embankment that provides cover for the fish.

Willowemoc Creek then flows past Cottage Street in Roscoe, the location of the "old" Dette fly shop next to the highway. A formal angling parking area, Riverside Park, is located downstream at a bridge crossing at the end of Cottage Street, at Stewart Avenue. Park there and fish downstream to Junction Pool, at the Beaver Kill. It's right near Roscoe's village strip. Three additional fly shops—Beaverkill Angler, Trout Town Flies, and Baxter House Outfitters—can provide fishing advice, flies, and tackle.

Beaver Kill

The Beaver Kill (aka Beaverkill or Beaverkill River), born from springheads in the shadows of the high peaks of Doubletop and Graham Mountains in the western Catskills, is arguably the most famous trout stream in the East. It's also one of the most famous trout streams in America. Its principal tributary, Willowemoc Creek, a charming quintessential Catskill stream, also boasts some of the best fly fishing in the East; it begins high in the Catskill Mountains, southeast of Doubletop.

Great trout-angling possibilities aside, the 44-mile-long river is filled with rising and willing trout. The rich angling history that defined the river, a heritage that reaches back well over a century, is, for many, as much a draw to the Beaver Kill as the stream's prolific fly hatches. Notable angling writers and prominent artists, from the early nineteenth century to contemporary times, have fished and described its waters.

The lore and literature surrounding the so-called early Catskill School of fly tiers, artisans who practiced their craft on the Beaver Kill and surrounding waters, lured many fly fishers to the region. Walt and Winnie Dette, along with Harry and Elsie Darbee, among others, sold flies to visiting Beaver Kill anglers. They learned their craft in the late 1920s by unraveling delicately tied Catskill-style dry flies obtained from Rube Cross, a contemporary of Catskill neighbor Theodore Gordon (1854–1915), often called (rightly or wrongly) the father of dry-fly fishing in America. Gordon also wrote extensively about the river.

Beaver Kill at Hendrickson's Pool. It might be argued that Beaver Kill is the most famous trout stream in America. That statement might be a stretch, but the river holds that degree of importance in fly-fishing history. Hendrickson's Pool is an easy-to-access roadside water located a couple of miles downstream from the Village of Roscoe.

It has been over 50 years since I first fished the Beaver Kill as a 15-year-old kid who roamed the area alone on a day's fishing adventure. William Schaldach's book, *Currents and Eddies* (1944), and, in particular, his chapter "The Bountiful Beaverkill" in that book had sparked a plan to fish the river. "The pull of the current," in Schaldach's words, became an obsession. A $5 bus ticket that transported me from my home in Binghamton, 65 miles to the west of the river, figured into my plans of experiencing a solo Beaver Kill fly-fishing adventure.

I fished alone for miles on the river downstream from the Village of Roscoe on that day. I didn't catch a single trout, but I did net a friendship with Walt and Winnie Dette after stopping in the shop in Roscoe that morning. Today, the Dette Flies shop is still alive and well, operated by the Dettes' great-grandson, Joe Fox and his fiance, who recently moved the store from Roscoe to an expanded shop in nearby Livingston Manor, across from the Willowemoc Creek, the Beaver Kill's major tributary.

Frequent month-long stays with the Dettes all through the rest of my teen years and through the 1970s provided fly-tying and fishing instruction, as well as many fond memories of my early days on the Beaver Kill and the fish that I caught. Marking the fiftieth anniversary of my first solo trip to the Beaver Kill, I decided to fish the river a few years ago. The river and the area have changed, yet the Beaver Kill remains a great fly-fishing destination.

During my teen years, almost all of my Beaver Kill fishing was limited to the lower Beaver Kill "big water," along a 5-mile stretch between Junction Pool (the confluence of Willowemoc Creek and the upper Beaver Kill, in Roscoe) and Painter's Bend. Most of my Beaver Kill fishing today is along that same section. The river upstream from Junction Pool, which is almost brook-like in character, is different from the big water in many ways.

Aside from brief public mileage in Rockland and stretches a few miles upstream at the Covered Bridge Pool at the Beaverkill Campground, almost all of the Beaver Kill water upstream from Rockland is private. A chain of historic fly-fishing clubs, some that go back to the 1800s, control the upper river. The Rockland PFR access points, located at points 1.5 miles and 2 miles north from the intersection of State Route 206 and County Road 179A ("Old Route 17") in Roscoe, are clearly marked by NYSDEC stream access signs along State Route 206.

A good strategy on the 2-mile Rockland stretch is to fish small traditional wet flies downstream along the riffles and pocketwater. Brown trout, rainbow trout, and a few brook trout willingly slam patterns such as Hare's Ear and Quill Gordon wet flies tied down to size 18. However, my friend Ayumi Ozeki extensively fishes a size 12 and 14 classic Catskill-style dry fly, the Oszeki Cree Wing, in that section of the Beaver Kill. Ayumi has netted browns up to 18 inches using his preferred 8-foot, 3-weight rods. I like 7- to 7.5-foot, 4-weight rods when sampling the charming, albeit brief, public upper Beaver Kill water.

I prefer to fish the limited public upper Beaver Kill, and the Willowemoc tributary, during late April to very early May, when the Catskill streams come alive with first mayfly emergences that arouse hungry trout. Be sure to carry in your box both dry and subsurface patterns that suggest these early bugs. The little Blue Quill (*Paraleptophlebia adoptiva*) and the Quill Gordon (*Epeorus pleuralis*) are the first mayflies that perk up not only the trout but also dry-fly anglers on both the upper river and the lower big water. You'll often encounter both flies emerging on the upper Beaver Kill at the covered bridge into mid-May, depending on the season.

The big water, the lower river below Junction Pool (commonly called "The Forks"), is an entirely different kind of stream. Nearly all of this section of the river is public water, clear downstream some 15 miles to the Beaver Kill's confluence with the East Branch Delaware River. Two Catch and Release sections are located on the lower river; they're open to year-round fishing. Most water can be covered with 8.5- to 9-foot, 5-weight rods.

Nearly every major run and pool downstream from Junction Pool is named. Some have appeared in Beaver Kill literature for over a century. You'll want to head for many of these famous and historic pools during the major mayfly and caddis emergences. They are all located along County Road 179A/State Route 17 and marked by signs erected by the Theodore Gordon Flyfishers organization, as well as NYSDEC signage.

Junction Pool is very popular with bait casters, especially on opening day of the regular trout season, when anglers gather in crowds. Newspapers often print opening day photos of Junction Pool and the gatherings that mark the beginning of the regular trout season in New York, on April 1. Even during my teen years, I never favored the deep-water pool that undoubtedly harbors big brown trout. However, the pools, riffles, and runs below Junction Pool still bring me great joy.

Ferdon's Eddy, located immediately downstream from Junction Pool, was always a favorite during the very early 1970s, when I fished it with Gary Clark, Walt and Winnie's grandson. The pool has a history with the Ferdon family, which operated a hostelry above the river that catered to the many famous anglers and vacationers before the Great Depression. The ruins of the old River View Inn can be seen along County Road 179A, not far from the Ferdon's Eddy angling access marked by an NYSDEC sign. Winnie Dette, a Ferdon before she married Walt in 1928, lived at the hotel while she was growing up.

Ferdon's Eddy is where the famous Hendrickson dry fly was born over a century ago. Roy Steenrod, a frequent guest of the hotel, named it for his fishing partner, Albert Everett Hendrickson, also a frequent guest at the River View Inn. Steenrod and Hendrickson got into a big hatch of *Ephemerella subvaria* mayflies. Rising fish rejected all the flies in their boxes until Steenrod went to his tying materials and arrived at one of the most famous Catskill-style dry flies. The new fly, created in 1916, resulted in fish-taking success for the two anglers.

The pattern, with a wood-duck wing, dun hackle, and light fox fur body, was christened the Hendrickson a couple of years later, in 1918. Incidentally, the Hendrickson emergence on the Beaver Kill is one of the river's most popular hatches.

The hatch can be encountered anytime from the third week of April into mid-May. The body of the male *E. subvaria* is a different shade that the lighter body of the female natural. It's much darker and reddish, better imitated with patterns such as a classic Catskill-style Red Quill dry fly, made famous decades ago by Art Flick, or the many contemporary patterns available locally. A classic Atherton No. 2 dry fly will also take fish. You'll want a supply of *E. subvaria* emerger patterns for the Hendrickson hatch.

The next major pool downstream from Ferdon's is Barnhart's Pool, my favorite pool on the river ever since I first fished it a half-century ago. Barnhart's begins roughly at the Sullivan County line, the upper boundary of the first Catch and Release stretch, created in 1965, which extends 2.5 miles downstream. Today, there's a nice-size parking area and a wide, mowed path that leads to the upper boundary at a signed NYSDEC parking turnout located on State Route 17. In the old days, we had to hack through field brush and briars to reach upper Barnhart's, or walk upstream a distance from Hendrickson's Pool.

I caught my first good Beaver Kill brown trout at Barnhart's, in June 1972. The 17-incher sipped in a small Conover dry fly, a pattern developed decades before by Scotty Conover, a member of the upper river's Fly Fishers Club of Brooklyn. A few caddisflies were buzzing around. The battle began along the shallow end of the pool's slick flats and ended downstream at Hendrickson's Pool, where I beached the fish. The crowd of anglers there admired the battle, although one older fly fisher named Ernie Maltz—"dean of the Beaver Kill" in those years, and a caddis hatch enthusiast—reprimanded me for not having a landing net.

In the early years, the Conover was the dry fly of choice for caddisfly emergences, but it's also a good general dry-fly attractor pattern. The Beaver Kill provides some excellent fishing during prolific caddis emergences. Several caddis species emerge and overlap throughout the season. One of the most popular is *Brachycentrus appalachia*, called Apple Caddis. I've encountered these apple-green-bodied adults and pupae as early as very late April, but they usually appear around the first week of May. You'll want a supply of both dry-fly and emerger imitations; local shops can fix you up with a number of patterns.

Of all the mayfly emergences I experienced on Barnhart's, none beats the Green Drake (*Ephemera guttulata*) and its somber spinner stage, called the Coffin Fly. Expect this bug to appear around the last week of May into the first week of June. Some years produce better hatches than other years. That day in 1972, my fishing partner, an older gent, and I witnessed one of the biggest Green Drake hatches that had occurred in decades. We both shook our heads when we witnessed thousands of the giant mayflies floating along the pool.

We threw every big dry fly we had at the bulging rises, but not a single fish showed interest. We figured out fast the browns were feeding on the emerging nymphs just below the surface, not the adults. If that happens, drift and strip a large dark-shaded nymph among the bulges. When the fish show interest in the large Green Drake duns, try a big dry fly with greenish-yellow wing hues. My good friend, Paul Weamer, uses a fly called Weamer's Green Drake Comparachute. A large White Wulff dry fly or a Dette Coffin

Beaver Kill at Horton Bridge. Horton Bridge reach is full of trout, and as a result, it's one of the most popular Beaver Kill stretches. (PHOTO VALERIE VALLA)

Fly will take fish during the impressive spinner fall, which can last until well after dark. John Collins created an interesting fly he named the Yearling Elk Coffin.

Barnhart's Pool spills into Hendrickson's Pool. It's one of the most gorgeous pools on the Beaver Kill, and a reach I've admired since the very first time I fished it in 1969. It was the downstream extent of my first solo journey, and I remember well casting over its deep water along the car-size, midstream boulders. Old Route 17 will deliver you to the pool, well-marked by a NYSDEC sign.

In his classic *Matching the Hatch* (1955), Ernest G. Schwiebert described an encounter with the March Brown mayfly, now classified as *Maccaffertium vicarium*, at Hendrickson's. The moderately large mayfly usually started appearing around mid-May. Schwiebert netted a 22-inch hook-jawed brown that splashed for the wind-blown bugs that skated along the boulders. The fish almost took the fight downstream to swifter water at Horse Brook Run. John Collins's Peacock March Brown is a good choice when that mayfly is on the water.

During the early years, Horse Brook Run, named for the little brook that joins the pocketwater fun, was known as rainbow trout water, although, during all my years fishing that run, I never caught one. However, you'll hear of a rainbow netted from time to time, no doubt a fish that ascended into the Beaver Kill from the Delaware River. I've experienced multi-fish days when fishing Horse Brook Run's pocketwater with small White Wulff dry flies late in the season.

I've also had success on Horse Brook Run fishing size 12 *Isonychia* nymphs designed by Walt Dette. It's still one of my favorite nymphs, and one of the very first nymphs Walt taught me to tie. A classic Lead Wing Coachman, fished along the water's edge, is also a good choice at Horse Brook Run.

Around the end of May and into June, you might notice *Isonychia bicolor* mayfly shucks along the shoreline rocks and debris, which the fast-swimming, minnow-like nymphs leave behind when they crawl out of the water and emerge as Slate Duns, as they are commonly called. Expect a second *I. bicolor* emergence on the Beaver Kill in mid-September.

Horse Brook Run riffles into Cairns Pool, historically the most-crowded pool on the river because of its easy State Route 17 roadside access. As Yogi Berra once quipped in a different context, "Nobody goes there anymore. It's too crowded." I landed my first Beaver Kill trout at the head of Cairns Pool when Walt dropped me off there after dinner one evening.

I've encountered fabulous fishing at the head of Cairns early in the morning, in mid-June. *Drunella* Blue-Winged Olive mayflies bring sipping trout to the surface. The famous Blue-Winged Olive dry fly that Catskill fly tier Art Flick created will take fish. Another good tactic is to drift a slightly weighted 14 AP Beaver Nymph through the riffles at the very head of the pool.

Ozeki Cree Wing (tied by Ayumi "Rocky" Ozeki) My friend Ayumi owns a "weekender" home in Roscoe, a short walk to the upper Beaver Kill. He embraced John Atherton's classic dry fly patterns that mixed and blended fly material shades to better project in his flies "the quality of life." Cree hackle does just that; the result was Ayumi's Cree Wing dry fly. Tied with Cree hackle tip wings, its body is formed with Hare's ear mask dubbing that includes short speckled hairs.

Peacock March Brown Dry (tied by John Collins) John's beautiful March Brown is tied with one of his favorite materials combinations. "I like to fish dry flies consisting of a colored turkey biot abdomen and dubbing to match," John said. Its body is tied with cinnamon peacock biot (obtained from adult peacock primary wing feathers), a very close match to a natural March Brown mayfly's bottom abdomen shade.

Yearling Elk Coffin Fly (tied by John Collins) John's coffin fly pattern, with its spentwings and well-placed tails, floats exactly where it should float on the water surface. Its tails are created with black faux bucktail or chinese boar, three hairs. The pattern's name is derived from its body material, Bleached Yearling Elk.

Female Beaverkill (tied by Frank Payne) This old Catskill dry fly classic goes back many decades. It was once one of the most popular Catskill patterns, in both its dry fly and wet fly versions. Its original recipe called for double-slip mallard quill wings (two slips on each wing side).

Wagon Tracks, the next pool directly downstream from the tail of Cairns Pool, is also crowded during the height of the season. Yet it offers great fishing, as do the remaining pools with the upper Catch and Release water: Red Rose Pool, Schoolhouse Pool, and Trestle Pool, the upper Catch and Release terminus.

You can find some great water downstream from the original Catch and Release mileage, particularly Painter's Bend. I have fond memories of Painter's Bend, named for the "panthers" that roamed the mountains in times past. Walt used to drop me off at the pool just before sunrise. I'd start there, drifting wet flies through the pocketwater along the stone road embankment, and net some mighty nice trout. By the day's end, I'd have fished upstream all the way to Hendrickson's Pool, and there Walt would retrieve me by dinnertime. Walt advised me to take a couple of dollars and have lunch at the Red Rose on my way upstream. That's still good advice; the Red Rose, once a well-known angler's eatery and lodge, recently reopened for business.

The Beaver Kill downstream from Painter's Bend, below Cooks Falls, has a number of productive runs and pools, including Cemetery Pool and Horton Bridge Pool, my favorites on the lower reaches of the river. The second Bever Kill Catch and Release stretch, designated in 1975, occupies water from 1 mile upstream to 1.6 miles downstream from the iron bridge at Horton. While the Beaver Kill mileage below Horton Bridge Pool holds trout, my fishing experience on the lowermost river is limited. That mileage tends to warm considerably by summer. Because of the thermal-stress issues, the Beaver Kill is closed to angling from the iron bridge at Horton downstream to the first State Route 17 highway overpass from July 1 to August 31.

Many more hatches than I've described keep Beaver Kill regulars happy throughout the season. Light Cahills (*Stenacron interpunctatum*), Little Sulphurs (*Ephemerella dorothea*), and October Caddis (*Pycnopsyche scabripennis*) are among them. And many more await the angler making a first trip to the Beaver Kill and Willowemoc. The best time to sample the famed Beaver Kill is the last week of May and first week of June, known to regulars as "bug week." Paul Weamer's *Pocketguide to New York Hatches* (2013) will serve you well.

Beyond the shops, the Catskill Fly Fishing Center and Museum, in Livingston Manor, along with the Willowemoc, is a must-visit. Public fishing access is right outside the doors. After experiencing the storied pools, the museum, and the Roscoe area itself, you'll catch "not only fish, but impressions," as William Schaldach once wrote. Just as I did, so many decades ago.

Big Pond

Big Pond, located about 12 miles or so north of Livingston Manor, inhabits both trout and warmwater species. Take Beaverkill Road, just down Old Route 17 from the Catskill Fly Fishing Center and Museum, to Big Pond Road. The popular launch site is located about a mile up Big Pond Road from its intersection with Beaverkill Road. You'll pass the well-known Wulff School of Fly Fishing facility on your way, as well as the popular Beaverkill Valley Inn that caters to fly anglers. Just before arriving at Big Pond, you'll notice the NYSDEC Little Pond Campground and Day Use Area, popular with anglers who desire a camp location while fishing area trout streams, as well as Big Pond.

Big Pond, a 51-acre pond stocked with rainbow trout, is best fished with a canoe or rowboat. Bass and pumpkinseeds that also inhabit the water are fun to catch during the summer season. The launch site is directly next to the road. Regardless of the time of

Big Pond, located not far from Livingston Manor, is an easy-access trout and warmwater species water. Canoes are easily launched from a roadside parking area. (PHOTO VALERIE VALLA)

Spottail Shiner (tied by Keith Fulsher) Keith created his Thunder Creek-style Spottail Shiner bucktail to suggest small spotted shiners (*Notropis hudsonius*). Natural spottail shiners inhabit a range of waters, from rivers and creeks to lakes and ponds.

year, but especially during fall foliage season, the pond and the parking lot are busy with hikers enjoying the trail near the pond. Parking can be a problem during the height of the vacation season. During the fall, fish the pond early in the morning. You'll sometimes encounter fish rising within casting distance offshore. Try small streamers fished near obstructions or along the shoreline.

Schoharie Creek

Ignored by Theodore Gordon, the presumed father of dry-fly fishing in America, and denied the fanfare enjoyed by its historic Catskill sisters to the south—the Beaver Kill, Willowemoc, Neversink, and Esopus—Schoharie Creek continues to elude fame but not development and floods.

Historically considered a family misfit, the Schoharie has been dominated by inconsistencies and problems. Over the past century, it has been alternately revered, studied,

Upper Schoharie Creek, at Elka Park. Headwater reaches on Schoharie Creek have a much different appearance from the oft-wide-open sections of the lower river near Lexington. The Indian Head Wilderness Area mountains backdrop adds to its charm.

loved, defended, and—in very recent times—cursed by those who live along its banks. Yet, for all its myriad problems and challenges, Schoharie Creek flows resolutely on against its backdrop of streams considered important in fly-fishing history.

In 1960, even Art Flick—the dean of the Schoharie and laird of the West Kill, who studied and safeguarded those streams all of his life—documented Schoharie Creek's wildly changing moods. As reported by John W. Randolph in his May 26, 1960, *New York Times* column, "Wood, Field and Stream," Flick had flown out of the stream the previous day and telephoned to announce that he had taken and released more than 30 trout between 2 and 3:30 p.m. The water had been high but clear that day, and Flick told Randolph that "anybody could take trout on March Browns and Gray Foxes." Flick further reported that 70 percent of his catch, attributed to a "good wet spring," was wild trout. Yet a little more than a year later, the Creek's tenuous conditions worried him.

In the September 5, 1961, "Wood, Field and Stream" column in the *New York Times*, Oscar Godbout acknowledged Flick as "one of the more knowledgeable fish and insect students" and quoted him as saying, "Our streams are really sick. They are hopeless. The water is 70 degrees every day." And so it was, and still is, with Schoharie Creek. Its moods, temperaments, and conditions change, not only from time to time but also, as with many trout streams, from one section of the stream to another.

Schoharie Creek flows just short of 100 miles from its source deep in the Catskill Mountains to its confluence with the Mohawk River. Its journey is interrupted once it feeds Schoharie Reservoir at Prattsville. Most of the fly-fishing activity occurs for trout in its upper reaches, well above the hamlet of Prattsville. However, a growing number of fly anglers also enjoy fishing for warmwater species on the Schoharie's lowermost reaches.

Schoharie Creek's headwaters and its tiny spring-fed tributaries arise in New York State Forest Preserve areas, not far from the remote and treacherously steep Platte Clove

Wilderness Preserve. The most remote of the Schoharie's upstream tributaries I've ever fished is the Roaring Kill—a small, wild brook trout stream that flows through hemlock and spruce stands a few miles from the hamlet of Elka Park. The tiny stream is a good late-summer destination.

Elka Park is located by driving 2 miles south on Bloomer Road from its intersection with State Route 23A, just east of the Village of Hunter, a popular ski resort location. First, you'll pass a large lumber yard along the way, as the road winds toward Elka Park Road. You'll pass over upper Schoharie Creek just before the Elka Creek Post Office at a bridge. Bypass the creek for now (we'll get to it momentarily).

From the Post Office on Elka Park Road, continue about a mile to Roaring Branch Road, a seasonal dirt road. In about another mile or so, you'll arrive at the Roaring Kill bridge crossing. Just beyond the bridge, you can park at a popular hiking trailhead.

Gazing downstream from the bridge reveals the brook as it tumbles over large boulders into pristine forest-lined glides and pools. It's a beautiful place to sit and have lunch.

But my favorite stretches are upstream from the bridge, where small, wild brook trout hide under deadfalls and undercut banks. The trout are very spooky, especially in late summer, but you can often spot them in the crystalline water, which remains cool. The brook can be explored quite a distance upstream before leaving New York Forest Preserve Lands. Camping is allowed within the preserve as long as you're at least 150 feet from the water.

For wild brown trout, you have to look back at the upper Schoharie Creek bridge crossing near the Post Office. Public water downstream from the bridge tumbles through an old low-water concrete dam and continues on. The section upstream from the bridge is a favorite. Once you've waded out of sight around the bend, you'll find hemlock and spruce trees hugging the right bank, offering good shade. Try small dry flies, blind-fished upstream along the runs and pools. The number of stream-bred wild brown trout that Art

Roaring Kill, about a quarter mile upstream from the bridge crossing. Anglers could spend a day trekking along the brook that flows out of Indian Head Wilderness State Forest lands, casting flies along small pools and deadfalls that hide small-yet-colorful wild brook trout.

The Falke Road reach, downstream from Mosquito Point Bridge, provides angling that is wide open riffles and runs. Wading can be difficult among streambed boulders and rocks. A wading staff comes in handy while sampling this stream reach. (PHOTO VALERIE VALLA)

Flick encountered on the Schoharie years ago has declined, but at the headwaters, you might net one—small but very brightly colored.

Downstream from the Schoharie's headwaters at Elka, PFR stretches are located in the Village of Hunter. This is not the most appealing section of Schoharie Creek. It's best to continue west on State Route 23A. The creek immediately downstream from Hunter is somewhat congested (there are dwellings in sight), but the water at the foot of a steep bank is worth a cast or two. There used to be a rope tied to a tree to help anglers get down to the stream bank, but now you have to carefully trek down the slope to reach the tumbling pocketwater, which offers plenty of places to drift sinking flies.

Farther downstream, scenic views of the creek improve as it goes in and out of sight of the road, with formal public fishing stretches scattered intermittently along its course. The East Kill tributary flows in from the north and passes under a bridge on State Route 23A before it meets Schoharie Creek at Jewett.

For nearly two months, the devastating effects of Hurricane Irene, which struck at the end of August 2011, turned both the East Kill and Schoharie Creek into a red-stained, flowing mud hole. The storm—called a "500-year flood"—was catastrophic, causing flooding levels never before seen or recorded, destroying roads and bridges, and nearly wiping out the entire village of Prattsville on lower Schoharie Creek. Thankfully, the East Kill and Schoharie have healed over the last decade since the flood.

After crossing over the East Kill, continue on State Route 23A a little less than a mile to a formal NYSDEC parking area marked by a large hanging sign. The riffle and runs there are full of *Isonychia* mayfly nymphs. It's a stretch where I fish a long-winged Leadwing Coachman wet fly.

Continue downstream less than 2 miles to the hamlet of Lexington, where Art Flick once operated his West Kill Tavern. Turn left off State Route 23A onto State Route 42.

You can either cross the river in Lexington and head south for a few miles to the West Kill or at the bridge crossing stay straight on to Country Road 13A to a formal NYSDEC angling parking area marked by a large hanging sign. If interested in fishing this section, do so in the early season before the water temperatures rise.

Downriver from Lexington on State Route 23A, for about 3 miles, a series of established NYSDEC parking areas and turnouts sit along the creek bank. My favorite lower Schoharie stretch of water is located just downstream from the Mosquito Point Bridge on County Road 2, located about 2 miles downstream from the State Route 23A/County Road 13A intersection at the last official parking area in Lexington.

Cross the bridge then to Falke Road, where you can access the stream. Try the section where the Little West Kill enters the Schoharie. You can also access the stream reach from the opposite side, on State Route 23A, at a turnout located a half-mile from the Mosquito Point bridge. Just down State Route 23A from that parking area, you will encounter a turnout where a monument was placed that honors Art Flick. It's worth stopping to see.

Schoharie Creek downstream from the Flick Monument stretch to Plattsville has never been good to me.

State Route 23A crosses another tributary, the Batavia Kill, 3 miles west of the Flick monument turnout, at the Prattsville area. Prattsville, on the doorstep of Schoharie Reservoir, looked like a war zone 2 months after being swept away by the 2011 floods. Collapsed homes sat in ruins along the Schoharie, and debris from demolished structures

Black-Nose Dace (tied by Mike Valla) Patterns intended to resemble natural black-nose dace minnows have been around a very long time, both bucktail versions and featherwing styles. However, Catskill fly tier Art Flick is most associated with a simple version he made popular in his classic *Streamside Guide to Naturals and their Imitations* (1947). Flick's original version was tied on short shank hooks, not long shank hooks used in contemporary styles. Flick also used different hair types in his early pattern.

Quill Gordon (tied by Mike Valla) It could be argued that this is the Catskill region's signature dry fly, the famous pattern that was developed by Theodore Gordon (1854–1915) around the turn of the century. Using stripped peacock eye quill dry fly body wasn't original with Gordon. Early British fly tiers used the material for fly bodies.

March Brown (tied by John Kavanaugh) Many March Brown patterns have been created over the years, particularly for Catskill streams. In correspondence, John wrote: "The pattern works for both duns and spinner stages of the March Brown. It's also my favorite big fish fly."

continued to pile higher many weeks after Hurricane Irene hit the region. The hamlet survived the destruction through intensive rebuilding efforts. There's a nice diner in town, for those seeking a good breakfast or lunch.

Those interested in what the Batavia Kill tributary can offer should head up State Route 23 to the Ashland area, from the State Route 23A intersection (see Batavia Kill page 282).

When fishing the Schoharie, some of us still stand by the traditional fly patterns Flick presented in his *Streamside Guide*, although many consider the Catskill-style flies antiquated. "So, what flies are you fishing on the Schoharie these days?" I once asked Judd Weisberg during an outdoor sit-down chat on a beautiful fall day with the river in sight. He told me, "My box is filled with Art's patterns and one or two contemporary flies thrown in with them." Like Judd, my fly box is also chock-full of Flick's dry-fly classics—flies such as the Quill Gordon, Red Quill, Dun Variant, and Gray Fox Variant. His Early Brown Stone wet fly is a favorite, too. During high water, early season fishing Flick's Black-Nose Dace bucktail takes fish.

Those few patterns worked for Flick throughout his lifetime, and they *still* work. In a May 18, 1958, *New York Times* article titled "Wood, Field and Stream," John W. Randolph wrote that Flick felt he could get through an entire summer fishing the Schoharie with only six dry flies—his favorite Gray Fox Variant and Dun Variant among them. In recent years, I've continued using a simple long-shank, long-winged Leadwing Coachman wet fly, along with Flick's Dun Variant, for the slate-colored *Isonychia* hatch they imitate. A 17-inch holdover brown trout slammed a Leadwing, on the swing, down near Mosquito Point on the Schoharie several years ago.

West Kill

For some Catskills-region anglers, fishing West Kill has more to do with the stream's rich fly-fishing history than an unlikely landing of a trophy-size trout. The little tributary creek is associated with fly tier Art Flick (1904–1985), a member of the so-called Catskill school of fly tiers.

Flick, best remembered for his classic book *Streamside Guide to Naturals and Their Imitations* (1947), lived in the hamlet of West Kill, several miles upstream from the stream's junction with Schoharie Creek near Lexington. Flick's Westkill Tavern, an inn that catered to fly anglers and grouse hunters, was located not far up the road from the confluence; sadly, the building burned to the ground in the early 1960s. Iconic figures, such as author and angler Ray Bergman, stayed at the inn.

While the larger Schoharie, where Flick accomplished much of his aquatic entomological collecting during the mid-1930s, is a more significant trout stream, it's no match for the West Kill's quaintness, especially its reaches upstream from the intersection of State Route 42 and County Road 6 (Spruceton Road). One of the most picturesque stretches of the creek is accessible from the Spruceton Trail parking area, 7 miles upstream from the State Route 42/County Road 6 intersection. A large NYSDEC sign clearly marks this as a fishing access site. A 1-mile walk upstream from the parking area takes you to beautiful Diamond Notch Falls, a great place for a lunch break. Fish downstream from the falls, which are impassable to fish.

I like to string up my 7.5-foot, 4-weght rod when fishing the upper stream reaches, drifting small nymphs or wet flies through the pools. Paying homage to Art Flick, I like his Early Brown Stone, a pattern mentioned in his book. It's a simple early-season wet fly tied with a stripped-quill body (from a Rhode Island red hackle) and two small dun

West Kill Creek, along Spruceton Road. West Kill spells Art Flick country, the iconic member of the so-called Catskill School of fly tiers; he lived and fished the little stream. Small brown trout inhabit its small pools.

hackle point wings laid flat. Soft dun hen hackle at its throat provides lifelike movement. Small dry flies skittered over the riffles work well later in the season. Old Catskill dry fly patterns, such as Deren's Stone Fore and Aft, a simple classic Brown Bivisible, or Conover, work well.

Small, spunky wild browns and brook trout are found in the upper reaches of the creek. NYSDEC generally stocks 500 to 700 8- to 9-inch browns annually in the creek's lower reaches. I've never caught rainbows that supposedly inhabit the lower creek. The stream runs in and out of PFR water not only in its upper reaches but also along its entire 11 miles. The best way to locate PFR stretches is to watch for NYSDEC signs posted along the stream.

When fishing the West Kill, I generally find myself getting in and out of my vehicle throughout the day, because some of my favorite PFR sections have relatively brief frontage, and they're well separated. One favorite is the stretch located about 2.8 miles up Spruceton Road, beginning at a small parking area just after the bridge. You'll see New York State Forest Wilderness Area signs across the road. Work your way upstream from the bridge.

There's also ample PFR water downstream from the hamlet, clearly indicated on the NYSDEC maps. I found a lot of that water to be more productive years ago, but surprisingly, you'll still catch fish. Catastrophic flash flooding from Hurricane Irene in August 2011 wiped out the road bridges all the way down to Schoharie Creek and heavily damaged the stream.

Visiting the ripped-apart stream shortly after the storm departed made me wonder how Art Flick would have felt, the conservationist that he was. Flick loved and cared for the West Kill. For decades, he planted willows along the creek each spring, as an annual

Deren's Stone Fore and Aft (tied by Frank Payne)
An old pattern originated by Jim Deren, who operated Angler's Roost in New York City, has fallen out of favor among modern fly fishers. Yet it is still effective on Catskill streams, particularly waters inhabited by brook trout.

Conover (tied by Bob Adams) A favorite of Scotty Conover, a member of the Brooklyn Fly Fishers Club on the Beaver Kill back in the 1930s. In *Tying Catskill-Style Dry Flies* (2009), a story is told how this author caught his first large Beaver Kill brown trout in Lower Barnhart's Pool, in 1972. The original pattern body, tied by Catskill fly tiers Walt and Winnie Dette, was created by mixing rabbit fur, seal fur, and red wool. However, the Dettes eventually switched to a simple muskrat and red wool blend. Golden badger is used at the fly's collar.

ritual. My own ritual is to visit the West Kill frequently and recall my meetings with Flick when I was a young boy. It's always nice to catch fish, but that's not why I cast flies on this historic little stream.

Batavia Kill (Greene County)

Circumstances other than fishing first led me to the Batavia Kill, a 22-mile-long trout stream located in the northeastern corner of the Catskills in New York. "Go to the abandoned quarry on the west slope of Cave Mountain," my Cornell University paleobotany professor insisted, "and there you'll find remnants of the 360-million-year-old Devonian-age plant fossils I lectured about."

Prepared for my two-day expedition at the quarry and packing a pup tent and a few cans of food, I had a classmate driving home for the weekend drop me off at the intersection of State Route 23 and County Road 17 (Jewett Heights Road, in Ashland, Greene County), not far from the quarry on Cave Mountain. I crossed a small stream on my hike up County Road 17 to the quarry. I never did find the fossil specimens I was hunting for that October weekend more than 40 years ago. But on my return hike back down the mountain road, I soaked my sore feet in the soothing stream, its name unknown to me at the time.

A few years later, however, I returned to that very spot on the stream, after researching its name, and this time, I was toting a fly rod. Since then, Batavia Kill, a tributary of Schoharie Creek, has been one of my favorite destinations.

These days, a NYSDEC public fishing sign at the bridge on County Road 17 marks the spot where I arrived at Batavia Kill that first time. The bridge is located less than 0.1 mile down the road from State Route 23. One of several state-designated public fishing access areas along Batavia Kill, this Ashland reach receives the bulk of the brown trout stocked in the stream annually by the DEC. The fish range from 9 to 15 inches; upstream in the Windham area, the stocked browns are smaller, typically 8 to 9 inches.

Batavia Kill at County Road 17 bridge crossing, near Cave Mountain quarry. Batavia Kill, a creek that shares the same name with a stream in Delaware County, is categorized by NYSDEC as Stocked. Its upper reaches inhabit a few wild fish. (PHOTO VALERIE VALLA)

Anglers exploring the stream should concentrate their efforts from the Ashland area upstream (east) to the headwaters. I've never had much luck fishing the middle and lower reaches. If you're more interested in netting wild brook trout and brown trout, try the headwaters above the small in-stream impoundment at C.D. Lane Park, which is 3.2 miles east of Hensonville via County Road 40 and then County Road 56 (Big Hollow Road).

There are not a lot of fish in the headwaters, but the pleasant surroundings along a short stream reach in the state-owned Windham-Blackhead Range Wilderness make the effort well worthwhile. From C.D. Lane Park, continue east on Big Hollow Road for 3 miles to a parking turnout that serves as a DEC trailhead for the trail to Black Dome Mountain. Expect to encounter hikers heading up the mountain trails but few anglers along the stream during the fall foliage season, when this forested area is especially scenic. A lovely footbridge crosses the brook just downstream from the parking area. It's a good place to enter the water.

Leave your chest-high waders at home—this is hip-boot water along the tumbling brook. I like to cast small dry flies, such as John Checchia's Little Green Stonefly, in the tiny pools during the autumn. Earlier in the year, stonefly nymphs work well.

Below the headwater reaches that flow through the wilderness area, the stream also courses through the New York City Department of Environmental Protection (DEP) Black Dome Valley watershed recreation unknit along Big Hollow Road.

The DEP has undertaken a variety of stream restoration projects and created numerous public angling access sites throughout the Catskills watershed. In 2001, the Greene County Soil and Water Conservation District, the DEP, local chapters of Trout Unlimited, and local volunteers all partnered to complete a cooperative Batavia Kill restoration project along Big Hollow Road, mitigating damage from the 1996 floods that severely eroded a mile-long section of the stream in that area. That cooperative effort stands as an example of the kinds of projects and advocacy that could benefit many other Catskills waters.

East and West Branches of Delaware River Tailwaters

The West Branch tailwater that departs Cannonville Reservoir at the Village of Deposit and the East Branch that discharges below Pepacton Reservoir at the Village of Downsville were once prime bass fishing waters, enjoyed by both fly anglers and bait casters alike. Impounding the upper East and West Branches of the Delaware River created Pepacton Reservoir in 1955 and Cannonsville Reservoir in 1964, located more than 100 miles from New York City. After departing the Pepacton, its waters flow through the East Delaware Aqueduct 25 miles to Rondout Reservoir, where it mixes with Cannonsville Reservoir's contribution and Neversink Reservoir's input. The creation of the Pepacton and Cannonsville Reservoirs, along with water obtained from other Catskill reservoirs, gave the Big Apple its drinking water; trout anglers unexpectedly got something else that was much more fascinating.

Even as far back as 1906, Catskill fly fisher and tier Theodore Gordon, sometimes referred to as the "Catskill Thoreau," lamented the damming of Espous Creek to create Ashohan Reservoir but recognized "the millions of inhabitants in New York City must be supplied with pure water." An ample supply of Gordon's "pure" Catskill water wasn't the only remarkable result of the Catskill reservoirs engineering triumph. Coldwater tailraces from Pepacton, Cannonsville, and Neversink Reservoirs transformed what were formally warmwater fisheries into world-class trout rivers.

It took time before the tailwaters from Pepacton and Cannonsville Reservoirs reached their full potential as waters now classified as Wild-Premier by NYSDEC. Periods of litigation over adequate water releases from the impoundments ensued as conservationists and anglers fought hard to ensure minimum tailwater flows.

When the quality of the tailwaters improved, the fisheries took a dramatic turn, resulting in expanded populations of large trout and the crowds of anglers who were after them. I smile when I read my old fly hatch journal notes from 1970, complete with scientific names and water temperatures, when I first floated flies on the popular West Branch tailwater from Deposit to Hancock as an enamored teenager. Only once in numerous trips to the river did I ever see another fly angler (and I still remember the exact location above Hale Eddy).

Big wild trout in the tailraces couldn't remain secrets forever. During the 1960s (and no doubt before), fly anglers were getting into large rainbows on the East Branch and downriver on the main stem at Long Eddy and the mouth of Basket Brook. Only a handful were even talking about the East Branch. I recall a couple of East Branch regulars who stopped by the Dette shop asking for Muddlers that they fished at night. Around 1969 or 1970, in my hometown newspaper, the *Binghamton Press*, outdoor columnist Frank Dolan wrote about a multi-pound rainbow taken on a Light Cahill, on the East Branch; I still remember that eye-opener of a story.

Fly fishers who stopped by the "old" Dette Flies shop during the months I stayed with Walt and Winnie during the early 1970s were heading to the Beaver Kill or Willowemoc. Some were angling for Shad on the East Branch. A few were sampling the East Branch at Shinhopple for rainbows but never in the numbers who fish the East Branch today. By the late 1970s into the 1980s, fly-fishing magazine pieces began to appear that trumpeted the East Branch and its big fish.

The West Branch's fishery potential was still ripening. One has to realize the reservoir wasn't put into service until 1964. What I most remember about the early days were the number of fall fish, not trout, that sucked in and mucked up a dry fly, that and persistently

Downsville Dam and its tailrace, at Village of Downsville. When the East Branch of the Delaware River was dammed in the mid-1950s, creating Pepacton Reservoir that served New York City's water supply needs, coldwater releases created optimum trout habitat.

high water. However, by the mid-1970s, word was getting out about large browns turning up on the West Branch along the mileage between Deposit and Hancock.

Float fishing, virtually unheard of during the 1970s and early 1980s, became increasingly popular during the 1990s. I can recall a pleasant May 1987 session on the West Branch upstream from Hale Eddy that I used to fish in my teen years when I didn't see one single floating craft the entire day during that successful Hendrickson hatch session. The relative solitude that many wade-fishing anglers once enjoyed is largely a thing of the past, and nowadays, boat traffic mingles with anglers on foot, resulting in oft-crowded conditions. Many traditional wade fishing anglers have reeled in and relocated to other Catskill waters empty of crowds and sometimes errant behaviors that large numbers of people sometimes bring to popular fishing locations.

Private sections that I once fished on the East Branch tailwater that were available to other polite anglers who asked permission to fish are no longer available. Trash, disrespect for private property, and other problems have increased the access challenge. I know of at least one altercation between a fishing guide and a private landowner that ended up in town court. The vast majority of guides attempt to be respectful of landowners, but those issues are there on the rivers.

In a way, the big-fish potential on the tailraces is both a blessing and a curse of sorts, for all users of the resource—both anglers and others. To be sure, the fishery generates income for the various towns that abut the rivers. Everything from corner pizza shops to campgrounds to fly shops benefit from what the building of the reservoirs brought to the area. The tailwaters may be reaching a point that requires a fresh look at the resource— admittedly, a very difficult proposition.

All of that said, one can certainly recognize a reluctance to bring any more attention to an already crowded situation not only on the West and East Branches but also the main stem of the Delaware downstream from Hancock. In this book, I'll mention only a couple of my favorite "starter" locations on both branches and on the main stem that have been well-known and publicized over for many years, and that I still fish today. However, readers still desiring an extensive treatment of the tailwaters, where and how to fish the system, should get a copy of *Fly-Fishing Guide to the Upper Delaware River* (2011), written by my friend Paul Weamer. Realize that some access changes have occurred over the ensuing years.

The fly hatches have been fairly consistent over the years, although some stream regulars have noticed mayfly hatch declines. There was some grumbling a few years ago that Sulphurs, in particular, inexplicably decreased on the East Branch. Anecdotal reasons ranged from natural fluctuations, abiotic impacts, or microhabitat changes. My favorite hatches on the Delaware system have always been the Hendricksons, followed by Sulphurs and Blue-Winged Olives, although the big Green Drakes bring up some remarkably big fish.

EAST BRANCH DELAWARE RIVER TAILWATER

Flowing nearly 34 miles from its discharge from the Pepacton Reservoir at Downsville to its confluence with the West Branch at Hancock, the East Branch is entirely categorized by NYSDEC as Wild-Premier and no longer receives hatchery brown trout stockings. However, 18 or so miles downstream from the reservoir, the East Branch weds the Beaver Kill, a river heavily stocked with brown trout, at the hamlet of East Branch at State Route 17.

As a wade angler, I've always favored the East Branch over the West Branch, particularly the upper section from Downsville to the junction with the Beaver Kill. Before heading for a trip to the East Branch and planning to wade fish, check online the USGS flow rates, measured at the hamlet of Harvard gauge station. Flow rates less than 500 cfs can accommodate wade fishing, but I prefer 350 cfs or less.

Drift boat float fishing is not advised below 500 cfs, although an increasing number of pontoon boats are floating the river, often to the annoyance of wade anglers. More and more former wade anglers are purchasing pontoon boats because wade access on private lands continues to diminish through posting.

However, there's enough PFR water and other unofficial public access reaches to keep me happy when I'm on the stream. A few are described here, but other unofficial access areas are available along the course of the stream. You'll want to make certain you don't wander into sections of the river that are private unless you have prior permission to do so. Be aware that as the popularity of the stream continues to grow, private riverbank lands that once provided angling access can suddenly become off-limits. It seems additional recreational second homes and small cabins appear every year along the river.

The East Branch tailwater is often described in two segments: the uppermost section upstream from its confluence with the Beaver Kill, and the lower river from the junction pool to Hancock. The lower river tends to warm significantly along its wide stretches during summer. My experience shows it is best fished early in the season, particularly during May into early June. The water temperatures on the upper river, particularly above Shinhopple, remain much cooler throughout the summer months.

Upper Segment "Starter" Stretches

From Exit 90 on State Route 17, the river flows along State Route 30. Before heading north along Route 30, stop by the gazebo located at a formal NYSDEC Beaver Kill parking lot near the exit. It's a bald eagle observation point that overlooks the river's junction with the East Branch.

East Branch of the Delaware River at Long Flat. A popular public fishing stretch, Long Flat along State Route 30 receives plenty of attention by fly fishers.

Crusher Pool: This reach used to simply be called the Sunoco station access point or Lower Wulff Pool access, but a formal parking area, now well-marked, provides access. On State Route 30, drive 0.2 mile past the Sunoco station that's located just off Exit 90, to the first official NYSDEC parking lot marked by a large hanging sign. Trout inhabit the deep, slow-moving pool, but bass also hang out in the area just upstream from the junction with Beaver Kill. Wading upstream is not much of an option but can be managed on lower-water conditions downstream from the pool. Better, easier-to-wade, and more productive reaches are upstream from this one.

Long Flat: From the Crusher Pool access point, continue north on State Route 30 just under 5 miles to one of the more popular reaches. A NYSDEC large hanging sign is along a parking turnout that can accommodate several vehicles. Expect a lot of company at Long Flat, especially during the late afternoons and evenings during the hatches and spinner falls. However, I've had the slow-moving, easy-to-wade pool all to myself during very early morning sessions. Adjacent landowners have experienced trespass issues in recent times so make sure you're aware of the well-marked PFR boundaries and private property signage.

High Power Line Pool: Located a mile up State Route 30 from Long Flat and near Terry's Campground, the Power Lines pool and downstream riffle, reached by a footpath, is another popular location. The footpath is located almost directly across the road from a large red structure next to Terry's Campground. Obscured by sumac growth, a NYSDEC yellow "footpath access" sign is nailed to a tree stump at the beginning of the path. Take note of the numerous posted signs on both sides of the easement path that leads to the river. You'll know when the fishing is productive by the cars that sometimes park on the road shoulder, and anglers gearing up for the rise.

It's easy to wade and cast to the fish that hold on the far bank that provides good shade cover. It's a good section to fish when Blue Quills, Apple Caddis and March Browns are on the water during late May into June. A nice run is located a few hundred feet upstream from where the footpath ends at the water. Be aware of private property and no trespass signs that are clearly posted in that area.

Shinhopple Bridge: The productive run at "Al's old place" downstream from the bridge crossing is located about 2.6 miles up State Route 30 from High Power Lines Pool. Al Carpenter's former fly shop building is at the corner of the bridge and State Route 30. His son, also Al, who owns Al's Sport Store and Downsville Motel upstream in Downsville, owns the property. I see and chat with Al frequently because his motel is my lodging of choice when fishing the area. He assured me that anglers are still welcome to park at the old shop parking area at the bridge.

The large, deep pool upstream from the bridge is not wading water. The run downstream from the bridge is wade-water that I first fished in June 1972 by hitching a ride with another fly angler, on-leave from the Navy, who stopped by the Dette Flies shop in Roscoe that day, and offered a ride to the section I had heard about. A beautiful rainbow came to my net that afternoon.

Corbett Bridge Reach: Continuing another 3 miles up State Route 30 will deliver you to the one-lane, interesting-looking Corbett Bridge. You'll pass a formal NYSDEC parking area called Thayer Hollow, marked by a large hanging sign, on your way to Corbett Bridge. I've never been overly excited about the river structure at Thayer hollow access, and most always bypass it in favor of sampling the Corbett area. The private property on the downstream side of the bridge was once a popular boat launching site but is now off-limits and posted.

Access is still available on the upstream side of the bridge for wade anglers. A very small parking area will accommodate a couple of vehicles. You'll encounter new posted signs, but the signage makes it clear fishing access is allowed. A short walk down a footpath past a couple of boulders will get you into the stream. A nice run and pool are located several hundred feet upstream. The stretch is my favorite for fishing the Sulphur hatch.

An official NYSDEC access area, marked by a large hanging sign, is located on River Road. Drive a short distance east after crossing Corbett Bridge to River Road. Go right 1 mile to the large parking area. You'll have to trek down a steep hill to reach the river.

Lower Segment "Starter" Stretches

In East Branch near the Sunoco Station, get on State Route 17 west. The East Branch Rest Area is located just short of 2 miles west of the State Route 17/State Route 30 intersection. The pool and its riffles and run are set back from the rest area but easily accessed. The reach inhabits trout but for years has been a popular area during May when Shad are in the river. During the early 1970s, I remember fly tier Walt Dette putting his wood-duck feathers and hackle to the side, shifting activity to tying garish Shad Flies for customers who typically were heading to the Rest Stop. Fly tier Art Flick stopped by one day, chatting about heading there for Shad, a fish he had yet to catch.

Several good access points are found in the hamlet of Fishs Eddy located a few miles downstream from the East Branch Rest Area. From the State Route 17/State Route 30 intersection in East Branch, take Exit 89 to County Road 28 at Old Route 17 next to the Delaware County DPW facility. A formal NYSDEC access site is marked by a large hanging sign. The parking area and footpath that leads to the river is located down a short dirt road along the DPW site. You'll encounter Eagle Scout hiking trail signage that follows the river downstream. Take note of the posted signs and private property upstream from that point. A nice pool will greet you that is often inhabited by brown trout rising to an evening hatch in early season.

East Branch of Delaware above Alice's Way, downriver from Fishs Eddy, is wide-open water. A land preservation agreement with Delaware Highlands Conservancy provides public fishing access.

Fishs Eddy, O&W Road: Good water can be encountered by returning to the intersection and crossing over the green Fishs Eddy Memorial Bridge and taking O&W road that follows the river upstream. Over 50 years ago, during the time I fly-fished that reach in my teenage years, I don't recall having any access issues. However, nowadays, the road is heavily posted, providing only intermittent access to the river. The best section, a nice run and riffle where I caught my first East Branch trout, is a couple of miles upstream. The road shoulder turnout at a "no dumping sign" became posted several years ago.

Partridge Island Reach: Plenty of access is instead available downstream along Old Route 17, downstream from the Old Route 17/County Road 28 intersection along the Partridge Island reach.

Partridge Island Cemetery: Drive west on Old Route 17 about 0.4 mile to Partridge Island Cemetery, the first access point along the road. Park on the road shoulder and make your way down to the stream via a footpath. The river at this point begins its flow around the longer of the two Partridge Islands, in two channels. The right channel is the better of the two. Another parking turnout on Old Route 17, along the road shoulder, is located a short distance west of the cemetery.

Partridge Island Walking Trail: Located 0.8 mile west from the Old Route 17/County Road 28 intersection (0.4 mile from the Partridge Island Cemetery), you'll encounter a large, mowed, grassy area on the left side of the road. It's marked by a handsome large green Eagle Scout project sign. The trail footpath follows a very steep hill that leads down below to the river and a very nice run. I generally get down to the stream by walking west along the trail to a drainage area created by old culvert. The right river channel at this point flows about three-fourths the way down the longer Partridge Island. A gravel bank area and run can be very productive during May.

Reichbach's Run: You won't miss Reichbach's Run because of the red sign mounted on a metal post next to the guardrail located on the left side of the road as you drive 0.4

Sulphur Hackle Stem Dun (tied by Bruce Concors) Bruce Concors, fortunate to own a getaway place on the East Branch of the Delaware, enjoys tying small size flies he's found to be highly effective on his home water.

East Branch Delaware Adams (tied by John Kavanaugh) John takes this fly out of his box when Green Drakes and Coffin Flies are emerging on the East Branch of the Delaware River. Its grizzly hen wings and palmered grizzly hackle over a White Coffin Fly-like body enable the fly to float well. John said, "I respectfully call it East Branch Delaware Adams."

B.G. Dun (tied by Dave Brandt) Dave Brandt (1944–2020), a Catskill fly tier and angler extraordinaire who passed away a couple years ago, was a friend to many, including this writer. A dry fly pattern he was most fond of was his B.G. Dun. The fly doesn't suggest a particular bug; it's just an all-around good fly to have while fishing the East Branch and other Catskill waters.

Sulphur Emerger (tied by Joe Fusco) Joe Fusco, an upper Delaware River enthusiast for many years, fishes his go-to Sulphur pattern with annual success along his favorite river stretches. Sulphur mayfly emergences on the Delaware system are highly anticipated by Catskill regulars. Every angler has a favorite pattern; this one doesn't let Joe down often.

IOBO Humpy (tied by Chuck Coronato) Chuck Coronato, a frequent Catskill region angler, would not be without his favorite, an IOBO Humpy. The fly uses only thread and a single CDC feather, making it a model of simplicity and within the skill range of nearly every tier. In correspondence, Chuck had this to say: "A fly that I have excellent luck with and wouldn't be without on the East Branch is the It Ought to Be Outlawed Humpy (the IOBO Humpy), originated by Frank Tucker. I learned to tie the fly from watching a Hans Weilenmann tutorial, so I tie it using the same procedure as Hans. My only difference with the way that Weilenmann ties the fly is that I leave a few stray fibers in the finished fly, rather than neatly trimming it. I believe that it fishes better with the extra movement of those stray CDC fibers." Chuck ties the fly on a TMC 102Y hook. When fishing, Chuck treats the CDC with Loon Locha floatant.

mile west on Old Route 17 from Partridge Island Trail. There's enough room along the guardrail for a couple vehicles. For years, this reach wasn't formally named. Signage also exists that designates the area protected by a Land Preservation Agreement with Delaware Highlands Conservancy. A trek down the steep hill will take you into the river and the two islands.

Alice's Way: The final location that provides access to the river in this area is located by driving 0.4 mile west of Reichbach's Run. It's located just before Tyler Switch Road, a private road near a small brook. A formally partially paved road at its entrance, now more of a grassy wide trail, is marked by a metal post covered with red reflectors and a now-faded "Alice's Way" sign on top. You'll see the white Land Preservation Agreement signage on the same post. The grassy road that continues along the river, following it upstream, is gated at the entrance, but anglers are allowed beyond it. A pleasant riverside picnic table just beyond the gate is a nice place to have your lunch. Please respect the property, and carry out what you carried in.

The river directly upstream from the entrance can be very shallow across its entire width on low-water conditions, with not much fish-holding capacity at those at minimum flow levels. It's best fished early in the season, and like many reaches this far downstream, significant warming can occur during summer.

WEST BRANCH OF DELAWARE RIVER TAILWATER

Contemporary fly fishers heading to the West Branch tailwaters might not realize the prior significance of the 17 miles that flow between Cannonville Dam at Deposit and Hancock, where it joins the East Branch. Before the dam was constructed, Binghamton area anglers, including my grandfather, headed to those stretches for some of the best smallmouth fishing in the East. The City of Binghamton is only 30 miles west of Deposit.

It attracted the iconic fly angler John Alden Knight and his son, Richard. In his book *Black Bass* (1949), Knight wrote about the "great deal of time" he and his son fly fished that mileage. He wrote, "It is not uncommon for us to hook and land seventy-five or a hundred bass on two rods in a single day." Not everyone welcomed the cold water that changed the river into a coldwater fishery, including my grandfather. Much has changed from those years, including attitudes about the fishery as it flows today.

The West Branch tailwater, like the main stem, is primarily a float-fishing tailrace, although wade fishing is still popular along stretches that provide public access. You'll encounter a remarkable number of drift boats on the river. If you're interested in wade fishing and the river is flowing over 800 to 1,000 cfs, relocate to another stream. My preferred rate is under 600 cfs, and the lower the better.

I can recall several instances in my youth years that I should have never attempted wade angling the river, given the unlikely potential to land a fish, and given the dangers of wading through high water. Back then, my puny 7.5-foot Cortland glass rod and level fly line was no match for the river at high water. Today, most anglers are using 9-foot or longer rods, matched with 5-weight to 6-weight and, in some instances, even 7-weight lines when anglers are casting gargantuan "flies." Like a few of my friends, I'm fishing dry flies with an 8.5-foot to 9-foot rod, with a 4-weight line and do just fine with it.

This is big water that inhabits big browns, water that's ideal for float fishing, especially when flows are conducive to those angling tactics. A friend of mine once counted over 50 floating craft passing by near Hancock. There was once a time that boat traffic fishing dropped off when cfs levels dipped below a certain level, but that is not so today. It seems if there's water at any level, there are boats. An inescapable situation these days.

West Branch of Delaware at Hale Eddy Bridge. Hale Eddy Bridge, located a few miles downstream from the Village of Deposit, is one of the more popular stream reaches. When water levels permit, wade anglers can easily fish the water. (PHOTO VALERIE VALLA)

Most wade anglers prefer the East Branch not only because of all the boat traffic encountered on the West Branch but also because the East Branch has better access for wade fishing, despite the loss of private land access, through posting, that occurs every year. However, I'll describe a couple of my favorite West Branch "starter" locations.

Deposit Sewer Hole and State Route 17 Reaches

During the early 1970s, we referred to the stretches both upstream and downstream collectively as the Route 17 high bridge runs and pools. The stretch upstream from the Route 17 bridge crossing in Deposit is more commonly called the Sewer Hole, or Deposit Sewage Treatment Plant Pool. The Sewer Hole exists into the Route 17 run and pool.

Nick DelleDonne fished a Hendrickson Comparadun to entice this West Branch brown trout at the Route 17 Bridge run.

Nick DelleDonne latches into a brown trout at the Laurel Bank Avenue stretch in Deposit. Laurel Avenue reach provides easy access. It's a good location to fish when Hendricksons are emerging.

The Sewer Hole is easily accessed by driving 0.3 mile down Laurel Bank Avenue from the bridge crossing at Oak Street in Deposit. A formal NYSDEC parking area called Laurel Hill Access is marked by a large hanging sign on the left side of the road. It's located just before passing under the Route 17 bridge. The lot can accommodate several vehicles.

Most of my fishing, over many years, is downstream from the parking lot at the Route 17 high bridge run and pool. A road shoulder, streamside parking area across from the Stanford Stone facility is located 0.2 mile down the road from Laurel Hill Access, just after passing under Route 17. My journal notes from 1970 show I fished that reach on multiple days during May and early June. Remarkably, after all the changes the West Branch has gone through surrounding water flows, the same hatches still occur pretty much on the same extended dates on that reach and stretches downstream. Hendricksons appeared into late May back then, as they still do now.

The extended emergence period on tailwaters is attributed to the coldwater releases and flows that are different from area freestone streams. I ran into Nick DelleDonne a couple of years ago on the pool during a substantial Hendrickson hatch that came off the water May 25, 2019. My notes show the hatch occurred on May 20, 1970, on that same area. Gray Fox, Light Cahill, and other mayflies float through that stretch during early late May into early June.

Hale Eddy Bridge

Hale Eddy bridge crossing is located about 4 miles from Deposit on State Route 17 East, or about 18 miles from the hamlet of East Branch on State Route 17 West. Parking is available at the bridge. Most anglers, however, fish the long pool downstream from the bridge. During low-water discharges, it's possible to wade portions of the river upstream from the bridge and fish all the way up to the riffle and run where Sherman Creek, a small tributary, enters the river.

Hendrickson (tied by John Kavanaugh) John's Hendrickson, tied in the Catskill style, is no doubt an effective pattern when *Ephemerella subvaria* emerges on Catskill waters.

Sulphur Transitional Dun (tied by John Kavanaugh) John uses the same technique as he does for his Hendrickson Transitional Dun.

Sulphur Comparadun (tied by Bill Shuck) The late Bill Shuck embraced his favorite Sulphur pattern—a comparadun style. Bill tied this fly in a variety of hook sizes, from a #12 through #18. He preferred Rusty brown UNI-Thread. Tails were created with two-four light dun or light blue dun microfibbets. Bill varied body shades, light yellow to Sulphur orange dry-fly dubbings to suit local and/or seasonal color variations.

Hendrickson Transitional Dun (tied by John Kavanaugh) John created his Hendrickson Transitional Dun from René Harrop's original concept and technique. He changed materials using trigger point fiber, which float great and are much more durable than CDC. This style of emerger has become John's favorite for all Catskill hatches he fishes.

Truform Hendrickson (tied by Paul Weamer) My good friend, author, fly tier, and now Yellowstone guide, Paul Weamer, developed his Truform Hendrickson during the time he lived and guided in the Catskills. In correspondence, Paul described his interesting pattern: "I came up with the idea for Truform flies sometime in the early 2000s, while my wife and I were living in our home on the Beaver Kill on a high bank along a Pork Island river channel. I loved parachute dry flies but was always troubled that they imitated a mayfly's legs by placing hackle on top of the fly's body rather than the underside as they are with real insects. I also desired to change the orientation of the wing to more closely match naturals."

Sherman Creek is about a half-mile upstream from Hale Eddy bridge crossing. Many years ago, my dad and I frequently bushwhacked along the length of Sherman Creek to reach the river, about a half-mile trek from Sherman Creek Road. Unfortunately, that alternative is no longer possible since the land along the creek is posted. We took that effort because the run downstream from the creek's mouth was usually very productive when water levels provided easy wade fishing. I spotted the first March Brown mayfly I had ever set eyes on along that riffle one Saturday morning over 50 years ago.

I also recall a tremendous Hendrickson hatch along the run, the first substantial mayfly hatch I had fished during those years. On May 10, 1987 (Mother's Day), while fishing with Don Henderson and Gil Ott at Hale Eddy, we encountered a nice Hendrickson hatch that produced a handsome 19-inch brown trout for Don that he enticed on a classic Red Quill dry fly upstream at the pool above Sherman Creek, as I recall.

Delaware River (Main Stem)

The "big water" of the Delaware, the main stem, is undoubtedly much easier to access and fish via float fishing. Drift boats can cover a lot of water between Junction Pool at Hancock and reaches far downstream. However, a couple of "starter stretches" with easy access, reaches I've fished for many years, are presented here.

JUNCTION POOL TAILOUT

The tailout run downstream from the confluence of the West Branch and East Branch is located just a couple of miles south of Hancock. From the intersection of State Route 97 and East Front Street in Hancock, go south on State Route 97 about 1 mile. Turn right on Bard Parker Road, then a left on Labaret Street. Take Labaret Street 0.2 mile to a gravel road on the right that leads to an official NYSDEC access parking lot and access point.

Main Stem of Delaware River at Lordville bridge crossing. Delaware River main stem is big water, best covered by float fishing. But some reaches can easily be fished by wade fishing provided water levels are not too high.

The tailout riffles below Junction Pool are popular with wade anglers.

The pleasant grassy area directly in front of the large parking lot has a few riverside picnic tables that overlook the deep Junction Pool. You'll often see drift boats moving through the expansive pool that holds trout. Wading isn't an option in the pool, but the tailout, located a few hundred feet downstream and within sight of the parking area, is easy to wade if the water flows are not too high. Fish the right bank area, looking downstream. Plenty of bugs that emerge during the season keep the fish happy.

Main Stem of Delaware River at Kellams Bridge crossing. Kellams reach, located 17 miles downstream from Hancock, can accommodate wade anglers if water levels are not too high. Under favorable levels, the reach can be fished from downstream of the bridge on the New York side. By crossing the bridge into Pennsylvania, and securing a fishing license for that state, the reach can be fished upstream from the bridge at the Soaring Eagle Campground.

KELLAMS BRIDGE

Kellams Bridge, a narrow suspension bridge, located about a mile south of Basket Creek on State Route 97 (17 miles south of Hancock), links New York State to Pennsylvania. The deep pool downstream from the bridge can produce during times the fish are up, typically during late evening into dark. The challenge is getting a cast out far enough toward the far bank area where some of the larger fish hold, and rises are often spotted at last light. Kellam's Pool was a favorite of Catskill fly-tiers Harry Darbee, Walt Dette, and fly-fishing guru A. J. McClane. I can recall many sessions at Kellam's when the stretch was good to me during late-evening outings. The pool is easily reached via a footpath located at the bridge that leads down the manageable hill to the river.

The strong current run directly upstream from the bridge, on the New York side, can be very difficult to fish, even with weighted nymphs. The left side of the river (looking upstream from the bridge) is more easily fished and approached from the Pennsylvania side. Access is available for day-users at the Soaring Eagle Campground, just beyond the bridge crossing, for $10. Campsites are also available at the facility that has restrooms and picnic tables. Little Equinunk Creek flows into the river at the campground. It's hard to predict exactly when it happens, but substantial March Brown hatches occur on the reach, typically during late May.

Basket Creek (aka Basket Brook)

Unfortunately, almost all of Basket's two branches are posted and private water, aside from a short stretch that flows near the State Route 97 bridge, about 17 miles south of Hancock. However, the mouth of the stream at the Delaware River not far downstream from the hamlet of Long Eddy can be very productive.

In late August 1967, my dad, his uncle Leonard, and I made a late-season trip to Basket Creek (which we always called Basket Brook, as locals still do today). We trekked down

Mouth of Basket Creek, a few miles downstream from the hamlet of Long Eddy. The riffle and run flows downstream from the mouth, at the far left of the photo.

Basket Creek is a tumbling Delaware River main stem tributary. Access is very limited in the brook itself. Good fishing can be had in the Delaware River, at the mouth of Basket Brook. Fish the riffles and runs downstream from the brook's mouth using caution while wading. (PHOTO VALERIE VALLA)

the hill next to the high State Route 97 bridge crossing where the brook enters the Delaware River not far downstream from the hamlet of Long Eddy. The other two headed to the stream's mouth while I wandered upstream a few hundred yards. Next to an undercut bank, in low water, I hooked and landed a large wild brown trout.

Later in September that year, we returned with my dad's fishing partner, George Kurbaba. By evening, we ended up at a local tavern in Long Eddy. The men sat at the bar and discussed fishing. The lady bartender overheard their chat and pointed out that the man on the dancefloor knew where to catch large rainbows on Basket. His name was Hap, or something like that. The man said he fished a large wet fly at night, a Black Prince, at Basket Creek's mouth.

Black Prince (tied by Mike Valla) Classic Black Prince wet flies have been featured in several books and other publications, going back many years. Author Ray Bergman (1891–1967) featured the fly in one of his color plates that appeared in his book *Trout* (1938).

Many years later, in the late 1980s, while on a Delaware outing with Phil Genova, I carefully waded the river during the evening, just downstream from the creek's mouth. At near dark, trout slammed my dry flies skittered across the riffles. It's dangerous wading, but on lower water, it's doable. I didn't own a wading staff in those years, but I never fish that river stretch now without one.

During those years, the only way to get down to the creek was from the north side of the State Route 97 bridge and a path that led down the steep hill. Today, access is available on the south side of the bridge, via Viaduct Road that leads down to a formal NYSDEC parking area marked by a large hanging sign almost directly under the bridge. A sign on State Route 97 just south of the bridge crossing will direct you down to the parking area.

A path from the lot that's obscured by a massive grove of obnoxious Japanese Knotweed will deliver you to the stream and access to the mouth at the river. However, an alternate path from the parking area will get you to the stream's mouth if the creek is too deep to wade, just upstream from the river. The path, often obscured, is located along private property fencing, just before the NYSDEC large hanging sign. Walk the path to the railroad tracks and, with caution, cross over the tracks. A small path continues down a very steep hill to the river and the creek's mouth.

If you're not experienced with getting down steep terrain, it's probably best not to attempt that route to the river. The same holds true for fishing the sometimes fast-flowing run below the creek's mouth. If you're not experienced wading such water, it's best to fish elsewhere.

East and West Branches of Delaware River and Tributaries above Reservoirs

EAST BRANCH OF DELAWARE ABOVE PEPACTON RESERVOIR

A short drive from Stamford easterly along State Route 23 will take you to the hamlet of Grand Gorge. A couple of miles south on State Route 30 out of Grand Gorge will take you to the tiny headwaters of the East Branch of the Delaware River at the Town of Roxbury, where it begins its 20-mile journey to the Pepacton Reservoir. It's both a hatchery trout (browns) and wild trout (browns and brook trout) fishery. The New York City Department

East Branch of the Delaware River, about a mile north of Margaretville on State Route 30. The East Branch of the Delaware above Pepacton Reservoir provides fishing for mostly stocked brown trout. This reach is near the mouth of Bush Kill, a small tributary that enters the river from the opposite side of the stream.

East Branch of Delaware River at Cold Spring Road Crossing. Cold Spring Road and the upper river reach is located several miles north of Margaretville, just downstream from Roxbury. The reach is best fished during early May into early June. (PHOTO VALERIE VALLA)

of Environmental Protection (DEP), the agency that regulates the water supply reservoirs, provides at least some public fishing access in the watershed.

East Branch Tributaries

Formal NYC DEP fishing access sites aside, anglers can also locate stream reaches on private yet non-posted lands where owners allow fishing. The courteous avenue is to ask permission when desiring to fish on non-posted private land. With a little exploring, the venturesome angler can also locate many such areas on tributary streams that feed the upper East Branch.

Before even thinking about sampling the small upper East Branch that flows through Roxbury, it would be a sacrilege to pass by Hardscabble Road, located along State Route 30 a couple of miles outside of the settlement. Signs will direct you to John Burroughs Memorial Park and Woodchuck Lodge, where the naturalist and philosophical essayist lived in 1910, within a mile of where he was raised on a farmstead.

A stop at Burrough's burial site and boyhood "Thinking Boulder," with its inset bronze memorial tablet, is a must-see. Take a break from fishing and enjoy viewing the photos at the kiosk or have a lunch break at the picnic tables. You might be tempted to fish Pleasant Valley Brook on your way up to the memorial area.

Nearly all of Pleasant Valley Brook, an East Branch tributary, is posted water. However, a brief reach of private yet non-posted water exists at the bridge crossing a short distance up the road from State Route 30. During a recent visit to the memorial site, I stopped at the bridge to have a quick look at the stream below the bridge. From her vantage point on the bridge, my dear wife spotted a large trout in the clear pool. Her eyesight is much better than mine.

I couldn't spot the fish and questioned her observation. But as is usually the case she shamed me into gearing up and insisted I take a few minutes to cast a line. I really didn't have an interest in fighting a steep bank with neck-high weeds and briars to reach the small pool. Casting a small Dark Cahill wet fly into the water resulted in a nice dollar-size wild brook trout.

Returning to State Route 30, and driving south a couple of miles into Roxbury, you'll pass Kirkside Park. The park is open free to visitors. Kirkside Park's entrance, marked by a sign right on State Route 30 in the heart of the town, is located on a 14-acre peaceful setting with winding, streamside walking trails along both sides of the East Branch. Its rustic little bridges add to its charm.

The park is more of a lunch stop than a serious fishing location. The brown trout are not large, but they are very colorful and eagerly strike small wet flies, including small-size Quill Gordons and Dark Cahills. Brook trout from the lower river reaches spawn in that area in the fall.

However, an East Branch stream reach located a short drive downstream from Roxbury, on Cold Spring Road, will provide a bit of solitude. Park at a bridge turnout and sample the riffles above the bridge. You'll encounter low-gradient, difficult-to-fish water downstream of the Cold Spring Road site. While DEP allows fishing access at the Briggs Road bridge crossing, I usually bypass that slow-moving stretch and instead head for Batavia Kill located several miles downstream from Roxbury at Kelly Corners (not to be confused with the "other Batavia Kill" located in Greene County).

Batavia Kill (Delaware County)

I like a Batavia Kill section located 3.2 miles upstream from the State Route 30/County Road 36 intersection. I've also fished downstream from the intersection, wading along the north bank of the stream to its junction with the East Branch. My Batavia Kill fly box is filled with Martinez Black Nymphs and Elk Hair Caddis dry flies. Brown and brook trout inhabit the little stream. Lime Sally stone flies and a variety of caddis flutter along the stream.

Upper Batavia Kill, in Delaware County. Sharing the same name with a creek in Greene County, this Batavia Kill lacks formal NYSDEC PFR water. However, a couple of stretches provide access.

Batavia Kill, classified as Wild-Quality water by NYS, is an important East Branch thermal refuge tributary. I can't say enough good things about the collaborative study NYSDEC Region 4 biologists and the Ashokan/Pepacton chapter of Trout Unlimited (TU) undertook to better understand trout movement and thermal challenges affecting the upper East Branch trout populations.

Temperature-monitoring studies, which were largely focused around the Town of Roxbury, were initiated in 2016 and continued annually into 2020. The team tagged and tracked both wild and hatchery-planted fish. The TU chapter also partnered with Delaware County Soil and Water Conservation staff, with the cooperation of private landowners, to undertake tree-planting initiatives along riparian sites that experienced elevated summer water temperatures.

Bush Kill (Delaware County)

Bush Kill (not to be confused with the "other Bush Kill" in Ulster County) is an upper East Branch of the Delaware tributary stream near Arkville that enters the East Branch of the Delaware a short distance upstream from Margaretville. Bush Kill serves as a spawning tributary for big brown trout that migrate upstream in the fall from Pepacton Reservoir. The creek falls under Special Regulations of little concern to most fly anglers. NYSDEC imposed creel limits of three per day and only one trout can be over 12 inches in length during the regular open season. The stream is open year-round, with Catch and Release only regulation is in effect between October 16 and March 31.

The only formal PFR water is located at Arkville. The main easement section is downstream from the State Route 28 bridge in Arkville, just up the road from Margaretville. Access the stream at the bridge crossing or from near its confluence with the East Branch of the Delaware about 1 mile north of Margaretville on State Route 30. The somewhat

Bush Kill at Fleishmann's Village Park. Sharing the same name as the small stream that flows through Ulster County, Delaware County's creek has limited PFR water but can also be accessed at Fleishmann's Village Park, located not far from Margaretville. (PHOTO VALERIE VALLA)

wide road shoulder can accommodate a couple of vehicles. However, access from that point is possible only at times when the river water levels are low enough to cross the river.

Other unofficial access points are available upstream from Arkville. From the Arkville bridge crossing, drive about 3 miles east on State Route 28 to a left on Old Route 28. Follow the road upstream a little less than a half-mile to an area you can park on the road shoulder. It's a good place to fish during the fall, drifting streamers through the runs and pool. Easy stream access is also available at the 5-acre Fleischmanns Village Park, located just a couple of miles upstream on the opposite side of the river on Wagner Avenue. It's also a good fall season fishing location.

I usually fish with 7-foot to 8-foot rods, with 4-weight to 5-weight lines on the Bush Kill. Bring a supply of caddis patterns during the spring, along with nymphs and Matuka streamers. Most of my fall fishing on the Bush Kill is with black streamer patterns. Ed Ostapczuk's Black Leach is a good choice to interest lake-run browns.

Barkaboom Stream/Mill Brook

Short access reaches can be found on a couple small tributaries that dump directly into Pepacton Reservoir, including Barkaboom Stream and Mill Brook. During the warm summer months, the lowermost East Branch of the Delaware reaches around Margaretville, a village just upstream from the Pepacton, experiences significant elevated water temperatures. However, cooler water can be found in Mill Brook and Barkaboom Stream tributaries that feed directly into the east side of the reservoir not far from Margaretville.

Millbrook, unfortunately, is almost entirely historic-yet-private Tuscarora Club mileage. However, short reaches can be found near its mouth with the Pepacton and also upstream at its headwaters where it flows briefly through NYS Wild Forest lands. Wild brook trout inhabit the upper stream. Anglers wishing to sample the brief lowermost

Barkaboom Stream, a tributary of Pepacton Reservoir. Quaint Barkaboom Stream is inhabited by wild brook trout. A portion of the brook flows through NYS Forest Preserve lands. Short DEP sections are located downstream.

Mill Brook at the DEP reach downstream near the reservoir provides a short stretch of water open to public fishing via a DEP permit (available free online). Unfortunately, highly productive Mill Brook water flows through extensive frontage owned by the Tuscarora Club.

stretch near the reservoir will need a free DEP permit, which can be easily obtainable online (see Notebook).

A short drive south along the reservoir from Mill Brook will take you to Barkaboom Road and Barkaboom Stream, a tumbling brook. Access is available in the upper DEP areas and the brief NYS Wild Forest reaches. I first discovered the stream several years ago while driving back roads. I pulled over to take care of an urgent need. While taking care of business, I peered over a very steep bank and had a hunch. I geared up, scaled down the rocky bank, and proceeded to catch a sizably handsome brook trout.

WEST BRANCH OF DELAWARE RIVER ABOVE CANNONSVILLE RESERVOIR

The West Branch above Cannonsville Reservoir is a completely different river when compared to the tailrace below the impoundment. Both brown trout and brook trout exist in the system, although brookies are much more common in the tributaries. While the West Branch is managed as a coldwater trout fishery, a scattering of warmwater species, such as bass and chain pickerel, also inhabit the river. Unlike the tailrace, which runs cold via discharge from the reservoir, the upper West Branch relies on spring seepages during the warmer summer months.

The main river itself is heavily stocked, and unlike the tailraces below the reservoir the system depends on significant numbers of hatchery browns, to maintain the fisheries. Stream-bred, riverine browns also inhabit the river (as opposed to lake-run browns that enter from the reservoir below). Over 16,000 browns from 9 to 15 inches are stocked along the stream that's easily accessed along State Route 10 that closely follows the river some 40 miles between Stamford and Walton. Access is not a problem. Six-pounders, while not common, have been caught in the stream.

West Branch of the Delaware upstream from the County Road 26 bridge crossing in Hawleys. The big, slow-moving, often-stained West Branch of the Delaware above Cannonsville Reservoir offers extensive PFR mileage.

Twenty-two miles of PFR water has been purchased by NYSDEC since 1948. Yellow signs with dark lettering clearly mark PFR frontage. Numerous parking turnouts exist along the stream, including five formal NYSDEC fishing parking areas (FPAs), clearly marked by larger hanging signs.

Some PFRs are distanced from State Route 10 and connect to the stream by gravel roads, paths, or tiny brooks. A favorite of mine is at McMurdy Hill Road. Park at the State Route 10 PFA, then walk the small brook to the river to reach some nice water. There's also plenty of precious water that is not formally PFR, but access is still permitted by private landowners who welcome anglers.

Speaking of anglers, there aren't many you'll encounter along the stream. I've never encountered a floating craft. I ran into only a couple of fly anglers during May last year who were scouting the stained water from the County Road 26 bridge at Hawleys, one of my favorite reaches. We were looking for Hendricksons (*Ephemerella subvaria*), one of the common mayfly hatches on the stream. It wouldn't happen that day. A serious drawback on that stream is the turbidity that occurs after rainfalls, along with rapidly rising water. Hendrickson fishing would have to wait for better conditions.

A few tributaries that feed the West Branch above the reservoir—East Brook, Town Brook, and Little Delaware River—are worth exploring while in the area.

East Brook, a West Branch of the Delaware tributary, is a wild brown and brook trout stream near Walton. It's lightly fished. The new NYS Inland Fisheries Plan classified East Brook as Wild-Quality. The criterion for that classification requires at least 300 yearling or older trout per mile.

Last late May, I encountered a Yellow Sallie (*Isoperla*) emergence on East Brook PFR water located downstream from the Macgibbon Hollow Road/County Road 22 intersection. Park at the intersection and walk down the tiny PFR brook to the stream. Another PFR located at the extreme headwaters is small water, yet fishable. There's room for one

East Brook at the Macgibbon Hollow Road reach. East Brook is usually lightly fished by fly anglers. NYSDEC reports that it inhabits a healthy wild trout population. (PHOTO VALERIE VALLA)

The lower reach of Town Brook, near its confluence with the West Branch of the Delaware

small vehicle to squeeze in next to the guardrail along County Road 22. There's also a nice reach downstream off Nichols Road. It's not formal PFR water, but it's not posted. The NYSDEC East Brook maps available online clearly show these areas.

The few upper PFR reaches on Town Brook rarely see a boot print. Last June, my wife, Valerie, and I made the brutal trek hundreds of feet through chest-high grass to reach the fishing easement reach located off the intersection of Red Rock Road and Town Brook Road. Easier access to Town Brook is located downstream along Clove Road at

Little Delaware River along the State Route 28 reach (PHOTO VALERIE VALLA)

the bridge (not formal PFR water, but it's not posted) or along Stamford River Road PFR near the junction with the West Branch. The PFR reaches are also clearly shown on the NYSDEC West Branch PFR maps available online. NYSDEC Region 4 biologists stationed at Stamford offices surveyed the little brook several years ago and turned up browns and brook trout. The stream is not stocked.

The Little Delaware River, more of a creek than a river, is a tributary that enters the West Branch of the Delaware River at the Village of Delhi. The stream is an off-the-beaten-track brown trout and brook trout creek. It receives only a couple hundred hatchery brown trout stockings every spring in the Delhi area. Brook trout inhabit the headwaters. While not a major fly-fishing destination, the creek-size stream can provide relative solitude when compared to other popular Catskill destinations. Don't expect banner, multi-fish days on the stream.

If approaching from the West Branch or the Delaware River areas at Walton or Delhi, the creek can be fished at PFR sections starting at Delhi then working upstream to Bovina. If approaching from the east, near the Pepacton Reservoir area, fish the head-waters at Bovina first, then sections downstream to Delhi. An official NYSDEC parking lot is located on the headwaters about 10 miles north of Margaretville on County Road 10 and about 15 miles east of Delhi via State Route 28 to Bovina Road.

A NYSDEC parking lot on the Little Delaware River is located at the corner of Cape Horn Road and Crescent Valley Road at a small bridge crossing, across from an old one-room schoolhouse. The water here is very small and difficult to fly fish upstream from the bridge, yet it is possible using a short rod, fishing nymphs through intermittent little pools and runs. The stream flows out of a very brushy, meadow-like area along the PFR stretch upstream. You'll encounter a small habitat-improvement structure with a small plunge pool, just upstream from the bridge, that often holds a couple of small brook trout. However, it's much easier to cast flies along the continuous PFR stretches that flow downstream from the bridge. I use a 7-foot, 4-weight rod when fishing the stream from this point downstream to the Bovina area.

Little Delaware River at the Cape Horn Road/Crescent Valley Road bridge (PHOTO VALERIE VALLA)

Flowing downstream from the headwater parking lot, the stream enters a pool below a bridge crossing culvert located 0.6 mile down Bovina Road. The stretch upstream from the bridge flows through a nice spruce-tree-shaded area that often harbors small trout. You'll see official NYSDEC public fishing signs upstream from the bridge but also posted signage that will remind visitors that access is limited to fishing easement only. Later in the season, during fall on lower-water levels, you'll often notice small trout that are skittish darting around in the pool. Stretches downstream from the bridge are also PFR water that departs away from the road.

E.C. Emerger Caddis (tied by Joe Fusco) Catskill fly fisher Joe Fusco likes this pattern when caddis are emerging. It floats well and is easily followed while drifting it across riffles and pools.

Another formal NYSDEC parking area is located a little over a mile downstream. A very steep path leads down a hill to the stream that flows well away from the road. The creek in that reach is more wide-open and more conducive to casting flies. Additional access areas are located downstream.

Bovina Road continues another 5 miles or so to the State Route 28N intersection. Take a right turn and drive about a little less than 4 miles to a road shoulder turnout that provides access to a formal NYSDEC-designated footpath easement. Small, round, yellow footpath markers lead down the hill to the stream. The stream runs along a streambank protected by large boulders. Fish the pool by casting nymphs up along the streambank.

Your fly box while fishing both the West Branch and its tributaries should carry an ample supply of caddis pupae and dry flies, as well as big streamers. Joe Fusco's favorite E.C. Emerger Caddis is a good choice.

Mid-Lower Hudson Valley Region

everal streams that flow in Mid-Lower Hudson Valley, on the east side of the Hudson River, originate along, or flow close to, the western borders of Massachusetts and Connecticut, along the Taconic Ridge. Bash Bish Creek and Roeliff Jansen Kill, near the Town of Copake in Columbia County, benefit from springheads that originate at Mount Washington in Massachusetts. South of Copake, in Dutchess County, other streams, such as Wassaic Creek, flow close to Connecticut. Ten Mile River is also in the neighborhood. Dutchess County also provides good fishing in streams such as Wappinger Creek, and there are others, too.

Some of the more unique trout streams, located on New York City Watershed Property, are found south of Dutchess County on the east side of the Hudson River in Westchester County, in the Lower Hudson Valley. Outflows from nine New York City Water Reservoirs provide 13 miles of public access water. The East and West Branches of the Croton River are no doubt the most popular, but the other outflows also provide good fly-fishing sport.

Bash Bish Falls, on the Massachusetts border near Copake, tumbles more than 1,300 feet then almost immediately into New York State as Bash Bish Creek. After traversing a gorge, the creek eventually joins Roeliff Jansen Kill at the base of the Taconic Ridge.

Roeliff Jansen Kill/Bash Bish Brook

I'm not sure what I like most about my good friend Bill Newcomb. He has a strikingly similar appearance to "Buffalo Bill" Cody, complete with a signature hat that he wears every day, which always makes me smile. A museum out West even offered him a job, as a stand-in for the famous Westerner from times past. Appearance aside, his soft-spoken charm and helpful demeanor is what Bill is most known for, and it is what I probably like best about him, if asked.

However, Bill is also admired as an ardent fly tier, fly angler, and student of fly-fishing history. He most enjoys fishing the little streams near the Town of Copake that he's enjoyed since boyhood. Among his favorites are the Roeliff Jansen Kill and Bash Bish Brook, a tributary. Both streams originate very near the Massachusetts border in roughly what can be considered the southeastern extent of the Capital Region. Their combined waters end up along the Lower Hudson River Valley region.

Roeliff Jansen Kill (known better among locals as the "Roe-Jan") begins its 56-mile journey near Austerlitz in Columbia County, eventually joining the Hudson River near the hamlet of Linlithgo. Flowing through both Columbia and Dutchess Counties, the Roe-Jan is a varied fishery that supports both warmwater species in its lowermost reaches and trout in its mid- to upper sections. The uppermost reaches are wild trout waters. NYSDEC stocks brown trout in areas downstream in both counties it flows through.

I hooked up with Bill recently near his home in Copake, where we looked over one of his favorite stretches at the 300-acre Roeliff Jansen Park, owned by New York State and managed by the Town of Hillsdale largely through volunteer efforts. The park is divided by State Route 22. The Roe-Jan cuts through the eastern 150 acres along an area of mowed fields, sheltering barns, playgrounds, and trails. The park is located less than a mile south of the State Route 22/State Route 23 intersection in Hillsdale.

Copake native Bill Newcomb on the upper Roeliff Jansen Kill. Bill Newcomb grew up in Copake and attended school on the banks of Roeliff Jansen Kill. I don't know what I enjoy more when I see my good friend Bill—walking his local streams or our frequent rendezvous at the local diners. Bill has fond memories of his times fishing his home "Roe-Jan," as it's often called.

Bill Newcomb on Bash Bish Brook, at Taconic State Park. Bash Bish cascades down a steep waterfall in Massachusetts, located a short walk upstream from New York's Taconic State Park and just up the road from Copake, Bill's hometown.

The stream, tiny in this area, cuts across State Route 22, then flows along the western 50 acres next to leased farm fields. The abandoned Harlem Valley Railroad bed, now a rail trail path, was acquired in the purchase of the expansive farmland property that almost ended up in the hands of developers. The result of the purchase ensured access to trout fishing along the Roe-Jan in that area, providing extensive frontage. Just downstream of the official public lands, along State Route 22, much of the stream flows along private property that's not posted. It's always best to ask permission to fish those sections.

The wild browns in the Hillsdale area are wild and challenging to entice. Bill most likely casts flies like classic Partridge and Orange or Queen of Water wet flies, but contemporary nymphs and flies will interest the fish. Anglers interested in fishing the stocked stream reaches should continue downstream to a couple of good locations located in both counties. Heading south of Hillsdale on State Route 22 in route to those stretches, stop by a beautiful brook called the Bash Bish.

From the entrance to Roeliff Jansen Park, drive a little over 3 miles south on State Route 22 to State Route 344. The road leads into Taconic State Park and a Bash Bish bridge crossing at the entrance to Copake Iron Works Historic site. Nice pocketwater, perfect for casting nymphs, inhabits wild brown trout. Another option is to continue up State Route 344 less than a mile to a large parking area that serves visitors to the park, mostly those interested in hiking upstream to Bash Bish Falls, which flows out of Massachusetts. It's quite crowded during the summer. A good strategy is to park at the lot, then fish downstream to the bridge crossing. Continue to the midsections of the Roe-Jan for larger water. Depart Taconic State Park on State Route 344, then bear left to State Route 22. Driving south about a mile will get you to the State Route 22/County Road 7A intersection in Copake.

A nice PFR section is located on Mount Ross Road, 13 miles or so south from the intersection. Continue on 7A past the Clock Tower Pub & Grill and Copake General

Queen of Water (tied by Bill Newcomb) Bill Newcomb, from Columbia County, New York, prefers to fish old, classic, soft-hackle wet flies on his home waters such as the "Roe-Jan."

Apple Caddis (tied by John Kavanaugh) John's pattern suggests the Apple Caddis (*Brachycentrus appalachia*). However, there's no doubt it can be fished on most any trout stream as a general caddis dry fly, regardless if that particular species inhabits a given stream. The bright post makes for an easy fly to flow on water.

Store. County Road 7A leads into County Road 7, where it eventually meets Mount Ross Road. Park next to the bridge. You can access the PFR section upstream from the concrete bridge along a footpath (you'll notice a small "fishing permitted" sign at the beginning of the footpath). The stream on the left side, looking downstream from the bridge, isn't official PFR water, but it's not posted. A footpath leads down the riverbank to nice water. Swing streamers through the pool and runs.

One other desirable PFR section is located downstream only a couple of miles, in the area that borders Dutchess and Columbia Counties. From the Mount Ross Road bridge crossing, return back to the intersection off County Road 7, then take a left on to Jackson Corners Road (County Road 2). Driving west, you'll pass under the Taconic State Parkway. In about a half-mile, take the first left on Academy Hill Road. In 0.2 mile, park along the road shoulder at the bridge crossing. PFR water flows downstream from the bridge. A footpath from the road shoulder leads down the streambank. It's a nice stretch to swing flies.

During early spring, toward the end of March, Little Black Stoneflies (*Taeniopteryx nivalis*) emerge on the PFR stretch at Mount Ross Road. Caddis hatches are plentiful on the Roe-Jan, along with the usual variety of mayflies that emerge on other New York trout streams. Terrestrial patterns can interest the wild brown trout on the upper reaches.

Wappinger Creek

From its source at Thompson Pond, near the hamlet of Pine Plains, the 41.7-mile Wappinger Creek flows south through Dutchess County to its confluence with the Hudson River at New Hamburg. The stream receives significant stockings of hatchery trout from NYSDEC. In a typical year, the southernmost reaches in the Town of Poughkeepsie receive both brown trout and rainbow trout. The upper sections that flow through the Town of Pleasant Valley, upstream from the dam in the Village of Pleasant Valley, receive only browns.

Some 16.5 miles of the creek, from New Hackensack Road Bridge in Red Oaks Mill upstream to East Branch Wappinger Creek in Hibernia, are stocked with nearly 13,000 trout. The headwater reaches inhabit wild browns and a few wild brook trout. Nearly

Hibernia Road crossing at the "Green Bridge" reach, in Salt Point, is a popular Wappinger Creek access point. Little Black Stoneflies (*Taeniopteryx nivalis*) emerge along this reach in March. Drift black stoneflies through the run upstream from the bridge.

4 miles of the upper creek near Stanfordville, from three-quarters of a mile downstream of Jameson Hill Road bridge in Clinton Corners upstream to Hunts Lake Creek, is categorized by NYSDEC as Wild-Quality and receives no stockings.

While only a small amount of official PFR water exists along the stream's total mileage, plenty of access is available at other public entry points along town parks and recreation areas, or non-posted lands where fishing is allowed. Three Wild-Quality section access points are available in the Stanfordville area, on the upper-creek section. Two are brief sections of PFR water, and two are along Town of Stanfordville parks. All are located within 4 miles of each other.

The short uppermost PFR stretch is located a short distance upstream from Stanfordville on Cold Spring Road. From Stanfordville, drive north about a mile up State Route 82 from its intersection with County Road 65 (Hunns Lake Road), then bear left onto Cold Spring Road. The access point to the PFR water is at an old, small cemetery located 0.1 mile up Cold Spring Road, on the left. The headstones that could use some loving care date back to the late 1700s and early 1800s. Trek down the steep-yet-manageable hill behind the cemetery to the water. A few runs and riffles flow through the brief non-stocked public easement stretch.

The next access point is located downstream just a couple of miles at the Stanford Recreation Park. From the State Route 82/Cold Spring Road intersection, drive 1.8 miles south on State Route 82 to a right turn on Church Lane. Take Church Lane 0.1 mile to a left on Creamery Way. The park is located just down the road. You'll notice a friendly "fishing permitted" sign at the bridge crossing near the park entrance.

During the off-season, no fee is required to park at the recreation lot. A small fee is required for day-use during other times. It's a great place for kids to enjoy a swimming area and playground during summer. The creek runs along the border of the park. Quite

Upper Wappinger Creek at the Stanfordville Recreation Park is small water that's easily accessed. Depending on the year and rainfall amounts, there are times during late summer that the stream flows are very low and mostly unfishable in this reach. (PHOTO VALERIE VALLA)

a distance of fishing frontage is available. Anglers can also fish downstream from the Creamery Road bridge crossing where the stream continues its flow behind the Town of Stanfordville garages. While fishing upstream along the park boundary, cast nymphs into the runs. A little dam exists that's used to divert water to a swimming area that creates nice habitat directly downstream. Swing small streamers while working your way downstream from the bridge.

Another public access point is located just a couple miles downstream from the recreation park. Exit the park and return to State Route 82. Drive a short distance south on State Route 82 to a right on Salt Point Turnpike. The Town of Stanfordville Wildlife Preserve is located a quarter-mile down the road, at a parking area next to a bridge crossing. The stream is easy to access by walking down a wide path along the fields that follow the creek. A nice run is located just downstream from the bridge crossing. Check the map that's posted on a kiosk next to a convenient picnic table at the parking area. A "fishing access" point is located on the map that makes for easy entry into the creek.

The next formal PFR section, a brief stretch, is located downstream from Stanfordville at a small bridge crossing at Jameson Hill Road. Return to State Route 82, then drive 0.7 mile south to a right turn on Jameson Hill Road. A small formal parking area is located at the bridge crossing. The creek here can be difficult to access and wade during periods of high water, especially during bank-full levels in early spring. The stream meanders downstream from the bridge and can be difficult to fish with flies.

Continue downstream out of the Wild-Quality reaches and into the Stock-Extended stretches by heading for the hamlet of Salt Point, located on the west side of the Taconic State Parkway. (If approaching downstream areas, take State Route 115 north from Poughkeepsie about 11 miles. From the Village of Pleasant Valley area, take County Road 72 north 6 miles or so to Salt Point.)

The Little Wappinger Creek, a tributary of the main creek, flows under the bridge crossing in Salt Point, at the State Route 115/Hibernia Road intersection. It's next to the red-painted Consigli Equipment building. A fast-flowing riffle flows downstream from a small, impassable dam located upstream from the bridge. The stretch downstream from the bridge is a nice section to swing small wet flies of streamers and worth a few casts before heading down to the main creek and a PFR section at a bridge crossing, located less than 1 mile down Hibernia Road. I call this the "green bridge" reach, a pleasant area to fish during spring and again in the fall.

Cross the bridge and park up at the Scout Road intersection, along the road shoulder. Walk across the bridge and get into the water upstream. You'll notice a closed gate at the bridge with a "no hunting sign" that closes off the area to vehicles and the wide path that leads upstream. Official PFR signage is posted along the trees upstream from the bridge. During late March into early April, clouds of Little Black Stoneflies emerge in that section. On one occasion in late March, I latched into a big brown trout a short distance upstream from the bridge swinging a Red Trude fly. An A.P. Black Beaver Nymph is a good choice when the Little Black Stonefly is emerging. Fly fisher, fly tier, and LaGrange resident Pat Crisci loves to fish a version of Cal Bird's Black Bird's Nest.

Another popular access point is located 6 miles in the Village of Pleasant Valley, downstream from the dam located below a bridge crossing at the Pleasant Valley Memorial Park on Main Street. The Cady Recreation Park, located a short distance downstream,

AP Black Beaver Nymph (tied Mike Valla) The AP Black Beaver Nymph is one of a series of AP Nymphs developed in the early 1960s by Andre Puyans. Tied with beaver fur dyed black, the copper-wire ribbed abdomen provides a hint of flash. The tails and wing case are crafted from dark moose hair.

Black Optic Bucktail (tied by Mike Valla) Bucktails and streamers that feature fly heads with eyes have long been popular for enticing a range of sport fish species. The eyes on this simple bucktail were created with gloss yellow and black testor enamel paints.

Black Bird's Nest—Variation (tied by Pat Crisci) Pat Crisci, from LaGrange, had this to say about his variation of Black Bird's Nest: "Throughout much of the Wappinger Creek, as with most coldwater streams in Dutchess County, New York, stoneflies are abundant year-round forage for resident trout. The Black Bird's Nest is a local favorite for imitating the large Black Stonefly Nymph." Pat created the fly's thorax with black hare's mask hair, loosely dubbed.

is also an access point. The short road that leads to the park and stream is next to the Pleasant Valley Town Hall off Main Street.

Additional angling access points also exist downstream from Pleasant Valley, including a PFR section in the LaGrange area. From Main Street in Pleasant Valley, drive south 8 miles or so south on US-44 to Degarmo Road to Overlook Road to State Route 55E. The PFR reach is downstream from the bridge crossing at Titusville Road. The area is somewhat congested with commercial buildings. Park along the Titusville Road shoulder near the bridge. The creek here is easier to fish on moderate water levels where a nice run flows downstream from the bridge. Swing streamers through the run.

Greenville Park, with a boat launch access area, is located just a couple of miles downstream. Once you get downstream from the park, in the Red Mill Oaks section, the water is marginal trout water during summer and best fished in the early season. Wappinger Creek flows below Red Mill Oaks as a warmwater fishery, although reports are made of trout catches in the lower reaches.

Use a 9-foot, 5-weight rod for most of the mid-lower reaches. I use a 7.5-foot, 4-weight rod along the Stanfordville stretches. Bring an assortment of caddis and the usual mayfly patterns as well as streamers.

Wassaic Creek/Ten Mile River/Swamp River

The quaint hamlet of Wassaic, located off State Route 22 in Dutchess County only a couple miles east of the Connecticut border, is better known for the significant role it played during the Civil War than its namesake stream, Wassaic Creek. In 1856, entrepreneur Gail Borden received a patent for condensing milk. By 1861, his New York Condensed Milk Company opened its first successful plant in Wassaic on the banks of the little stream, manufacturing much-needed milk that could be preserved for long periods of time and transported many miles for consumption by the Union Army. Evaporated milk, "Elsie the Cow," and Elmer's Glue that the Borden Company is known for came later.

The old factory still stands in Wassaic along its creek (now occupied by another industry), along with nice streamside picnic tables and historical displays at the entrance to the buildings. The creek that originates several miles upstream northwest of State Route 22 flows downstream between the factory building and railroad tracks picks up water from a small tributary. It then continues down along Wassaic Town Park for a distance, providing access for both anglers and families.

At the factory building entrance, off Furnace Bank Road and Main Street, cross the stream to Nelson Road and take a quick left on Borden Lane. A short drive around the rear of the building will deliver you across a small bridge to the park and playground. Try fishing small streamers though the stream along the park boundary during spring and nymphs in the pocketwater upstream from the bridge crossing. While not great in numbers, wild brook trout and wild brown trout inhabit the creek in its headwaters.

The creek widens and becomes more substantial a couple of miles downstream. You can access the creek via a small, formal NYSDEC parking lot directly on State Route 22 a short distance downstream, marked by a large hanging sign. A steep-but-manageable hill leads down to the stream from the lot. Good dry-fly fishing can be had along the pool that exists from an upstream riffle.

The creek continues its journey downstream a couple of miles until it eventually joins Webatuck Creek and creates Ten Mile River, categorized as a stocked stream dependent on hatchery brown trout, about 4,000 are stocked annually. Continue south on State Route

Wassaic Creek reach at Wassaic Town Park, near the old Borden plant. Easy access is available at the former Borden plant and at the town park. (PHOTO VALERIE VALLA)

22 from the NYSDEC parking lot a little over a mile to Sinpatch Road. In less than a half-mile down Sinpatch Road, cross the river near the Taconic Disability Development Service and Tenmile River Rail station. A small parking area marked by stones at the Webatuck Creek bridge crossing on Creek Road (across from the Disability facility) is a good access point for the streams. Webatuck Creek is also categorized as a Stocked trout stream. It annually receives around 1,700 browns.

One of the more popular Ten Mile River access points, however, is farther downstream at the NYSDEC Wassaic Multiple Use Area. It's located a mile or so downstream from Sinpatch Road on State Route 22 and a couple miles north of the hamlet of Dover Plains, across from Willow Lane. It's marked by a NYSDEC large hanging sign. Park next to the kiosk at the entrance. A dirt road leads across a large field past a gate and small weather station several hundred feet to the stream but is restricted to vehicles unless you have a permit. The long walk to the stream along the road is easy and not an issue. Long,

Located a couple of miles north of Dover Plains, Wassaic Multiple Use Area provides access to Ten Mile River. Access the river by parking at the Multiple Use Area and walking a few hundred feet down the dirt road that exits the parking area. A footpath at the end of the dirt road leads to the stream.

slow-flowing pools inhabit the browns. Other access is available at the J. H. Ketcham Memorial Park in Dover Plains. Take Mill Street in Dover Plains off State Route 22 a half-mile or so to Ketcham Park.

Besides Wassaic Creek, Ten Mile River is fed by other tributaries, including Swamp River located just a few miles south of Dover Plains. Take County Road 62 (Olde Route 22) off State Route 22 to a Swamp River bridge crossing located 0.9 mile from the State Route 22/County Road 6 intersection. A small NYSDEC parking lot marked by a large hanging sign is just beyond the bridge. The stream flows through New York State Lands, reached

Snowshoe Hendrickson Stillborn (tied by Pat Crisci) Stillborn mayfly patterns are popular among fly tiers. Pat ties his with a reddish-brown goose or turkey biot abdomen and a thorax created with a mix of fiery brown rabbit and seal furs, roughly dubbed.

by a footpath from the parking lot that leads a few hundred feet to the water. A NYS Lands fishing access sign is posted on an ash tree at the water's edge. Swamp River flows downstream from the bridge less than a half-mile then enters Ten Mile River.

Dutchess County resident, fly tier, and fly angler Pat Crisci had this to say about one of his favorite patterns, Snowshoe Hendrickson Stillborn: "On Ten Mile River and its tributaries, Wassaic Creek, and Webutuck Creek, the most reliable mayfly hatch from year to year has been *Ephemerella subvaria*—the Hendrickson hatch. When it's 'on,' the fish show a decided preference for this fly. The Snowshoe Hendrickson Stillborn imitates a crippled insect struggling to lift itself from the water."

Croton River Branches/Amawalk Outlet

The East and West Branches of Croton River that flow into and out of New York City reservoirs, as well as Amawalk Outlet, have been a magnet for anglers residing in the more populous areas of New York. Tucked away in Putnam and Westchester Counties, the streams provide relatively quick access for New York City residents and those who reside in surrounding cities and towns. However, anglers from outside the metropolitan area also cast their lines on the streams that flow along New York City's watershed property. You'll need to obtain a NYCDEP permit to sample the Amawalk and Croton branches, available for free online.

Within the NYC watershed property system, fly anglers can experience varied management categories that range from Wild-Quality to Stocked-Extended to Stocked. Regulations also vary, depending on what stream reach you're fishing. Catch and release, artificial lures only and daily harvest limits regulations are found on the varied stream segments.

WEST BRANCH OF CROTON RIVER

Upper West Branch: The uppermost Croton River reach begins downstream from Boyd Corners Reservoir in Putnam County. Completed in the late 1800s, the small reservoir is located about 50 miles north of New York City. The short half-mile-long stream reach that flows into West Branch Reservoir is categorized by NYSDEC as Stocked water from Kittredge Bridge, off State Route 301, upstream to Boyd Corners Reservoir. The stream

West Branch of Croton at the Wild-Quality stretch, near Cherry Hill Road. Anglers after the possibility of netting a wild brown trout should head for the Cherry Hill reach. (PHOTO VALERIE VALLA)

exits the reservoir and flows briefly along East Boyds Road to a State 301 bridge crossing. The stream enters flatwater a short distance downstream from the bridge and widens by the time it hits Kittredge Road bridge. NYSDEC categorized the stream as Stocked. The short section receives about 800 brown trout annually during March and April.

The best water for fishing nymphs along the streams meager half-mile is upstream from the State 301 bridge and a short distance downstream. Park at the State Route 301/East Boyds Road intersection along the road shoulder or at a parking turnout located 0.1 mile up East Boyds Road, on the left. You can also park downstream from the dam, along the road, but make sure not to block the yellow gate barrier at a DEP dam access road. You'll encounter clearly written DEP signage that informs anglers that fishing isn't allowed for a short distance below the dam. Make sure to check the USGS water discharge information. It can be a torrent, and largely unfishable, but it is usually easy to fish the pocketwater with nymphs. It's best sampled early in the spring or in the fall.

Midsection West Branch: The stream reach downstream from West Branch Reservoir provides a little over 2 miles of fishing access before the stream enters Croton Falls Reservoir. This stream reach, located in the Town of Carmel area, is not stocked. Good fishing for wild browns in a pleasant woodland setting can be enjoyed throughout the season. NYSDEC reports that brown trout run up from Croton Falls Reservoir to spawn in the nursery waters this reach provides.

A good access point at the lower area is along Drewville Road (State Route 36) at a bridge crossing located at the Cherry Hill Road intersection, located 1.1 miles west of County Road 35 (Stoneleigh Avenue) in Carmel Hamlet. Park next to downstream side of the bridge (a small parking area is also located a short distance up Seminary Hill Road next to the bridge, on the opposite side).

You'll encounter signage that reminds anglers that this stream reach is categorized as Wild-Quality. A footpath leads upstream from the bridge (on the left side). Remnants of an old bridge that once spanned the stream are located a short distance upstream from Drewville Road. Nice pocketwater is located upstream from the old bridge crossing.

Access is also available upstream near the dam, at a parking area located across from Meadowlark Lane on US-6. From the downstream access point at the Cherry Hill intersection, drive about a mile and a half north on State Route 36 to US-6. Take a left and drive a little less than 4 miles to the dam area. You can park near the dam spillway. Note the signage that restricts fishing close to the dam.

Lowermost West Branch: The lower West Branch reach exits Croton Falls Reservoir and flows for about a mile before joining the East Branch of the Croton River. NYSDEC categorized this reach as a Stocked-Extended, Catch and Release artificial-lures-only stretch. It's located in the Town of Carmel in Putnam County in its upper part and the Town of Somers in Westchester County in its lower area. Both wild and holdover stocked brown trout inhabit the short stretch. Around 1,100 browns are typically stocked annually. Access the stream along Butlerville Road or on State Route 34.

If approaching from I-684 at Croton Falls, take State Route 22 to US-202 to Croton Falls Road. Head less than a mile northwest from the US-202 intersection to a left on Butlerville Road. Park at the bridge crossing along the road shoulder, just past a baseball field. Another parking spot marked by a NYSDEC large hanging sign is located along the road shoulder northwest on County Road 34 (Croton Falls Road) from the US-202 intersection, just past a large New York State Electric and Gas (NYSEG) electrical complex. The Butlerville Road access, located a half-mile downstream from Croton Falls Dam, is one of the more popular access points. The stream reach downstream from US-202 is flat water, deep, and sometimes holds very large trout. The late Keith Fulsher, known for his classic Thunder Creek bucktails series, preferred that stretch over others upstream.

EAST BRANCH OF CROTON RIVER

The East Branch of the Croton River is divided into two sections. The lowermost 2.5-mile reach is from its confluence with the West Branch and entry into Muscoot Reservoir in Croton Falls upstream to Diverting Reservoir. The uppermost 2.4-mile reach flows from East Branch Reservoir to Diverting Reservoir in the Town of Southeast, located in Putnam County. Both sections are classified as Stocked-Extended.

The lowermost stretch is easily accessed a short distance from the West Branch stretch in Croton Falls. From the Butlerville Road/Croton Falls Road mentioned previously, a quick drive southeast along Croton Falls Road will get you to an East Branch bridge crossing off US-202. Ample parking is available upstream from the bridge, along US-202 northeast to a second bridge crossing at Stoneleigh Avenue. From that point at the bridge crossing, a 5-mile drive north on US-202 will get you to the Village of Brewster and a popular upper reach that flows downstream from East Branch Reservoir, located near the intersection of Sodom Road and Brewster Hill Road. The stretch is located only 1,000 feet or so downstream from the dam and just downstream of the State Route 22 overpass. Park along Sodom Road near the bridge crossing.

You'll encounter a variety of hatches on the Croton River watershed—everything from Quill Gordons and Blue-Winged Olives that appear in April into May, leading to Sulphurs that typically arrive in mid-May. Carry mayfly dry flies that are popular on the Catskill area streams. Most of the same hatches emerge in the Croton system, some more important than others. Caddis is also important, including *Hydropschye* pupae and *Chimarra* that tend to show up around Hendrickson hatch time. Have Elk Hair Caddis

East Branch of Croton River at the Sodom Road bridge crossing. One of the most popular East Branch reaches is at Sodom Road bridge. Terrific runs and riffles are easily fished with nymphs and small streamers. Dry flies also take fish.

Dynamite Harry-Sulphur Variation (tied by Michael Johnson) Michael Johnson, who spends much of his time on the Delaware River, ties some of the nicest contemporary dry flies I've seen. His Dynamite Harry-Sulphur Variation will no doubt tempt trout on any New York stream, including the Croton streams. Michael reports that the original tier who developed the Dynamite Harry is Jorge Danielsson. Tier Davie McPhail created a variant using CDC tailing fibers. Michael tied the Davie McPhail version for Sulphurs.

dries on hand. Blue-Winged Olives will also take you into the fall months. On higher-water conditions, you'll want to cast streamers that can get down deep.

AMAWALK OUTLET (MUSCOOT RIVER)

It's surprising that Amawalk Outlet has received so much attention and care over many years given its brief 2.7 mileage that connects Amawalk Reservoir to Muscoot Reservoir in Westchester County.

Rich Norman, who relocated from Westchester County many years ago to Batten Kill country just up the road from my home, fondly recalled an early 1970s stream session assisting a group of the Croton Watershed Chapter of Trout Unlimited members who called themselves the Amawalk Rock Rollers. The industrious group heaved and set rocks to help stabilize the banks. The Rock Rollers, from the twenties to the eighties in age, also did work on Cross River Inlet. Today, the New York City TU Chapter is involved

Vinny Cagnina and Willy Jacobs fishing Amawalk Outlet on an early April day

with stream-bank plantings of willow and dogwood along the Outlet, a cooperative effort with the Arbor Day Foundation.

Coldwater releases from Amawalk Reservoir ensure good brown trout survival rates. A Special Regulation stream since the early 1960s, NYSDEC has classified the entire reach as Wild-Quality. The stream reach isn't stocked but has received hatchery browns in past years. It's a very nice stream that's blessed with both pools and tumbling water runs. Hendricksons, Sulphurs, and Tricos are among the hatches that bring trout to the surface. Subsurface nymph patterns can entice the wild browns in early season when the Little Black Stoneflies start showing.

I ran into anglers Vinny Cagnina and Willie Jacobs fishing the Outlet on April 2 a year ago. It was one of those bright, blue-sky splendid days when anglers are reminded how nice it is to be on the water after a long winter. Vinny first hooked into a monster-size fish that turned out to be a big sucker. However, a short time later, I watched him hook and land a beautiful wild brown the stream is known for.

The best water on this Lower Hudson Valley stream can be accessed by heading to Wood Street in Katonah, a hamlet located 15 miles or so east of Peekskill and about 20 miles southwest of Danbury, Connecticut. If approaching from State Route 35 (Amawalk Road), drive south 0.3 mile on Wood Street to a small road shoulder parking area marked by a NYSDEC large hanging sign. You'll pass the Mildred B. Lasdon Bird Sanctuary on the way, as well as a couple of other small parking turnouts, before reaching the primary parking area at a bridge crossing. Well-worn paths lead along the stream from the uppermost road turnout just down the road from the sanctuary.

Very nice tumbling water exits the pool before it turns at an old mill dam site marked by bankside rocks. Fish small streamers through the pocketwater. A long, flat pool that's good dry-fly water is upstream from that point. The pools and water downstream from the bridge crossing are also nice. Anglers who fished the Outlet over the last 50 years might

Besides pools, Amawalk Outlet has nice riffle and pocketwater structure.

comment that the almost smothering dense thickets of invasive multiflora rose along the stream didn't exist in their early fishing sessions on the stream. The prickly briars are a nuisance to anglers walking the banks and footpaths.

Other streams worth exploring if in the area are short sections of Titicus River outlet and Cross River outlet, both part of New York City's water supply system. NYSDEC classified both outlet streams as Stocked. Titicus River, stocked annually with rainbow trout, can be sampled along a half-mile stretch from Titicus Reservoir to Muscoot Reservoir in the Town of North Salem. Access the stream from State Route 22. NYSDEC reports some wild brown trout inhabit the reach. Cross River, in the Town of Bedford, flows about a half-mile downstream from Cross River Reservoir to Muscoot Reservoir. Like the Titicus River outlet, Cross River outlet's short reach, accessed along State Routes 22 and 35, is also stocked with rainbow trout.

Long Island Region

The Long Island Chapter of Trout Unlimited created a very useful manual for those venturing on the spring creeks. The manual describes, in detail, the various "beats" that flow on the Connetquot and Nissequogue, along with other useful information for all the streams.

Carmans River

Carmans River, a fresh water stream for its first 8 miles before flowing into an estuary in its final tidal water 2 miles, is one of three spring creeks on Long Island where fly anglers can latch into trout. There's little doubt it's the best of the three when considering overall water quality. It's rife with insect life, too. Unlike its sister spring creeks, the Connetquot River and the Nissequogue River, there are no assigned fishing beats that must be reserved in advance. However, like the other two spring creeks, wild trout also inhabit its waters. A Catch and Release stretch on the upper reach helps protect wild brook trout population.

Angler interested in fishing Carmans should head to Southhaven County Park, located just a couple miles south of Yaphank off Victory Avenue. Yaphank is located more than half-way east out on Long Island, so expect to drive through heavy traffic at times on your way to the Carmans and nearby Connetquot River. You'll encounter signs to the main entrance to park. A small fee is required for parking. There was a time when only elite members of a private sporting club could enjoy the 1,320 park acres and stream that are now in public hands.

Like many spring creeks, bankside growth can cause difficulty laying out casts along the still, clear water that harbor brookies. The relatively shallow water in the upper reach makes for easy wading and in-stream casting to avoid getting hung up on vegetation. However, some of the streamside vegetation provides a beautiful backdrop to the angling experience, especially when the Blue Flag Iris flowers greet you at the water's edge.

NYSDEC classifies two reaches of trout water on the Carmans River. The upper Wild Trout section from Long Island Power Authority (LIPA) transmission lines at Gate G upstream to Yaphank Avenue is the Catch and Release stretch. The Stocked-Extended section runs from the cement dam upstream to LIPA transmission lines at Gate G. The stream typically receives NYSDEC stockings of both brown trout and rainbow trout. About 1,000 browns ranging from 9 to 15 inches are stocked along with an equal number of 9-inch to 10-inch rainbows. Wild brook trout average about 7 to 8 inches in size, but larger fish are sometimes encountered.

Your fly boxes should contain an assortment of patterns that are typically fished during seasonal hatches that are encountered on New York's free-stone waters. Carmans River is a fertile stream that provides everything from Little Black Stoneflies in March to an assortment of mayflies. Hendricksons to Grannom caddis to Sulphurs to late season Tricos keep both trout and anglers happy. Fantastic mayfly spinner falls bring trout to the surface, too. The Brown Drake hatch and spinner fall during late May into June bring hungry trout to the surface. My good friend, Bob Lindquist, a very knowledgeable Carmans River enthusiast, fishes two of his favorite patterns on the stream: a small-size Parachute Caddis and Sailboat Dun are effective flies.

Blue Flag Iris flowers greet anglers who cast their lines on Carmans River. Known for its water quality and abundant insect life, the Carmans River is different from other Long Island spring creeks with no assigned fishing beats. (PHOTO BOB LINDQUIST)

Connetquot River

Located west of the Carmans, near the hamlet of Oakdale at the Connetquot River State Park Preserve, the Connetquot River, or the "Conny," as its often called, also provides a spring creek experience on Long Island. Like the Carmans, its history as a fly-fishing destination is fascinating. In the early 1960s, New York State purchased over 3,000 acres of land from the exclusive Southside Sportsmen's Club. The club was handed a 10-year lease after the sale, so it wasn't until 1973 that the stream was open to the public. Before that time, only the wealthy and famous going back to the late 1800s, including US presidents, could enjoy the interesting resource.

The Conny has experienced its ups and downs over the years, and the most notable was the presence of infectious pancreatic necrosis disease (IPN) in the stream hatchery. The hatchery that once dumped in large numbers of trout into the stream was shut down for several years and not reopened until 2016.

During the years prior to 2006, before the hatchery was shut to rid the disease, the Conny was considered a joke of sorts. The trout were almost tame, large, and extremely easy to entice with just about any fly pattern anglers threw at them. You could have probably taught a monkey to fish the water and walk out with success on a first-time visit. My friend Teddy Patlen likes to tell the story about a trout that came swimming right up to him, nosing his boots, almost like a pet.

The stream no longer receives the large number of fish stockings that occurred in the old days, but trout that are stocked occur downstream from the new hatchery, now supplied with water from artesian wells. However, some very big rainbows and browns inhabit the Conny. Brook trout are also present, and if caught in the upstream stretch above the hatchery, they must be carefully released. While seasoned fly anglers often shun the stream, it's a good place to introduce anglers new to the sport.

Fly anglers interested in sampling the Conny must secure a fishing reservation by calling 631-581-1005 on Sunday at 8:00 a.m. one week in advance of the fishing week.

Teresa Manocchia and Gregory Lopez on a Connetquot fall day. (PHOTO ADRIANO MANOCCHIA)

The fly-fishing-only stream has strict guidelines (such as a barbless-hook-only rule) while fishing one of the 30 beats available. Make sure that you review the Connetquot River fishing regulations before visiting the stream.

You can't reserve a specific beat section. They're assigned on a first come, first served basis. The various beats range from wading areas to platform/bank sites to deep-water boat stretches. A nice map of the stream and all the beats and their designated uses is available online (see link at the end of this section).

Beats are available during two sessions: 8 a.m. to noon, and noon to 4 p.m. During April through September, a beat time from 4 p.m. until sunset is available. In addition to a NYS fishing license, a $25 fee is required per session.

A good range of mayfly species hatch on the Conny. The olive hatch that emerges throughout the season is a favorite among some regulars. Tricos should occupy your fly box if fishing the stream during August into September. Ant patterns work well, too. Besides dry flies, bring an assortment of small streamers and nymphs. A 9-foot, 5-weight rod is a good choice on the stream.

A map of the stream beat stream locations is available online at https://parks.ny.gov/documents/parks/ConnetquotRiverFlyFishingInformationMap.pdf.

Nissequogue River

Once in the hands of the Brooklyn Gun Club during the late 1800s, then a few years later known as the Wyandanch Club, New York State acquired the over 500 acres in 1963. Now named the Caleb Smith State Park Preserve, the stream that flows through its lands is popular with fly anglers looking for a spring creek experience on the north shore of Long Island. Head to the hamlet of Smithtown and access the park at 581 West Jericho Turnpike. The entrance is next to Willow Pond, a park fishing site reserved for youngsters ages 15 and under. The 8.3-mile-long Nissequogue River flows through the park on its way to Long Island Sound.

Nissequogue River regular Tom McCoy on lower beat #7. Once private waters in years past, Nissequogue River is open to the public at the NYS-operated Caleb Smith State Park Preserve. (PHOTO SUE MCCOY)

Tom McCoy caught an 18-inch brook trout that ate a size 16 Iris Caddis on upper beat #7. Colorful brook trout swim in the stream's waters. (PHOTO SUE MCCOY)

Like the Connetquot River, the Nissequogue fly-fishing-only stream at the park operates on a reservation system with 13 beats available on a first come, first served basis. Call the park at 631-265-1054 for more information. The beats are somewhat longer stretches than provided on the Connetquot River. Some sites are available for wade fishing while others are platform-fishing sections. While brown trout and brook trout swim in its waters, some regulars look forward to enticing the rainbows. Some natural reproduction occurs in the stream, but almost all trout encountered are hatchery fish.

Parachute Caddis (tied by Bob Lindquist) Bob likes to tie his Parachute Caddis on an Ahrex 521 hook, using Semperfi Nano thread. The pattern's tail is Zelon. Its wing is formed from snowshoe rabbit foot hair. Bob uses EP fibers for a post.

Sailboat Dun (tied by Bob Lindquist) One of Bob's favorites for Long Island spring creek fishing is a Small Sailboat dun. He ties the wing with EP fibers or snowshoe rabbit.

Blue-Winged Olive Comparadun (tied by Bill Shuck) Before he passed away, Bill Shuck (1939–2019) handed me a very nice Blue-Winged Olive Comparadun. Bill enjoyed much success fishing it on a variety of waters, big and small. Bill was an excellent fly tier, good friend, and a beloved member of the Flymph-tying community

Warmwater Fly Fishing

New York has ample opportunities for fly rodders interested in targeting warmwater species, in all regions. Some of the more interesting spots are located in the Allegany watershed, particularly the lakes that inhabit "the fish of 10,000 casts," the muskellunge or more muskie, as it's known to conventional anglers and fly fishers alike, which are the crown jewels, and to catch one of those large predator fish on a fly is a real accomplishment. Of course, other warmwater species, such as bass and pike, also inhabit a group of lakes clustered together in the southwestern corner of New York.

Among some 13 lakes and 19 rivers scattered around New York identified as inhabiting muskellunge, Chautauqua Lake and the Upper Niagara River are no doubt the most renowned in Western New York. However, smaller lakes located in Chautauqua County receive fingerlings reared at Chautauqua State Fish Hatchery located on Chautauqua Lake. The hatchery also contributes fingerlings that are stocked on the Great Chazy River, a Northern Lake Champlain tributary. Like the muskellunge granddaddy river of them all in New York, the St. Lawrence River that flows along the Canadian border, Upper Niagara River has a self-sustaining population. Allegany River and neighboring Susquehanna River are also favorite musky waters, as well as a small lake in the Finger Lakes Region, Waneta Lake (see page 333).

If you're targeting muskellunge, you'll be well served by reading Rick Kustich's book *Hunting Musky with a Fly* (2017). Understanding muskellunge behavior and what fly tackle is required to enhance chances for success, particularly what types of terminal leaders and flies work best, are requisites before heading out on the water. There's a difference in what rod weights, lines, terminal leaders, fly sizes, and so on are typically used when comparing the large lakes and rivers with smaller muskellunge inhabiting tributaries (see Grasse River in Adirondack/St. Lawrence River section).

Muskie hunters utilize a variety of gear, all depending on experience, preference, water types, and conditions. A common terminal rig is a small section of 40-pound to 50-pound test fluorocarbon off the fly line. A short 10-inch section of metal leader bite guard is attached to the fluorocarbon butt leader, via a barrel swivel. Rio and Scientific Angler manufacture pre-made "predator" leaders, complete with loop butt, wire bite guards, and snap swivels for fly attachment, but they're pricey.

Musky fly fishers commonly use 9-foot or 10-foot, 9-weight rods. Flies are gargantuan contraptions, some even a foot-long. However, these big, difficult-to-cast creations are not the only flies that will successfully take fish. Check Rick's book for photos of effective patterns and their recipes.

Findley Lake

Tucked into the extreme southwest corner of New York, in Chautauqua County, not far from the Pennsylvania border, 292-acre Findley Lake inhabits muskellunge, tiger muskellunge, northern pike, largemouth and smallmouth bass, walleye, black crappie, bluegill, yellow perch, and pumpkinseed. Since 2009, the small lake has received 8-inch hatchery muskellunge stockings. In 2022, 1,450 muskies were stocked.

Head for the Village of Findley Lake, in the Town of Mina, just a few minutes off US-86, a short drive west of the City of Jamestown. You'll pass over Chautauqua Lake

Findley Lake, located in the extreme southeast corner of New York, inhabits a wide variety of warmwater species, including muskellunge. (PHOTO VALERIE VALLA)

to get there. A very nice public boat launch is located at the north end of the lake, in the Village of Findley Lake at the State Route 426/430 intersection. Anglers can cast from shore, but a watercraft is required to adequately cover water where the fish are.

Chautauqua Lake

At over 13,000 acres, Chautauqua Lake boasts an impressive warmwater fishery, with every imaginable species inhabiting the water. Home of the only pure muskellunge hatchery in the state, at Prendergast Point, Chautauqua Lake's muskie population also serves as a resource for eggs and fingerlings reared for stocking into other waters. The hatchery and its boat launch entrance are located 3.9 miles north of the State Route 394/US-86 intersection on the west side of the lake. While many anglers first equate the fishery with muskellunge, bass and other popular warmwater fish also await fly anglers.

The south basin is shallower, with a mean depth of 11 feet, with lots of weed beds. The north basin water depth averages 19 feet and has weed beds in the shallow water bays but some deep 75-foot holes also exist in the basin. With three public boat launches in the south basin near Jamestown and four in the north basin, access is not an issue. NYSDEC lists all the launch areas and directions at: https://www.dec.ny.gov/outdoor/23907.html#Ellery.

Chautauqua Fish Hatchery, located on Chautauqua Lake near the Village of Mayville is the only DEC hatchery that raises pure-strain muskellunge. Eggs are collected from Chautauqua Lake muskellunge and occasionally from other waters. A boat launch is located close to the facility.

Chautauqua Lake at Long Point State Park. The lake has long been considered the muskellunge epicenter in New York's Western Region.

While boat fishing is undoubtedly the best way to adequately sample Chautauqua Lake, shoreline frontage is available in some areas for limited wade fishing. Long Point State Park, located off State Route 430 at Bemus Point, popular with swimmers who enjoy the beach, is a very nice facility with plenty of frontage. A boat launch is also available at the park.

Some of the smaller area ponds, like nearby Bear Lake and Cassadaga Lake, are more friendly to fly anglers fishing from canoes or small watercraft. Those waters also inhabit muskellunge and other warmwater fish.

Bear Lake

Bear Lake, located north of the Village of Stockton, just a few miles from Chautauqua Lake, is a pleasant warmwater destination that is user-friendly for fly casters desiring to fish from small watercraft. Bear Lake is a Kettle Pond, formed back in geologic time from big hunks of melting ice. Very limited shoreline fly casting is possible at the NYS-DEC boat launch, located on the north end along Bear Lake Road. It's better fished by canoe or kayak along the shoreline rife with weed beds and lily pads that provide cover for bass, muskies, and panfish. Some 500 muskellunge are stocked in the water annually.

Cassadaga Lake

Anglers targeting bass and muskellunge on Bear Lake should also consider trying canoe- and kayak-friendly Cassadaga Lake since it's located only a couple miles from the Bear Lake boat launch and less than 4 miles from Stockton. Head for the Cassadaga Middle Lake Boat Launch located on County Road 48 (Glasgow Road) by driving a couple miles to Frisbee Road from the Country Route 380/Cassadaga-Stockton Road intersection in Stockton. Drive about a mile to Frisbee Road, then take a right on Glasgow Road.

Bear Lake, located in the Western region near the Village of Stockton, is a small 114-acre "Kettle Pond" that inhabits muskellunge and other warmwater species. A small watercraft is needed to adequately cover the water.

Cassadaga Lake, a chain of three separate waterbodies, is another Western region muskellunge water located a short driving distance from Chautauqua Lake. The water is popular with recreational paddlers as well as anglers.

The boat launch, popular with recreational kayakers, is located at the bridge crossing. A kiosk at the launch has a nice map of the three connected "lakes," as well as posters that describe the fish species that inhabit the waters. NYSDEC typically stocks 250 muskellunge in the lake chain. Both largemouth and smallmouth bass inhabit the waters.

Waneta Lake

Located a couple of miles west of the Town of Tyrone, 780-acre Waneta Lake is a productive warmwater fishery in Schuyler County. While Waneta Lake is located not far from Keuka Lake, it's not considered one of the Finger Lakes because it drains to the south, not north, as is true with the Finger Lakes. While a few smallmouth bass live in its waters, sizeable largemouth bass inhabit Waneta Lake. NYSDEC reports the lake has abundant largemouth bass populations with ample numbers in the 4-pound range. However, the muskellunge populations in the lake have drawn attention from both anglers and NYS fisheries biologists. The muskellunge population is maintained through hatchery stockings although some natural reproduction exists. Over 4,000 muskie fingerlings are stocked annually in the lake that connects with Lamoka Lake via a 0.7-mile channel that flows through the Waneta-Lamoka Wildlife Management Area. The lakes are rife with vegetation, both invasive Eurasian watermilfoil and native aquatic plants.

The lake receives fluoridone treatments to help control watermilfoil. Plenty of native, weedy vegetative cover exists that harbors gamefish and prey. Biologists have given the lake impressive attention. Muskellunge population numbers have been tracked for decades. Muskellunge in the 30-pound-size to 40-pound-size range swim in Waneta Lake. An adequate forage base comprised of alewives and sawbellies exists in the waterbody.

Access to Waneta Lake and Lamoka Lake is via formal NYSDEC boat launches and the connecting channel and bridge, located on County Road 23, 2 miles west of Tyrone. Parking and launching are located on both sides of the road. Low-profile boats can pass under the bridge via the channel that connects the lakes.

Since virtually all of Waneta shoreline is occupied by private cottages and summer homes, aside from the southernmost section, access other than at the boat launch is difficult. However, a couple of wide road shoulder turnouts enable small-craft anglers

Waneta Lake and its connecting water body, Lamoka Lake, in the Finger Lakes region, is popular with anglers targeting muskellunge and bass. Waneta Lake has received significant attention by NYS fisheries biologists who, over many years, have been monitoring and tracking muskellunge populations.

to access the south end of Lamoka Lake at Mill Pond, a connecting waterbody at the hamlet of Bradford.

From the NYSDEC boat launch site on County Road 23, drive west 0.6 mile to a left turn on West Lake Road. You'll pass Wildlife Management Area signage on your way. A small shoulder pull-off is located 3.8 miles down West Lake Road. Access to the lake at this turnout is fine for canoes or kayaks. Wade fishing is marginally possible by getting down the footpath to the water. A larger road shoulder and cleared waterside area that is an adequate launching area for small boats is located 0.2 mile down the road, just north of the hamlet of Bradford.

Mohawk River (Lower Warmwater Section)

While trout are the primary target fish on the Mohawk River upstream from the City of Rome, significant warmwater fly-fishing opportunities exist downstream. While the reaches that inhabit trout are located north of the City of Rome, beginning it the upper areas in the Adirondack Region foothills, the warmwater section flows through both the Central Region and Capital Region. After the Mohawk dumps water into the barge canal, it maintains its identity and departs on its own for a while, finally becoming one with the canal at St. Johnsville, some 60 miles before it hits the Hudson River at Waterford, near Pebble Island State Park located in the Capital Region.

The Mohawk along the barge canal is an entirely different fishery, requiring different flies and fishing strategies for warmwater species. One of the most knowledgeable Mohawk River warmwater anglers is Rob Streeter. A passionate angler, hunter, and conservationist, Rob recently retired from the *Albany Times Union* newspaper, as the outdoor correspondent for many years. His recent book, *The Greats of Adirondack Fly Fishing*, also gives a nod to William Scripture's contribution to Mohawk River fly-fishing lore.

Mohawk River at the lower Clarke Avenue access area, near the river's confluence with the Hudson River in the Capital Region. Smallmouth bass as well as carp are abundant. Easy access to the river is available for wade-fishing anglers.

Rob Streeter on a stretch of the lower Mohawk River. Besides bowhunting for whitetail deer, or stripping streamers on Lake George for lake trout in early spring, Rob targets the plentiful population of smallmouth bass on the lower Mohawk River. (PHOTO ROB STREETER)

Mohawk River's smallmouth bass are big and feisty. (PHOTO ROB STREETER)

Rob, who lives less than a mile from the river and grew up on it, was kind enough to allow me to pick his brain about fishing the big water of the Mohawk River, sections I never fished and never realized the interesting potential they hold for fly fishing. The flies he uses on the Mohawk while casting for bass are also interesting, and a couple are included here.

Spring and fall are the best times to go after bass on the big water. Rob's experience shows that late June to late August are the most difficult times to latch into the bass that are feeding deep in the water on crayfish. However, once late August and early September arrive, he keeps his eyes on the water for perhaps the most anticipated events of the year: the outward migration of juvenile herring that send big bass into a feeding frenzy. Schools of bass work collectively to herd the little herring into vulnerable positions in the water.

Jerk Fly (tied by Rob Streeter) Rob's Jerk Fly is another creation that entices herring-eating bass. The pattern gives the impression of a wounded herring, something an opportunistic hungry bass can't resist.

Baby Herring (tied by Rob Streeter) The annual outward migration of juvenile herring during September sends big bass into a feeding frenzy. Rob created his Baby Herring pattern when targeting herring-devouring bass. According to Rob, successful fly fishing for smallmouth declines between late June into late August. But once late August arrives, his eyes are peeled for the herring feast.

Carpnado (tied by Pat Cohen) One of Pat's original carp patterns, it's intended to suggest a wide range of aquatic critters—everything from crayfish to small leeches to nymphs. He typically ties it on a size #6 Bolie Long Partridge brand hook. Large black bead chains are tied in at the head. The fly is intended to ride hook point up, to avoid snags on the water bottom where carp feed. Hook shank length tails are tied with a variety of marabou colors—including brown, orange, olive, and black. Marabou also forms the body that's ribbed with Brassie copper wire. Rubber legs are positioned rear and front. Clumps of peacock herl form a "wing case." Pat's own Cohen's Carp Dub, from Hareline, is twisted, attached, and groomed at the front.

Creature Damsel Nymph (tied by Pat Cohen) Pat's Creature Damsel Nymph has creature-like features, for sure. While Pat tags the pattern as suggestive of damsel flies, its striking eyes make it a great attractor pattern.

While Rob typically casts conehead rabbit streamer patterns during spring and crawfish patterns (like his "Crawdaddy" fly) during summer, he ties on a surface fly he calls a Baby Herring or his Jerk Fly during the juvenile herring hatch. Rob's highly effective Jerk Fly gives the impression of a herring wounded by a bass on the prowl.

Rob prefers 10-foot to 11-foot, 7-weight fly rods while fishing the Mohawk for not only bass but other warmwater species that inhabit some of his favorite sections.

Rob has fished the Mohawk out of a variety of watercraft; boat fishing is for sure the best method to fish the lower river. Rob recommends visiting the New York State Canal Corporation website that provides valuable information concerning access and boat-launching points: https://www.canals.ny.gov/maps/index.html. A popular launch site is at the river's mouth, at Peebles Island State Park.

Wade fishing can be difficult, but there are a few sections that can accommodate wading anglers or casting from close to the river shore. The Lock 7 water below the Vischer Ferry Power Plant is popular with conventional tackle anglers who target northern pike by casting lures from shore during the spring and fall. That stretch is best fished by boat, but casting by wading out a few feet is possible during appropriate water levels. Both hikers and anglers are welcome at the overlook trail that leads from a visitor's parking area at the power plant on Sugar Hill Road off Riverview Road in Rexford. It's located about 14 miles upstream from the river's mouth near Peebles Island State Park.

An area that's easy to wade is located near the mouth of the Mohawk, a short distance upstream from where it joins the Hudson River in the vicinity of Peebles Island State Park. Both smallmouth bass and loads of carp inhabit the usually very shallow-water, wide reach at the north end of Simmons Island. Access the river via the Clarke Avenue access parking lot, located behind the U-Hall center on Ontario Street, in Cohoes. From the State Route 787/State Route 470 (Ontario Street) intersection, go east about 0.2 mile and take a left on Clarke Avenue next to the U-Hall center. Clarke dead-ends close to the water. A crushed stone path provides direct access to the river that's usually quite shallow for a distance, if not completely dried before the main channel is reached a couple hundred feet from the bank.

Chenango River (Lower Warmwater Section)

Outdoor columnist Frank Dolan's July 11, 1971, article in the *Binghamton Press* newspaper, titled "A Midsummer Night's Stream," gave readers insight into smallmouth bass fishing on the Chenango River within the Binghamton, New York, city limits. Dolan interviewed me for the story and wrote, "He gives the Latin name for the fly and describes

Lower Chenango River at Binghamton, in New York's Central Region. While the upper headwaters of the Chenango River are inhabited by trout, the lower mileage is prime smallmouth water. The lower section at Binghamton experiences blizzards of Whiteflies (*Ephoron*) mayflies in August, as well as big *Hexagenia atrocaudata* drakes and spinners.

it as a type of large mayfly. He said it usually emerges in early August. He said the fly usually hatches at night but the spinner begins to fall spent on the water at 7:30 each evening."

The large mayfly that I had described to Dolan some 50 years ago was *Hexagenia atrocaudata*. An enthusiastic teenage fly angler, I was more than willing to share my knowledge of Chenango River smallmouth fishing. The *Hexagenia* spinner flights on the Chenango, a river that flowed practically in my backyard, signaled an annual transition from late-summer trout fishing to bass angling.

I have a crystal-clear memory of the day I stuffed a large mayfly imago into a large glass aspirin bottle and mailed it to mayfly taxonomist B. D. Burks in Illinois for identification. A response from Burks was most welcome: he wrote that the beautiful male specimen was being retained for the national collection. Prolific *Ephoron* hatches also brought Chenango bass to the surface during August. Since my Binghamton home was so close to the river, I was able to spend many enjoyable late-summer hours pursuing smallmouth feeding frenzies when I couldn't be on a trout stream.

A few years ago, I decided to return to the lower Chenango River and cast a line on the bass waters that I first fished in the early 1970s. What is the river like now? Are the hatches still there? What about "my" little island? Such thoughts brought back precious memories of when I had built campfires on the island and fly-fished for bass long into the night.

The best access to the stretch I once fished, upstream from the Bevier Street Bridge, was from the east side of the river along Chenango Street, a few hundred feet north of Blanchard Avenue, where I once lived. Accessing the river used to require carefully dropping down a very long, steep, slippery bank just opposite my island. That hasn't changed. Now, all these years later, I shake my head in wonder at how I used to descend the bank in the evening and then crawl out of the river and back up the hill after nightfall.

The stretch is now more easily accessed from the west side of the river, in low water, along Otsiningo Park. The park grounds, once the site of an eighteenth-century Indian village, were only in the design concept phases in 1971. While the Chenango in that area was still within the city limits, it was empty of congestion and other river users back in the year I first fished there.

Remarkably, the river today remains much the same as I remember it. My little island is still there, and so is the tailout of the pool that used to draw feeding bass at dusk. And, most important, the hatches are still prolific. I saw the *Hexagenia* imagos hovering above the water with up-and-down mating movements just as I remembered. And the *Ephoron* mayflies (White Flies) still swarmed in great numbers. It all brought a smile to my face. But were the bass still there? My first cast brought a chub to a large, bushy brown Bivisible. Oh, how I used to hate the chubs that slimed up my flies as I pursued big smallmouth. The second cast ended with a scrappy Chenango small mouth. My smile broadened.

Lake Lauderdale

Tucked along State Route 22, a mile and a half or so west of Shushan, and the Batten Kill River, a lovely 63-acre "lake" awaits fly anglers interested in casting for warmwater species. Largemouth bass, northern pike, crappie, and tiger muskies inhabit the water that's better described as a pond. You'll likely run into more swimmers at the small swimming beach pond than anglers casting flies. It's a nice facility managed by Washington County, complete with a picnic area and places to launch small watercraft. I've used both a canoe and my beloved Hornbeck on the water.

Lake Lauderdale, a Capital Region warmwater fishery in Washington County. NYSDEC's surveys of the small lake have shown a healthy population of bass swim in its waters.

Flies that resemble baitfish entice various warmwater species that inhabit Lake Lauderdale (tied by Andreas Andersson).

Lake Lauderdale creates the headwaters of the Owl Kill, a trout stream with limited access downstream from the Village of Cambridge. The lake can be reached by driving north on State Route 22 from Cambridge. Just short of 4 miles, you'll see a sign on the right side of the road that will deliver you to the beach area and facility.

During summer, Lake Lauderdale, like Cossayuna Lake, provides a welcome retreat from the inner-tube floaters and all that theme-park-like madness over on the Batten Kill during summer months. The largemouth bass fishery is excellent. A few years ago, NYSDEC did a boat electrofishing study on the lake to assess the largemouth bass population. Bass collected showed a balanced size-range structure from 4 to 18 inches, with weights exceeding 5 pounds.

Cossayuna Lake

When late-summer heat arrives in bucolic Washington County, New York, more than a few fly anglers avoid area trout streams, such as the Batten Kill. The "rubber and plastic hatch"—recreational tubers and kayak floaters who overwhelm the river at that time of year—steer many fly rodders to their favorite area bass streams and ponds.

Washington and adjacent counties are blessed with many good bass waters, such as Saratoga Lake, Glen Lake, and Lake George. However, smaller countryside lakes, such as Cossayuna Lake in the towns of Argyle and Greenwich, provide excellent opportunities for not only largemouth and smallmouth bass but also other species.

The lake supports healthy populations of bluegills, pumpkinseeds, yellow perch, northern pike, and other species, such as tiger muskellunge, a sterile-yet-fast-growing cross between northern pike and muskellunge. New York State has been stocking tiger muskellunge around the state since 1968, providing a unique-yet-challenging prospect for fly anglers who enjoy tossing big flies with heavy rods. The state obtains fry from New Jersey's Hackettstown Fish Hatchery. From these fry, New York's South Otselic Hatchery annually raises some 90,000 9-inch-long tiger muskies for statewide distribution.

The elusive "tigers," sometimes caught by accident by anglers targeting bass, are hard to come by, but largemouth bass and bluegills abound throughout Cossayuna's 661 acres. The maximum depth of the lake is around 20 feet, but the section to the south is much shallower. Most anglers head for what some call "the bass factory," the weedy and shallow south end of the lake. Public access to the lake, however, is located at the no-fee north-end boat launch, located off East Shore Road. This hard-surface ramp is operated by NYSDEC and has parking for 30 cars and trailers. This site is accessible for persons with disabilities.

Reaching the productive south end of the lake via the boat launch makes for a long haul for those paddling kayaks or canoes, but it can be done. Conventional anglers launch small johnboats, square-stern canoes with small electric motors, and even large bass

Paul Siniki, a bass enthusiast, fly fishing Capital Region's Cossayuna Lake. A public boat launch maintained by NYSDEC provides easy access to the lake's abundant bass population. Many area anglers fish Cossayuna Lake in hopes of landing an elusive tiger muskellunge.

Cossayuna Fathead Minnow (tied by Mike Valla)
Designed by the author to suggest natural fathead minnow (*Pimephales promelas*), a baitfish widely distributed throughout the country, including New York. You'll often find ice anglers on Cossayuna Lake fishing fathead minnows. The tail is tied with olive cashmere goat. Wings are created by layering dyed yellow-brown bucktail with dyed olive-brown bucktail. A small amount of Blue Ice Dub Shimmer Fringe fibers is added for flash.

Fruit Cocktail Whit HairBug (tied by Dave Whitlock) Dave Whitlock, who passed away on November 25, 2022, created many effective bass patterns, including his aptly named "Fruit Cocktail Whit HairBug."

boats that allow for a quick return to the boat launch after an outing in the evening, the best time of day to get into bass during sunny summer days. Bass tend to sulk in deeper, cooler water during the bright summer weather, but in late afternoon and evening, they venture out to the shallows, where they prowl for food.

On a couple of occasions, I've arrived at the boat launch and discovered that the lake's wind-churned waters were too rough for my lightweight Kevlar Hornbeck canoe. On such occasions, I've elected to fish near and around the small island that's easy to reach directly across from the boat launch. The island blocks some of the wind.

Five- and 6-weight rods are generally fine here, but if you target tigers, go with a 7- and 8-weight rods. The tiger muskies like large bucktails retrieved for long distances through the water. A size 1/0 Platinum Blonde is a good choice. For bass, try optic bucktails, such as the Cossayuna Fathead Minnow, in sizes 6 through 10. The pattern features a yellow eye dotted with a black pupil and an olive bucktail wing, accented with bluish Krystal Flash. Get a supply of Dave Whitlock's multicolor Fruit Cocktail Whit HairBug poppers for top-water fishing next to the shoreline obstructions and lily pads.

Several directions will deliver you to Cossayuna Lake, depending on the approach. If approaching from the Village of Greenwich, take Cottage Street (off Main Street) to County Road 49 to County Road 48. Drive to the north end of the lake along County Road 48 to a right on East Lake Road. The public boat launch is less than a half-mile down East Lake Road, marked by a large NYSDEC sign.

Round Lake

Located 20 miles or so north of the City of Albany, on US Route 9, Round Lake is a popular warmwater fishery with area anglers targeting both bass and northern pike. A shallow lake with a mean depth of only 7 feet and a maximum of 20 feet, Round Lake provides good habitat for anglers seeking a warmwater fly-fishing experience. A formal NYSDEC boat launch and small parking lot located directly on US Route 9 in the Village of Round Lake.

Round Lake, located a short distance north of Albany in the Capital District. Known for its population of bass and northern pike, Round Lake also inhabits tiger muskellunge. A modern public boat launch is located along US Route 9.

Weekends are popular with both anglers and recreational craft enthusiasts. Arrive at the parking lot early on weekends to ensure room to park a vehicle, although several long slots are reserved for boats and trailers. Use big streamers for pike but smaller-size patterns for bass; both topwater bass bugs and sinking flies will bring attention from the bass.

Eagle Lake/Putnam Pond

From the State Route 74/State Route 9 intersection, heading east toward Putnam Pond Campground, you'll pass by Eagle Lake and its NYSDEC public boat launch in 8.6 miles. Anglers heading into Rock Pond in search of brook trout (see Rock Pond, page 199) often stop by Eagle Lake because it's located along the same route. Putnam Pond is the gateway waterbody next to Rock Pond. NYSDEC stocks brown trout in the small pond-size Eagle Lake, but it's better known as bass and yellow perch water. You'll be able to launch your canoe within minutes since Eagle Lake and the launch is right off State Route 74. I often stop by and cast a few loops from the dock on occasions when I'm heading for Rock Pond, in the Pharaoh Lake Wilderness.

Putnam Pond, located in the Putnam Pond State Campground, is the gateway waterbody for anglers desiring to trek into Rock Pond and Grizzle Ocean (see pages 199 and 201).

Putnam Pond inhabits sizeable largemouth bass.

Eagle Lake, in the Adirondack Region, is an easy-access pond located in the Adirondack Region on the way to Putnam Pond Campground.

Putnam Pond, a warmwater Adirondack Region fishery, is the gateway into Rock Pond and other area remote trout ponds.

Lake Durant, a warmwater fishery located in the heart of the Adirondack Region near Blue Mountain Lake, is easily accessed at the NYSDEC campground.

Lake Durant

Located in Hamilton County, in the Town of Indian Lake off State Route 28, Lake Durant is known for its largemouth bass and tiger muskellunge fishing. Anglers who travel to the Saint Regis Canoe area or tourists who are heading to the fabulous Adirondack Museum, at Blue Mountain Lake, pass by Lake Durant on their way. Recently renamed Adirondack Experience, the Museum on Blue Mountain Lake is a must-see while camping and fishing Lake Durant since it's located only a few minutes away up the road from the State Route 28/State Route 30 intersection in the hamlet of Blue Mountain Lake.

Lake Durant and its NYSDEC campground and day-use area, with a boat launch, is located about 50 miles northeast from Exit 23 off I-87 at Warrenburg. The scenic drive to Lake Durant follows the Hudson River, the same directional route along State Route 28 that is used to reach trout destinations in the Siamese Ponds Wilderness area, such as Thirteenth Lake (see page 149). You'll want to paddle a canoe along the weed lines while tiger muskie hunting Lake Durant. There's no need to bring your own craft as canoe and kayak rentals are available at the camping and day-use area. The camping fee is $20 to $25 a night. Both tent sites and RV sites are available. ReserveAmerica handles reservations.

The pleasant, nearly 300-acre lake has ample weedy cover for the tigers and bass. NYSDEC maintains the tiger muskie population by stocking nearly 1,500 of the sterile hybrids, a cross between pike and muskellunge. Panfish are also fun to entice with flies.

Also check out the Adirondack Experience website, a good diversion from fishing while in the area. A virtual tour of the facility is available online.

St. Lawrence River and Massena Tributaries

The 700-mile St. Lawrence River starts its journey to the Atlantic Ocean at the northeast end of Lake Ontario. For just over a hundred miles, the river borders Canada. Every imaginable warmwater fish species, including muskellunge, swim in the waters. Perhaps the most popular area of the river, with both tourists and anglers alike, are the Thousand Islands. Spread over 50 miles, the archipelago of actually 1,864 islands attracts visitors from around the globe. Fish aside, the beauty of the Thousand Islands itself and its historic features, such as the Antique Boat Museum in Clayton and Boldt Castle at Alexandria Bay, are enough to entice vacationers to sample its fishing potential.

The Saint Lawrence is usually thought of in three segments: the upper, the middle, and the lower. The upper Thousand Islands area runs from Cape Vincent at Lake Ontario downriver to Morristown, upstream from Ogdensburg. The lower area runs from Iroquois Dam (just upstream from Waddington) to the Moses-Saunders Power Dam near Massena.

The middle corridor between both ends runs through Ogdensburg downriver past Galop Island and Lisbon Town Beach. The middle area is my favorite area because it's less developed, less congested, and

Northern pike is a popular gamefish in the Thousand Island area along the St. Lawrence River. (PHOTO VALERIE VALLA)

Boldt Castle, located on an island on the St. Lawrence River, is a popular tourist attraction in the Thousand Island area at Alexandria Bay. Boat anglers, including fly fishers, cast lines along the many islands in the area.

relatively free of the hustle and bustle of the more popular vacation areas upriver near Alexandria Bay and the core of the Thousand Islands. Relative solitude aside, a disadvantage of the Ogdensburg corridor is the lack of fishing guides, boat rental establishments, and various other amenities available in other river areas, although very nice riverfront lodging is available in Ogdensburg.

UPPER RIVER CORRIDOR

The uppermost river area between Cape Vincent and Alexandria Bay, flowing past Clayton, is also very nice, and you'll have no problem securing a charter boat guide in that reach and in Alexandria Bay in the heart of the Thousand Islands. The Village of Clayton holds special significance; the New York State muskellunge record, set in 1957, a whopping 69-pound, 15-ounce beast, still stands. It was caught in the vicinity of Clayton.

While there are a couple of charter boat operators located along the Thousand Islands upper river corridor section who are familiar with fly fishing, the majority are conventional tackle anglers who target northern pike, walleye pike, bass, or muskellunge. However, they all have knowledge of the river and where fish are typically located. You'll have to bring your own gear, and fly-fishing know-how, but they can put you over fish and likely habitat.

MIDDLE RIVER CORRIDOR

Conventional tackle angler Jerry Kroeger II grew up in Ogdensburg on the middle corridor and fished it since his youth years. Jerry knows every nuance about the corridor and the changes that have occurred over the years. His knowledge of the Ogdensburg water is vast, from the reed stand shallows to where the deeper holes are located.

If you're targeting muskellunge, "the fish of a 1,000 casts," the reed stands on the east end of Wheathouse Bay are a good place to start. However, you'll want to be on that

Fly fishing near standing reeds at the east end of Wheathouse Bay in Ogdensburg, for muskellunge, the "fish of 1,000 casts." The big muskies are there, but latching into one with a fly isn't always easy. (PHOTO VALERIE VALLA)

The bay at Whalen Park, near Massena, inhabits carp and other warmwater species. Canoe or kayak launching is easy at the park, putting fly rodders on the water quickly.

water very soon after the musky season opens, which is June 15. For a short window of time, the big fish can be very close to shore in relatively shallow water before they head to deeper water within a couple of weeks. You can get by with 8- or 9-weight rods and a floating line casting big muskellunge fly patterns. Northern pike are also in the area. Another good location is the eddy directly under the international bridge, on the east side.

Another likely pike and musky holding area is located in a deep hole, just east of the international bridge locally referred to as St. Hospital Bay. The 16-foot-deep hole is located next to land that once housed a psychiatric center until it closed in 1983. A short distance downriver from St. Hospital Bay is Galop Island. The head of the island is well worth fishing; the north shore channel is popular with conventional tackle muskie hunters.

Anglers who are bringing along small craft, such as canoes or kayaks, can cast near shore at Lisbon Beach and Campground Recreation Park located directly across from the east end of Galop Island at 9975 State Route 37 in Lisbon. A boat launch is available at the park. Anglers with smaller craft should also head downriver to the Massena area and sample a few of the St. Lawrence River tributaries.

LOWER RIVER CORRIDOR

The lower river corridor that flows past the Village of Massena is a lake-like section where fly anglers can get into phenomenal warmwater-species-fishing experiences. Even if you don't hire a charter boat guide, or don't have access to a floating craft, there are a few areas that wade angling is possible, mostly at public parks and along the very nice riverside trails that are easily accessed.

The kayak launch at Whalen Park, located on State Route 131, will get anglers into a small bay frequented by carp, bass, and pike. If you're targeting pike, May would be a good time to try the section accessed near Massena Town Beach, located just up the road from Whalen Park. Anglers equipped with a canoe can fish the bays along the Richards

Grasse River at Veteran's Memorial Park in Massena. Smallmouth bass are numerous at the Grasse River Veterans Memorial Park stretch. The bass are typically on the small size, but they provide good sport. (PHOTO VALERIE VALLA)

Landing Dike Trail, a crushed-stone, flat, multifunction path that runs along the St. Lawrence from the Massena Intake Dam past Massena town beach. The bays along the trail upriver from the beach would be a good choice.

During a most pleasant breakfast chat with Massena area outdoor journalist Don Meissner, I learned much about what the Massena area on the St. Lawrence River has to offer anglers of all types. The big river aside, Don is most passionate about the tributaries that

St. Regis River, at the Town of Brasher, is a popular muskellunge area. Camping is available next to the river at Jelly Bean's Campground. The 86-mile-long river eventually flows into the St. Lawrence River at the hamlet of St. Regis, in the St. Regis Mohawk Reservation.

Muskellunge inhabit the St. Lawrence River tributaries near Massena. This muskie was hooked on a 6-inch-long, colorful fly. Not all musky flies need to be massively long. It depends on the particular water body. To the author's surprise, the fish broke loose but came right back after the fly that was still dangling free in the water. Again, the musky broke free, but the fish just wouldn't give up! A third hit soundly hooked the fish. (PHOTO VALERIE VALLA)

Big flies like these, yet not excessively large, attract muskellunge on Massena area tributaries. Unlike the gargantuan muskellunge flies used on big lakes, smaller and easier-to-cast flies will interest muskies on smaller rivers and tributaries in the Massena area.

Alex Krywanczyk nets a frisky muskie for the author on a tributary of the St. Regis River, not far from Massena. Alex, who isn't a guide but just a good guy, is so passionate about muskellunge he has one tattooed on his right shoulder.

enter the Saint Lawrence in the Massena area. "The tributaries provide fantastic fishing for anglers interested in fishing out of small boats or canoes," Don said. Don understands well the big St. Lawrence River in the Massena area, too.

Don is about as enthusiastic an angler as I've ever encountered; his enthusiasm for Massena's fishing opportunities easily excites his audience. "Anglers can fish around here with success not only during the popular spring and summer but also well into the fall, even into November on the local St. Lawrence River bays," Don mentioned. Pike and bass can thrill both small craft and canoe anglers in solitude during the late fall. Wade fishing in some bay areas is also possible.

There was no doubt after meeting Don, and experiencing a muskie hunt myself, that he was spot-on about the fishing potential in his area. He about guaranteed I could get into muskies there; he was right. While the big St. Lawrence River provides a healthy muskellunge, pike, and bass population, fly anglers visiting the region can also enjoy fishing the tributaries that flow into the big water at the City of Massena. Sizeable bass inhabit the Raquette River system. The Grasse River warmwater section downstream from the Village of Canton and St. Regis River in the Town of Brasher are popular with anglers who target muskies. Camping sites and a couple of small cabins are available on the banks of the St. Regis River at Jelly Bean's Campground, located near the bridge crossing in Brasher Falls.

The upper Grasse, from Degrasse to Pyrites, is considered a coldwater fishery. Lower Grasse River, from Pyrites to the mouth at Massena, is a warmwater fishery more easily fly-fished out of small boats and canoes. Wade fishing is possible at some stretches. Riffles at Veterans Memorial Park, located near the corner of Andrews Street and Main Street in Massena, can be wade-fished for the small bass that inhabit that reach. Boat launches are located at several locations, all the way upstream to the Village of Canton.

A popular canoe and small craft launch site is located a couple of miles downstream from Canton at the Upper and Lower Lakes Wildlife Management Area on State Route 68, marked by a NYSDEC large hanging sign. An informational kiosk is located at the entrance. Both flatwater and riffle sections occur through this stream reach. Other launch areas and descriptions of the river can be found at the NYSDEC Fishing and Canoeing Grasse River informational online page. It provides a complete list of watercraft access points and other useful information:

Great Chazy River

Unlike the natural muskellunge populations that thrive in Saint Lawrence tributaries in the Massena area to the west, Great Chazy River relies on stocked fish from the Chautauqua State Fish Hatchery. NYSDEC typically stocks over a thousand 9-inch fish annually. It's been discovered that some of the Great Chazy muskies that make their way into Lake Champlain end up in Vermont's Missisquoi River. Natural populations, thought to have been eradicated by the late 1970s, were once present in Lake Champlain and both Great Chazy River and Missisquoi River. Rock bass and smallmouth bass are also popular target species on the Great Chazy River.

The river is easily reached by taking Exit 42 on I-87 at the Village of Champlain. Drive about 3 miles west on US-11 to its intersection with St. Johns Road, at the VFW building bridge crossing, as a starting point. Floating craft put-ins typically occur at bridge crossings. Although sometimes difficult to manage, it's possible to drag a canoe to the stream at that point, directly upstream from the US-11 bridge at the VFW area.

Depending on water-level conditions, I've read some muskie anglers launch small floating crafts farther upstream at the Lavalley Road bridge crossing, reached by driving about 3 miles south on St. Johns Road to Lavalley Road. The serpentine river flows some 5 miles between the two bridges, making for a long trip.

Speaking only as an observer who visited the area, launching even a canoe at the Lavalley Road crossing seems difficult yet possible. If water levels permit, the bridge crossing at Creek Road, accessed downstream from the US-11/St. Johns Road intersection a few miles down Perry Mills Road can be wade fished. Local kids routinely catch

Great Chazy River at Creek Road bridge crossing near Champlain. While the North Branch of the Chazy River is popular with trout anglers, by the time it reaches the hamlet of Moores area and continues as the Great Chazy River, warmwater species inhabit its waters, including muskellunge.

rock bass in that area. Much easier Great Chazy River canoe launching access is located downstream from the Village of Champlain.

A stream reach popular with recreational kayakers is located in the lowermost area, accessed at the public boat launch downstream from the Village of Champlain near Coopersville, at Lake Champlain's Kings Bay. The launch is accessed at 34 Laventure Drive, off Lakeshore Drive (County Road 22). Anglers can make their way upstream into easy-to-paddle waters. For a longer downstream 5-mile angling journey, launch a canoe at the Bill Earl Park, located on River Street near the bridge crossing Elm Street bridge crossing off US-9. The float will take you through seemingly isolated agricultural areas as you cast for bass and other fish.